D1126281

Dance in Chains

Dance in Chains

Political Imprisonment in the Modern World

PADRAIC KENNEY

OXFORD
UNIVERSITY PRESS

OXFORD
UNIVERSITY PRESS

Oxford University Press is a department of the University of Oxford. It furthers
the University's objective of excellence in research, scholarship, and education
by publishing worldwide. Oxford is a registered trade mark of Oxford University
Press in the UK and certain other countries.

Published in the United States of America by Oxford University Press
198 Madison Avenue, New York, NY 10016, United States of America.

Library of Congress Cataloging-in-Publication Data
Names: Kenney, Padraic, 1963– author.
Title: Dance in chains : political imprisonment in the modern world / Padraic Kenney.
Description: New York, NY : Oxford University Press, 2017. |
Includes bibliographical references and index.
Identifiers: LCCN 2017008883 (print) | LCCN 2017010949 (ebook) |
ISBN 9780199375745 (hardcover : acid-free paper) | ISBN 9780199375752 (Updf) |
ISBN 9780199375769 (Epub)
Subjects: LCSH: Political prisoners—History. | Imprisonment—Political aspects—History. |
Dissenters—History. | Political prisoners—Poland—History. |
Political prisoners—Northern Ireland—History. | Political prisoners—South Africa—History. |
World politics—1900–1945. | World politics—1945–1989. | World politics—1989–
Classification: LCC HV8706 .K46 2017 (print) | LCC HV8706 (ebook) |
DDC 365/.45—dc23
LC record available at https://lccn.loc.gov/2017008883

1 3 5 7 9 8 6 4 2

Printed by Sheridan Books, Inc., United States of America

CONTENTS

Acknowledgments vii

Introduction: Where a Free Man Can Abide with Honor 1

1. "But I Have No Wish to Be Discharged": When Imprisonment Became Political 9

2. Night and Fog: The Regime and Its Captives 36

3. "Everyone Learned Prison": Becoming a Political Prisoner 61

4. "You Have the Consolation of Being Very Much in the Fight": The Cause in Prison 89

5. "How to Free Your Prisoner": The Personal and the Political of International Prisoner Support 117

6. "A Close-Knit Group, Chosen with Care": Community and Order in the Political Camp and Prison 144

7. "I Was Confusing the Prison": The Contest in the Cell 174

8. "Why Wouldn't I Laugh, When I Win Either Way?": The Hunger Strike 205

9. "This Purgatory Is Useful": How Prison Forges Politics 232

Conclusion: The Politics of Prisoners' Stories 262

Epilogue: "Nobody Survives Guantanamo": A Political Prison
   Today   268

Notes   283
Archives Consulted   321
Index   323

ACKNOWLEDGMENTS

Nearly thirty years ago, during what turned out to be the last days of communist rule in Poland, I was living in the city of Wrocław, then a center of youth opposition to the regime. Politics were less on my mind than my impending wedding, but the signs of anti-communist opposition were everywhere. I frequently spotted posters and graffiti calling for freedom for Sławomir Dutkiewicz, an activist on a hunger strike. I learned later that he and I were the same age, both twenty-five that summer. He was from a Pomeranian village and had a small farm. At university, he joined a student-based human rights movement called Freedom and Peace, which staged protests against the military draft and the oath to the Soviet Union that soldiers were required to take. As a farmer raising a family, Dutkiewicz was exempt from the draft, according to Polish law. But he was a peace activist, so they drafted him anyway; he refused to serve and was jailed, tried, and sentenced to three years' imprisonment. Almost immediately, he began a hunger strike (and a shaving strike too, thrashing around in the prison barber's chair so violently that the razor would have decapitated him). He was force-fed, so his hunger strike lasted the better part of a year. To say the least, we spent that summer of 1988 in different ways.

Nine years later, I finally met Dutkiewicz, in his auto-body shop in Sopot on Poland's Baltic coast, as I was researching a book on the social movements that brought down communism in Central Europe (*A Carnival of Revolution*, 2002). The political prisoner began to occupy my thoughts precisely because the experience was so alien. I conducted dozens of interviews with people who had, at one time or another, been in prison for their opposition to the regimes of the Soviet bloc. The more I learned about opposition movements and their protest strategies, the more I realized just how much harder it is to imagine or understand the experience of imprisonment for a political cause. Political imprisonment pervades the memories of so many families in Poland; my mother-in-law (whom I introduce in Chapter 9) twice went to prison as a Solidarity activist in the 1980s, and her father, a fighter in the resistance to Nazi occupation, perished in Auschwitz.

This book seeks to demystify the political prisoner, posing and answering new kinds of questions about those who spend time in prison for political reasons, whether interned for a few weeks or for decades; in the dark basement cell of a fortress prison, a makeshift barrack, or a modern prison facility; as a communist, a pacifist, a guerrilla fighter, a priest. I am not interested, here, in whether the causes they have fought for or the methods they have chosen are right or wrong. My purpose is not to chronicle either abuses of human rights or any political struggle. Perhaps this book will be of use to the would-be political prisoner searching for models of action; perhaps, too, it might help political leaders understand why they do what they do—though I hope they will not find any "best practices" here. Indeed, one conclusion is that political incarceration is likely to fail to achieve its goals.

So many friends and colleagues in Poland, South Africa, Ireland, Northern Ireland, Great Britain, and the United States have contributed in some way to this research that I cannot possibly acknowledge them all. One of the great pleasures of this research has been discovering a network of prison historians, who understood the hazards and joys of this research better than anyone: Anna Muller, Will Murphy, Neo Legkotla laga Ramoupi, Anna Bryson, Stuart Finkel, Jeff Hardy, Steve Soper, and Alex Lichtenstein. I treasure the many conversations with patient and thoughtful friends: Bob Blobaum, Maria Bucur, John Connelly, Marek Czapliński, Max Paul Friedman, John Hanson, Róisín Healy, Darek Jarosz, Bill Johnston, Lara Kriegel, Marcin Kula, Ed Linenthal, Rick Lippke, Ethan Michelson, Andrzej Paczkowski, Wayne Reeves, Rebecca Spang, Kacper Szulecki, Mary Werden, Marcin Zaremba, and especially my father, Michael Kenney; so many other colleagues at the University of Colorado and at Indiana University have been steadfast in their interest and wise counsel at every stage. Two colleagues who have themselves been political prisoners, Hamid Ekbia and Kaya Şahin, offered perspective and encouragement. Verne Harris, Łukasz Kamiński, Laurence McKeown, Krzystof Persak, Mirosława Pałaszewska, Oleh Razyhraev, and Richard Whiteing provided crucial advice and assistance with sources. I have learned so much from the students in my undergraduate seminars on political prisoners, too. Thank you all! I have presented this research to dozens of audiences and received valuable suggestions and advice from so many. I must mention the one group whose warm support meant a great deal: the former prisoners who now work as guides at the Robben Island Museum, with whom I spoke at an early stage in my research.

The American Council of Learned Societies, the International Research and Exchanges Board, and the Fulbright-Hays Faculty Research Abroad Program all provided fellowships that enabled me to conduct research in Poland.

A grant from the Council on Research and Creative Work at the University of Colorado allowed me to turn my attention to Ireland and Northern Ireland. A grant from the College Arts and Humanities Institute at Indiana University enabled me to complete research in Dublin and London. The New Frontiers in the Arts and Humanities program provided generous support for research in Johannesburg, Pretoria, and Cape Town. The Wits Institute for Social Research (Johannesburg) and the Centre for African Studies at the University of Cape Town provided research bases in South Africa. A fellowship from the Moore Institute for Humanities at the National University of Ireland in Galway allowed me to think it all through again.

As this research has taken me down many new paths, I was fortunate to have the assistance of a number of student researchers: Anna Arays, Katie Hiatt, Nicolas Hidalgo, Andrew Jacobs, Megan Kelly, Daniel Mark, Ruthann Miller, and Jonathan Warner. I am especially grateful to my colleague Betsi Grabe for her reading of an essential source in Afrikaans. Marie Deer gave this manuscript its first thorough reading.

A version of Chapter 1 appeared as "'I Felt a Kind of Pleasure in Seeing Them Treat Us Brutally': The Emergence of the Political Prisoner, 1865–1910," in *Comparative Studies in Society and History* 54:4 (2012), 863–89, published by Cambridge University Press. Some of the material in Chapter 2 appeared in "'A Parade of Trick Horses': Work and the Physical Experience in the Political Prison," in *Global Convict Labour*, ed. Christian G. de Vito and Alex Lichtenstein (Leiden: Brill, 2015), 380–99.

At Oxford University Press, Susan Ferber has been the best and hardest-working editor I could have wished for. Anonymous readers delivered extremely thoughtful reviews, and the book is much the better for it. Any shortcomings are of course my own.

Many a family vacation over the last decade has included detours to visit a prison museum. Netflix sent a few too many prison movies in the mail. And I'll admit that torture and hunger strikes are difficult topics of conversation at the dinner table or while running errands around town. Through it all, Izabela has been more than patient, not to say indulgent. Thank you for sharing this history with me.

Dance in Chains

Introduction

Where a Free Man Can Abide with Honor

You have done nothing wrong—though to be honest, perhaps that's a matter of perspective. You marched in a demonstration, or you attended a meeting, or you wrote an essay that appeared in an underground journal, or you merely possessed a copy of that journal. Or maybe you really did break the law. You planted a bomb, carried a weapon, plotted an assassination, managed secret funds, advocated revolution—but you know this was in the service of a just cause, a struggle so that others could live more freely and have the rights they deserve. Perhaps you were just a sympathetic bystander, or perhaps an officeholder who became a victim of regime change. Regardless, what you did or did not do had political meaning and a higher purpose. Surely that puts your deeds, your words, and your allegiances in a different light. One thing is for sure: you aren't a criminal.

And yet you are fingerprinted, examined, interrogated, and stripped by armed officers. Perhaps you are beaten, taunted, threatened, bound. You have lost mastery of your life and must wear a uniform that marks your helplessness. You might face execution or merely a short detention, but you do not control your fate. And the regime you oppose, or merely disapprove of, is no longer an abstraction; it has you under its control. The terms of that control are both brutally explicit—guards might laugh that your life is now in their hands and that the only way to leave is "feet first"—and terrifyingly uncertain.

On the other hand, you can't be surprised. Imprisonment is one of the known consequences of opposing this regime. Objectively, you could even say that the state is acting in accordance with its established principles. These are the terms of political conflict. And you are a political prisoner.

Is there any figure in the contemporary world who inspires greater respect than the political prisoner? The women and men who are such prisoners have been locked away for professing their ideals or for demonstrating disagreement with a regime, and their suffering transcends their particular beliefs. They mark the limits of modern states' willingness to tolerate difference of opinion or belief.

1

Henry David Thoreau's claim that "prison is the only house in a slave state where a free man can abide with honor" has echoed for prisoners and their supporters around the world.[1] Prison, according to this line of thinking, ennobles the "free man." And yet, how can someone spend months, years, even decades locked away from family, friends, and supporters for no personal gain? It is one thing to fight for one's beliefs, but how can suffering in forced passivity be worth it? How could the experience not destroy one's spirit, body, and sanity?

Nevertheless, to be on the state's list of those considered sufficiently dangerous to be removed from society confirms one's commitment to a cause. In the spring of 1982, as the Polish communist regime interned nearly 10,000 members of Solidarity, Warsaw personages who had not yet achieved this badge of honor began to wonder how they might, with minimal physical risk, provoke the police into detaining and interning them, too. Some, according to legend, began carrying around a toothbrush and a change of underwear, displaying them to friends to prove that they mattered enough to fear the unmarked car or the midnight doorbell.

For some prisoners, the ongoing contest with the regime and the camaraderie with their fellow prisoners inspired a kind of joyful irony. Ludwik Waryński, the founder of the first socialist party in the Polish lands, inspired the title of this book with a song he composed in Warsaw's Citadel in 1885:

> Rise joyfully to the dance, you of rebellious faith.
> Turn and turn again, with joy. O Warsaw, O Kara!
> The enemy has for us chains and fortresses aplenty,
> But we are joyful, as our chains ring out a *mazurka*.[2]

The "Mazurka in Chains" became an anthem for Polish socialists, both in the exercise yards of prisons close to home and in the Kara Mines of Siberia; other songs, dances, and marches would break out in other prisons over the years. The positive emotions of the political prisoner—admiration, desire, and joy—stem from the belief that one can pursue politics in the prison cell. The confrontation with the state and its carceral institution is complex and multisided. Guards and interrogators, prison administrators, and prisoners, both political and criminal, all negotiate the rules that bind the political prisoner and the roles that the prisoner plays.

Opposition movements vary widely in their level of organization, their resources, their ideology, and their aims. Modern states also advance a range of ideologies and differ in their capacities and their willingness to use instruments of force against opponents. Where the two collide emerges the political prisoner, who exemplifies what the state can do and what the opposition is willing to do. In the terms of Irish revolutionary lore, the political prisoner demonstrates who can endure (or inflict) the most. As states and their employees confine and handle their opponents, prisoners and their supporters try to make sense of confinement and relate it to the cause or struggle that has put them behind bars. Together, they produce politics in the cell. To understand that politics beyond simple terms like "repression" and "resistance," this book investigates the multifaceted social and political relations enacted in this grim and hidden space.

In all but the cruelest of regimes, opposition movements have seen prison as a valuable part of the struggle. Political prisoners have inspired fervent campaigns domestically and around the world, beginning well before Peter Benenson launched Amnesty International in 1961. The image of the steadfast prisoner enduring privations and injustice behind bars with dignity crystallizes the twentieth-century struggle for social change and human rights. Yet thinking of political prisoners as "good people held by bad regimes" tells us nothing interesting, or even true; this book does not ask the reader to identify with the politics of any of its protagonists. Plenty of men and women imprisoned for their political actions—like Slobodan Milošević, Saddam Hussein, and Adolf Hitler—do not inspire esteem. Yet they too are a reminder that in any intense political struggle—for or against democracy, independence, human rights, civil rights, a civilization—some protagonists play their roles behind bars. With increasing regularity since at least the 1920s, prison years have become a useful qualification for high office. The resumés of John Vorster and Nelson Mandela in South Africa, Éamon de Valera and Martin McGuinness in Ireland/Northern Ireland, and Józef Piłsudski, Józef Cyrankiewicz, and Tadeusz Mazowiecki in Poland, among other state leaders, include this designation.

Given the great diversity of regimes and of oppositional ideologies, is it possible to reach general conclusions about the experience of political prisoners? Are there common practices and repertoires that they share? What can political incarceration accomplish, for the state or for its opponents? What does the political prisoner, alone or with others, do in the prison cell, and how do those actions matter? This book explores each of these questions. It argues that the political prisoner is neither necessarily heroic nor mere collateral damage but a potent figure in modern contentious politics.

The topic of political incarceration in the modern world is a huge one, and this book examines it through three large cases rather than by a global survey of prisoners. The latter approach might have turned the book into a superficial catalog of woe, in which numbers and names substitute for any sustained argument. The three cases—Poland, Ireland (and Northern Ireland), and South Africa—share several traits and yield a broad range of experiences. Each has seen a number of generations of political prisoners under a variety of regimes over the course of a century or more. These regimes range from Nazi rule in occupied Poland through the Apartheid state in South Africa to the democratic, though militarized, United Kingdom during the Troubles in Northern Ireland. Each country, indeed, has seen frequent regime change. In the 1860s, where this book begins, none of these countries even existed: Ireland was part of the United Kingdom, Poland was mostly part of the Russian Empire, and South Africa was subject to the British Empire. The spectrum of those imprisoned is equally broad; sometimes bitter opponents might be found in the same prison, as when white South African communists encountered extremist nationalists, Polish nationalists were jailed with Nazis, or Irish Republicans shared space with Ulster Loyalists.

As all of these countries are now open democracies, documents on their political prisoners are largely accessible. This book is based on research in two dozen archives and libraries in five countries, including prisoners' letters, diaries, petitions, and memoirs; the reports of informers and police; assessments by prison officials and by representatives of central government; and the documents of social movements. These perspectives build a collective portrait of the modern political prisoner—a figure who has not receded into the past, as analysis of a fourth case, the detention facility at Guantanamo Bay, will show.

To choose a set of cases is to exclude others. Most societies have at least some political prisoners. In many of them, the practice of political incarceration is as long and as widespread as in the cases examined here. Broadly, cases can be divided along a few axes. First, European regimes developed the necessary ingredients for identifying political prisoners earlier than regimes elsewhere. This is not to say that societies in Africa or Asia did not both generate and repress opposition. But political prisoners as such are produced by modern states and by oppositions with access to media and party structures.[3] Thus, the story in what would become South Africa picks up only in the first decade of the twentieth century. A parallel to this is the case of Vietnam where political prisoners began to act as a group within prison only in the early 1900s.[4] The same is true in Iran, where prisons really became centers of political activity when communists organized in the 1920s and 1930s.[5] While a system of state prisons developed somewhat earlier in Argentina, the story of political prisoners there appears to have developed only in the early twentieth century, as anarchists and communists—both prevalent among European migrants—organized.[6]

Within the European context, political prisoners emerged roughly in the mid-nineteenth century in a number of cases. Political prisoners have been chronicled, though not placed at the center of analysis, in France.[7] Scholars examining the topic have generally asked how states, police, and prisons have operated rather than exploring the category of prisoners themselves.[8]

A second way to categorize cases of political incarceration is to consider how sensitive regimes are to societal pressures. Authoritarian regimes are very likely to incarcerate a broader set of opponents than liberal or democratic governments and also to think differently about them. The prison guard may not be any less cruel in a "liberal" prison, but the mechanisms of sentencing, release, and information likely vary between authoritarian and more liberal governments.[9] This book draws attention to similarities by focusing on experiences inside prison. One distinction that is not fully captured in this book is that some authoritarian regimes—China certainly, and perhaps North Korea—make it more difficult for political prisoners to differentiate themselves from ordinary prisoners. Political prisoners act separately even when the "political" category is not recognized, but this appears from the fragmentary evidence to have been much harder to accomplish in the prisons and camps of Mao's China.[10] As historians broaden the study of political prisoners, each national history will no doubt contribute new perspectives to the arguments presented here. This book aims to illuminate the relations in which political prisoners everywhere are enmeshed.

More than portraying particular prisoners, this book is about political relations within prisons, among prisoners, and between prisoners and the regimes that confine them. The prison figures prominently in the literature on the modern state, but that literature tends to leave these relations hidden or assumed. Four important theorists dominate thinking about the prison. Erving Goffman described it as a "total institution," in which a variety of people are brought together under "a system of explicit, formal rulings and a body of officials" and required to follow "a single rational plan purportedly designed to fulfill the official aims of the institution."[11] This definition accurately describes the modern prison and helps elucidate how the prison is like a camp, a hospital, or an army barrack. But it inhibits analysis of the experiences of a group that seeks to exploit the institution.

More recently, the field of prison studies has been heavily influenced by Michel Foucault and Giorgio Agamben. The concepts they offer, however, have proven of little use in illuminating the specific experience of the political prisoner. The scholarship on prisons does not generally make a distinction between criminal and political prisoners, so Foucault's work in particular is often generalized.[12] Both Foucault, in *Discipline and Punish*, and Agamben, in *Homo Sacer*, portray worlds in which prisoners are closely observed (Foucault explores the prison as a "panopticon") and acted upon, with little or no agency of their own. They are examined, measured, and reduced, in Agamben's powerful phrase, to "bare life."[13] This approach helps enormously to explain the prison as the instrument of a modern regime that seeks to control its human resources, but not to make clear what political prisoners do and how their community acts. The prison Foucault and Agamben explore is one that sentences, punishment, and observation have rendered dead certain, yet for political prisoners, uncertainties outweigh certainties. Consider how much may be unknown to the political prisoner, in contrast to the typical criminal convict: Does law apply to me? Will

I be charged, or tried, or sentenced? How long will I be here? What do "they" still want to know about me? Does the cause still live on outside, or have arrests revealed that we were infiltrated and corrupted? Can I trust my cellmates or the person tapping on the wall from the next cell? These uncertainties shape, and in fact constitute a central purpose of, political incarceration.

Complementary to the total institution of the watchful state is an all-encompassing concept of resistance. Pushing back against the pessimistic view of total control, scholars like James Scott offer insight into the ways that even the "weak" can resist the hegemonic power of those above them.[14] The state, for Scott, desires that its people, like other assets, be "legible," their actions and characteristics easily accessible and able to be counted and utilized. The subject—a landless peasant, a citizen of an authoritarian state, an inmate—follows a "hidden transcript" that subverts the visible relations of power. Scott restores agency to his subjects, but the concept of resistance needs to be used with caution. This book will focus more on the idea of control—over the space one inhabits, one's body, one's relations with others and, finally, over the narrative of one's incarceration. Whereas the regime, through prison, seeks to assert control, deny agency, and erase even the possibility of redemption or transformation during or after incarceration, political prisoners ultimately overturn this with their own narratives; this is the power of political imprisonment.

This book begins by situating the political prisoner in the modern world, a new development in the history of incarceration. Chapter 1 argues that political prisoners appear in the second half of the nineteenth century. Earlier "imprisoned politicals" regarded prison as a hindrance to their politics; the new political prisoners in British, Russian, and African prisons were among the first to make the place of their incarceration a site of struggle in their campaigns. In the half-century before World War I, states showed some uncertainty about how to treat their incarcerated opponents whom previously they had exiled or summarily executed. In petty conflicts over roll calls, over a fork for one's dinner, or over the wearing of handcuffs in public, individual prisoners as well as regime officials and prison administrators worked out what it meant to be a political prisoner and developed a modern understanding of incarceration.

Political prisoners, of course, exist because a regime has put them behind bars. Chapter 2 explores the mechanisms of control that this institution exerts upon its inmates. Regimes subjugate their captives and seek to isolate them from politics by immersing them in uncertainties. Prison personnel constantly disrupt prisoner routines and impose their own seemingly arbitrary order; they foster mistrust among inmates and both brutalize and infantilize them. The chapter concludes by examining the practices and intended effects of torture. The regimes of a second period of political incarceration, stretching from World

War I through the 1950s, exhibited little of the hesitancy that their predecessors did; torture is one manifestation of this.

Chapter 3 tackles the question of who is a political prisoner. The answer depends in large part on subjective perception. Separating prisoners into "terrorists," "criminals," and "prisoners of conscience," for example, is an exercise in political preference, not definition. Instead, this chapter examines how political prisoners themselves have shaped and defended the term. The ways of initiation into the cell community and its practices, and the ways that future prisoners think about and prepare for prison, reveal the outlines of a political category. The chapter introduces two groups against whom politicals define and defend themselves: criminal prisoners and guards. Associating politicals with criminals allows regimes to make them indistinguishable, so politicals have to maintain the line of defense vigorously. One might expect that political prisoners would try to indoctrinate criminals, but politicals more often perceive criminal prisoners as diluting the community and undermining its character. Guards, in turn, provide a positive opportunity: by fooling, humiliating, or educating the daily face of the regime, political prisoners affirm and develop their identity.

In addition to the regime and the prisoners themselves, political movements outside the prison shape political prisoners' behavior and identity. The political prisoner and the movement draw strength from one another: the prisoner needs human interaction, comfort, and material support; the movement values the symbolic power of its living martyrs and the experience they gain inside. Chapter 4 considers how prisoners interact with the movements that claim to represent them and how communication works across a supposedly impenetrable boundary. Letters to comrades outside, and the occasional escapes, bind movements together as surely as do actions undertaken outside to assist those inside. Chapter 5, in turn, examines the role played by international movements of prisoner aid, from the Irish-American groups of the nineteenth century, through the "Red Help" movement that assisted communists in the interwar years, to Amnesty International today. Such movements are an important factor in the third era of political incarceration, beginning in the 1960s, in which ideas of rights become more visible both outside and within the prison. As they assist and defend political prisoners, rights movements shape the way others see political prisoners.

The last four chapters investigate how political prisoner communities produce new political realities as they organize and protest the rules of the prison and the politics of the regime. Chapter 6 offers a genealogy of prison organization, including prisoner-of-war camps and military structures, showing how these shaped new kinds of prisoner organization that emerged during and after World War I. The interwar years saw the development of extensive social structures, such as food-sharing communes, study groups, and creative circles. These groups manage elaborate forms of communication and distribution of goods.

Chapter 7 shows how prisoners respond to the illegibility that prison regimes impose upon them. They seek scraps of normal existence, engage in clandestine communication, deny or subvert their identity, and even destroy that identity—feigning madness or attempting suicide, for example. This search for control thus makes the prisoner illegible to the regime and forms the basis for the survival of political movements in prison. Indeed, political prisoners are most visible to the world outside when they engage in collective action. Some protests aim to confuse or deny control over the prison, such as by storming the prison gates to be let in or refusing to wear prison clothing. Chapter 8 details the best-known type of prisoner protest, the hunger strike. This is the most dramatic protest in which prisoners engage and also represents the height of prisoners' efforts to remove themselves from the authorities' reach, asserting control through an action that is both incomprehensible and unpredictable.

Many of the movements whose activists and supporters have been imprisoned have subsequently taken power, including nationalists, communists, and democrats in subsequent regimes in Poland; nationalists in Ireland and in Northern Ireland; and the African National Congress in South Africa. Chapter 9 turns to a crucial link between the prison cell and political change. Through basic education, discussion circles, and other forms of self-organization among prisoners, the prison experience can become a crucible of commitment to the cause, what has been dubbed the "prison university." The cell experience creates not only political activism but also activism of specific kinds, such as negotiated and nonviolent responses to repressive regimes.

An epilogue considers the present and future of political incarceration and tests the framework this book offers against the notorious case of the Guantanamo Bay detention camp. It compares the experiences and actions of prisoners and guards at Guantanamo to others in modern world history, while asking what is implied by calling Guantanamo a political prison.

Even the select settings chosen here, followed over the last century and a half, yield an account crowded with different stories. If the commonalities have any purchase at all, the details of individual biographies and national histories should be less important—but they nevertheless help to make the experience of imprisonment more palpable. That, too, is a purpose of this book. Political opponents of all stripes are still going to prison, all over the world, in the name of causes that may inspire admiration or scorn. Shedding light on their cells should make them recognizable and make it possible to see more clearly the ever-proceeding dance in chains.

1

"But I Have No Wish to Be Discharged"

When Imprisonment Became Political

On her first encounter with the Warsaw Citadel, in 1893, Zofia Grabska felt no fear of being imprisoned in the famed dungeon; she expressed only "embarrassment that by such a stroke of luck I had come to the Tenth Pavilion, where so many genuine heroes had spent time, and from which Traugutt and his comrades had gone to their deaths." The twenty-one-year-old found herself on sacred terrain, inheriting a space occupied by true Polish patriots like Romuald Traugutt, leader of an uprising in 1863. In vain she searched the walls for any graffiti left by her predecessors. "Gradually, I fell into a mood appropriate to the place. This mood satisfied the hunger of my soul. I had been worn out by everyday concerns and didn't have a clear knowledge of what I desired and in what direction I should go. Now, I began to fear that the mistake would be swiftly uncovered and they would release me too quickly from the Citadel."[1]

Grabska came from a noble family active in social causes and politics. She was in some ways a typical detainee of the time, a young recalcitrant from a good home, imprisoned by the Russian state to be taught some manners. The soldier who escorted her to her cell lit the lamp and made the bed for her, using sheets Grabska had brought from home. Soon, General Brok of Warsaw's Russian command paid a visit. As Grabska learned, the Citadel offered three different meal plans for peasants, townspeople, and nobility. She had no objection to belonging to the last category and didn't mind watching a soldier perform household tasks for her. Prison proved quite agreeable—but when the first dinner was brought, she refused it on the grounds of being given a spoon as her only eating utensil. Instead, she opened her suitcase, removed the dinner and flatware her mother had packed for her at the manor house that morning, and ate this meal instead.

The old and the new collided in this encounter of a young, well-born socialist with one of the Russian Empire's legendary places of incarceration, as established traditions of resistance and repression began to slip away. Grabska was a member of the Polish Socialist Party, founded less than a year before. She was a modern political activist in a premodern cell. Looking into her first cell, she glimpsed a heroic past; her gentle treatment echoed social traditions against which she and her comrades fought outside. Prison was but a temporary sequestering, with home life not too far away. By the time she wrote her memoirs decades later, political prisoners were no longer the stuff of legend but a standard feature of the political landscape, and the prison was no longer a place for picnic dinners.

The hospitality afforded Grabska did not herald great leniency. Although she was not executed, she was sent on to St. Petersburg, far from her mother's parcels and the intervention of friends. A second arrest soon after her release the following year resulted in a two-year Siberian exile. Yet—characteristically for the not-quite-modern political prison—her class meant nearly as much to the regime as did her crime. Both the punishment and the attendant amenities signified the state's evaluation of her position in Polish society. Like exile, that punishment reflected how a state could be policed and kept ordered. Until the last third of the nineteenth century, those incarcerated for engagement in political activities generally shared several basic characteristics: they were nobles, or at least well born; they were treated individually, because they rarely represented any organization; and they found themselves quickly on the way out of prison: to freedom, to exile, or to the gallows or guillotine.

The history of the incarceration of individuals for beliefs or actions against the state or comparable authority stretches far back before the modern era. Jesus Christ, Saint Peter, and Socrates—to take examples from just the ancient world—are sometimes described as political prisoners.[2] Attention to commonalities across time can be useful, not least because modern prisoners themselves are aware of the parallels and have found comfort, for example, in reading of the Passion of Christ. But such exemplars do not help to pinpoint what changed in the modern era. Consider instead the so-called Age of Revolution. In Britain, members of the London Corresponding Society were widely persecuted in the 1790s for their advocacy of radical ideas. These prisoners, and their freethinking successors through the Chartists of the 1840s, knew they were different from other prisoners in the nature of their transgressions and in their comportment under lock and key. They often expected and demanded treatment appropriate to their station in life.[3] The state, too, recognized that difference. For example, it allowed such prisoners to conduct business or entertain their friends in their cells. Many familiar elements, such as a common ideology, experience of collective action, and awareness of the state (as opposed to a single tyrant), appear in this prisoner–regime relationship. Yet to imagine that a continuum of slowly evolving experiences links all those who would speak truth to power or exercise their human rights and freedoms is to miss what makes the modern political prisoner something new.

The fundamental difference is between a politics *against* the prison and a politics *of* and *in* the prison. Before the mid-nineteenth century, prisoners incarcerated for political acts or ideas sometimes accepted their fate and sometimes protested it, but the prison itself appeared to them as a hindrance to their activities or as a representation of what was wrong in the political and social order. They could be called simply "imprisoned politicals," for their incarceration posed an obstacle to their political work. The political prisoner, in contrast to the imprisoned political, imposes his or her politics onto the prison, using it as an instrument of political activity. Some can act with impunity, while others, suffering severe restrictions, isolation, and hardships, can conduct but the barest outlines of a political struggle. Still, they aspire to a politics in and of the prison rarely if ever essayed by detained opponents of earlier eras.[4]

This chapter outlines what changes in the nineteenth century introduced the modern political prisoner. How was Zofia Grabska, in short, different from those whose graffiti she sought?

Imprisonment, Exile, and the Political

Few imprisoned politicals in early nineteenth-century Britain achieved as much fame from prison as did Henry Hunt, who was locked up at Ilchester in 1819 for advocating parliamentary reform during the so-called Peterloo demonstration. Defying the privations of the Ilchester "Bastile," as he called it, Hunt smuggled out a pamphlet, "A Peep into the Prison," that exposed the conditions he and his fellow prisoners endured. The pamphlet enjoyed wide circulation and had some impact on prison reform. Yet Hunt, as he describes the food, the furnishings, the sufferings of other inmates, and the petty cruelties of the wardens, gives no hint of a community of like-minded prisoners, nor any evidence that imprisonment contributed to his political struggle. Indeed, Hunt's repeated references to the limits placed on visits by his friends make it clear that prison interrupted his politics.[5] The prison, for Hunt and other radicals, exemplified what was wrong in England; William Cobbett could thus argue that the politicians and their cronies, and not the incarcerated debtors and petty thieves, were the real criminals deserving of a prison cell.[6] This politics against the prison, in varying degrees of radicalism, characterized not only the imprisoned political but also his comrades outside prison. Of course, the prison was intended by the state precisely to hinder the actions that provoked arrest and internment; the imprisoned political could not yet see a way beyond the boundaries set by the regime.

A quarter century later, John Mitchel, a barrister from Ulster, was drawn into the ferment of Irish nationalist politics in Dublin and became the movement's leading journalist. A grand jury charged him with sedition in April 1848; the charge was amended to treason. Mitchel was sentenced to fourteen years' transportation (forced exile). The crime for which he was convicted was manifestly political, and the sentence was among the harshest that could be exacted—and yet he was not truly a political prisoner. Mitchel's *Jail Journal* became a classic of Irish nationalist literature, making its author one of Ireland's iconic martyrs. The title, however, is a misnomer: Mitchel devotes barely a paragraph to his time in a prison cell and begins with the morning he leaves Newgate Prison. En route to the Dublin quay to be shipped to Bermuda, Mitchel travels alone, under special surveillance. Once aboard the ship that was to take him into exile, he quickly effaces his status as captive by engaging the ship's captain in learned conversation.[7] Mitchel's writings from abroad, for newspapers read by thousands, made him a category of one, either a treasonous individual or a tragic-heroic martyr, depending upon the reader's perspective.

Exile like Mitchel's effectively sundered the ties between the individual and the sentencing state. The state manifestly exerted its power over the individual in the courtroom, on the transport ship, and at the border; it often dictated how the exile would live. Siberian exiles were often restricted to one village or required to report regularly to a local police chief. Australian exiles arrived with papers that might send them to prison or to hard labor.[8] Yet though the chain of command typically led to the same ruler, prisoners were effectively removed from the state against which they had acted and could thus no longer hope to inspire unrest in the societies they had left.[9]

Political exiles might not have to cross their country's borders. Tens of thousands of Poles and Russians endured transport to Siberia, especially after the Polish uprisings of 1830 and 1863; toward the end of the century members of nascent anarchist and socialist groups joined them.[10] Exiles generally lived freely where they were assigned and reported regularly to local authorities.[11] By contrast, convict laborers in Australia, especially those sentenced for ordinary crimes, were virtually enslaved on farms and plantations.[12]

Transport did not differentiate between political and ordinary crimes. George Rudé, in his study of those transported to Australia from the British Isles over the eight decades that system was in effect, estimated that just over 2 percent of 162,000 individuals transported could be placed in a category of "social" protesters, ranging from participants in local insurrections to arsonists and maimers of wealthy landowners' cattle.[13] Suppressing a wave of insurrectionary violence in Ireland in 1822–23, for example, British courts tried some 4,000, convicting just over 500; of these, 90 percent were transported.[14] Leaving aside whether such men and women, who took oaths, attended meetings, or were found carrying arms, were really political offenders, the state clearly had little interest in keeping them around, whether for reformation or as cautionary examples. The prison, in this process, was a temporary stage in the course of punishment, lumping political offenders together with criminals in their removal from society. Having imposed severe punishment on them, the state had no long-term interest in their persons.

Exile of protesting individuals might appear to be the logical outcome of a modernizing state's efforts to manage nascent social and national revolt, a pruning of disorderly growth in society's garden.[15] The nineteenth century was indeed the century of exile, as states acquired, at about the same time, both the power to suppress rebellion or conspiracy (with standing armies and police forces) and extensive territories (colonies or remote hinterlands) to which they could send vanquished foes. However, a practice in which the state relinquished direct control over its opponents was inadequate to the concurrent expansion of state power and aspirations. At the same time, target territories no longer wished to receive boatloads of societal rejects, and states questioned whether exile was an efficient use of transport and of land. Not that exile disappeared as a form of social control: when the British were phasing out the practice, beginning in the 1850s, France was just beginning to implement it, and the French would continue to use penal colonies until after World War II; British India would soon transport Indian rebels to the remote Andaman Islands; and Siberia would remain a destination for Russian and Soviet convicts until the late twentieth century. However, considering the tens of thousands of individuals whom Britain had transported to distant lands in the nineteenth century, the decline of exile signifies a crucial shift in the way political prisoners were regarded and treated. The prisoner kept close to home in a state institution would be able to serve some use for the modern state.

The early modern prison, unlike its modern counterpart, was locally controlled, loosely regulated if at all, and privately run. In Britain through the early nineteenth century, the jailer derived his income from any fees he could extract from those placed in his charge.[16] Russia, meanwhile, had much less use for prisons at that time, as the serfs were tied to landowners and subject to their idiosyncratic systems of justice. Prison, it seems, was a place avoided not only by the offender but even by the courts, which mostly issued either a sentence of corporal punishment or immediate release.[17] In Asia and Africa, prisons were often decidedly temporary institutions.[18] As a means of sequestration, banishment was preferable to prison for both the prisoner and the state.

No neat dividing line exists in the history of political incarceration. Modernizing European states gradually developed and expanded institutions to house, discipline, and reform criminals. The prison as a centrally controlled state institution emerged globally over a century and a half, spreading from northeastern Europe in the eighteenth century to Asia and Africa in the early twentieth century. By the mid-nineteenth century, all countries in Western Europe and North America boasted a network of state-run institutions employing a variety of techniques to control and transform their residents.[19]

The prisoner-state relationship was concurrently shaped by the emergence of political parties and organizations. The modern political organization, hierarchical and united by common ideas and tasks, matured around the world between the 1860s and the 1910s in the context of dynamic urban centers, increasingly literate communities, and rapid communication technologies. Parties, associations, trade unions, and the like espoused relatively coherent ideologies that they could use to challenge the state. Socialist and nationalist organizations developed by the 1870s into mass movements with a permanent place in the political landscape, even where they were illegal. New kinds of political organizations forced liberal and autocratic regimes alike to reexamine policy toward their opponents.[20] This era would see the first concentration camps, the first genocides, and the first civilian refugees. It is not surprising that political prisoners would take their place on stage at the same time.

Concurrently with the prison, movements arose to aid prisoners and to expose the conditions they suffered. Agitation or organization on behalf of prisoners emerged at the intersection of two trends. On the one hand, the humanitarian impulse, deeply rooted in traditions of religious charity, acquired secular form in the era of liberal civic association.[21] Prisoners were a riskier group to assist than, say, orphans or the poor, but they fascinated liberal society, both as a spectacle and as a wayward citizenry who could be reformed. Offering food and clothing to prisoners became an acceptable avocation for the urban middle class in cities like London and Antwerp. Prison visiting boards, unpaid civic organizations that monitored prison conditions and received prisoner complaints, usually reporting to a judge or magistrate, flourished in the early nineteenth century.[22]

The story of prison reform began with advocates like John Howard, whose 1777 treatise *The State of the Prisons*, based upon visits to prisons around Britain, set the parameters of debate: what is the prison for, and how should it achieve these aims? These questions animated liberals in Northwest Europe and North America to experiment with systems of discipline and punishment for the wayward and the transgressor.[23] While some focused on how the institution could remake the criminal, others concerned themselves with the experience of the inmate. Groups like the Society for the Moral Improvement of Prisoners in the Netherlands, inspired by religious faith and civic impulse, publicized the dire straits of common prisoners and sought to ameliorate their suffering.[24] Occasionally a former prisoner—likely an imprisoned political, not a typical debtor or common criminal—might join such campaigns, but this work was overshadowed by the greater program of making the prison achieve the state's objectives.

Until the mid-nineteenth century, campaigns on behalf of prisoners were unlikely to advocate freeing them except to alleviate suffering. But in the Italian States and France after the 1848 revolutions, and in Ireland after the Fenian Rebellion, supporters demanded freedom for their incarcerated comrades, drawing on the accumulated knowledge and rhetoric of the prison reformers. A new word entered the lexicon of prison campaigners: amnesty. This cause allowed defeated revolutionaries a secondary goal and eventually brought some victories. Famous early examples were the amnesties of French emperor Napoleon III. In several decrees from 1852 to 1859, he offered freedom to thousands of participants in the 1848 revolution. Six years later, the emperor offered amnesty to insurgents in Algeria.[25] These acts of clemency resonated across Europe, where political causes were becoming organized movements. Thus, amnesty emerged as a theme among Fenian supporters. The Reverend John Spratt issued a cautious appeal to Queen Victoria in a speech at Dublin's Temperance Hall in October 1869. Careful to disavow any association and abjuring any untoward "language of defiance," he nevertheless offered pointed praise for Napoleon III and decried the "bitter sufferings the Political Prisoners have already undergone."[26] The defiance Spratt deplored was much in evidence elsewhere, as the movement for a Fenian amnesty divided between radicals and moderates, attracting police attention.[27]

Thus, imprisoned politicals could be the object of a campaign to free them. Such figures could be cast as martyrs for their causes, around whom the movement could coalesce. While prisoners in general had already become an object of charity in the eighteenth century, the era of revolutions in the early nineteenth century brought fame and attention specifically to politicals. The earliest such campaign on behalf of a group of imprisoned politicals was likely that for imprisoned Italian revolutionaries in the 1840s (assisted by the publication in many languages of Silvio Pellico's memoir of imprisonment), followed soon after by French opponents to Louis Napoleon in the 1850s. These drew international support, especially from the British public.[28] Paradoxically perhaps, prisoners became more interesting politically when they became less accessible. Celebrity prisoners of the early nineteenth century did not need anyone to call attention to their plight, in the way that lesser figures hidden away in state prisons needed to be remembered. For some movement activists, prisoners were another marginalized or forgotten group in need; for others, they symbolized a struggle for one kind of liberation or another.

In the eyes of the state, the modern movement-based politicals looked very different from their predecessors. The individual pamphleteer or the cattle rustler might be easily neutralized. A few months in jail awaiting trial, a miserable berth on a ship bound for Melbourne, a set of leg irons in a carriage headed beyond the Ural Mountains, or a hangman's noose would bring a swift end to the problem. Behind every such troublemaker the regime might suspect a con-spiracy, but one with shallow roots. Late nineteenth-century civil society pre-sented new challenges less easily vanquished.

States responded unevenly at first, as prosecution was constricted by what his-torian Seán McConville calls the dilemma of the "chivalrous state."[29] Lawmakers recognized prominent political dissenters as being of the same class and even disposition as themselves, and so politicians often tended toward leniency, even in cases of violent opposition. Regimes considered the inherent qualities of the well-born prisoner to outweigh their deeds or ideas. "It is difficult," observes Otto Kirchheimer in one of the first studies of political crime, "to prosecute a heretic while explicitly recognizing the purity of motivation which triggered this action."[30] His phrasing makes clear that the regime is responding to an indi-vidual, not a movement. But as much as a ruler might grant leniency for—or, conversely, inflict exceptional, sadistic punishment on—a noble gadfly, the repressive apparatus of a modern state would hardly be likely to treat the mem-bers of a political party in personal terms.[31]

The rise of constitutional liberalism after 1848 also hemmed in European states, which hesitated to punish political transgressors seriously. Kirchheimer cites the case of Paul Déroulède, whose right-wing Patriots' League plotted the overthrow of the French Third Republic in 1899, leading to his arrest. Even as he demanded to be tried for treason, Déroulède was acquitted merely of a mis-demeanor before a high court banished him from the country.[32] That leniency of European rulers in the nineteenth century, an era of national uprisings and anarchist plots, was as much the product of confusion as of benevolence or class solidarity. The abilities of the police to monitor and arrest suspected subversives outstripped, for a time, the interest that the legal and executive apparatus had in prosecuting those whom the police put at their disposal. This had little to do with popular pressure; rather, states prioritized order and thought it sufficient to try (and execute or banish) a leader or remove miscreants from sight.

Premodern incarceration looks in some ways like exile, even when it was not a first step toward exile. The premodern imprisoned political could simply be forgotten. Walerian Łukasiński suffered this fate. An army officer linked to the Freemasons and other secret organizations in Warsaw during the reign of Russian emperor Nicholas I, Łukasiński was sentenced in 1824 to fourteen years' imprisonment, with the proviso that he could not be released without personal approval from the governor general of the Kingdom of Poland. In fact, he died in the Shlisselburg Fortress outside St. Petersburg in 1868. Over the decades, he was occasionally glimpsed by other prisoners, but he was as distant from subse-quent generations as if he had been exiled.[33] Though Łukasiński ostensibly rep-resented a movement of disaffected, liberal nationalists, he was really a personal captive of the ruler, held indefinitely. He was not on public display, nor was he of any interest to the sovereign.[34] Why Alexander I kept Łukasiński in Shlisselburg rather than exile him to Siberia or have him hanged remains obscure; given the utter isolation of his sentence, the location made no significant difference.

The creators of the modern prison vigorously debated the correct approach to social control and the best means to create what Michel Foucault called "docile bodies." The debate about means contained a debate about purpose: could criminals really be transformed by prisons into useful, respectable citizens, or should they simply be confined as punishment and a prophylactic measure? Were the oft-invoked principles of moral improvement and compassion real or a smokescreen for the vengeful exercise of state power?[35]

Such debates relate only indirectly to the question of how to deal with political opponents, some of whom a state might choose to tolerate. Imprisonment of a political opponent obviously promises a different sort of security from that afforded by locking up a murderer, and the beneficiary of this security is as much the state or the sovereign as it is the people. Politicals were also unlike debtors, common denizens of nineteenth-century prisons, for there is no obvious way for the political prisoner to make amends. The modern political prisoner challenges, both implicitly and explicitly, the very ideas of discipline and reform. By the last third of the century, prisons had become a place to keep political offenders as well as criminals; the question was in what sense they were separate or different.

The Bold Fenian Men

In January 1868, the frigate *Hougoumont*, the last convict ship from Britain, arrived in Western Australia carrying nearly 300 convicts. As states turned from expulsion toward monitored, proximate incarceration of political offenders, the age of the modern political prisoner subject to the legal and punitive apparatus of the total institution began. The category could be seen even in law. In 1880, the Russian authorities in Warsaw, establishing guidelines for the Citadel (and subsequently other prisons), acknowledged the category of "political prisoner." The rules were somewhat ad hoc and were in any event superseded by a comprehensive regulation five years later. However, the 1880 regulation recognized, both in permitting and in forbidding certain rights, a collective identity. On the one hand, politicals were to be separated from criminals and allowed to walk on the prison grounds together. On the other hand, they were forbidden from submitting petitions as a group, an action they were likely to attempt.[36]

Whether the state was lenient, chivalrous, or simply ill-prepared, it experienced socialists, nationalists, and other organized political movements as new challenges. Among the first movements furnishing political prisoners in the modern sense were the Fenians, who succeeded Mitchel's Young Irelanders in the struggle for Irish freedom in the 1860s. The Fenian movement—formally the Irish Republican Brotherhood—resembled other late nineteenth-century movements across Europe in its emphasis on conspiracy, organization, and armed struggle. In cooperation with comrades in the United States, the Fenians planned an uprising in Ireland for 1865, but their plans were discovered and most of the principals arrested. James Stephens, one of the founders, was detained in November and held in Richmond Bridewell prison in Dublin with a few of his comrades. Less than two weeks later, he escaped with the help of his guards and friends outside and left the country. The cells of the forty or so left were reinforced with iron, and trials before Special Commissions took place within a month. The trials—which featured Fenian leader Jeremiah O'Donovan Rossa defending himself with incendiary speeches—convicted many movement leaders.[37] By the end of 1866, more than 750 Fenians were imprisoned, most in England; hundreds more followed over the next two years as further Fenian plots were uncovered. More than a hundred received sentences ranging from several years to life incarceration.[38]

The Fenian prisoners, Seán McConville argues, "did not grasp the opportunity to continue their fight within the prison walls . . . . Prison had yet to be viewed by the militant as a theatre of revolutionary war."[39] Yet the Fenians did forge a new collective political identity in British prisons, becoming more than imprisoned politicals. Some came to see the prison itself as a place in which one acted as a political; for them, as McConville puts it, "captivity became an opportunity as well as an incapacity."[40] Prison proved an arena for the contest with the British government. If the Fenians did not continue an active campaign against the regime from within their prison cells, their incarceration was nonetheless something more than the lonely martyrdom it had been for their predecessors. In small ways, they reformed a political community within the English prisons.

For the British, this bounty of captives far exceeded those from earlier protest movements such as the Chartists. The incarceration of an entirely homegrown, mainly English, movement like the Chartists would likely have been uncomfortable for the British regime and public, but the Irish could more acceptably be arrested, tried, and imprisoned en masse. The option to transport them, though, was rapidly disappearing. So the British authorities devised novel restrictions, as they clearly expected the Fenians to conspire in prison. Even when sharing cells, therefore, detainees were not allowed to speak with one another. Contact during exercise was similarly restricted. Newspapers were forbidden, and prisoners could only write letters intended for delivery outside the prison.[41] Fenian actions inside and outside prison reinforced British fears that they posed a danger even when incarcerated. These prisoners, authorities decided, were a dangerous group in and of themselves, wherever they were.

Less than two weeks before the *Hougoumont* sailed for Australia, an armed attack on a police van freed two Fenians recently arrested in Manchester. The

Fenian campaign of prison rescues culminated in an amateurish plot to free Richard Burke from Clerkenwell Prison in December 1867. Burke, a prominent member of the Brotherhood, had helped to plan the Manchester rescue. His comrades planned to rescue him by blowing up (from the outside) a wall of the prison's exercise yard. The explosion, on the afternoon of December 13, killed and wounded a number of people in the prison's vicinity, but rescued no one. The attempt unleashed rumors that a wave of Irish terror would engulf Britain with assaults on other prisons. The police began to round up anyone of whom they were suspicious, and they increased surveillance; guards in prisons where Fenians were held began carrying arms.[42] Thus for the British public and authorities, just as for the Fenians, the prison became a focus of political relations.

As a group, the Fenians seemed far more dangerous than had John Mitchel. Exile would not make them disappear from public memory; besides, their attacks had challenged state institutions directly. Thus incarceration became the method not only to contain political unrest but also to attempt to erase the cause. Yet the British met their match in Fenian leader Jeremiah O'Donovan Rossa, who well understood the propaganda value of prison. Offered passage to Western Australia, Rossa refused, recalling later: "I felt a kind of pleasure in seeing them treat us brutally in England, and I could not enjoy this feeling under similar treatment in the Antipodes."[43] Proximity to one's own community, in

Fig. 1.1 The Fenian bombing of the Clerkenwell Prison, December 13, 1867. From *Illustrated Police News,* December 21, 1867. Courtesy of the British Library.

other words, allowed the prisoner to furnish a spectacle of repression and suffering that would not be visible in distant exile. To be a prisoner on one's home turf, or close to it, afforded some political benefit from the regime's treatment. O'Donovan Rossa's prison memoirs, unlike those of Henry Hunt, keep the collective always in view.

O'Donovan Rossa's defiance of authorities, and his sense of his position within the prison community, steadily escalated. At Portland prison, he and his comrades found no Roman Catholic priest, nor an appropriate place of worship; their protest yielded permission to choose one among them to read prayers and scripture in the cellblock corridor on Sundays. This exercise in self-organization became a protest, as the reader, Denis Mulcahy, took care to choose texts with "denunciations of tyrants and oppressors . . . and blessings for all who suffered persecution for justice sake [sic]."[44] On the relatively limited ground of religious faith, the authorities granted the Fenian prisoners the right to govern themselves and thus to articulate a collective identity in incarceration.

Still, O'Donovan Rossa and the others had to work out what being a political prisoner entailed. The guards at Portland chose two prisoners to clean the outhouse every three weeks. When O'Donovan Rossa's turn approached,

> I told my companions I would refuse, and some of them remonstrated with me. Mr. Luby observed that obedience and subordination were more than anything else in accord with the dignity of the cause of our imprisonment, and in this I agreed with him. John Mitchell [sic] submitted to the prison discipline, he said, and did his work like any other convict, but I could never realize to my mind John Mitchell's shoveling the dung out of a privy.[45]

Two questions were at issue here. First, does obedience or disobedience bring greater dignity to the prisoner? The Fenians came to agree on obedience; other groups of prisoners drew different conclusions. The second question concerns the individual prisoner's responsibility to his comrades. O'Donovan Rossa relented when another comrade pointed out "that some four or six of our party had cleaned the closet before me, and my refusing to do it would look as a reflection on their spirit or a presumption of my own superiority."[46] Both sides looked to Mitchel's experience, but in the end, the desire to maintain solidarity prevailed. Soon, O'Donovan Rossa was breaking stones in the prison yard at record pace, showing himself to be, he tells a prison officer sarcastically, "a gentleman convict." He would not remain so; when ordered to break stones in Chatham Prison in early 1868, he flung his hammer over the prison wall and was chained to the floor of his cell as punishment.[47]

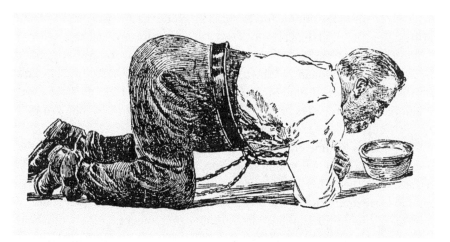

Fig. 1.2 Jeremiah O'Donovan Rossa in Chatham Prison, 1868. From John McGuffin, *Internment* (Tralee: Anvil, 1974), plate 1.

One sure marker of political detainees—both imprisoned politicals and political prisoners—is that they are constantly wondering about, negotiating, or defending a status that is only partly visible. Whether it is the way they are detained, the charges laid (or not laid) against them, their station in life, or their views, something indicates to such prisoners, to the state, or both that they could be called political. Jeremiah O'Donovan Rossa was not the first political captive, but he may have been the first to contest the incarcerating regime, together with a larger group, for an extended period of time, and to recognize how valuable his imprisonment was to him and his cause. The Fenians spent up to six years in prison, treated largely as a group even as they were frequently moved around the English penal system. Their incarceration delineated the boundaries of collective action within and without the prison cell. The British eventually succeeded in suppressing the movement, but O'Donovan Rossa would become a legend from the moment his prison memoirs appeared.

During these years, the British authorities discovered that the imprisonment of a large number of political opponents had led them into a trap. They recognized the group as distinct and worthy of special opprobrium. Yet in consigning them to prison, they aimed ostensibly to treat these men like any other convicts. This is the classic dilemma of the modern repressive regime: it wants to single out political offenders for punishment, but it also fears drawing attention to them. The British found it a difficult position to maintain. Seán McConville describes the British government's Fenian dilemma: "The doctrine of 'no political prisoners here' was the official line, but neither officials nor politicians believed or acted as though it were true." By 1870, he notes, the Fenians had won the category in all but name.[48] While O'Donovan Rossa's protests surely had some effect, the authorities no doubt feared the publicity consequences of any mistreatment. To hold such prisoners was a necessary inconvenience, subject to constant pressure from the prisoners, from movements advocating freedom for the prisoners (or trying to free them), from sympathetic or hostile publics, and from political leaders. Prime Minister William Gladstone had little choice but to grant an amnesty; a first group of Fenians went free in 1869, followed by a second group, mostly expelled from the country, in 1871.

The patterns hammered out during the Fenian years were repeated in the next episode in Irish political incarceration, that of the so-called Dynamitards in the 1880s. The authorities' security concerns were much greater, and public opinion more severe, in the case of these men who set bombs in railway stations, on bridges, and in other public places in England. These men—six of whom were tried in 1883–84 and served about fifteen years—acted like and were treated as political prisoners. In Chatham Prison, they were the "Special Men" and were constantly harassed under the guise of security; for example, guards observed them hourly during the night and let the metal inspection flap on the door fall shut with a clang to prevent the prisoner from sleeping. The authorities even selected reading material—nursery rhymes and anti-Papist tracts—to further torture the Dynamitards.[49] They endeavored to treat them like ordinary dangerous criminals while also distinguishing them; this was made easier by the evident severity of the Dynamitards' actions. Though a number of the prisoners went mad, one, Thomas Clarke, carried on a constant correspondence with his fellow prisoners, even publishing a clandestine newspaper from the prison's print shop.[50] The Dynamitards' experience is a reminder, however, that the resourcefulness of the political prisoner was still set against a much more powerful state.

The Mazurka in Chains

In the Russian Empire, in the same decades, the balance also began to shift from exile toward political imprisonment. Socialists were central actors in this drama, slowly altering the political landscape of a society where political opposition had been so clearly identified with the nobility. As they sought explicitly to build alliances across classes and to remake the political and economic order, socialists undermined the ability of regimes to differentiate among oppositions on the basis of class.

Socialist parties emerged across Europe in the decade after the defeat of the Paris Commune in 1871, another clear moment marking a transition toward the era of organization and ideology.[51] In Poland, indeed throughout the Russian Empire, the first socialist party was Proletaryat, founded by Ludwik Waryński in 1882.[52] Members of Proletaryat who went to prison were also pioneers, facing an autocratic state quite different from that which imprisoned the Fenians. Waryński's party was preceded by informal groups of socialist students and workers who held clandestine meetings in Warsaw in 1878–79, until nearly all its leading members were arrested. Significantly, the prosecutor branded them as an association that does "not act as individuals but in complete agreement with one another."[53] The Russian state, like its counterparts elsewhere, was beginning to articulate this concern more clearly.

The socialists, yet lacking a collective name, became stronger in prison. One, Zygmunt Heryng, discovered that despite the rigors at the Warsaw Citadel, he and his friends could publish several issues of a newspaper, "The Prisoner's Voice," which reached, so he claimed, the workers of Warsaw, Łódź, and even Kraków, across the border in the Austrian Empire. The prison director, Aleksandrowicz, had a deal with the prisoners: he would only serve them meat cutlets on holidays or in case of an inspection, and in exchange he would turn a blind eye to their activities. He instructed Heryng "not to knock too loudly [on the walls], because I could get the gendarmes upset and cause [the director] trouble."[54] Still, by 1881 Heryng and more than a hundred of his comrades were en route to Siberian exile, and the movement vanished.

Waryński revived Polish socialism with a vengeance; after a brief but impressive series of strikes and protests, he and his comrades would fill up the Citadel. Though Proletaryat organized strikes and published a newspaper, its greatest impact came through its prison experience. The Russian authorities, grappling with a wave of assassinations, treated its captives with some ambivalence. Six of Waryński's comrades were convicted of participation in specific acts and hanged. Party leaders were exiled instead, perhaps because the Russian authorities still differentiated between violent acts and intellectual leadership.[55] Veteran socialist Feliks Kon could see how much changed, as the regime grappled with the spread of socialist groups, by comparing two experiences a decade apart. Early in his first prison sojourn in 1884, Kon refused an order from Lieutenant Fursa, the infamous chief of the Citadel, to prepare for an interrogation downtown. Kon knew he could not be taken by force, lest the spectacle of a prisoner in chains provoke a street protest. The standoff was only resolved by Fursa's superior, General Unkowski, who promised that books and letters would be delivered to Kon's cell.[56] Though just twenty years old, Kon already knew what he could demand and what he might hope to receive within prison. What is revealing is not so much the leniency with which Kon was treated but the informality of the rules that allowed even a young socialist Polish Jew to win the attention of a Russian general and gain concessions.

Ten years later, back from Siberian exile, Kon found himself again in the Citadel. This time, he received a printed copy of the prison regulations, which warned: "Whosoever has come here should forget who he was, and remember only that he is a prisoner."[57] The message mirrored a lesson in Waryński's "Mazurka in Chains": to be in prison was a special identity in itself. The regime was not thinking of its captives as wayward noblemen or foolish youth, nor as terrorists to be strung up or shot. Instead, they were prisoners, located in and defined by a specific place. Kon and his comrades (now of the Polish Socialist Party) thus entered into a new relationship with their captors and the regime.

By this time the Russian Empire was awash in political parties, as well as a growing variety of civic associations, especially in the Polish territories. The early 1890s saw street protests and marches become a regular feature of Warsaw's public life. Out of this milieu came Zofia Grabska. After several months in the Citadel, she was transferred to the Kresty, a huge prison complex in the center of St. Petersburg. Decades later, she maintained that this prison had made her a socialist. The prison library kept her supplied with books that surely would not have passed a review board—like Chernyshevskii's *What Is to Be Done?*, the bible for many a budding socialist in the Russian Empire. "The pride and joy," she recalled, "that I will no longer be 'a marriageable girl,' that I will become (because that's what I had decided) a creative force, at least in some modest way, leading humanity to a better tomorrow, so brightened my cell that I simply came to love it. No longer was I in such a hurry to leave the prison."[58] Grabska's comment resonates with O'Donovan Rossa's a quarter-century earlier: being in prison brought a certain satisfaction. The Fenian focused on the fact that his imprisonment made the regime uncomfortable; the Polish socialist recognized that it could transform her. Both were writing from the perspective of national liberation movements and realized that prison contributed to that struggle.

At the turn of the century, the Polish Socialist Party (PPS) grew exponentially from a tiny band of intellectuals into a sizable social movement with ties to labor activism across the Russian Empire and beyond. The few hundred socialists of the 1890s became thousands by about 1903; factory workers increasingly peopled a party that had long been dominated by intellectuals. Anti-war protests in 1904 and the outbreak of revolution in January 1905 brought the socialists onto the streets; by the end of 1905, the PPS and its trade union boasted tens of thousands of members and supporters. Socialists would become the Russian Empire's first significant community of political prisoners.[59]

The prisoners' relationship to their political traditions changed. The legends that had haunted late nineteenth-century Polish prisoners were the men who had left the cell for the execution yard or Siberia. By 1900, prisoner legends came from the present. One such legend was Józef Piłsudski, the socialist who would later lead Poland to independence. In the 1880s, he spent three years in Siberia before going into exile. In 1900, though, his marginalia (written in pin pricks) in prison library books excited rank-and-file socialists like Marian Płochocki, revealing that their leader was with them.[60] Prison was an integral part of the struggle against Russian rule as its participants moved in and out with regularity, effacing the boundary between the cell and the street.

Polish socialists thrived and gained self-recognition in prison. Indeed, Warsaw prisons in the first decade of the century seemed almost to be under the control of the socialists and communists, who communicated with one another at will. Printer Wacław Koral, a communist first arrested in December 1901, felt overwhelmed with anger and the need to protest his incarceration in Pawiak Prison, so he began a hunger strike. On the third day the door opened and a

Fig. 1.3 Postcard by Jerzy Soszyński/George d'Ostoja, c. 1908. The caption reads: "Why do you long for home, for home? Isn't it better for us behind bars, behind bars?" Courtesy of Archiwum Akt Nowych, Warsaw.

guard tossed in a small package containing bread, sausage, and a note from a party comrade: "Stop the protest and accept prison regulations. You won't beat the walls down with your head. You are yet needed."[61] Emperor Nicholas II could still execute opponents or send them to Siberia, but Polish socialists had incorporated the prison experience into their political world, using it to work out their ideas, in interactions with each other and with guards and criminal prisoners.

The transformation of the prison owed something to the diversification of the political prisoner community. Koral was one of many workers who joined the students who had previously made up the bulk of socialist prisoners. An anecdote recounted by another worker illustrates how this new makeup changed the balance of the prison. One day in the spring of 1906, two prisoners escaped from the Citadel, unnoticed until the soldiers staffing the prison conducted a count and realized that they would be held responsible for lax security. "Then," recalls Bronisław Fijałek, "a distinguished middle aged worker, the leader of the catacomb prisoners, whom everyone respected," summoned the officer in charge and assured him: "'We know that you're a very good man, and you've done nothing bad to your soldiers or to us. If you agree, we'll arrange so that there will be no prisoners missing when your watch concludes, and you won't be held responsible." During the count, Fijałek and another skinny prisoner slipped through a secret passage between cells to be counted twice; the officer gave them "an almost imperceptible, grateful glance." The prisoners repeated this maneuver at every count until a day when a more sadistic team was on duty and was allowed to "discover" the disappearance of two prisoners. Fijałek gives the story a fairytale ending, as the cruel head guard understood the lesson and "softened."[62] In Fijałek's surely dramatized account, a worker enjoys the respect of both his political comrades and the prison authorities. He and other workers are key to the control of the prison; Fijałek implies that their affinity with Russian soldiers contributes to this. The worker does not object to imprisonment as such in his speech to the commanding officer, but points out that the prison is partly under the prisoners' control and could be used to deliver a socialist message.

"Control" should be understood in limited terms; even in this time of revolution, criminal convicts constituted the bulk of the prison population.[63] While political prisoners experienced a profound transformation in their place in the prison, the authorities would have considered this empowerment secondary to the massive growth in the prison population as a whole. Still, the fact that politicals could be numbered in the dozens or even hundreds in one prison, and that workers easily outnumbered the intellectuals, would have been obvious to prison officials and guards.

The Prison Becomes a Political Tool

In the British Empire as in Russian Poland, the first decade of the twentieth century saw new, unfamiliar groups crowd into the prison cell. They undermined established relations, forcing prison authorities to understand their charges not as an assortment of dissenting gentlemen, seditious newspapermen, or merely the belligerents of a marginal nation. Rather, the prison would contend with collectives that conceived of their place of incarceration as a site of contention with the regime. Beyond asking for privileges or improvements in their condition, these prisoners built a community within the prison walls that came to be just as important to the movement as their activity outside.

In 1899, the British Empire embarked on a war with the independent Orange Free State and the Transvaal Republic in southern Africa. The ensuing three-year conflict, the Second Boer War, proved complicated to win, as Afrikaans-speaking farmers waged guerrilla battles against British troops with some success. Beginning in December 1900, British forces evacuated hundreds of thousands of Boer and African settlers from large swaths of territory in the Transvaal and the Orange Free State and interned them in concentration camps, where tens of thousands died.[64] The ostensible purpose was to control a hostile population and protect it from the effects of the war.[65]

The concentration camp inmate is not necessarily a political prisoner. Men, women, and children rounded up for their ethnicity or their residence, or in retaliation for the actions of others, do not become political, nor behave politically, simply because a regime distrusts them. "Prisoner of politics" more accurately captures the fact that while politics accounted for their plight, it was not their own politics that led to their internment.[66] As a matter of course, the British forces in the Transvaal also rounded up subversive elements and imprisoned them as "political prisoners."[67] They faced quite a different problem in the Western Cape than elsewhere, for this was territory that had been under British control for a century; it followed that political opponents were committing treason. Detained treason suspects—newspaper editors, clergymen, teachers—began to fill up the jails; courts martial convicted over 9,000 individuals.[68] Local officials, meanwhile, struggled to determine what treatment "political offenders" merited and how they were treated and classified in the United Kingdom.[69] How did those convicted of sedition, like newspaper editors, differ from armed rebels who were convicted of high treason? Both were exempt from hard labor, and though there were several dozen executions, the authorities generally interpreted the regulations with leniency. Thus, they allowed prisoners to wear their own clothes, to receive or procure their own food, and to write letters and receive visitors with frequency, following regulations in force in England.[70]

In the midst of a war, these special cases posed a tough challenge. In July 1901, Assistant Resident Magistrate of Tokai Prison H. Orpen passed on a request from the "High Treason Prisoners" that they be allowed to procure their own beds, since the "imprisoned Editors" had received permission. This seemingly innocuous request alarmed Under Colonial Secretary H. B. Shawe, who wondered how the two sets of prisoners had been able to compare conditions; Orpen had been sent the high treason group on assurance that they would be held incommunicado. In any case, Shawe continued, these prisoners were not "quite on the same footing" as the editors, given their more serious crimes.[71] Both Shawe and Orpen were trying to parse categories but also to blur them, using an occupational reference ("editors") in place of a penal one. Confined in the same place under the same martial law, the prisoners were nevertheless separated into men of action and men of words. Thus the boundaries of the political and the obligations of the regime remained uncertain.[72] The deference to the political prisoner, even far from home and of another nationality, is reminiscent of that shown by Russian administrators to Polish prisoners at the same time.

Yet prison authorities discovered that sedition prisoners (not all of them newspaper editors) caused problems that "ordinary civil prisoners" did not: they wrote a lot of letters. In the normal course of prison administration, reviewing the letters written or received by prisoners would not be an onerous task. Now, complained Orpen from Tokai Prison, "the censoring of letters . . . is becoming a very formidable business," one he hoped to avoid if "prisoners are told exactly what they may and may not write about."[73] Orpen and Shawe were attempting to assimilate what they assumed to be an exceptional and temporary category of inmates to the expectations and routines of the colonial prison.

Thus the criminal justice system encountered literate men and women, community leaders, property holders, often holders of official positions, presenting demands that would be perfectly appropriate outside prison walls. Their treatment derived as much from presumed class affinities as from penitentiary considerations. The crimes, in their bulk, may have been unfamiliar or repugnant, but the individuals themselves and their needs—to read and write, to smoke, to maintain a circle of friends, to have access to certain comforts—were comprehensible.

After the Fenians regained freedom in the early 1870s, British prisons saw few imprisoned politicals for decades. There were the handful of Dynamitards, and Oscar Wilde, whose 1895 poem "The Ballad of Reading Gaol" became a classic of prison literature and was often read in prison cells but was not a source of politics. The real successors to the Fenians did not appear until October 1905, when Annie Kenney, a millworker and leading activist for suffrage in the Women's Social and Political Union (WSPU), was arrested along with WSPU co-founder Christabel Pankhurst on charges of obstructing a political meeting in Manchester. Over the next nine years, more than a thousand suffragettes went to prison. Most, in the early years, were offered the option of paying a fine and chose incarceration instead. For the suffragettes, prison became an integral part of their political struggle.

It is not surprising that a political movement should benefit from the symbolic power of the imprisoned comrade. Often enough, imprisonment has been tantamount to martyrdom. For the Fenians or the Polish socialists, prison was more explicitly useful, as prisoners themselves could join the battle with the state alongside their comrades still at liberty and build stronger movement ties within the cell. The British suffragette movement, however, is difficult to imagine without prison. Imprisonment and physical torment furnished narratives of power and resistance essential to the movement's cause. In the WSPU's struggle, the prison cell emerged as a terrain of political contestation in its own right.

The suffragettes' political campaign was premised upon the idea that women, whom the political sphere excluded and the legal code marginalized, owed no fealty to state institutions. At the same time, as many leading suffragettes were educated and privileged, they were able to manipulate and challenge expectations in prison in a way that ordinary criminal convicts or the Fenians could not. The choice between paying a fine and accepting a prison term was easy, since the former would nullify the crime, and these women had not made a forgivable error but had deliberately damaged property to create a public nuisance. So, too, a successful defense at trial ran counter to the suffragettes' aims. Released under the so-called Cat and Mouse Act of 1913, women simply violated the release terms and returned to prison. "Prison was the goal," writes Sophia van Wingerden; she records one suffragette's despondent remark upon being released: "But I have no wish to be discharged."[74]

In their quest for prison, the suffragettes exploited a narrow window of opportunity. An authoritarian regime offers many routes to prison but limits access to public opinion. A citizen in a democratic society who would go to prison, on the other hand, is likely to have to resort to violence to be treated as a dangerous political opponent. In order to make themselves fully recognizable political prisoners, the suffragettes needed not only a coherent cause and unfettered media but also a cooperative regime, one that could see them as sufficiently dangerous to incarcerate while being unable and unwilling to silence them. Only under such circumstances was it possible for Mary Leigh and Charlotte Marsh to climb to the roof of a building in Birmingham where Prime Minister Herbert Asquith was speaking, in September 1909, and break the roof slates with an axe, hurling the pieces to the street below. The act itself might have been possible anywhere, but it would have been either unintelligible or much more severely punished. The WSPU could be confident that Leigh and Marsh would be imprisoned; indeed, it published an account of Leigh's hunger strike while she was still behind bars.

Fig. 1.4 Cartoon from *The Irish Citizen*, August 30, 1913. The image evokes an attack on Hannah Sheehy-Skeffington by a Dublin policeman, for which Sheehy-Skeffington was imprisoned. The label on the sword, "Cat and Mouse Persecution," refers to the law by which suffragette prisoners who began hunger strikes were released until they recovered their health and then reimprisoned. The drawing is captioned: "That weapon always wounds the hand that wields it." The figure to the right is an Egyptian Pharaoh, evoking the Biblical persecution of the Jews.

The British suffragettes were the first to articulate explicitly the practices and goals of politics in the prison. Their model crossed easily to Ireland, where Mary Leigh was among those arrested and imprisoned. The leader of the Dublin campaign (which began in summer 1912) was Hanna Sheehy-Skeffington, the daughter of a Fenian who had been imprisoned several times during the Land War of the 1880s. Her husband, Francis Sheehy-Skeffington, would go to prison in 1915 as a conscientious objector. Indeed, the pacifist movement across Britain during World War I bears the stamp of the suffrage campaign. Hundreds of men filled prisons that in some cases had been emptied especially for them, amid public hostility as great as that faced by the suffragettes. They refused to accept prison discipline and used the prison to further the politics that had brought them there.[75]

The Birth of *Satyagraha*

The most direct descendant of the British suffragettes was Mohandas Gandhi. The passive resistance movement in the Transvaal, of which Gandhi was the most visible actor and most impassioned advocate, developed nearly simultaneously with the suffragettes' campaign of civil disobedience yet also drew lessons explicitly from it—as did the British regime.

In August 1906, the British government in the Transvaal and Natal provinces issued a draft ordinance, which eventually became the Asiatic Registration Act, requiring all Asians to re-register and to acquire passes similar to those required of Blacks the previous year. Significantly, the act surfaced as Gandhi campaigned for the restoration to Indians of the right to vote. In a speech to the Hamidiya Islamic Society in Johannesburg on September 11, Gandhi urged his listeners not to register and pledged to go to prison himself rather than obey the act.[76] Two days later, assembled members of the British Indian Association were reminded of a recent, similar confrontation with the "Boer Government," when several dozen traders, arrested for lacking a license, declined to post bail and went to prison. Hajee Habib, urging support of a resolution pledging the same tactic, provoked applause with the cry "the time has come to go to gaol, and go we will."[77]

As Gandhi pondered this act of civil disobedience, the example of the suffragettes was clearly on his mind. In a letter that October from London to H. S. L. Polak, the editor of *Indian Opinion*, he enclosed news clippings about the suffrage campaign and followed up with a column entitled "Deeds Better than Words." Recounting stories of imprisoned suffragettes, he remarked: "They are bound to succeed and gain the franchise, for the simple reason that deeds are better than words. Even those who laughed at them would be left wondering. If even women display such courage, will the Transvaal Indians fail in their duty and be afraid of gaol? Or would they rather consider the gaol a palace and readily go there? When that time comes, India's bonds will snap of themselves." "Going to gaol," he wrote elsewhere, "is a unique step, a sacred act, and only by doing so can the Indian community maintain its honour."[78] Imprisonment was for Gandhi a mark of having become a political person. One might even say that imprisonment bestowed citizenship, by establishing a particular relationship with the state. If that state ignored them or denied them civil rights, members of marginal groups could set the terms of the state's relations with them from prison.

Going to prison was hardly novel. Gandhi referred in his essays for *Indian Opinion* to many other historical precedents, especially the imprisonment of Henry David Thoreau and the struggle of English dissenters of the seventeenth century, but the suffragettes provided the closest parallel of an entire community represented in the prison. But how did a community reconstitute itself in the prison cell? How should an individual, or a community, experience prison so as to create a politics in prison?[79]

The Asiatic Registration Act took effect on August 1, 1907, and the first "passive resister," Hindu priest Ram Sundar Pundit, was arrested in November and sentenced to one month in jail. By this time, Gandhi and others were picketing registration offices. The arrest brought a strike by Indian shopkeepers, more pickets, and more arrests. The problem for Gandhi was that the arrest of a respected priest provided the movement with excellent propaganda and inspiration, but it also deprived them of a leader. During his weeks in prison, Ram Sundar Pundit offered to those outside messages of encouragement, but no new politics. He reported that he was reading poems extolling the prison-going tactic in *Indian Opinion* and assured his readers that "there is no hardship in gaol. I see even women here. No one should feel anxious on my account. I feel as if I am in a palace."[80] He played the role of an imprisoned political well, but Gandhi knew from his observation of the British suffragettes that a political prisoner could be something more. That December, the Transvaal government arrested some 2,000 nonregistered Indians, including leaders of the resistance movement.[81] Gandhi himself received a sentence of two months' imprisonment in the Johannesburg Fort. In a series of articles he wrote for *Indian Opinion* upon his release, Gandhi described the criminal inmates (with some distaste), the prison layout and conditions, and the administration's treatment of its new charges, aiming to calm the fears and steel the resolve of the hundreds he hoped would follow him to prison.

Gandhi also used his time in prison to work through his idea of *satyagraha*, nonviolent resistance. Thus, he tried to reconsider the problem of prison food from the perspective of resistance and personal cleansing. The Indian prisoners found they were classified with the "Natives" in prison, made to wear an "N" on their clothing, and limited in their food rations, unlike "European" prisoners who received bread, porridge, meat, and soup regularly. When Gandhi submitted a petition on behalf of nearly a hundred prisoners to the director of prisons, the Indians were granted permission to receive bread and other items, and to cook (and spice) their own food. Yet Gandhi wondered: did this "point . . . to a deficiency in our satyagraha"? Prison, by its nature, presented many hardships, and "if there were no hardships, what would be the point of being imprisoned?"[82] Gandhi understood that prison mattered, beyond the state-ordained purposes of punishment and rehabilitation, and beyond the opportunity to manifest martyrdom. But did his successful struggle for better food negate the political purpose or strengthen it? Gandhi began to think through these questions, which continue to resonate with political prisoners, only weeks after he first emerged from prison.

Gandhi was torn between the natural desire to make his stay in prison as comfortable as possible and his belief in the value of hardship. While he accepted that the travails of prison life contributed to personal growth and reflection, he was uncertain how to incorporate them into political struggle. His first two-month sentence ended after just three weeks. Rearrested in October, Gandhi served two months in prison; a third term, of three months, followed in February 1909. The Indian prisoners were assigned to hard labor, most of it outside the prison and thus in public. Work in prison could be imagined as liberating or confining, as a submission to authority or as an assertion of one's humanity. Gandhi's dilemma was made more difficult by the fact that, like the suffragettes, the *satyagrahis* did not claim to reject the state but simply refused to obey certain laws. "We bear no ill will to the Government," Gandhi wrote after his second imprisonment. "We do not regard it as an enemy. If we are fighting it, it is with a view to correcting its errors and making it mend its ways. We would not be happy to see it in difficulties."[83] At this point, he was only beginning to realize both the potential and the obligations of imprisonment.

A minor scandal erupted during Gandhi's third imprisonment, when he was brought to Johannesburg by train to testify in another prisoner's case and forced to walk handcuffed from the train station to the nearby prison. His colleague H. S. L. Polak fired off an outraged letter to a friendly journalist, listing the indignities Gandhi had suffered. The prime minister's office, squeezed from both sides, responded to the official queries by asserting that this was normal practice but that "Mr. Gandhi was however allowed to draw his sleeves over his handcuffs and to carry a book, which concealed the fact of his being handcuffed." Gandhi explained the matter differently to his *Indian Opinion* readers: "Thinking probably that I felt ashamed of the handcuffs, [the warden] asked me to hold the book with both hands, so that the handcuffs might not be seen. I was rather amused at this. To me the handcuffs were a matter of honour." He added that the book happened to be Tolstoy's *The Kingdom of God Is within You*, implying that the incident afforded him an opportunity to focus on his own personal growth.[84]

Such negotiations over the politics of the prison set the terms for the century ahead. Does the regime need a political prisoner to appear in public—and if so, to appear humbled and constrained, or to be treated with respect? How is a

prisoner like Gandhi different from "ordinary" prisoners, and why is this distinction important? How should a prisoner act in order to call attention to a cause?
It is striking to find that even the most famed nonviolent protester did not have
ready answers. Gandhi filed petitions to assert the right to different treatment
before reflecting that it was more proper to accept the hardship that prison dealt
out. The authorities assured each other and the public that Gandhi was afforded
every appropriate accommodation in prison, while also endeavoring not to treat
the Indian prisoners differently.

Gandhi may have been vexed by his inability to accept what prison offered,
but he found he could not. He and his fellow *satyagrahis* not only protested the
food but demanded respect for Ramadan, the right to sacred clothing and beards,
access to visitors, and so on. They complained about being forced to strip naked
upon arrival in the prison and that protests were dealt with brusquely.[85] Every
instance of rough or coarse handling, especially of Gandhi himself, seemed to
occasion a letter to the press or to officials at all levels. Both sides suspected dis-
honesty. The British Indian Association complained that the regime had made
"every effort . . . to insult and humiliate Indian prisoners who . . . for the sake
of conscience, prefer to accept the penalties of the law."[86] The governor of the
Transvaal, Lord Selborne, in turn, observed: "Mr. Gandhi, when he voluntarily
sought imprisonment, did so of course knowing that he could not expect treatment in any way different from that accorded to other prisoners."[87] Neither side
was being fully honest, as each embraced the difference of these prisoners while
also insisting on their conformity.

Upon replacing Lord Selborne in May 1910, Herbert Gladstone was soon
greeted by a memorandum from the South African prime minister's office assur-
ing him that "the so-called Indian passive resisters are not differentiated against
in the Transvaal prisons. They are, however, constantly complaining."[88] In seeking to extricate his administration from this impasse, Gladstone realized that
repercussions could affect the whole British Empire. He sympathized with the
Union government, constantly defending its penitentiary practices in the face of
"the general ignorance of the public in prison matters, and the usual tendency to
disbelieve and discount official statements"—and the prisoners' access to a free
press. Gladstone's previous role as Britain's home secretary gave him "practical
experience of prison responsibility," he wrote to Prime Minister Louis Botha, as
"the same situation arose on the prison treatment of the suffragettes."[89]

Thus, like Gandhi, Gladstone turned to the suffragette precedent to understand how the modern political prisoner challenged the state. He, too, observed
that prisons had to be governed by general rules and that political prisoners were
particularly well equipped to demand exceptions to those rules. He advised
against the tactic of adamant refusal to negotiate. Instead, administrators should
"admit the desirability" of any demand and either adopt it or show concretely why

it simply was not possible. Prison administration, he continued, had tied itself in knots trying to avoid accommodating Ramadan or to ignore complaints about "polluting" prison tasks. He proposed that the only relevant test of any demand was, "Is the particular prison treatment necessary and justifiable?" Honesty and clarity, he argued, would "completely outflank... the attack." Though he had not been so successful in dealing with the suffragettes, Gladstone was the first in the South African administration to accurately perceive the nature of the contest and to recognize that prison rules were a means, not an end. Gandhi, too, had reached this conclusion and incorporated it into his concept of *satyagraha*.

Gandhi and his followers would continue to court imprisonment for another three years, with varying success.[90] Blacks who opposed the analogous pass laws would take up that struggle, intermittently, for the next eight decades. Gladstone's precepts would not have been acceptable to many of the incarcerating regimes of the twentieth century; Gandhi's ruminations on accepting hardship would have seemed quaint to the victims of those regimes. Yet by 1910, in industrial, democratic Europe, on its autocratic peripheries, and in its colonies, the basic relationship between the political resister-turned-inmate and the state that sought to sequester and control such an opponent had taken shape.

2

Night and Fog

The Regime and Its Captives

As a total institution in a modern state, a prison regime imposes and maintains order among its inmates. Yet order and discipline, though they might suffice in the task of governing criminal convicts, surely are subordinate, in the case of political prisoners, to the goals of gaining and denying information. All modern states seek to know those under their control; in the case of political prisoners, they want to know as much as possible in order to destroy real or perceived existential threats. The challenge of and need for information varies across regimes. Some of the regimes studied here—the Russians or the Nazis in Warsaw, and to some extent the apartheid state in South Africa—sought to control a population that was mostly hostile. Even regimes that can claim to be acting in the interests of the nation assume they face a substantial network of political enemies. They tend therefore to arrest more people than they have information about. Order and discipline make extracting the necessary information feasible.

By incarcerating opponents, the state gains control over the bodies and voices of prisoners in ways that neither execution (which creates martyrs) nor exile can achieve. This control allows states to categorize or name their captives as threats to civil security, as criminals, or as nonpersons. The state thus renders them something different from what they themselves claim to be. This struggle over naming the prisoner, however, makes little sense if the prisoner can simply refute the label. Political prisoners are not simply victims of cruel punishment; they are people whom a regime has made a special commitment to incarcerate. A modern state may deny the category, but it still pays these men and women special attention and arranges their incarceration in particular ways that may only appear mercurial.

Political incarceration attacks prisoners' sense of control over their lives. It seeks to induce uncertainty among prisoners as to the state's intentions and even to the prisoners' identity. If the practices of order and discipline could be called strategies to make prisoners legible, then a second set of practices—the focus of this chapter—create illegibility. Political incarceration has the effect of making prisoners illegible to themselves and to their comrades inside and outside the prison. To understand prisoner protest strategies in later chapters, we need first to understand the practices of the prison regime.

Prisoners of Stalin's Gulag adopted the habit of referring to the world outside as the *bolshaia zona*, the big zone, a vast prison that contained the smaller prison they inhabited. They understood that as radically unreal as the prison world might seem, it was still an institution of the society that created it. Its inhabitants, no matter how socially enlightened, found a world that stubbornly mirrored the one they had left—and indeed exceeded it in the rigidity of social hierarchies. Jean Hart, a white journalist for the Johannesburg magazine *Drum*, spent one weekend, sometime in the 1950s, at Hillbrow police station for having "supplied blacks with liquor" at a party. As it happened, she personally knew one of the black prisoners assigned to clean her cell. "Once, when she was shuffling around my cell on her hands and knees, she looked up at me and said 'Who says stone walls do not a prison make nor iron bars a cage?'"[1] A white liberal, Hart found herself literally standing over a black servant, one whom she had tried outside to regard as an equal. White prisoners in South Africa were usually kept separate from black prisoners, and the regime rejected their efforts to be united with their black comrades from the movement. Their guards would be white as well, while menial staff would likely be black, like domestic servants. Hart's acquaintance neatly deconstructs social distance with a literary reference, but she is still the one on her knees.

Gender, too, pervades the prison experience, both among prisoners and across the entire institution. Because men and women are always in separate cells, and often in separate prisons, served and interrogated most often by functionaries of the same sex, gender relations are hidden. Yet as suffragette Hanna Sheehy-Skeffington observed, the prison is, with the possible exception of the army barrack, "the most masculine place under the sun."[2] She meant only to draw attention to the lack of women doctors, inspectors, and prison administrators in British Ireland. Nevertheless, one could extend her point: prisons were and are regimented places in which people with weapons and keys confine those who have neither. From that basic expression of power stem all the relations within the prison's walls.

The Rules of the Institution

With its ubiquitous regulations, posted on cell walls, handed to incoming inmates, or manifested in shouts, orders, and punishments, the prison may appear like a factory where menial workers follow a clearly dictated script. The earliest regulations for political prisoners, as in British Ireland in the 1860s and in Russian Poland in the 1880s, by contrast, read like guidelines for gentlemen. They consisted primarily of rights, such as the rights to have books, to exercise separately from criminal prisoners, and to write letters, but they also enumerated responsibilities, such as keeping one's cell clean.[3] After World War I, restrictions took the place of rights. A guard in a Stalinist prison, challenged to conform to the regulations posted on the cell wall, indifferently replied that these were for the administration only and that prisoners have no rights.[4]

In the modern political prison, the nature and implementation of rules are fundamentally uncertain.[5] Political prisoners for the most part enter without definite information about the duration and severity of their detention, which most criminal prisoners possess. Prison life for the political inmate rests not on codified rules, nor precisely on custom, but on what can seem to be arbitrary power—"caprice and whim," as South African prisoner Robert Sobukwe put it.[6] Uncertainty naturally accompanies arrest and is further manifested in the obscurity of rules and unpredictable treatment in prison. Prison memoirs are replete with examples of Orwellian illogic enforced upon inmates, such as Moses Dlamini's recollection of a head guard accusing his charges of attempting an escape through an old crack in the ceiling.[7] This outburst manufactured uncertainty: because Dlamini's cellmates would know that none of them were guilty of the ludicrous charge, they could not be certain what constituted guilt and even whether that mattered to the regime. The categories of "guilty" and "innocent," so vital to a prisoner's life, lost their currency.

From within the prison cell, the workings of the institution seem as illogical as they are impenetrable. Trying to make sense of this foreign institution and find some consistency despite the changing of guards, administrators, and prisons, the prisoner is uncertain which rule or restriction is a random display of power and which is part of a calculated campaign to warp reality. What constituted a threat, and what was simply the normal working of a bureaucracy? Prisoners cannot easily judge which is which. A Polish Home Army partisan, imprisoned by the Soviets in 1945, related how after months in solitary confinement he received a visit from an armed escort to take him outside. As the soldiers urged him, in Russian, to walk, he knew he was about to be executed. Sent back to his cell, he puzzled over their intentions: were they trying to frighten him or playing mind games to break him? The next day, the soldiers came again, and this time one asked if he felt stronger and could walk. Suddenly he understood that he was finally being permitted his daily walk per regulations, nothing more. "How often does an inexperienced prisoner misinterpret such minor incidents?" comments Barbara Skarga, herself a survivor of prisons and camps, who retells this story.[8]

Just as they try to make sense of the fragmentary sights and sounds reaching their cells, prisoners also piece together the motivations of their captors from stray and often unconnected pieces of evidence. Naturally, they assume the worst. As Peadar O'Donnell admitted during the Irish Civil War: "If I got wondering when I heard steps in the passage: 'Now is this my dinner, or is it word that I'm to be shot? is this a raid in the early morning or are they going to take me out and shoot me?' then I'd tear myself to pieces."[9] O'Donnell, like other inmates, discovered time and again the corrosive marks left by prison and its practices on the human mind.

Change, not consistency, is the key feature of prison rules as experienced by politicals. Guards at Johannesburg Fort in the early 1960s made arriving politicals stand in formation. "They had a lovely way of confusing you," recalled a Pan-African Congress activist. They shout 'four, four,' and just as you try to stand in fours they shout 'two, two.'"[10] Besides demonstrating the guards' ability to remake rules, the confusion destroyed even the tiniest shred of social bonds among entering prisoners. The uncertainty of prison treatment drove a group of Robben Island prisoners to submit a petition to the prison's governor in October 1972. "There are few things more irritating and provocative than caprice on the part of warders and the contradictory instructions we have to follow," they wrote. "As prisoners we are leading abnormal lives, and the behaviour described above aggravates our plight considerably. We are presently at the whims of individual warders who make little attempt to acquaint themselves with the practice followed by their predecessors."[11] They cited the guards' changing rules on whether they could hang out their washing to dry, whether they could walk in the mornings, and whether they could enter their cells during the day. This apparent randomness disturbed the prisoners as much as being deprived of specific privileges or rights. The court case that resulted did reduce the arbitrary power of guards and make heretofore hidden regulations available to the prisoners.[12]

Jan Krzesławski well understood that inconstancy as he offered readers a tour of the cells of Russian Poland in 1911: "Prison life tends to be regulated by rules which are usually different for each prison. Sometimes the regulations are displayed in each cell, but it quickly turns out that they are quite incomplete, and the prisoner learns only what his responsibilities are, knowing nothing about his rights. That second, more interesting part of the regulations can usually be found in the prison chief's office. Sometimes the prison has no regulations at all, or the rules are so contradictory that everything depends on the will, or rather the whim, of the prison chief."[13] Like his colleagues on Robben Island, Krzesławski personalized the prisoner's plight, yet he also knew he could encounter it in any prison. Inconsistency was not a failure of the system to be repaired by an administrator but a characteristic inherent to the system.

Surveying the history of political incarceration suggests that uncertainty evolved from genuine confusion on the part of the regime into a conscious tactic. Prison officials in the early twentieth century simply did not know how to manage the growing category of political prisoners. As revolution swept the Russian Empire in early 1905, the Central Prison Board struggled to set rules for political prisoners coming under its care in large numbers. While there were new, permissive regulations, the old ones had not really been enforced, so any regulation would look like a crackdown. The Prison Board decided instead to suspend regulations in favor of temporary guidelines.[14] A few years earlier in South Africa's Cape Colony, the colonial secretary and his subordinates tried to figure out what rules applied to prominent Boer citizens who had been detained as "Martial Law Prisoners." Could they smoke? Receive visitors? Send out lengthy letters? There seemed to be no regulation that could adequately address such uncategorizeable cases, and so state officials had to treat each individual challenge separately.[15] Those responsible for Gandhi's followers in the Transvaal or the suffragettes in England and Ireland were similarly perplexed and always a step behind the prisoners.

The modern incarcerating regime, by contrast, specializes in regulation and categorization. The particular category to which a prisoner belongs does not matter as much as the fact of its assignment. The prison regime determines the criteria by which prisoners are distinguished from one another, beginning with the frequent placement of those arrested as political opponents among convicted or suspected criminals—or below criminals. At Robben Island, entering prisoners were usually placed in the 'D' category, the lowest, for purposes of determining privileges. Ordinary criminal prisoners generally received 'B' category placement, from which they could move up or down depending upon their behavior. This system equated the politicals with the worst criminals, for whom rehabilitation was unlikely. Placing politicals in the 'D' category underscored a crucial point: rules were at once both rigid *and* capricious. That there could be no exceptions indicated that prisoners' actions could not matter. Protests against the 'D' category could be understood as demands for greater privilege, except that these same prisoners, aware that privilege was based on race and thus contrary to their politics, emphasized that they did not expect special treatment.[16]

A similar use of arbitrary categories appears in the notorious prison regulations introduced in Poland in 1931. The reform eliminated any residual recognition of political prisoners and their *komuna* (the self-government discussed in a later chapter), ending the prisoners' right to wear their own clothing and many other privileges or rights they previously enjoyed. It even introduced mandatory prayer. But these were things for or against which one could fight. The leftist prisoner support group Red Help raised alarm over a more insidious change: "Political prisoners will be broken up into national and other groups depending on the will of the prison head."[17] Separating Poles, Jews, and Ukrainians from one another, the regime used labels that these communists or socialists either rejected or at least considered secondary to political or economic divisions. The nationalist dictatorship of this period perceived Polish society in these terms; imposing them upon prisoners not only made them legible in regime terms but also illegible to one another. Prisoner-generated categories threatened the system, while regime categories hindered the prisoner community's desire to organize itself and to educate less politically conscious comrades.[18]

That these categories were fundamentally about illegibility was made clear by Heinrich Himmler. A Nazi decree of December 1941 established the category of "Nacht und Nebel"—Night and Fog—prisoners, a special category of political prisoners primarily from France, the Low Countries, and Scandinavia. To quote Himmler's accompanying instructions: "The Führer is of the opinion that in such cases [of political opposition, especially by communists] penal servitude or even a hard labor sentence for life will be regarded as a sign of weakness. An effective and lasting deterrent can be achieved only by the death penalty or by taking measures which will leave the family and the population uncertain as to the fate of the offender."[19] In Night and Fog camps, prisoners wore the red letters "NN" on their backs, also signifying "name unknown" (Latin: *nomen nescio*). By denying the *Nacht und Nebel* prisoners the right to write or receive letters, to contact other prisoners, and even to work outside prison, the Nazis effaced their existence. There could be no image of dignity and suffering for a cause; the "NN" on their backs simultaneously connected them and rendered them anonymous.[20]

Absence of information is a central feature of extrajudicial internment—under martial law, in particular. Detainees most likely do not know where the convoy carrying them is headed, what the terms of their detention are, or if anyone else knows. The "disappearing" of opposition activists in Argentina in the 1970s is an extreme version of a common phenomenon. In a sense, "disappeared" prisoners who have been killed remain prisoners as long as their fate is unknown to others.[21] When South Africa declared a state of emergency in 1960, the decree made it a crime for anyone to report that a family member or acquaintance had been detained.[22] Even when strictures are less severe than in these cases, detainees and the public know very little. This is why prisoner support groups devote so much energy to gathering and publicizing the names and locations of the interned.

"Do You Belong Here?" How Political Incarceration Works

Arbitrariness, capriciousness, and internal inconsistency are operations of prison. While no regime outlines a plan to be unpredictable, the patterns are consistent enough as to be intentional. The practices of the political prison regime, as applied by guards, administrators, and the system as a whole, destabilizes prisoners' lives and minds. Five aspects of prison practice can be distinguished.

First, arrest and incarceration stun the new inmate, opening the gates to a world that is deliberately alien. John Laffin's claim that the political offender is "usually arrested . . . by night," in contrast to the daytime arrests of those suspected of ordinary crimes, does not stand up as a general rule, but his larger point is sound: surprise, shock, and confusion accompany the passage from freedom to incarceration.[23] Solzhenitsyn's accounting of the arrests during the Great Purge in the Soviet Union is echoed in Adam Michnik's observation that a dictatorship brings "the terror of the doorbell."[24] Whether or not a regime opponent expects a knock at the door, that moment still produces uncertainty and anxiety about what will happen next.

The prison's essential alienness militates against any sense of familiarity, thwarting prisoners' search for stability. The lack of ordinary sensations made "Gaweł," in a Polish Stalinist prison in 1953, almost infantile in his

> hunger for color. The prison world was gray, somber, and colorless. The prisoners wore the same gray clothing. The prison guards wore dark green uniforms. The nurses and doctors wore white coats. Only one of the exercise yards had any greenery—and they rarely took us there. They sometimes gave us scraps of cloth from the tailor's shop to dust our cells. Once I found among these scraps a small piece of pink fabric. I liked it so much that I hid it among my things, but I could not stop thinking about it. Every few days I would take it out—secretly, so my comrades in suffering would not make fun of me—look at it for a while and hide it again.[25]

Frequent, abrupt physical relocation to a new cell or new prison further deprived prisoners of their sense of the space around them. Erasing the advantages of prison experience, any change in routine imposed costs that prisoners could not easily recoup. A new cell "introduced an element of doubt," as apartheid opponent Baruch Hirson puts it. "Tactics and moves had to be learnt afresh and, given the constraints of the prison system, that could be unsettling."[26]

This unfamiliar world is yet supposed to become normal, an effect especially important in the case of political prisoners. Prisoners lose their names, and the institution's rituals encourage the nameless to accept their fate and their identity. On Stanisława Sowińska's first day in prison, the former communist dignitary heard a guard ordered to get prisoner #4.

> A second later someone snapped his fingers at the door. Then clicked his tongue. Then whistled.

"Why don't you come when I call you?"

"You're calling me—you're calling me that way, like a dog . . ."

"Shh! Don't speak out loud—it's forbidden! You can only speak in a whisper, and only when you are spoken to. Those are the rules here. When you hear the door opening, you must run to the window and stand there, back to the door, with raised arms. You can't turn around, you can't lower your arms without permission. Understood?"[27]

These instructions made some sense: having imprisoned many from among its own elites, the communist regime did not want its former comrades to know who else was in prison. Not much had changed when Marek Kulczyk was interned in 1981, though: "What terrified me the most in prison was the treatment of a person like an object. It was awful because it had been perfected. When the guard came for me, he did not use my name, rarely said 'you,' but most often 'Come,' and motioned with his finger. I didn't know where I was going—to see a visitor, to interrogation, to the doctor, maybe to be beaten up."[28] The order of political prison stripped new inmates of any scrap of evidence of their individuality.

The use of numbers or other identifiers in prison is a logical way to keep track of an ever-changing population. Each encounter with a prison functionary, however, underscored not just who had the power but also the normality of incarceration. A conscientious objector taken to Northampton Prison in 1917 found himself tested like the Apostle Peter:

Having been weighed, washed, measured, Bertillioned, ticketed and docketed, I was informed by the clerk at the prison gate that he had seen me before. Of course he had not, but that was merely a formula used to secure an admission of a previous sentence. I had been in my cell about two hours when the Chaplain entered and made precisely the same remark—that he had seen me before. "Surely, I know your face," he remarked; and that with such an air of conviction that to deny a previous acquaintance with him seemed to border on rude contradiction. This, of course, was also the outcome of a cut and dried arrangement to secure an admission of a previous sentence. At six o'clock on my first morning a warder flung a piece of tarred rope into my cell and slammed the door without a word of instruction. I rang the bell three times, not knowing what I had to do with it. The warder came at last and threatened to report me for ringing "needlessly." "You're an old-timer, and know all about it," he said. Finally he initiated me into the mysteries of oakum-picking, having failed in his object to obtain the admission that I had previously been in prison.[29]

The Stalinist regime was much more direct, as Father Tomasz Rostworowski noted. Guards asked prisoners "What are you in for?" over and over again, simply forcing them to characterize their actions in the regime's terms, such as "for anti-state activity"; next would come the question "Do you belong here?" The answer revealed the prisoners' acquiescence or resistance to their new selves.[30]

A second aspect of prison practice is surveillance, a feature inseparable from prisoners' confinement. In contrast to the Panopticon in which all prisoners' cells are constantly watched, or to the exercise yard beneath a watchtower, the greatest impact of surveillance actually derives from its uncertainty. Prisoners could not know whether their cells were bugged, whether there was a cell informer, whether someone was peering in the spyhole (or was about to look), or whether a cell search was imminent.[31] These uncertainties resemble more farfetched worries that prison officials could read inmates' minds or interpret their mumblings in sleep. Regardless of what the authorities could actually do, prisoners experienced an unsettling loss of privacy. Control of the prisoner tempted authorities to find innovative ways to invade their private space. Stanisława Sowińska received each day a certain number of squares of toilet paper in Mokotów Prison in 1949–50. Every morning, before she emptied her chamber pot, a guard would first count the used pieces, to be sure none had been secreted away for writing material.[32]

The use of informers brought the regime deeper into the cell community than it could come with guards, whose visits rarely lasted for more than a few minutes. An informer undermined political prisoners' efforts to protect their stories about themselves, disrupting even those cells where no informer had visited.[33] In Stalinist Poland, the often indiscriminate arrest of people from a wide range of milieux—party members and Gestapo officials, army officers and Home Army partisans, businessmen and priests, armed youth and opposition intellectuals— made it both more necessary and easier to insert an informer into a cell community of those awaiting trial. Prison communities that were more tightly knit, such as those on Robben Island or among interwar Polish communists, could more readily verify a newcomer's identity, perhaps with the help of comrades outside. Stalinist-era prisoners had only sporadic contact with the outside and thus had to rely on telltale clues, such as someone who was moved frequently from cell to cell, or alternatively someone left in one cell for a long time despite evident misbehavior. They noted their cellmates' demeanor to gauge whether they had really returned from an interrogation or if it had been a debriefing instead. A staff doctor in Rawicz Prison would tip off prisoners by announcing to a cell "It stinks in here!" or, if he noticed two informers present, "It really stinks in here!"[34]

Informers were often fellow prisoners hoping for lenient sentences in return, but some were employees of the Ministry of Public Security.[35] Besides eliciting information for interrogators, they sought to play on prisoners' psyches, encouraging them to confess or wearing down their hopes of evading punishment. Informers' tales of the cell relationship offer further clues to the way the state understood its political inmates and the space they inhabited. "Jerzy" was only the latest in a string of informers to share a cell with Zygmunt Augustyński, an editor of an opposition newspaper arrested in 1946. At first, Augustyński was cautious, telling Jerzy that "whether our relations will be good depends upon us not discussing the cases for which we have been detained." Jerzy himself cautioned Augustyński against revealing anything, "not wanting," he told his bosses, "to create the impression that I care."[36] Even the simple trick of pretending not to want any details, Jerzy was convinced, would eventually encourage Augustyński to talk. To further relax his vigilant cellmate, Jerzy began a conversation about how informing might work: "We discussed the possibility of someone being placed [in the cell] who could provoke him to reveal aspects of his case. We hypothesized on this at some length, taking as possible examples me in his case, or him in my case." Already Jerzy saw Augustyński's weak spot, concluding that night interrogations with certain "rigors which he clearly fears could bring him to the breaking point" would be appropriate. The interrogator probably followed Jerzy's advice, as Augustyński began speaking in great detail about his case the very next day.[37]

More was going on than just extracting information and breaking someone through lies and torture. To accomplish his task, Jerzy subverted the cell relationship, asking the initially suspicious Augustyński to imagine himself as an informer. This stripping away of the prisoner's legibility was not just hypothetical; the mutual suspicions of the pretrial cell could lead a prisoner to suspect himself as well as everyone else. Natoo Babenia, an experienced Umkhonto we Sizwe saboteur, recalls the poisoned atmosphere in Durban's Point Prison in 1963. A new arrestee would be confronted upon entering a cell: "'Who are you?' Silence. It was terrible. 'Why do you not talk?' Silence. People were too scared . . . . No one really knows who the others are, what you have said and whether you are already an *impimpi* [informer]. It was terrible. You could talk as much as you wanted. There were no cops to stop you. But no one spoke because we did not trust each other."[38] With each prisoner "selfish and scared," one could not even trust oneself, let alone anyone else. Distrust, for men and women who embarked upon their path to prison in the company of like-minded comrades, devastated their very political identity. Who was the prisoner tapping in the next cell, claiming comradeship? Had others confessed under torture, or was that just what one was supposed to think? Even visitors could not be trusted.[39]

Six weeks after helping to break Augustyński, Jerzy was sharing a cell with another suspect in the same case, Father Leon Pawlina. He found an unexpected ally in the third man in the cell, who joined in Jerzy's efforts to convince Father Pawlina to stop fabricating stories in his interrogations. While Jerzy offered to help him plan his confession better, the third cellmate recounted his ordeals in an isolation cell. "I think," concluded Jerzy, "that Father Pawlina will eventually give in to our persuasion, because he says he's exhausted and is afraid of the isolation cell."[40]

The informer usually appears in prisoner memoirs or letters as a measure of the author's perceptiveness and honor. However, prisoners' attempts at a battle of wits with their interrogators were more likely to be undermined by their inability to recognize who was who. Sometimes they had suspicions, but much of their intimate lives spilled out anyway: their private methods for recognizing informers, plans for foiling interrogation, personal fears, moral failings, and personal complaints. In the informers' telling, their victims were often undone by their faith in intuition. The informers claimed to be able to see through their cellmates' strategems. Thus one describes his victim "skillfully masking his undoubtedly hostile political views behind empty slogans about democracy, socialism, Marxism. Only when he talks about attitudes [in society] and similar topics can one skillfully sense the almost ungraspable masking of his real political opinions."[41] This particular victim was General Stefan Mossor, arrested in 1950. To another informer, Captain Szymon Segal, Mossor frankly admitted that he had to suspect him, because of course he would be assigned a cellmate the Stalinists trusted. But after seven weeks together "I have managed to get to know you a little and to reach the conviction that you are at the least not a sneaky person, but sincere, and you don't behave at all like the way I imagine an informer would."[42] By the end, after his trial, Mossor was so talkative that the informer who earlier bragged about his skills was pleading for mercy: "our ears are ringing."[43]

Whether an informer is real or imagined, suspicion hinders the creation of a community among political prisoners. Mac Maharaj recalls an encounter on his way to prison after sentencing in 1964. The newcomer, in the truck transporting them to Cape Town (and Robben Island), stood out: "Soft spoken, shining skin, and none of that harassed, unkempt look of the usual prisoner . . . . Something doesn't fit. How is it that Raymond Nyanda has clean clothes, shoes, socks, a jersey and a canvas jacket?" Nyanda introduced himself with a plausible story. The others began to question him intently, but Maharaj fretted. "It is becoming an interrogation. Suspicion churns through my mind. I must ward off an interrogation. We must not arouse Raymond's suspicions. We need to find ways of establishing whether he is a plant and what his mission is. The trip becomes nerve-racking. We are unable to talk freely, share experiences, and bond as freedom fighters."[44] Maharaj's choice of this anecdote to introduce a book about Robben Island suggests he saw the regime's influence as profoundly disintegrative, even when he himself outwitted it.

Regimes use informers to gain useful information or to spread false information that enhances the regime's power over its opponents. Political prisoners can incriminate themselves, admitting to things they might withhold in interrogation; they might also possess information about comrades outside, though that knowledge's value quickly fades. The strategic goal of disrupting relations among prisoners probably has a longer-lasting effect. The cell community is atomized, causing "a rejection of cell mates and an acceptance of the enemy."[45] Instead of a community, there are individual inmates uncertain about those around them and about themselves.

Alongside practices designed to make prisoners uneasy in the spaces of prison and unsure of the people around them, a third aspect of political imprisonment makes prisoners uncertain of time and consequence. A formal arrest usually comes with a charge, but many regimes employed internment (that is, detention without intent to file charges), which gave the state greater flexibility. Outside prison, internment indicates to society that law provides uncertain protection, as it can be superseded by emergency decree; those detained or interned also lose the sense of time that comes with the normal machinations of justice. In communist Poland, the system of detention without charges for up to forty-eight hours was simple enough for the state to circumvent. A newly freed detainee would be met on the sidewalk outside the police station jail by a new set of policemen, invited into their car, and driven to a different police station to spend another forty-eight hours.[46] There might be more efficient ways of isolating opponents, but this ritual made the detainee a participant in the state's performance of arbitrary yet deliberate rule without limit.

Locking up citizens in this way deprives them of a certainty on which those arrested for ordinary crimes can rely: a trial. Detention or internment by emergency decree makes incarceration dependent on the decision of one person— the minister of justice, the head of state, or a completely unknown bureaucrat or police official. Where a trial, even a charade of a trial, yields a rehearsal of evidence, the chance to speak, and some kind of decision, the decision-making process of detention remains opaque and can last for years.[47] The prisons of Stalinist Poland offer a good example. A review of the investigative wing of Mokotów Prison in May 1953 found that sixty-two men and women had been held without charges for at least two years and some for nearly five years.[48]

A trial—often announced suddenly, leaving the prisoner no time to prepare— did not necessarily relieve the sense of loss of control. In Polish Stalinism these were called "toilet trials" because they were sometimes conducted summarily in the cell, with the accused sitting on the latrine. Władysław Bartoszewski claims that when his trial was announced the orderlies had just begun serving lunch down the corridor; when he returned from the courtroom upstairs with an eight-year sentence, his soup was still warm.[49] From beginning to end—whether the end was summary execution, a sentence, or a surprise release—arbitrary exercise of power is one of the defining features of political incarceration. This

mode of action allows the state to control the time of its inmates as fully as it
controls the space they inhabit.

Even the sentenced prisoner could not be sure of time's passing. Henryk
Nakielski sat on death row in Mokotów Prison for a whole year not knowing
his sentence had been commuted long before. Władysław Gomułka—who
had been the most powerful man in Poland until 1948—ranted to his captors
a few years later that "basically [I] have been arrested in order to do time . . . .
Apparently [I] didn't spend enough time in prison before the war, so now I have
to make it up."[50] In Northern Ireland, those younger than eighteen when they
committed their offenses received "indeterminate" sentences. Even older prisoners who received life sentences could not be sure what that meant, as British
law left ambiguous the circumstances governing eventual release and judges
neglected to specify minimum years to be served.[51] South African Hugh Lewin
put it best: "The indefiniteness was the worst part of it: nothing certain, no fixed
point around which to structure your thoughts and actions, only an aimless
vacuum of uncertainty and silence."[52] The lack of a sentence or endpoint underscores the extralegality of incarceration and differentiates many political prisoners from most criminal prisoners.

Prison labor also contributes to the sense of being outside time. Labor for
ordinary prisoners might have a rehabilitative purpose or at least an economic
one.[53] For political prisoners, labor was more likely to be punishment, like the
oakum-picking in British prisons, stretching on without evident outcome. In the
early years on Robben Island, the "high security prisoners" (Nelson Mandela
and other leaders) worked on the "knap line," breaking stones with hammers.
Ostensibly they produced gravel for the island's roads, but the small scale of this
hidden operation belied this purpose. Neville Alexander acerbically noted that
the piles of rocks produced there, or at the lime quarry in which prisoners began
working in 1965, had little value on the island and could not be transported to
the mainland, so it lay in heaps eroded by wind and rain. "The pointlessness of
the whole thing," he wrote, "weighs heavily on the prisoners."[54] The humiliation
of a lawyer or schoolteacher, and the reinforcement of hierarchy, were at least
as important as any possible transformation, since the prisoners were not being
prepared for later careers. On Robben Island, work did not rehabilitate or provide economic gain for the institution or the laborer.

Fourth among the prison practices was the use of political incarceration specifically to dehumanize the prisoner. There may be no more dramatic example
of this than the arduous boat ride to Robben Island. Most prisoners had never
seen the ocean or been on a boat, and many became quite seasick; there was also
nowhere, in the early days, to relieve oneself. Moses Dlamini, who made the trip
to the Island in 1964, recalls the warders mocking the new arrivals, saying they
smelled like shit. "This was true," he admits.[55] On the island, Neville Alexander

saw how brutality broke down civilizational barriers, the "atavistic destructive-ness" of the warders "dehumanising the Black." Men unused to prison—"sensi-tive people"—are "confronted with naked brutality, the complete senselessness and absurdity of human existence in these conditions." Civilization disap-pears: "the resulting savagery on both sides is one of the most traumatic expe-riences a human being can have, one of the most demoralising phenomena a prisoner has to live through and to witness."[56]

Thandi Ruth Modise put it slightly differently in a suit she and other women in Pretoria Central filed against the minister of justice and the commissioner of prisons in 1981. Protesting the "torture" of isolation, calling it "the most serious attack upon my mental, spiritual and physical well-being," she singled out one particular treatment: "Since the 8th May 1981 my supper has been put on the floor. This is a change from the erstwhile system in terms whereof I would actu-ally be handed my supper directly. I found this new practice, if it be a new prac-tice, to be utterly degrading and strange to me. I do not know what the reason is for being treated as an animal."[57]

Stanisława Sowińska also found she was denied human dignity. On her first morning in Mokotów Prison in 1949, a guard taunted her explicitly to under-score her fall from power. After she had folded her pallet neatly, the guard threw it on the ground: "Make your bed properly! Or maybe you would like to send for your maid? The lady isn't used to work!" Told to clean the cell without supplies,

Fig. 2.1 Prisoners arriving on Robben Island, 1960s. Courtesy of UWC-Robben Island Mayibuye Archives.

Sowińska ripped her shirt into strips to wash the floor and toilet. Next came a new inspector who found a piece of straw on the floor: "Aha! The dirtiest cell, the dirtiest prisoner in Mokotów is Sowińska! And she's supposedly a woman! Shame!"[58] Humiliation and degradation thus aimed to undermine the moral and political power claimed by regime opponents. Prisoners like Modise and Sowińska, accustomed to testing political limits as movement leaders or activists, lost their bearings and their claim to human dignity.

Fifth in the prison practices, the modern political prison questions prisoners' sanity and even their ability to act. The most infamous example of this tactic is the use of the psychiatric ward in the Soviet Union under Leonid Brezhnev. The regime labeled some political opponents schizophrenic and isolated them in hospitals. In so doing, they reassigned political opponents to a category neither criminal nor political and declared repressive measures medically necessary, not punitive.[59] While no other regime used this method systematically, the threat of losing control of one's identity, and possibly one's mind, terrified political prisoners. It also had a clear sociopolitical motive. As Bogdan Ciszak observed when he was abruptly transferred from a Polish prison to a psychiatric hospital in June 1982: "Keeping us in a psychiatric hospital allows the regime to spread the idea that the state of our mental health explains our actions before martial law."[60]

The regime did not need to hospitalize inmates to render them helpless. Any restriction—the imposition of silence; the denial of reading material or permission to study or choice of music to listen to; being required to stand at attention, or to pick up one's food tray from the floor—infantilizes the prisoner. As Caesarina Makhoere reflected: "The effect that this is having upon me is that I am beginning to feel that I am perhaps unworthy. I have a very poor image of myself."[61] In similar terms Con Lehane, testifying before an Irish commission on political prisoners in 1936, described the atmosphere at Arbour Hill:

> The whole atmosphere of the prison is designed to affect the prisoner mentally. Minor and childish ways of humiliating men were tried as, for instance, the refusal to allow prisoners to write letters in ink. It could well happen that the general atmosphere of the place—the solitary confinement, the unbroken silence—and the fact that exercise could only be had on conditions so limited as forced the prisoners to refuse it—would have such an effect on men, particularly on men accustomed to working in the open air, that a very short period there would affect their mental stability . . . the conditions could only be described as a cleverly calculated system of mental torture.[62]

The order of a prison is most effective when it is not fully legible to the political prisoner. Denying rules and practices could confuse political opponents as to what the regime knows. Names that could not be spoken, languages not to be used, prisoners not to be seen, rules not to be posted, and prisoners categorized according to administrative whim keep the regime in control and prisoners disoriented. Moreover, they weaken the ability of prisoner communities to recognize themselves, of prisoners to distinguish among themselves, and of their supporters outside to understand what was going on. Like a black hole, the political prison produces no information for observers. The last words to a departing prisoner in Stalinist Poland, cautioning him or her not to discuss conditions or divulge the names of prison staff, were "After all, we have not met, have we?"[63]

Torture in Silence

Not every political prisoner undergoes torture, even in the broadest sense. Prisons utilize torture both alongside interrogation and as a form of ritualized punishment, irrespective of law and regulation. As Darius Rejali argues in *Torture and Democracy*, torture practices are best understood as prisoners see them, subinstitutionally. He quotes a prisoner of war (POW) at the Tokyo War Crimes Trial: "Every guard was a law unto himself."[64] Torture can be anticipated but its contours remain uncertain, appearing between the lines of interrogation manuals and in prisoner testimony.[65]

The torture of political prisoners—distinct from their general ill-treatment— is not a constant. Insofar as it is intended to elicit information, torture occurs mainly at the beginning of incarceration, during interrogations before trial. Sentenced prisoners also experience punishment, such as solitary confinement, that might be indistinguishable to them from torture. Not all physical pain is inflicted to gather information—but all contributes to disorientation, from the ritual beating at entry to prison, to interrogatory torture, to ordinary, random acts of sadism.

When there are no criminal prisoners to keep the politicals in check, as in interwar Poland's Bereza Kartuska camp, in Stalinist-era Fordon Prison, in Long Kesh, or (eventually) on Robben Island, guards implement their own hazing rituals. The new arrivals, stripped naked, might have to run a gantlet of stick-wielding guards. Body searches are part of this ritual and can escalate well beyond simple humiliation to degradation. A guard might probe an inmate's rectum for contraband before using the same finger to check his mouth. Black South Africans were made to strip and dance the *tauza*, a humiliating acrobatic routine designed to shake loose contraband while providing guards with entertainment.[66]

Such brief rituals of physical and mental torment establish a clear and inviolable hierarchy, demonstrating how power inside prison is different from that outside. These rituals also have a carnivalesque quality: those who were free and

Fig. 2.2 In May 1954, *Drum Magazine* (Johannesburg) published an exposé of prison conditions, including Bob Gosani's clandestine photographs of the *tauza* routine inside Johannesburg Central Prison. As ZB Molefe explains, "The action of the dance was intended to dislodge anything illicitly placed between the legs or backside. The warder watched the prisoner intently and nodded as the naked man looked around him. The prisoner then picked up his clothes from the ground and walked on while the next man in the queue ran up to repeat the routine." Molefe, "An Appreciation," in *Tauza: Bob Gosani's People* (Cape Town: Struik, 2005), 20. Reprinted from Norman Phillips, *The Tragedy of Apartheid: A Journalist's Experience in the South African Riots* (New York: David McKay, 1960).

mocked state power are brought low and humiliated, while their tormentors flaunt their own freedom.[67] Torture, though, differs from hazing in that it rises above the "ordinary" punishment that is part and parcel of the daily prison experience. Like hazing, it conveys that the incarcerating regime is superior in force, holds different values from those it imprisons, and has higher-order needs that require the inflicting of pain. Hazing merely enforces collective degradation; torture degrades and dehumanizes the isolated individual. In Polymeris Voglis's words, it "unmakes the prisoner's world."[68]

Prisoners tend to write very little about the experience of torture. They report torture and help to publicize instances of it, but their memoirs usually remain silent about specifics. Jacobo Timerman, who devotes some time to this experience in his account of Argentinian prisons in the 1970s, tries to offer an explanation. "In the long months of confinement," he writes, "I often thought of how to transmit the pain that a tortured person undergoes. And always I concluded that it was impossible." Timerman's memoir is unusually blunt, yet on this topic he switches abruptly to the third person:

> A man is shunted so quickly from one world to another that he's unable to tap a reserve of energy so as to confront this unbridled violence. That is the first phase of torture: to take a man by surprise, without allowing him any reflex defense, even psychological.

Timerman notes that while some prisoners begged to be spared and others cursed their captors, he allowed himself to be led passively to the torture room. With the same detachment, he describes the torture almost clinically, in short sentences of self-interrogation:

> What does a man feel? The only thing that comes to mind is: They're ripping apart my flesh. But they didn't rip apart my flesh. Yes, I know that now. They didn't even leave marks.... And what else? Nothing that I can think of. No other sensation? Not at that moment. But did they beat you? Yes, but it didn't hurt.

This dialogue, for Timerman, makes sense only among the free, for within prison, torture was simply not something prisoners talked about. It was so intimate they used a euphemism instead, such as " 'I had five days on the machine.' "[69]

Thoughts of torture can generate an obsessive anticipatory fear. Even for the prisoner who passively submits to torture, the experience is both a physical and mental contest. Those who are able to talk about it gain clarity. In February 1942, Halina Barylewska-Hajdo smuggled notes from Pawiak Prison to inform underground comrades and her family about the interrogations she was undergoing.

"One thing they told me," she wrote, "is that they don't believe what I'm say-ing and will not leave me alone. I will be silent, I will be strong. Don't worry. Beating has a good effect on me, because I bite my tongue all the harder."[70] She had learned something about herself presumably impossible to imagine before arrest. Torture itself she surely expected from the Gestapo, but the effect of the experience would have been harder to foresee.

In stories like these, torture is the test of one's commitment to the cause and to one's comrades. Facing a police force sometimes equal in brutality to the Gestapo, Stephen Biko of South Africa's Black Consciousness Movement pro-fessed to welcome torture's clarifying effect:

> If they talk to me, well I'm bound to be affected by them as human beings. But the moment they adopt rough stuff, they are imprinting in my mind that they are police. And I only understand one form of deal-ing with police, and that's to be as unhelpful as possible. So I button up. And I told them this: "It's up to you. " We had a boxing match the first day I was arrested. Some guy tried to clout me with a club. I went into him like a bull.... Now of course they were observing my reaction. And they could see that I was completely unbothered. If they beat me up, it's to my advantage. I can use it.[71]

By the time this interview appeared in print, Biko had been beaten into a coma in a police station and left to die in the back of a Land Rover, but the bravery of figures like him become legendary, their stoicism discussed in cells, their terrible ordeals the subject of underground broadsheets.

Torture thus frames political imprisonment even when it is absent. Like prison itself, torture brings exhaustion, isolation, and emotional hardship, but it also makes death palpable, whether the prospect is real or rumored. Outside the everyday experience of incarceration, torture imposes order. A closer examina-tion of three cases in which torture ceased to be a hidden, ordinary occurrence and became disturbingly visible, helps to contextualize this practice.

In May 1926, Józef Piłsudski led a coup to restore stability and morality to the Polish state. The "sanacja," or "cleansing," regime he installed, while democratic in form, became increasingly authoritarian. The repressive measures culminated in the creation of a concentration camp at Bereza Kartuska in 1934, preceded by a wave of arrests of centrist and leftist politicians in the fall of 1930. The increas-ingly paranoid interwar Polish regime faced an emergency that was diffuse. A series of armed attacks by Ukrainian nationalists in July 1930 had set the govern-ment on edge, and an election was called in November after that government fell. There was, however, no ticking time bomb, to use the scenario often pro-posed by defenders of torture. During the week of the election, police across

Eastern Poland rounded up activists of the Western Ukrainian Communist Party (Komunistyczna Partia Zachodniej Ukrainy, KPZU) and of the Communist Youth League of Poland. After some time in local jails, the activists were taken to Security Police headquarters in the town of Łuck, where officers systematically tortured them. The goal was clear: both organizations had been outlawed, and the police sought information about party activities and leadership. Most of the prisoners were either Jewish or Ukrainian and thus, to the regime, outside the Polish nation, which needed to be cleansed of foreign bodies.

Decades later, Szymon Dobrzyński of the Youth League vividly recalled the waterboarding torture nicknamed "Paraguay" (others recalled it as "Uruguay"). Others mentioned beating on the soles of the feet—what the police called the "Polish Rubber Industry," or *pe-pe-ge*—and beating of the testicles, or the "omelette." At least one woman was raped, and Stefan Bojko, a KPZU leader, died.[72] Another prisoner, Rozalia Szczyrbowa, recalled how Comrade Ozjasz Szechter "organized moral resistance," telling stories of heroic revolutionaries; "he taught us that one should rather choose death than to reveal to the enemy the smallest secret."[73] Szechter's interrogation broke him as well: carried half-dead from the interrogation room, he managed to whisper through bloodied teeth to his comrades, who had heard his cries under torture, "Everything came out."[74]

Stories of torture in Łuck caused a furor in the press and in Parliament, and led the minister of internal affairs to shut down the Łuck Security Police office in early 1931. The incidents in Łuck, meanwhile, became a rallying cry for the revolutionary left. The torture became visible at the 1933 trial: when assembled prisoners began to sing in the Łuck courtroom, their guards proceeded to beat them. Dobrzyński recalls: "For us, it wasn't so terrible to be beaten with nightsticks." But when he saw tears rolling down the face of a journalist from the socialist daily *Robotnik*, "I realized that this had a devastating impression on the audience."[75] The regime had achieved its aim, as torture became a demonstration of pure control, indifferent to public interpretation.

"Łuck" became synonymous with repression, as when prisoners at Grudziądz warned in a protest letter five years later that "Our prison has become a Łuck." They had been punished for demanding a visit from the prosecutor (responsible under Polish law for handling prisoners' complaints): guards had stripped, beaten, and choked them and applied tortures like standing on a board placed on a prone prisoner's stomach.[76] At Grudziądz and elsewhere, prisoners called this kind of treatment "*defenzywiackie*": characteristic of a security police interrogation room. Prison brought punishment, but torture of this kind was expected only in the context of emergency information-gathering. The scandal, in other words, was that prisons became like police stations.

A similar pattern played out in the most serious torture scandal during the Northern Irish Troubles, when the Royal Ulster Constabulary was accused of systematically torturing IRA internees. Everyone knew that detention usually entailed a beating: the masculine world of police and paramilitaries practically required physical confrontation. But this internment was different. In the wake of a series of bombings and armed attacks, the British Army swept up over 300 men across Northern Ireland on the morning of August 9, 1971. After two days, interrogators selected fourteen captives for additional treatment. Each was wakened in the middle of the night and hooded with a heavy blue cloth bag that made it difficult to breathe. Helicopters took them to an unknown location—some guessed Scotland—where for six days they were beaten, deprived of food and water, denied access to toilets, forced to stand in excruciating positions, and subjected to unbearable white noise. From time to time there were interrogations. As abruptly as the treatment began, it ended with transport back to prison in Belfast.[77]

These prisoners were much more fortunate than their predecessors in Poland. Within days, they had all filed statements through their lawyers, and some met with a sympathetic Member of Parliament. The British Home Secretary convened a Committee of Inquiry, which reported to Parliament in November. Two years later, courts awarded the prisoners £10,000–15,000 in damages for "inhuman and degrading treatment." As in Poland, this torture was a public spectacle, with only a performance of secrecy masking a punishment that was meant to intimidate and disorient. Several prisoners believed that they would be pushed from the helicopter into the sea, as was occurring at the time in Argentina (though none make this connection explicit). Kevin Hannaway was in fact pushed out of the helicopter—landing on the grass four feet below. Michael Donnelly heard voices in the helicopter saying "Throw him out." "Before I went into the 'copter," he added, "I was asked if I could swim." Francis McGuigan had evidently heard rumors: he "believed we were going to be thrown from the helicopter, as had been happening to ones earlier."[78] Every bit of information became crucial; several prisoners mention desperate efforts to read documents handed to them after the hoods came off. At Patrick McNally's last interrogation before returning to prison, the "big grey hard fella" questioning him gave him a sheet of paper. "He asked me to sign it. I told him I couldn't see. I got it and tried to read it. He got annoyed. I waited until I could see, then I could make out 'boots and socks,' so I signed it." Others recall being unable to spell their names.[79] They battled for shreds of recognition, trying to put a name to what they saw or heard and to gain some mental bearing.

Torture made the mental contest with the British interrogators harrowingly physical. "They forced me to stand against the wall in the search position, [braced on my] fingertips," recalled Francis McGuigan.

> I refused to do this. Each time I rolled into a ball. They kept kicking and beating me. I took a breather against the wall—then I discovered they

weren't kicking me any more and I decided to stand against the wall and get a break. . . . I was fully conscious of someone standing behind me all the time watching what I would do.

Michael Donnelly describes the experience as lasting for days:

> I was taken outside the room and along a corridor into another room and made to stand against the wall as one is made to do for frisking, only I was made to stretch my legs and arms so far apart as I could get them. My feet also had to be as far from the wall as possible.
>
> I was made to remain in this position for at least two and at most four days with the hood on. I lost all track of time, but there is no doubt that I remained in this position for days. If I did not keep my head straight I was hit with a fist on the small of the back to make me straighten up. If I did not keep my back rigid I was "thumped" again in the small of the back.[80]

All the while they tried to determine who their torturers were and then struggled to narrate the experience clearly and to make sense of the performance the unseen guards forced upon them. The torture of August 1971 was an experiment not only to see if such treatment could effectively elicit information or deter opposition but also to work out the staging of torture in a modern democracy.

At about the same time that the Troubles in Northern Ireland were testing the limits of British treatment, the apartheid government in South Africa embarked on a similar campaign to enforce order. The Terrorism Act of 1967 created a broad definition of terrorism and prescribed indefinite detention for those suspected of it. Order in the prison would thus uphold order in society, and torture was a crucial part of that order.[81] One case, the mistreatment of several dozen men and women in 1969–70, reveals the nature of South African torture. The case began with the arrests, in May–June 1969, of twenty-two African National Congress (ANC) activists for work in a banned organization allegedly preparing a campaign of sabotage and terror. The security police, like their British counterparts, devised a torture system that combined total isolation with elaborate physical cruelty. In affidavits collected for the defense, the accused talked about their experience in graphic terms. They described a room with blacked-out windows and a small pile of bricks in the middle of the floor. Recalled Elliott Tshabangu,

> [Major Theunis] Swanepoel told me that whether I liked it or not I would stand on these bricks and never leave that small room before

I speak, I will stand on these bricks till I speak, even if I last two weeks . . . . In that small room there was a round electric light and the heat of the light burned my skull . . . . The pain of my feet caused by these bricks, endless questions from the police, punches, claps, insults, my moustache plucked out . . . all these sufferings did drive me to a point where I could not distinguish between night and day.

Another victim, Rita Ndzonga, refused to stand on the bricks.

One of the white Security police climbed on a chair and pulled me by my hair, dropped me on the bricks. I fell down and hit a gas pipe. The same man pulled me by my hair again, jerked me, and I again fell on the metal gas pipe. They threw water on my face . . . . I managed to stand up and they said "On the bricks!" I stood on the bricks and they hit me again while I was on the bricks. I fell. They again poured water on me. I was very tired. I could not stand the assault any longer. I asked to see Major Swanepoel. They said "*Meid, jy moet praat.*" (Girl, you must talk.)[82]

During the trial, as the accused and witnesses alike recounted interminable interrogations punctuated by beatings, the state's case collapsed amid patently flimsy evidence.

This trial raised the question of what constitutes torture and what place it had in the investigative process. Relatives of the detained asked the judge to issue a restraining order to prevent further mistreatment. The judge refused, on the grounds that further interrogations might not take place.[83] The security police, in turn, told of cooperative, even friendly conversations. Swanepoel, interviewed a year after the trial, claimed interrogations had led to friendship with detainees:

A detainee can ask for anything he likes to eat . . . . I will take him to a restaurant because, as I say, I want to win a man's confidence and swing him away from communism . . . . One wants the person who is questioned to become a friend. I have seen this happen time and again. People I have questioned have come back to me regularly if they have personal problems or if they have information for me. They come and visit me at my home. Do you think this would happen if you tortured someone?[84]

One of the detainees, John Schlapobersky, exposed the mental breakdown that torture induced. His testimony highlighted how personal torture is, and how it made him dependent upon his torturers.

Swanepoel and his partner terrorised me with threats, revilement and castigation. The other two pairs entered into a "conspiracy of kindness" through which I became dependent on their personal concessions and "small charities." My awareness of what was happening did not enable me to control my emotional and psychological needs. As Swanepoel's brutality wore me down, I became steadily more dependent on the false concern of others. When they were convinced of my dependence, after three days, the "soft pairs" withdrew their concern, became brutal and threatening, and switched roles with Swanepoel who, in turn, became concerned and paternalistic.

At the end of four days I felt disorientated. The distinction between sleep and waking life was dissolved. I walked into walls whilst asleep on my feet, and whilst awake on the chair found reality imbued with macabre dreams from semi-consciousness. I felt an inclination to trust Swanepoel as a "father figure" and this threw me into confusion as to what was real about me. I saw myself as a "sinner" and believed I had committed some hidden crime which we, the police and I, were now hunting down—for my own sake.

After Schlapobersky was examined by a doctor at the request of the British Embassy, and cleared for further detention, Swanepoel took revenge: "I was put on my feet again and kept falling asleep on my feet and walking into the wall, waking when I banged against it. I could not see clearly. I could not focus my eyes. . . . I think my identity was so detroyed I would have done almost anything asked of me." Indeed, Schlapobersky soon signed a statement prepared by the security police.[85]

The dance of interrogation in which roles frequently shifted created ambiguities as well as certainties. While the prisoner began to doubt his own innocence, observers, including even judges, doubted whether interrogation could constitute terror. Questioning in and of itself, even a lengthy session, was not in and of itself torture. Why should time or the elaborate edifice of paternal role-playing make the experience torture? Rejali details the physical and psychological effects of forced standing, placing it clearly in the torture category.[86] Hilda Bernstein, an anti-apartheid activist who fled South Africa in 1964, describes the nuances of torture eloquently:

There is no means which can be used to classify degrees of torture, nor is there any standard of endurance to inflicted pain or mental suffering. The public demands that if a political prisoner claims he has been tortured, then he must have some horrible physical details to recount. "Were you tortured?" the reporter asks the released prisoner. And it is not enough for him to reply "Solitary confinement is torture," or "I suffered terrible mental torture." The press wants something more solid: electric shocks, lashes, the rack.

Bernstein concludes with a dramatic assertion that gets at the heart of the prison experience: "Uncertainty itself is torture."[87]

These three cases help to define torture as continuous directed, intentional coercive measures linked in some way to the extraction of information or the modification of attitude. Torture establishes and reinforces a dependent relationship, based on fear and disorientation, of the prisoner to the interrogator/captor, whether that person works for the police, the ministry, or the prison. The tortured prisoner then brings those mental states to the broader prison experience.

Political incarceration prompts questions about the very nature of human agency. Does good behavior buy freedom, or would resistance win concessions? Would a confession have the desired effect of lessening the rigors of one's time in prison, or extend the indefinite incarceration?[88] What about silence? When Kazimierz Świrski, who had worked for the anti-communist underground within the regime's secret police, was arrested in 1947, he determined to "be silent, silent, silent. To forget the past until death. Only under interrogation did I realize that complete silence for me would mean death. They told me they could do with me what they liked because, they said, 'you are ours, you belong to the Security Bureau.' "[89] Neither option seemed correct, and prisoners lacked the information to make decisions. Stanisława Sowińska, hearing from her interrogator that her stay in prison depended upon her responses, lay awake that night pondering: "So there exists some consequential word, and if I guess it, that word will open the gates and free me?"[90] No matter what the prisoner's goal, the nature of political incarceration obscured the path toward it, or at least seemed to place it outside the ability of the prisoner to achieve it.

The apparently arbitrary or even capricious acts of administrators, interrogators, and guards do impose order on the political prison and may help to achieve the regime's goal of controlling opposition. But within the prison, they fundamentally erode the prisoner's sense of self. Prisoners become illegible to themselves and to others. Just as every attempt to deny prisoners their identity as political is linked to the violence that keeps them incarcerated, so too can acts of physical force, such as torture or prison labor, be understood as blows against prisoners' recognition of who they are and what their actions have meant. These twin forms of repression shape the way that political prisoners respond to prison.

3

"Everyone Learned Prison"

Becoming a Political Prisoner

Crossing the cell's threshold, the new prisoner suddenly uncovers a new world. Prison paradoxically makes the political struggle fresher and more palpable. Outside, there is always the fear of arrest and worries about getting family or friends in trouble. Now, those doubts and preoccupations seem far away. The struggle against power embodied in the political activity that led to detention or arrest becomes manifest, while some entirely new social relations take shape. Among the opposition outside, there may have been debates about the relative value of work in the underground, in the legal opposition, and behind bars. The dilemmas now are different: is it better to stay with imprisoned comrades or to try to get out? More generally, how should one act behind bars?

Chris Giffard, a twenty-seven-year-old member of the African National Congress (ANC) detained in December 1987, confided to his diary a week later:

> At last I don't have to pretend to be an "armchair revolutionary" any more. I can understand, tho', how people <u>are</u> broken by this whole process—i.e. starting to question their own motives + aims. But I'm quite confident still at this stage, even tho' not one person I can talk to agrees with me in any way. I must say it is a strange sensation to say to someone from "Veiligheids" [Security]: "I am a member of the ANC and the policy of my organisation is . . ." It's a flooding relief after so many years.[1]

Giffard welcomed the chance to finally introduce himself to the regime, even though many ANC detainees, both white (like him) and black, had died in detention in recent years.

Even those who could not afford to affirm their politics could feel, upon entering the prison, "more curiosity than fear." Thus Tomasz Rostworowski, a priest engaged in the Polish underground, entered the security police headquarters in Łódź in January 1950. He had often passed the building with a prayer on his lips for those incarcerated in its dungeons; now he would be one of them.[2] As his role in the movement and his relationship to the regime changed with detention, he, like Giffard, derived some comfort from joining those he had prayed for.

For both men, the act of entering prison divided their political lives. Rostworowski embraced new pastoral duties, ministering to his cellmates. Giffard, who enthusiastically tried to make contact with "comrades" in adjoining cells, saw prison transforming him from an ordinary white dabbler in oppositional politics into someone to be taken seriously. His palpable pride at having proven himself echoes the reaction of an unnamed "young painter" whom Antoni Lange observed chained to a metalworker outside the transit prison in Warsaw in 1907 as they awaited transport to Siberia. He had probably done no more than attend the occasional socialist meeting; now he "rejoiced like a child, so much did the situation amuse him, and cried out happily 'I'm in chains! In chains!' "[3]

More than pride and curiosity marked the threshhold from freedom to incarceration, of course. The belief that this step brought new obligations and opportunities surely differentiated the political prisoner from a criminal or from an imprisoned political. Yet as much was lost as was gained. A generation before Giffard, another white South African, Hugh Lewin, had entered Pretoria Local, soon to be sentenced to seven years under the Sabotage Act. For Lewin, prison was a place of emptiness, the bare walls reflecting the prisoner's absence of identity. Lewin's sense of despair and the terrifying interrogations he endured shook his very understanding of himself as a political being. Marek Kulczyk, interned and beaten in Warsaw's Mokotów Prison in 1982, similarly describes his feelings of powerlessness, of being reduced to just an object.[4]

Diaries and memoirs, which (along with letters) make up the bulk of the evidence of prisoner experiences, are nearly all composed by those who have survived their punishment, mentally and physically. Their recollections are thus a record of their success in overcoming powerlessness or despair and making meaning out of their experience. Even more, these documents are the place for justifying one's choices. The prisoner becomes political through accepting or embracing incarceration and then enacts it in a private or public text. Most political prisoners do not keep diaries or write memoirs, though a significant number—in particular those from Robben Island, Long Kesh, and the prisons of interwar Poland—have been interviewed. These writings sustain the collective, shared experience of political imprisonment. Strikingly, memoirs and diaries like those of Rostworowski, Kulczyk, Lewin, and Giffard trace a solitary process of joining a collective. At the moment of encountering pure, unmediated authority, these writers are alone with their prayers and fear, cut off from friends and comrades. Through writing, they place themselves back into a political cause and movement.[5]

This chapter explores the path to becoming political within the prison. It begins with the sources that help future prisoners to imagine and learn about life in the cell. The experience of others (encountered in books, in the movement, in the cell, or at home) initiated them into the ways of life in the prison and outlined their new identity. Gender shaped how political prisoners encountered the prison and its inmates, as did class and race. Prisoners understood the term "political," and the problem of acting politically while incarcerated, in varying ways. The chapter then considers how political prisoners marked the borders separating them from ordinary criminal prisoners and from guards, the two groups they encountered daily. Criminal prisoners appear as a category both radically different from and yet also constitutive of the political. Prison guards, the most immediate representative of the regime, force politicals to imagine and perform the category they seek.

How to Be a Political Prisoner

Political prisoners and future prisoners can choose among many different strategies for moral and physical survival. The three national traditions that supply this book's examples each appear to furnish a different prisoner archetype, distinguished by relationships to punishment and to the captors. The examples of Mohandas Gandhi and Nelson Mandela evoke a South African model of personal dignity and gentlemanly behavior. Both men made only indirect references to racial difference and implied that they expected their jailers to accord them respect. Thus Mandela, in a 1976 letter to the commissioner of prisons:

> I have never regarded any man as my superior, either in my life outside or inside prison, and have freely offered this cooperation in the belief that to do so would promote harmonious relations between prisoners and warders and contribute to the general welfare of us all. My respect for human beings is based, not on the colour of a man's skin nor authority he may wield, but purely on merit.[6]

Both men assumed equality as a natural outcome of their own position.

The Irish model, in turn, seems to favor a willful, almost reckless defiance. Bobby Sands, his legend fueled by his death in the 1981 hunger strike, towers above all others, but earlier hunger strikers like Terence MacSwiney in 1920 or incorrigibles like O'Donovan Rossa also fit the mold. Each, in different ways, is a teacher and a community leader as well as an unwavering opponent of the regime. The unified rage against injustice within prison and without yields a deep connection to the national cause; Sands, for example, composed poetry in Irish and taught the language to others.

A third type, the stoic prisoner bearing punishment in silence or heading to the gallows with a song on his lips, directs attention to the evil of the regime. The Polish case yields several examples, such as Ludwik Waryński, the early socialist who perished in 1889, or Witold Pilecki, executed in 1948. Irena Cieślińska-Skrzypiec, a former partisan in the wartime underground, argues that suffering in silence in the Stalinist prison was a moral choice.

> It was easier for me to get through my prison episode, since as a political prisoner I did not have to be ashamed of or condemn my past, or have regrets. On the contrary, confidence in the rightness of my decision to work in the conspiracy . . . just gave me strength, and privately mobilized me.[7]

Shaped by this history of martyrdom, many detainees in December 1981 braced themselves for being taken to dig a shallow grave in the woods.

But is it fair to take whole national cultures and look for them in the prison experience? Many prisoners have taken it for granted that the soul of the people resides in prison. True representatives of the people must therefore possess characteristics drawn from a common tradition. The lens of comparative politics might also be applied to regime-opposition relations: perhaps the class or ethnic makeup of the two sides, or the political system in power, induces different kinds of relations. Certainly a stoic face before execution makes little sense if the regime does not choose to execute or apply excessive force against its prisoners; when torturers and executioners have free rein, by contrast, moral superiority is more difficult to project.

Arguments against national models seem stronger, though. It is easy enough to find counterexamples (quiet leaders in Long Kesh, angry ones on Robben Island) in any culture. In their search for models, prisoners could turn to literature, from the Bible to more modern texts: Arthur Koestler's *Darkness at Noon* for Robert Sobukwe, Nikolai Chernyshevskii's *What Is to Be Done?* for Zofia Grabska, or the prison diaries of Ho Chi Minh for Gerry Adams.[8] Ukrainian partisans in Poland's Bereza Kartuska camp in 1935 were forced to read the collected works of Józef Piłsudski, evidently because the guards hoped this would teach the prisoners respect for Poland's political authority. The Ukrainians were surprised to discover that the dictator who incarcerated them offered so much practical advice on underground work and life in prison. As one of them commented: "It was just as if they had given an imprisoned thief technical manuals."[9]

More important, if the public outside the prison looked for national heroes, fellow prisoners were more likely to remember and describe their leaders— Mandela, Sands, Waryński, and others—as clever managers of communication, community, and resistance strategies within the prison, not simply as paragons of national or other virtues. Authority in the prison cell draws upon characteristics that also make a successful movement leader outside prison, not necessarily the more dramatic traits that might make a prisoner famous. Prison authority, forged under extreme conditions, provides in turn a firm basis for authority outside the prison.

Although for most prisoners the shock of incarceration slowly yields to a sense of oneself as a political prisoner, some begin preparing for the cell even before their first arrest. Patrick "Terror" Lekota, first imprisoned as a student activist in 1974, recalled in an interview not long after his release: "When I went to Robben Island I didn't like going to jail but I was also proud of the fact that I was walking in the footsteps of the proud defenders of our people who had been there before, in particular, that here was an opportunity to meet some of the tried and tested leaders of our people."[10] In the mind of the teenage Tokyo Sexwale, Nelson Mandela was present in the courtroom where Sexwale was tried, in the movements to which he belonged, among the people he knew. Sexwale's encounter with Mandela in person on Robben Island in 1977 was a culmination of those experiences.[11] For both men, a distant hero-model made the life of the political prisoner comprehensible, even if they could not imagine the actual experience. Sexwale freely admitted that the Nelson Mandela he had fantasized was not like the man he actually turned out to be in prison. This contrasts with far more graphic imagery available to teenagers in Northern Ireland. Demonstrations in the Falls Road area of Belfast or in Derry would sometimes feature a marcher dressed as a Long Kesh protester, wearing only a dirty blanket, or photos of injured or starving prisoners.[12] Such images made the prison experience palpable to viewers.

For young Jacek Kuroń, growing up in Nazi-occupied Poland, prison seemed a test of manhood. His father scolded him for poking his nose into the underground conspiracy: "You foolish brat, it's better to know nothing, because one day they'll come for you, they'll start beating you, they'll stick matches under your fingernails, and you'll tell everything." Not yet ten, Jacek became obsessed with mastering this promised torture. He stuck matches under his fingernails, held his hand in the flame, cut himself. Thirty years later, writhing in pain from an untreated kidney stone in a communist prison, he finally felt "happy": he knew he was surviving the worst possible pain and could not be broken by torture.[13] Those tests, decades apart, seemed for Kuroń to frame his path toward true political prisonerhood. By the time he was a teenager, he was getting more encouragement from his father. Shortly after the war, Henryk Kuroń offered Jacek

Fig. 3.1 Marcher dressed as a Republican blanketman. Falls Road, Belfast, October 1981. Courtesy of Pacemaker Press International.

this advice: "Don't ever smoke, because in prison it is tough to quit." The elder Kuroń's counsel contains several striking paradoxes as well as a shared conception of prison's place in a political life. Both he and his son supported the communist regime at the time. If prison was inevitable, it was not because the regime was likely to turn against them, but because the path of political awareness must lead to the gates of prison. Henryk Kuroń also implied that one should prepare for prison. By denying oneself pleasure in the present, one could anticipate and mitigate the necessary discomforts of future incarceration.[14]

Political prisoners might be divided into two groups. Some, though they know that they could be persecuted by the regime for their political beliefs, still experience a transformative shock when they arrive in prison. Others have

Fig. 3.2 Taken with a clandestine camera in Białołęka Prison, 1982, this photo became known as "The Magnificent Five." From left to right, Solidarity activists Henryk Wujec, Lech Dymarski, Janusz Onyszkiewicz, Jacek Kuroń, and Jan Rulewski. Photograph by Jan Krzysztof Kelus. Courtesy of FOTONOVA Agencja Prasowa.

long journeyed to prison in their imaginations. The cell is for them a culmina-tion of the life path they have chosen. In their memoirs and letters, members of both groups most often portray themselves as willing participants in the prison community; whether only the willing leave traces or the willingness becomes a necessary part of a reconfigured story is another question. Thus the terrified novice becomes a curious apprentice, and steely resolution replaces dread. Still, interviews, diaries, and even secret communications rarely convey disgust at the prospect of wasted years or horror at what lies ahead. Instead, they seem to share the sentiments of Antoni Lange:

> For the first time in my life I was imprisoned. In theory my thoughts had been in the direction of illegality, but in practice I had not yet reached that intersection where the only road open is to prison. Simply put: I had never been active in politics and undertook no activities; I was a sympathizer . . . . This abstract position meant that though prison constrains one, I regretted that I had so late begun to explore the mysteries of the dungeon . . . . The prison is the heart and soul of Russia. Who has not been in prison does not know or understand her.

Thus I am grateful to that capricious and unknowable power ... which sent me to the highest school of Russology. The secret of prison so interested me that, though I could easily have taken the opportunity to escape, I did not do so, and remained in Warsaw, awaiting the decision of God and of Skalon.[15]

The cell might have been merely another test of his convictions, like speaking at a rally or being handed a gun. Yet those milestones in an oppositionist career take place amid comrades and within a movement's structures. Even if one imagined that prison to be simply a duty to one's cause, as many did, it was endured within an enveloping state institution that controlled one's fate. "To survive in a system like this," writes Hugh Lewin,

> you must do two apparently contradictory things. On the one hand, you must accommodate to the system sufficiently for you to be able to ride with it and not be ground down by it. This ... requires that you somehow maintain a balance between appearing to be acquiescent to the system and losing your self-respect in doing so. On the other hand, you must constantly fight the system, cheat it at every possible stage, and find as many ways as possible of beating it—which also requires that you maintain some balance between success and failure, for to be beaten too often is demoralizing.[16]

The conflict that Lewin described requires political prisoners to evaluate every choice they make. Should one become accustomed to prison or reject it? Could one deny prison's physical power, or should one embrace its cold reality? The home-cooked meal or letter from home might domesticate the prison cell, but a political prisoner, some believed, ought to resist the temptations of that "other planet of life."[17] Few politicals came both to symbolize and to accept isolation as clearly as did Pan Africanist Congress (PAC) leader Robert Sobukwe, whom the South African regime imprisoned on Robben Island but held incommunicado from his fellow PAC members and all other prisoners there. Sobukwe lived in a little hut he could furnish with the help of friends and supporters outside. In his sixth year on the island, Sobukwe wrote to Benjamin Pogrund, who had offered some domestic comforts. Sobukwe happily accepted a bedspread but wrote that pictures for the walls would not be "necessary, Benjie. You see, all these, after a time, become part of the environment. And it is a jail environment. And there is something in me which does not wish to forget that either."[18]

Even one's physical appearance could provoke political reflection. Some prisoners sought to make the distress of prison physically evident, revealing evidence of mistreatment at trial or upon release. The matted hair and skinny chests of the IRA prisoners who refused to accept prison clothing during the Troubles sent such a message. But to wear the prison so visibly also meant surrendering control of one's body to the institution. To look "normal" despite harsh prison conditions, on the other hand, denied the prison's power to destroy what was human. Ewa Ludkiewicz was summoned from Fordon Prison to be a witness at the trial of Władysław Śliwiński in 1950. Awaiting her turn to give testimony, she was placed in her old cell in Mokotów Prison, where

> the girls decided, and I agreed, that I should look as good as possible. Let no one think that I am at all broken, or torn up, or crushed—and maybe that will also boost Władek's spirits. All together they cleaned up my suit, which was made from excellent wool . . . . They put my hair in curlers for the night, and in the morning styled it beautifully . . . . It's humorous, but knowing that I look good gave me courage.[19]

Ludkiewicz was not doing this to bolster her own case but to convey something about herself and about prison to a fellow prisoner on trial and to the regime. Preparing a cellmate for a public appearance was equally important for the other prisoners, who in this way also sent a message about their community. It was as obvious to Ludkiewicz that she should refuse to show the effects of incarceration as it was to men in the Irish Republican Army (IRA) that they should embrace or magnify them. Though they expressed it in different ways, both men and women insisted that appearance was one of the few things under their own control. Managing their bodies for particular effects also expressed a sense of their own dignity. In such ways, social relations brought from outside inform the roles that political prisoners learn to adopt.

Instructions for the New Prisoner

The making of the political prisoner begins with the oppositional movement itself. Modern political prisoners occupy spaces hallowed by predecessors who both inspire and help their successors prepare for this role. Much has been written about the prison narrative as a literary form that lays bare a suppressed life.[20] Such narratives are also a means of communication within a political movement. In them, the prisoner recounts experiences in detail to make the prison imaginable. The narrative furnishes some of its readers with a template onto which they might imprint their own experiences. While prison narratives predate the political prisoner, earlier narratives had an individual, romantic function: whether addressed to the nation, to the king, or to fellow adherents to an idea, they did not invite or expect others to follow. If anything, they might serve as a warning.

The modern instructional narrative, by contrast, assumed that members of a movement would go to prison in small groups over a longer period of time. This can be seen from the early twentieth century onward, with such groups as the suffragettes, the *satyagrahis*, or the Polish socialists. Activists in these movements needed such a prison manual.

In filing reports in *Indian Opinion* after each of his internments, Gandhi aimed to make the prison familiar to his followers—middle-class shopkeepers and traders with much to risk. He did not shy away from the unpleasant experiences, the forced stripping or the execrable, sometimes culturally offensive, food. His accounts helped fellow *satyagrahis* to understand how they could take those indignities and make them assets. In this, Gandhi's aims differed somewhat from those of his contemporaries in the militant suffrage movement who aimed to make prison shocking to the general public so as to advance their cause. Gandhi's reference to prison hardships similarly linked the prison struggle with the struggle outside. The indignity of nakedness, he showed, was not unlike the indignity of registration. Opposition to registration therefore made it necessary to endure with dignity the humiliation of being stripped.

Besides rendering the prison experience accessible and politically usable, prison narratives and instructions sought to limit the institution's damage to the movement. Before Wacław Koral encountered his first prison interrogator, in 1902, he had already consulted a Russian-language pamphlet entitled "How to Behave at Interrogations"—one of the earliest examples of this genre.[21] Throughout the questioning, Koral claimed no knowledge of the socialist movement, but when it came time to sign the interrogation protocol, he took care to put his name immediately after the document's last word, so that nothing could be added. "Then the gendarme smiled ironically and remarked: 'Yes, I can see that you know nothing.'"[22]

Precise guidelines were especially necessary when the line separating movement prisoner from informer or police spy was blurred or uncertain, and when the costs of not recognizing or being unprepared for danger were highest. A higher probability of unrest may also have necessitated such instructions. All of these conditions held true in Nazi-occupied Warsaw, where the underground Polish government issued "Prison Instructions" in 1942. "Maximum safety and efficiency," the document states at the outset,

> can be achieved when there is the most precise cooperation between the outside world and those imprisoned. These instructions contain rules that are not always given justification, yet they should be followed, because the lack of commentary is usually warranted by the need to maintain conspiratorial methods and means of operation. The fundamental premise of these instructions is that it is better to do nothing

than to act in violation of safety principles and thus risk a cascade of betrayals.[23]

Much of the instruction is focused on two points: never confide in anyone, even one's best friends, and acquaint oneself with prison rules on letters and packages. The document even provides a formula for composing a *gryps*, a smuggled note, in the interest of ensuring that the necessary information is transmitted as efficiently as possible. Yet new prisoners faced the greatest test in interactions with fellow prisoners and the Gestapo. Here the advice is brutal and direct:

> Beatings do not occur according to any clear rule. It is better to endure a beating while denying everything and be sent to a camp than to avoid a beating by admitting [to charges], causing the incrimination of others and going to the firing squad [anyway]. One should never agree to a set-up [a confrontation with comrades outside prison] in hopes of escape or with the intention of misleading the interrogators. The result will be the exposure of others and, sooner or later, execution. One should testify briefly, boldly, and decisively. Pathos is pointless, as no one will appreciate it. Tears only irritate the interrogators, who are incapable of emotion.[24]

Through such documents, every reader becomes a political prisoner, battling in his or her mind with the interrogator. Though torture and death did not loom before all future prisoners, many would have had occasion to rehearse the prison encounter. Armed with these instructions, they could enter the interrogation room or the cell prepared to withstand the prison's attempt to change them.

In addition to explicit instructions like these, letters from prison or post-release reflections constitute the most accessible form of shared experience. More often, surely, advice passed unremarked in conversation, its traces occasionally surfacing in memoirs. When Zdzisław Jędrzejewicz first entered a cell in Kielce Prison in 1949, a new cellmate immediately asked him whether amnesty had been declared and one could thus admit to doing underground work. But he was prepared: "Never ask about anything and say nothing about oneself, until you have gotten to know the people in your cell . . . . You will come to recognize with whom you can talk only about health, or the weather, or women—but not about the cause." Jędrzejewicz explains the problem of informers at some length before noting: "I knew all of this from friends' stories."[25] Those stories had given him clear categories that he could recognize in the cell. The prisoner with a cause remains silent, while others who are either not political or worked for the other side distinguish themselves by talking. The ideal political prisoner was one who anticipated the obligations of that role, as well as the threats to it.

Of course, those who previously read prisoners' memoirs are likely to be the ones who eventually wrote about their own experiences. Baruch Hirson had prepared himself for years before he found himself in Pretoria Local in 1964. Having "read many accounts of jail in books and journals, fictional and real," he writes, he "thought I knew what to expect when I was arrested."[26] IRA leader Gerry Adams concluded upon reading Ho Chi Minh's diaries and poetry (published in English in the 1960s) that "some things are universal."[27] At least, the perception that they are universal is what matters. Would-be prisoners read about others' experiences in the hope that familiarity with the rules of entry and the language and customs of the territory would help avoid eventual embarrassment.

But the aspirant would find that the category of "political prisoner" simply did not exist outside of prison walls. The environment, the social relations, and the psychological pressures of the prison were all utterly new and shocking, even if the cell held familiar faces. Upon entering, prisoners hoped to learn from their cellmates. This communal learning process distinguishes the political from the criminal. The criminal prisoner is likely to have no interest in helping a new prisoner adapt; indeed, the world of the criminal prisoner depends upon a carefully maintained hierarchy of knowledge and power.[28] The political prisoner in such an environment receives no privilege nor instruction, as Marek Kamiński, a sociology student at Warsaw University, found in a criminals' cell in 1983. His cellmates recognized his difference, nicknaming him "Student" and tolerating his collection of data on the informal rules of the prison world. But they had no reason, beyond individual friendship, to assist him.[29]

The community of political prisoners is often riven by nearly insuperable divisions, as between Loyalists and Republicans in Northern Ireland, or ANC and PAC members in South Africa. Yet hierarchy of experience matters greatly. In 1940, Władysław Bartoszewski was an eighteen-year-old novice in the Warsaw underground, among several thousand Polish intellectuals deported to Auschwitz. Prisoners were allowed to read German newspapers together. "I also read them aloud, in such a way that everyone knew that I didn't take the contents seriously. 'My dear,' the [barrack] clerk told me. 'You read the German papers, but this way . . . you risk death.'"[30] Bartoszewski could still be an intellectual, he learned, but would have to learn the customs of the territory in order to stay alive. After Auschwitz, Bartoszewski would spend much of the Stalinist years in prison, too. Decades later, on the night the post-Stalinist regime rounded up Solidarity activists in December 1981, he packed once more for prison. His preparation reflected forty years of experience. "What does an experienced prisoner think about at such a moment? A sweater, warm underwear, a coat—that's what's necessary. Blankets? No, there are blankets in prison. No need to take any money—just a comb and a toothbrush. I'm ready. It took but a minute."[31]

At nearly sixty, he would be one of those conveying their experiences to a new generation in the internment camps, just like Andrzej Jakubowicz, a trade union leader from a locomotive factory. Jakubowicz taught his cellmates everything from how to organize one's days in prison to a method for cutting bread with a prison-issue spoon.[32] The intergenerational conversation within the cell fostered a sense of the praxis of political incarceration. No matter how much one had read or seen, the cell community created the prisoner.

"Everyone," concludes Jerzy Stokowski, "learned prison."[33] In 1952, the summer after he graduated from university, Stokowski was arrested for oppositional activity. His memoir of those days largely follows convention, as he points to more experienced prisoners who offered advice, like two friends who warned him not to talk about the world outside or about his case. As Stokowski explains, "I soon came to understand that prison is not at all the place where, as I naively assumed, one could feel free, voicing one's views and thoughts and telling political jokes. I had to learn to be cautious." He also learned how to sleep while feigning conversation during interrogations and what to expect in other prisons, too.[34] Stokowski describes in unusual detail his entry into a world ruled by criminal convicts. His cell in the Mostowski Palace was ruled over by Maks P., a communist veteran of pre-war prisons and himself a prison official in 1945–46. Maks P. might have seemed a candidate for the role of tutor, but he allied with the criminal element in the cell. He organized what he claimed were traditional games among the prisoners: beatings with wet towels, sexually humiliating rituals, kangaroo courts for novices. These marked the cell as foreign, even as the sight of those sharing Stokowski's political disposition promised community. The symbolic entrance to this new world was a towel thrown across the threshold at the newcomer's feet. A novice would instinctually pick it up and hand it to its owner, for which the punishment was a beating. An experienced (criminal) prisoner, or one forewarned, knew to wipe his feet on the towel, saying "The filth of freedom I leave behind me."[35]

"Ordinary Decent Criminals": Politicals on Foreign Territory

The entry to the cell was thus an encounter not just between a novice and an unfamiliar world, but between an institution created for criminals and those who felt themselves to be of another class entirely. One might imagine that a committed political activist would seize the opportunity to proselytize an untutored criminal cellmate. Outside prison the political activist labors to reach the often indifferent, apolitical mass of society. Now a representative of these masses sits a few feet away, with plenty of time to talk; surely even the shyest enthusiast would seize the moment. And yet the gulf between the two only hardened in prison, confirming the political prisoner's sense of difference.

In 1932, a group of women communists in Piotrków Prison confronted what they considered to be an ambush set by prison authorities. As they described it in a letter smuggled to their party comrades outside:

> The administration launched a general attack last summer. During our [daily] walk, criminal women with children sat at some distance. Since [our leadership] considered it appropriate not to react at that time, we accepted this sitting. This spring the mothers also came during our walk, but instead of sitting at a distance, they began to walk with us. We reacted immediately to this new attack by leaving our walk. On the next day the mothers sat at a distance [again] . . . . A few days later besides the mothers came another criminal woman without a child, and began to walk with us. We assessed this as a new attack; by accepting such a walk we would be accepting a walk together with criminals. The administration would gradually send out new women, and made this intention clear to us. We were forced to leave the walk.

Noting that similar infiltration was occurring in the baths and during the shaking out of bed linens, the women announced a total boycott of walks.[36] Given the deep isolation these women felt, and their commitment to communism, their aversion to any contact with fellow prisoners who deserved some sympathy, if not political education, is striking.

Similarly hostile interaction occurred in other settings where political prisoners were thrown in with others. Thus Elsie Mathibedi complained from Pretoria Central Prison in 1982: "I am unhappy of being sentenced for sweet nothing," noting her "greatest amazement to find that a political prisoner was being mixed with other ordinary prisoners in this prison. I am saying this because I never experienced it before."[37] The shock that Mathibedi and the Piotrków women felt stemmed from a sense that the prison was for the criminals and the administration should provide a haven for politicals. When Władysława Osińska gave birth to a son in Mokotów Prison in 1949, she was moved to a cell for mothers, where the criminals "ran the show, and laughed at us for being losers."[38] The knife fights and gang rivalries of criminals had set the tone in the same prison four decades earlier, reported socialist Jan Sosnkowski, but the criminals left him alone, regarding him as a "good little urchin."[39]

The gap between political prisoner and criminal arises, in these instances, in moments of physical encounter. In other cases, class clearly shaped attitudes toward criminals, as in the strikingly similar responses of two noblewomen. Countess Constance Markievicz entered Kilmainham Prison in the days after the Easter Uprising of 1916 with a death sentence; that sentence was eventually commuted on the grounds of her gender, and she was moved to Mountjoy Prison. Though the conditions there were appallingly filthy, she recalled the harshest punishment to be that she, a "patriot rebel," had to share space with "low class criminals" and listen to their "disgusting jokes."[40] Zofia Grabska was similarly incensed by the conditions in detention after a demonstration in Warsaw in 1894. Unlike her previous experience in the Citadel, she had to share a cell with common criminals. A literary comrade struck up conversations with the ordinary prisoners, but not Grabska: "Everything disgusted me. My socialist convictions did not fill me with understanding for these lost daughters of the people, these victims of the capitalist system."[41] The squalor that might be tolerable on its own was compounded by the sense that women of lesser breeding seemed to find these conditions acceptable, perhaps normal, leaving noble prisoners out of their element.

This disgust did not necessarily fade with time and the decline of the nobility. Marek Kulczyk, who enjoyed good relations with the criminals in his cell in 1982, during Poland's martial law, nevertheless protested when he and nine other politicals were suddenly moved to the criminal wing.

> We refused dinner and sustained the hunger strike until we returned to "our" wing. We were summoned to the counselor of that wing . . . . The explanation that we are politicals and want to be placed together with politicals worked like a red flag on a bull . . . . He said that we are emphasizing our political status only because we are disgusted by the criminals and that we want to gain some privileges.[42]

ANC men on Robben Island, who claimed that kitchen workers gave names like "sodomy" to the dishes they prepared, expressed their revulsion to and alienation from a world where the criminal ruled.[43]

Such stories belie a suspicion that the authorities manipulated the environment to make political opponents uncomfortable and had more trust in criminal convicts. Kulczyk's counselor would probably endorse the term "Ordinary Decent Criminals," which British officials in Northern Ireland used to emphasize their aversion toward the incorrigible IRA prisoners.[44] So would a wardress in the Johannesburg Fort, who upbraided ANC women who "have been arrested for rubbish, because they will never get the thing they are fighting for," while the drug dealers and the like "at least were trying to make a living."[45] As Władysław Bartoszewski put it: "Thieves are in any case well-liked in prison. They're always planning something, they always have ideas. A small-time thief is always welcome. The same is true for swindlers, and even those convicted of sex crimes, as long as they didn't harm a child. These are all ordinary human affairs, and the prison guards even like them. They aren't hardened criminals. The politicals are the criminals. The prison guards didn't want to have anything to do with politics—they feared that."[46] Unlike their nineteenth-century predecessors, prison officials viewed the politicals as alien. Expedience, comprehension, and even fear influenced officials' identification with the criminal denizens of the institution. Politicals, for example, were more likely to refuse menial work, such as sweeping corridors or cooking and distributing meals; as a result the kitchen, the laundry, the corridor, and often the cell itself came under the control of the criminal.

Politicals and criminals, wrote Gustaw Daniłowski during the heyday of socialist revolution in Poland, were like "two foreign tribes separated by a mountain chain."[47] Socialists mistrusted those who did not perform honest proletarian labor, while criminals interpreted socialism to mean the destruction of the system on which their livelihoods depended. Thus, commented Daniłowski, "to break a political's bones without laying a finger on him, it was enough to put him among the criminals."[48]

Both sides had an interest in convincing the authorities to maintain the separation between them. Politicals felt they could not trust criminals to be discreet; they also feared that authorities would take advantage of any rapprochement to erase hard-won distinctions. But criminals had further reason to resent politicals, whose arrival might result in restricted freedoms for criminals.[49] Thus each side built the barrier higher: the criminals restricting their contact to trade in cigarettes and the occasional passing of messages, the politicals protecting their honor and safety. Stefania Sempołowska, Poland's great prisoner-rights activist, understood the moral costs of this conflict clearly, recalling with embarrassment a moment during her own brief sojourn in Warsaw City Jail in 1909, when

> one of our companions . . . brought joyful news to our cell: "I managed to fish out a political from cell 4 [the prostitutes' cell], and we'll get her moved to a political cell." This . . . was a grievous fault on our part, as we threw into these women's faces the fact that in the depths of our souls we regarded them as such low, unworthy companions. That without considering a value of another person, we assign them names like "political" or "prostitute." We reacted this way instinctively.

Sempołowska's justification was that she and her socialist comrades believed that the other women could live with prison conditions that politicals could not tolerate.[50]

Władysław Szczypa, arrested by the Austrians in 1918, began ingratiating himself with the ordinary prisoners from the moment he entered Lublin Castle. They, in turn, showed him deference as soon as they heard he was a member of the Polish Military Organization, addressing him as "sir," a word rarely heard in a prison cell. Szczypa decided "not to show them the difference between us and to treat them like comrades in misery." He gave the guard money to buy tobacco for all prisoners and taught them checkers. In return, the prisoners excused him from cell chores and brought him his meals. But when after six days he met the magistrate, he didn't hesitate to complain about being stuck in a cell with "thieves and bandits." The shocked magistrate immediately transferred him to a political cell.[51] Likewise, Father Tomasz Rostworowski, after three years in prison, shared a cell with and ministered to a number of prisoners, some of them criminal. When Rostworowski and two other priests petitioned for the return of their breviaries, they were rewarded by being placed in a new cell by themselves. Apparently forgetting their previous companions, they celebrated Mass together and rejoiced at finding a communion wafer in one of the breviaries.[52]

The gulf between politicals and criminals was cast in sharp relief in large communal cells. Polish prisons featured such spaces even into the communist period, unlike British or Irish ones. Politicals there could use criminal prisoners' customs to protect themselves. When Janusz Horodniczy, then seventeen years old, entered his first prison cell, "someone threw a towel at my feet, and I picked it up and politely returned it to its owner. Someone else growled 'greenhorn!'" The thrower was in this case another political; Horodniczy's cellmates thus made sure they were not being sent "some criminal snitch." Thus Horodniczy's gaffe made him welcome.[53]

While the South African apartheid regime avoided mixing races in cells, white politicals in Pretoria prisons and black political prisoners anywhere often found themselves surrounded by criminal prisoners. Criminal gangs dominated Robben Island prison society in the early 1960s; in the politicals' view, the criminals clearly allied with the guards. Memoirs by ANC prisoners portray the two groups as radically different: politicals sing freedom songs while criminals do not; criminals engage openly in homosexual behavior while sex involving politicals is never mentioned.[54] After the alliance between criminal gangs and guards fell apart in 1964, Moses Dlamini recounts, criminal prisoners approached the politicals asking if they could be called something else, proposing "economic saboteurs." The politicals rejected this characterization, as it implied a political motive. Then, Dlamini recalls, "one peasant suggested that they be called '*abento zabo*' (that is, those who have been convicted for their own things). The criminal convicts heard this and became excited. They like to be called 'abento zabo.'"[55] This compromise maintained a distinction from politicals, who had been convicted for acting in the cause of others. In a prison where politicals were in the ascendant, criminals placed their identity in the hands of the politicals.

In Pretoria, Hugh Lewin found that white criminal prisoners sought a physical attribute for political prisoners, as if discomfited by the absence of race. "Hey man," said one to Lewin, "you kommies all wear glasses, man."[56] Lewin could not help but see the prison hierarchy as racialized: "At [Pretoria] Local Prison, however grim our condition, we had been daily reminded of the fact that we were white and therefore, inevitably, privileged. In our special section of what was basically a black jail, we had always been aware of the difference in treatment between us and the blacks.... Now, in the all-white society of Central, it was our turn to be the blacks."[57] Like blacks, Lewin implies, politicals could not improve their status through better behavior. One could perhaps use the Zulu terminology invented on Robben Island and say that because politicals were not "abento zabo," their behavior in prison was irrelevant to their reform. Only their behavior outside prison could matter.

Even in late communist Poland, when class distinctions had become much less visible in regime-prisoner relations, criminal prisoners respected politicals as different from them. In a cell in Mokotów Prison, Marek Kulczyk says "the criminal prisoners treated me well, since I was a man from another world, like a foreigner from a respected country."

> Once just before a "raid" the guard opened the door yelling "Thieves out!" When we were out in the corridor [my cellmates] told me that I shouldn't have come out, since I'm a political. And they were right. Whenever I wanted to study, I could always use the table—and the table is a sacred thing in prison, practically an altar. Not everyone can sit there. Meals, the most important prison activity, are celebrated at the table, but I was allowed to read and write there several hours a day. This wasn't just enjoying one's rights, this was a privilege. Another example, maybe even greater: when I was studying they turned down the radio, or even switched it off. Usually it played full blast.[58]

Thus the presence of a political prisoner transformed the space of the cell in the eyes of its native inhabitants.

In Irish and British prisons, the sectarian nature of political conflict tended to keep criminals and politicals separate. Parents of convicted criminals in Northern Ireland sometimes tried to get their sons into sections of the prisons for politicals, hoping that their influence might steer them toward a more honest life.[59] Yet there is little evidence that even IRA prisoners did much to educate their ordinary prison mates.

Prison officials faced a complex challenge in managing their inmates. Like the leaders of any authoritarian institution, they sought to maintain and extend order by coopting certain subjects. Assuming that all inmates were inclined to violate the institution's rules, they needed to decide which transgressions could be most easily controlled. Efforts by prison authorities to maintain a balance between politicals and criminals depended upon external politics and on the relative size of the groups. To take two contrasting examples from different Polish regimes: In 1907, Jan Kwapiński moved to a new cell in Warsaw's Arsenal Prison, where he found that criminals outnumbered his comrades nearly four to one. The czarist government, he explained, "tried specially to annoy us by putting us politicals among criminals." The cell leader (a criminal convict) ordered Kwapiński to carry out the latrine bucket and to clean the cell. Criminals, Kwapiński quickly learned, did not have to do anything, so he refused. When the guard punished the cell leader for maintaining a filthy cell, open conflict between politicals and criminals broke out until three large cells were set aside for the politicals. Still, the authorities placed three trusted criminals in each cell.[60] The political prisoners calculated that the regime desired order (and perhaps cleanliness) more than it needed to vex the politicals. Marek Kulczyk reports a different attitude toward order and balance during martial law in 1982. Political internees in Łęczyca Prison were not permitted to work for fear they would be better able to communicate with one another. In addition, the authorities sowed discontent, hinting to the criminal convicts that Solidarity had scuttled a planned revision of the criminal code and that politicals received superior packages from their families.[61] Whereas in 1907 the authorities did not fear the influence of their political charges, in 1982 they clearly did.

Just as regimes believed it was necessary to segregate politicals from the public, the authorities needed to protect ordinary, rehabilitatable prisoners from dangerous political influence. In 1950, the communist regime in Poland decided to separate long-term political prisoners from the rest. "Immediately after the removal of that category," claimed Hipolit Duljasz, then director of prisons in the Ministry of Public Security, "operative work [that is, efforts to gain information] got off the ground, and positive [cooperative] prisoners revealed themselves."[62] Duljasz focused on the incorrigible opponents of the regime, who could influence not only criminals but also less important politicals serving short-term sentences for relatively minor transgressions.

The authorities feared the politicals' leadership potential. Yet evidence of cooperation between criminal and political prisoners, which might create a formidable unity in resistance to the regime, is rare. The codes of behavior and concepts of honor that each group possessed created moments of détente and allowed individual criminal prisoners to cross over and be accepted, but the border remained. Tales of mass conversion, like this one from Janusz Horodniczy, the teenager in the Jaworzno internment camp in the early 1950s, sound unconvincing:

> [the criminals] began to adopt our ideals as the only correct ones . . . .
> We transformed our thief colleagues, inculcating our ideas in them. Of

course, not in every case. But we held together tightly, and definitely held moral sway over the criminal minority.[63]

Horodniczy's boast is framed more as an indictment of the regime, whose hold over the criminals is no match for the superior ideas of his colleagues. And despite the supposed "moral sway," Horodniczy got a prison tattoo, something few politicals did.[64] His memory of political influence likely reflects the youthful camaraderie he felt with those peers with whom he shared prison hardships. "I deeply believed," Horodniczy writes, "that in these conditions we were all equal."[65] Presumably hierarchy returned when the conditions changed. The socialization within prison and the treatment one endured left little doubt who was who.

The Distance from Cell to Corridor: Guards and Prisoners

While political and criminal prisoners skirmish along the border between them, there is always the eye at the keyhole, and a figure at the end of the exercise yard. The guards and orderlies had much in common with the criminal convicts; for both, prison was a familiar place with daily routines. Like the criminals, prison workers tended to be less educated and to distrust political motives. They were also paid by the regime and inclined to see the politicals as a threat to their livelihood. Despite the threat that political prisoners were assumed to pose to the regime, there is relatively little trace of routine scrutiny of prison workers for their reliability. One scrap of evidence comes from Stalinist Poland, where the Ministry of Public Security administered a political exam to over 7,000 prison workers. It found that while almost all held membership in the Polish United Workers' Party, fewer than half scored "good" or "very good" on the exam, and close to 1,000 were illiterate or nearly so.[66]

Insofar as the category of political was itself uncertain, prison guards policed its border. They could decide who among the prisoners was reliable and to what category they belonged. Janina Jelińska tells a story of a fellow prisoner given extra exercise time for health reasons, sometime in the late Stalinist period (1952 or 1953). The block orderly stopped her to ask why she was in prison: was she the wife of a colonel? a landowner? a capitalist or speculator? Finally he burst out: "I've figured you out . . . you are surely an intellectual, and got mixed up in politics. No more extra exercise!"[67]

This encounter points to the threat that political prisoners posed to their guards. In the big picture, the political prisoners' challenge to the regime raises the possibility, however distant, of those in power being replaced by those in prison. But at the individual level, in the exercise yard, that potential is reduced to an intimate conflict between one guard and one prisoner. The potential for reversal of roles is a fundamental characteristic of political incarceration, one that is irrelevant to the criminal convict who likely has no wish to run the state or its institutions. The latent possibility of overcoming one's incarceration and turning the tables determines much about the experience of political imprisonment.

The Irish struggle for independence offers several dramatic reversals. The fighters of Sinn Fein had fought the British since the Easter Uprising and waged the revolution as much in the prisons as across the countryside. The deaths of hunger strikers Thomas Ashe in 1917 and Terence MacSwiney in 1920 focused that struggle for independence on prison cell dramas in England and in Ireland. Even during the Revolutionary War, guards and staff in Irish prisons were likely to be Irish and faced pressure from prisoners and from those outside to turn against their British employers. Frank Gallagher, in the midst of a hunger strike in 1920, noticed the effect this pressure had:

> But for the friendly warders this strike might have been already broken . . . . If they had tempted the men, some might have failed; and if any had failed, many would die, because the failure of the few would encourage the British to test every man to the uttermost . . . . The warders tempted the men in the other strikes . . . . But today they have been leavened with the mass of the people and it is no longer hard to make them understand.[68]

As Max Green, head of the General Prisons Board, observed, all were aware that those then in prison might soon be masters of Ireland and were thus "very much inclined to avoid conflict with the Sinn Fein prisoners at all costs."[69]

While similar tensions could be seen in Polish prisons in the last years of Russian rule, Polish independence was not as clearly in the offing. Some guards were Russian (just as some staff in Irish prisons might be English); they might still help Polish prisoners out of pity, for extra cash, or in class solidarity.[70] One such guard, Sierakowski, had treated prisoners at Sieradz Prison with particular brutality before a change came over him. Approaching a communist beginning a new stint in prison, Sierakowski whispered in his ear, "Now I am a different man—I'll do anything for you." Indeed, with his help this prison seemed to be under the control of the political prisoners, until Sierakowski lost his job for smuggling out three comrades dressed as guards.[71]

The fluidity of a political regime and the uncertainty of the outcome of a conflict shrink the distance between guard and prisoner. In a relatively stable state, or one with overwhelming power, a guard's feeling of national or class affinity is overshadowed by the influence of the state apparatus. In late czarist Poland or British Ireland, guards could not be certain that they were on the correct or safe side.

Few cases in the history of political incarceration more resemble the 1971 Stanford Prison Experiment—in which psychologist Philip Zimbardo randomly divided a group of student volunteers into prisoners and guards—as do the internments of the Irish Civil War (1922–23). The conflict with the British ended suddenly when an Irish delegation signed a treaty in London in December 1921, relinquishing the demand that a Republic of Ireland consist of the entire island. To many, this seemed a betrayal of the cause and so they fought on; men and women who had fought alongside them against the British now captured and interned their former comrades.

The vice chairman of the General Prisons Board wrote to the Ministry of Home Affairs in December 1922 to warn of the dangers of dealing with anti-treaty women prisoners. They are, he wrote, "of the class that have always claimed treatment as political military prisoners. This class, although accorded this status and placed in the custody of very strong military forces, have succeeded, as Government are aware, in many prisons in not only wrecking those prisons, but in making their safe detention a matter of the very greatest difficulty."[72]

The shock of similarity pervades memoirs of the period, like that of Peadar O'Donnell, whose journey through prisons and camps across Ireland in 1922–23 was haunted by anticipation of being put to death. He seemed to know every soldier and prison official guarding him. One jolly evening of storytelling in Finner camp, in mid-1923, came to an abrupt end as O'Donnell was struck by the thought: "the whole situation was unreal. Why should I be in here with these lads as my jailers?"[73] Emblematic of this incongruity, for O'Donnell and many others, was the deputy head of Mountjoy Prison, Paudeen O'Keeffe. A coarse and larger than life figure, he had fought in the independence struggle alongside many of his charges. He willingly passed on messages to prisoners from families he knew. Yet he was also there to wake four leaders of the anti-Treaty Republicans in their cells and lead them away to an early morning execution in December 1922.[74] Distance between prison and prisoner widened after most treaty opponents were released in 1924, with far smaller numbers incarcerated over the next two decades.[75] The sense of chance that Peadar O'Donnell experienced gave way slowly to the logic of the legitimate state.

At the other end of the spectrum from the camps of the Irish Civil War lies Robben Island. No matter how much Nelson Mandela commanded respect among prisoners and guards, it was implausible that he or any of his comrades could trade places with their jailers.[76] The young, mostly uneducated Afrikaaner wardens on Robben Island looked upon their charges with incomprehension, while their charges found the warden culture utterly foreign.[77] James Gregory, a warden who arrived on the island in 1968, recalled the stark categories into which wardens placed the prisoners: they were all terrorists and Poqos, a reference to the military wing of the Pan Africanist Congress; then, depending on their race, they were simply kaffirs (black) or koelies (Indian); there was no other possible distinction.[78]

Degraded and labeled, prisoners struggled to resist racial slurs that denied them their political status. Moses Dlamini claims that guards deliberately circulated stories of politicals' criminal exploits or, conversely, displayed compliant criminal prisoners as politicals during a Red Cross visit to the island.[79] Guards ridiculed the very idea that political prisoners might be different from the stereotyped uneducated black, illiterate and unfamiliar with modern technology. Stanley Mogoba recalled gathering with some other prisoners in the Robben Island library and overhearing a guard exclaiming through the window: "My God, the Poqos are sitting on a chair."[80] A favorite game in the mid-1960s was to frame political prisoners as class impostors: "All teachers must come this side," guards would ask newcomers, then inquire of each: "Have you got a driver's license?" Those who dared to assert that they had the same skills as whites would be assigned to "drive" heavy wheelbarrows in the quarry.[81] Guards feared those who advanced claims to equality, which upset a social order and erased the border between political and criminal. If the gulf between prisoner and guard seemed threatened, the latter tried to protect it by humiliating the politicals and reasserting that prison is by definition a place for criminals.

Prisoners, for their part, equated the guards with the criminal prisoners. As Mosibudi Mangena put it (in Afrikaans), both had a *"tronk gedagte"*—a prison mentality. Mangena could not hide his condescension toward poorly educated guards. He recognized that they were simply ill-equipped for the job as their training, which focused on "anti-social" criminal prisoners, had not prepared them for the literate political prisoner.[82]

Perhaps because their very humanity depended upon their separate identity, the political prisoners of Robben Island took it upon themselves to educate their guards. Neville Alexander, author of a clandestinely prepared "dossier" on Robben Island, described this work as "one of the greatest diversions (though often a tedious, irritating chore) .... They have to be taught (1) ordinary manners; (2) the basic equality of human beings; (3) the prison regulations, with special reference to the limit of their power; (4) English (in most cases); and (5) the real history of South Africa."[83] Alexander here neatly reversed the pecking order: instead of guards teaching new prisoners the ways of prison (perhaps with the assistance of criminal convicts), here the politicals became the hosts and accepted the chore of teaching the rules and customs of their home.

Robben Island prisoners struggled for much of the 1960s over the terms of address in the prisoner-guard relationship. A black prisoner was expected to address a guard as "baas"—master; in turn, he was a "kaffir." According to

Alexander, his comrades won a decisive battle over *baas*; he calls this an elimina-
tion of "caste rules."[84] As for *kaffir*, Canzibe Rosebury Ngxiki relates a story from
1966 or 1967 indicating how prisoners enforced respect. One day, while Ngxiki
was working on a road crew, a guard called him a *kaffir*, then hauled him to the
prison's head when he protested. Reporting the slur, Ngxiki had the satisfaction
of watching the commanding officer berate and humiliate the guard.[85]

Prisoners played with the categories they were assigned. Indres Naidoo,
learning that a friend had just arrived on Robben Island, shocked prisoners
and guards alike by acting like a guard: he simply walked into the canteen and
yelled for him.[86] No one manipulated categories with greater self-assurance
than Nelson Mandela, who coolly asserted his own superiority to prison personnel and presented a model to other inmates. Guard James Gregory observed
this on his very first visit to Mandela's wing. His superiors had warned him to
avoid conversation lest he be drawn into some nefarious plan, and yet none of
the prisoners even looked up as he locked their cells, marking him as a nonen-
tity. A few years later Mandela took advantage of an encounter with the notori-
ously cruel Colonel Badenhorst, commanding officer on Robben Island, during
an inspection of the prison by a visiting panel of judges. The judges suggested
Mandela might want to meet with them privately, but he confidently replied: "In
fact I shall only be too pleased to have both General Steyn [Commissioner of
Prisons] and Colonel Badenhorst here as I address you on some of our concerns. As you might expect, many of our complaints relate directly to the general
state of our imprisonment here and it is only right they should be here to reply
to those criticisms." Badenhorst exploded angrily, thus substantiating Mandela's
concerns and precipitating the colonel's departure from Robben Island a few
months later.[87] The high civilizational barrier that divided regime from prisoners in apartheid South Africa afforded political prisoners a chance not only to
differentiate themselves but also to best both the guards and higher authorities.

To resist these categories was to assert the collective category of the political. In a remarkable 1972 petition to the prison head, discussed in the previous
chapter, forty-six Robben Island prisoners laid out the paradox inherent in their
treatment. "We have been told time and again," they wrote, "that each prisoner
is on his own and cannot speak for and on behalf of another. We are given to
understand that the reason for this attitude is to prevent the formation of gangs
and gangsterism in prisons." They recognized that a key goal of incarceration
of political opponents was to disaggregate them and thus render their community nonexistent. "In fact," the letter continued, "we have been treated as a group
by the authorities." They listed some of the epithets ascribed to them (Poqos,
terrorists), amounting to "a group or clan of prisoners separated from ordinary
prisoners." They have been unlabeled and relabeled, given names that should
not unite them. Rejecting these terms, the petitioners assert their own: "we DO

Fig. 3.3 Nelson Mandela and Walter Sisulu in Robben Island prison yard, 1966.
Courtesy of UWC-Robben Island Mayibuye Archives.

form a group of people bound by interests and convictions which transcend personal considerations or individual gain."[88]

Race also provided a source of unity for prisoners in Nazi-occupied Poland. There, racial categories were less clearly defined; the initial shortage of German personnel as the occupation expanded in the first two years meant that some guards could be Poles. Mira Zimińska-Sygietyńska, a renowned film actress, encountered one in the corridor as she carried out the latrine bucket one day. The guard, Mossakowska, shoved her to the wall, shouting, "Out of my way, you idiot!" Zimińska-Sygietyńska returned to her cell vowing revenge, but that evening Mossakowska apologized. "She sat on my bed and said 'I beg your forgiveness, Ms. Mira, please. I have to be cruel, do you understand, I have to be cruel.'" She and the prisoners participated in a charade of conflict intended to hide the real hierarchy, so that a prisoner of national reputation like Zimińska-Sygietyńska could remain insignificant in the eyes of the administrators, and a politically sympathetic guard could retain her job and her ability to help prisoners.[89]

By 1941, Pawiak prison no longer employed male Polish guards, but they remained in the women's section of the prison, and some Poles worked as clerks

in the administrative offices. Opportunities for manipulation were infrequent—
though the sheer cruelty of the Nazi prison sometimes opened a tiny crack for
expressions of sympathy, perhaps politically motivated. "Some guards are very
good," wrote one prisoner in a desperately optimistic communiqué smuggled
from the torture chambers on Szucha Avenue in 1943. "One can see they agree
with us communists in their hearts. One can feel it in the way they treat us, in the
amount of food."[90] Rhetorically, Polish prisoners weakened guards' authority by
giving them sometimes macabre nicknames that spoke at once of brute force
and intimacy: Strangler, Goldentongue, Thumper, the Arm, Uncle.[91] Unable to
subvert their torturers, prisoners could at least domesticate them.

Some political prisoners surely enter prison believing that they can now
engage the regime they oppose in close combat. Instead, they discover that "the
regime" is an abstraction and the guards are the real face of power, especially
after interrogation and/or sentencing. Some prisoners wondered whether conflict with guards even mattered or merely distracted from the struggle for the
cause. But such conflict was often the only way to affirm that one's incarceration
is political. The Troubles in Northern Ireland yielded particularly acute prisoner-
guard conflicts for just this reason. The mostly Protestant guards represented the
enemy to their IRA wards (while Loyalists regarded them as betrayers of the
nation). Perhaps because the struggle was with both the state and part of society,
the guards were a necessary enemy.[92]

The stakes in Long Kesh and other prisons were therefore high. IRA prisoners
maintained a strict military hierarchy and expected that their commanding officer would even have a say in which guards could patrol and when. The fire that
destroyed part of Long Kesh in October 1974 originated in a protest when senior
officials refused to remove a guard who had insulted a prisoner. "This is a long-
standing arrangement between our staff and the prison regime," Gerry Adams
wrote in his regular column in an IRA paper at the time. "Our people have never
abused it and the ordinary screws [guards] . . . willingly work this procedure. It cuts
down on any real aggro between them and the POWs." As Adams shows, the rules
of behavior implicitly named the categories, too: they were prisoners of war on one
side, facing guards who were "ordinary," like the Ordinary Decent Criminals. The
"screws" themselves recognized this. As one told journalist Chris Ryder:

> If they continue to get their demands met then the prisoners will soon
> be running the prisons. Either you have a prison or you don't. There
> should be no half measures. When the ordinary criminal gets caught
> he accepts the fact that he is going to be deprived of his freedom as a
> form of punishment. Special category prisoners [as IRA and Loyalist
> prisoners were designated from 1972 until 1976] believe they have the
> right to engage in violence and yet not be responsible for their actions.

Thus the prisoner-guard conflict threatened the institution itself. By asserting their control over personnel, and reducing guards' roles to formal tasks like escorting prisoners for visiting hours, the prisoners sought to transform prison into something like a POW camp, which merely sequestered its inhabitants from battle. This required negotiation at the highest level and maintenance of the invisible barrier between guard and prisoner. Both prisoners and regime attempted to patrol this border—for example, forbidding conversation between prisoners and their escorts.[93]

To the IRA prisoners of the Troubles, the contest with guards impacted both the war against the British occupying regime and the conflict with the Loyalists of Ulster. Because guards traveled between work and home, they also represented what the prisoners could not have—freedom. (On Robben Island, by contrast, prison staff lived nearby, though of course they could travel to the mainland.) Republicans reversed that freedom to entrap the guards with intimidation. One guard recalled the "chilling" atmosphere after the hunger strike of 1981. As the rules relaxed, IRA prisoners retaliated against "the bastards, the hard men," through psychological intimidation.

> A prisoner would ask a prison officer something on the wing, then [the officer] would be confronted by fifteen of them, all silently staring at him . . . . it was chilling. At night there would be one officer on the wing with everything locked up—it was an evil environment. Someone would shout out the officer's home address; someone else, the colour and make of his car; someone else, the registration number of his car; someone else, his wife's name.[94]

These seemingly casual comments hinted at a level of surveillance of guards and their families that matched what the prisoner in a cell felt. "I don't like the colour of curtains your wife has up now in that front room of yours," a prisoner might say, "don't like that shade of green at all," or "Those wee bikes are a good price now, it must have cost you a penny or two." Such intimidation served to soften up guards for small favors like smuggling packages or gathering information about the prison.[95] It also reversed the relationship, putting guards under prisoners' control in a way quite different from the educational methods on Robben Island. A 1976 IRA pamphlet ridiculed the work performed by the guards, implicitly questioning why incarceration even existed:

> COMPOUND DUTY—You stand outside the Cage in a sentry box and do the running and see to the prisoners' complaints.
> LOOK-OUT DUTY—You stand in a watch-tower all day long on your own and watch the wee men walking around the cage.[96]

The IRA sometimes arranged for hated guards or administrators to be executed, a tactic also employed in Nazi-occupied Warsaw. Like the intelligence prisoners gathered about guards, this reestablished the prisoner as part of the movement that continued outside prison.[97]

Trying to make the guards experience what the prisoners did, some prisoners and their visitors subjected guards to physical ridicule. On three occasions in August 1976, prisoners at Magilligan Prison overpowered guards and stripped them naked; an IRA statement explained that the action was directed at the prison system of strip-searching itself, not the individual guards, who would now understand the humiliation prisoners underwent. In another incident a group of women visitors, relatives of Loyalist prisoners at Long Kesh, stripped two prison officials to their underwear, and then a man accompanying them took photographs.[98] By stripping them of the uniform that signified their authority, prisoners and their allies could strip the guards of their prison power.

The language one guard used to describe the struggle over civilization with prisoners echoes the terms used by politicals for criminals. Prisoners, he said, "tried to bring you down to their level . . . . the language, foul, obscene language. And unfortunately some Prison Officers, to make themselves understood and to get things done, came down to that level too."[99] From the prisoner's perspective, too, guards embodied the culture of the institution they served. The guards who treated them as objects or as part of the criminal prison did as much to strip them of identity as did the regime. They addressed prisoners by number, or by the first letter of their last name, or with a whistle; they stripped and searched their bodies; they observed them on the toilet or in the shower; they read letters and searched through meager possessions.[100] Of course guards were thus carrying out the orders of the prison administration—sometimes with sadistic fervor, but sometimes, no doubt, with disgust or with empathy.

In the end, the prison guard is trapped, with no goal beyond that assigned by the regime. This paradoxically puts the political prisoner at some advantage. Reflecting on his imprisonment during the Civil War, when he narrowly escaped execution, IRA officer Ernie O'Malley saw his goal as follows:

> it is the duty of prisoners to prove that they cannot be influenced by their surroundings, or affected by the personalities of jailers. A prisoner must reverse their whole system, place them in the position of prisoners, make them concentrate on petty doings and sayings, limit their minds to the confines of prison walls. Make the enemy feel a jailer but be free himself.[101]

Or, as a guard in Bydgoszcz Prison explained to Wojciech Duklanowicz in 1982: "You understand, you are the heroes, and we are the captives—get it?"[102]

4

"You Have the Consolation of Being Very Much in the Fight"

The Cause in Prison

One day in Pretoria Central, after years away from family, friends, and the anti-apartheid movement, Hugh Lewin unexpectedly found himself unsupervised in the prison carpentry shop, where there was a telephone. Cut off from the world for so long, he suddenly felt an almost vertiginous freedom at hand. Other prisoners distracted guards, and he grabbed the phone. But after so long he didn't even remember how to dial a telephone, let alone remember any relevant numbers. Finally he recalled the work phone of a lawyer friend and managed to reach him at his desk. The friend was clearly shocked by this illicit contact, and Lewin had first to assure him he wasn't asking for assistance in escaping, nor to undertake any illegal task for the cause, but merely for some news. In response, the friend offered some lame bits of his family's doings. No, interrupted Lewin, I was hoping for some information about world events. But his friend could recall nothing and had no newspaper at hand. Lewin hung up sobered, having learned only that the world was not waiting to hear how he was making out in prison.[1]

Political prisoners' isolation is compounded by a heightened sense of importance. They are fortunate when they can still imagine that the world outside remembers and supports them. Like most martial-law prisoners from the Solidarity movement, Marek Kulczyk had been energized by the months in prison. But when release came, in February 1983, he was unprepared: "I left all broken up, somehow disintegrated." He had counted on all his comrades leaving together, especially as the regime had denied his requests for furlough. Once he was out, he was alone: "Many of us, I included, had believed that since we were in prison we were the center of the universe. We connected our protests with world politics . . . . But now it turned out that very few people cared about prison and prisoner issues." Work as an underground printer had landed him in prison, but time in prison prevented him from returning to the movement;

now marked by the police, he could only lead them to others not yet exposed. Riding Warsaw's trams, Kulczyk overheard conversations about everything but the struggle of interned Solidarity activists. "I still felt myself to be part of that collective, and believed that I had a duty to spread the word about everything they were doing, all their protests."[2]

As inconvenient a burden as political inmates are for the state, they also seem a questionable burden for the cause they stand for. In the prisoner, the movement gains a living martyr, with some propaganda value. But that same prisoner presumably has some qualities useful in the struggle against the regime that would be lost in the prison cell. Incarceration effectively removes activists from circulation, often well beyond their release. The gulf between the political prisoner and the world outside can often prove too vast to overcome.

For the politicals, the feeling that prison and society were in harmony, and that the nation waited for the internees' release, faded with time. Activists who left Polish prisons in the years 1984–86 experienced profound isolation among an apathetic population. Edward Nowak recalls feeling, in 1985, "ten times worse than during the year-and-a-half in prison right after martial law was introduced. It was more difficult: the feeling of isolation, of being deserted, a feeling of a certain helplessness, a feeling that—well, for whom are we doing this?" Back home in Kraków he and his comrades were no longer seen as martyrs or brave voices, but as nuisances.[3] For an underground movement, an ex-prisoner is "burned," unable to rejoin comrades still evading regime surveillance.[4]

Hugh Lewin's friend could perhaps be forgiven, as sympathetic as he was to the cause, for very few white South Africans ever entered prisons. At least until the 1980s, the apartheid regime largely succeeded in projecting the impression that prison was something that happened to black oppositionists. In fact, the success of many regimes depends on the population believing that incarceration for political beliefs only befalls people very different from them while at the same time policing themselves lest they cross some line. Thus the isolation of the political from society can become complete.

Even in communities in which the prison struggle was familiar, the cell was far removed from ordinary life, and often quite misunderstood. Even those who might aspire to the experience visualized a place of unrelieved horror; of course prison often was, but there might be no correlation between the imagined and the real. The prisons of martial-law Poland, for example, became legendary in part through prison songs that spread to opposition circles outside. One such song recited well-known internment camps: "Kamienna Góra, Głogów, Opole, Strzelce, Nysa are camps wild and harsh/Where our tormenter with a shout summons us to roll call." Listening to high schoolers sing this one around a campfire a few years later, former internee Krzysztof Turkowski began to giggle and confessed: "I'm really sorry, but listen, when I think of the bananas, the oranges [in care packages], well I just laugh."[5] The women in the prisons of the Irish Free State felt a similar dissonance. As Christmas 1931 approached, Sighle Humphreys confided to her journal her relief that there would be no holiday parcels. "So many people would feel that it was up to them to send the 'poor martyrs' in Mountjoy something at Christmas time. The last Christmas I was here I ate more than I ever would outside."[6]

Whether they received packages and letters or suffered alone, political prisoners lived in a world beyond the grasp of most of their fellow citizens. Whatever else a movement loses when its leaders and enthusiasts go to prison, it faces the difficult challenge of keeping them relevant to the cause. Some of those who are incarcerated might seek to influence the direction of the movement; others might simply hope that their plight inspires solidarity. The twin tasks of communication across the prison wall and representation of the prisoner as martyr and as movement member have remained constant regardless of technological advances. The letter and the package, the brief visit and the occasional escape are still the connective tissue between the political prisoner and the modern oppositional movement.

The Art of 500 Words

More than any other action, the individual political prisoner is associated with writing, as an act of both solace and liberation. Prison writing—ranging from graffiti and clandestine notes to letters, diaries, and more formal writing, as well as legal complaints and other correspondence with the regime—resists the silencing that prison regimes impose.[7] In most prison experiences examined here, writing is severely restricted and often close to impossible. It must be carefully hidden from guards' prying eyes. Nonetheless, many prisoners have been able to pen letters, diaries, poetry, and even novels, and often to smuggle that work out while they remain inside.[8] Without doubt, incarceration gives the writer new stature and the words greater force. This was true equally of Mandela's *Long Walk to Freedom*—produced in secret, discussed with comrades, buried in the exercise yard, smuggled out, and published in London—as it was of Adolf Hitler's *Mein Kampf*, composed in relative comfort in Landsberg Prison in 1924.[9] The reading of each gains in power because of the author's experience; the critique of the regime, even if it is not direct, becomes sharper.

Prisoners wishing to communicate with family or their political movement have two options, each presenting particular difficulties. The first is the smuggled note. Movements have relied on these to monitor prisoners' survival and to ensure that comrades were not broken by the experience or isolated from decisions made outside. Each such missive imposes risks and demands an enormous amount of energy. Wanda Wilczewska of the "Prison Unit" in Pawiak Prison scolded her comrades outside in the spring of 1944 for becoming too reliant on the smuggled note:

> Listen, we've got to reorganize our current system. What we have now is some kind of joke and can't continue like this. You don't understand the conditions under which we operate and conduct on us experiments that have to end badly. Lately you have been working on the Majer [Wilczewska writes this in code] case. You send him identical letters via four different routes . . . . On each message is the note "Write only via this route." This all reaches us and gets to the same person . . . . At the moment *all* our routes are good. They are so good that it is a scandal to endanger them for one and the same matter.[10]

From the perspective of the movement, redundancy of vital messages surely seemed necessary. After all, a previous system had broken down in 1941 when it turned out that all messages were being intercepted by a Nazi posing as a special envoy from the exile government.[11] To a prison community as well coordinated as the one in Pawiak, however, such multiple messages were at best a distraction, at worst a threat.

A well-oiled prison structure might have hundreds of literate, well-connected comrades overloading the channels to the outside with their messages. Imprisoned in Mountjoy Prison in the Civil War, Brigadier Sean Harling broke with IRA discipline to send out his own letters through a "private line." Upbraided by his superiors, he retorted:

> Though your officers would not trust me with regard to sending out purely personal correspondence without first having been censored by them, they are ready to trust people they do not know with important despatches for GHQ [General Headquarters]. I will, if you wish, give my word of honour that I will not send out any letters for any man in the Prison, and also that any letter I will send out will be purely personal and will not contain any reference to any military matter.[12]

To the individual prisoner the smuggled note was a lifeline, but to the movement it brought danger, too. Each communication tested clandestine structures, jeopardized contacts outside, and could make regimes more suspicious and diligent in their efforts to stop every hole.[13]

Prisoners could not always afford to evade official scrutiny by sending smuggled notes; they had also to communicate through the prison system. All prisons set rules on letter writing: how many, how frequently, and to which addresses. At one extreme were the Nazis, who forbade some political prisoners from sending or receiving any letters at all.[14] Other prisoners, in Auschwitz and other camps, were permitted formulaic postcards in German. In any prison it would be forbidden to write frankly about one's health, experiences in prison, or life inside. Even a privileged prisoner like Breyten Breytenbach, a South African poet imprisoned for terrorism in 1975–1982, vividly recalls the strain and degradation of adapting to the strict 500-word limit on the one letter he could receive and the one he could write each month. They

> naturally had to be very bland—not referring to any specific conditions or events behind the walls. These were censored by the section sergeant first, then the officer responsible for security and, in the case of politicals, certainly also by the security police . . . . A letter I'd written to my mother was refused because in it I referred to *tronk* instead of *gevangenis*—the familiar "jail" instead of the fancier "prison." Exceptionally I'd be allowed to rewrite the letter, omitting the offending word . . . . Another time [the security officer] came, proudly fluttering his handiwork: my mother, not quite used to having a son inside, and loquacious by nature, had tried ducking under the 500-word barrier by writing ever smaller toward the end of her page (like whispering), but Major Schnorff had cut her off in mid-air with a pair of scissors, exactly at the 500-word mark.[15]

Censorship denied information but also left prisoners in the dark as to what was allowed in a letter, or even whether a letter had been sent or confiscated. On Robben Island, James Gregory revealed the rules to some prisoners: by offering them the chance to rewrite withheld outgoing letters, he claims, he allowed them to learn what was forbidden and to avoid forfeiting a privilege that came once a month or even less often.[16] Yet his advice also reminded prisoners of his watchful eye and censor's pen. Benevolent control was still control, delineated by administrative action and dependent as much upon individual whim as upon the rulebook.

Official channels, with their attendant uncertainties and exacting guidelines, are a necessary evil. Whether the unofficial letter is tossed over a fence, slipped into a visitor's pocket, sewn into the lining of clothing,[17] or handed to a bribed guard, the risks and rewards involved are very different from the letter humbly submitted to the prison administrator. "I think you ought to write one letter thro' the ordinary post," wrote Sighle Humphreys to her mother in May 1928, "just saying how you are, as I might get it."[18] Humphreys likely recognized that administrators might otherwise wonder at the lack of correspondence. The official channels offered a banality that might be comforting to the nonpolitical family member or friend, allowing them to avoid the topic of prison altogether. But in truth, the alien world of prison translates poorly into any kind of letter, its deprivations, cruel games, and coping strategies almost impossible to explain.[19]

Nelson Mandela masterfully deployed official and unofficial channels against each other. Upon receiving the 1979 Jawaharlal Nehru Award for International Understanding, he prepared a gracious and thoughtful five-page letter of thanks, reviewing the history of struggle in South Africa and the legacies of Gandhi and Nehru. He sent this officially, yet kept a copy. When after

Fig. 4.1 Gryps from "Bohun" in Białystok Prison, 1928. The holes indicate this was sewn into the lining of clothing sent out to be laundered. Courtesy of Muzeum Niepodległości, Warsaw.

five months he finally learned that the letter had been denied and would have to be rewritten, he "decided to use my own channels" and re-sent it.[20] His letter contained no vital information and simply acknowledged a public event that had already transpired, and so Mandela recognized that its confiscation seemed all the more outrageous. He thus strategically called attention to censorship and repression; since he could expect that the letter would be publicized by its recipient, he also demonstrated his ability to evade prison control in order to carry out movement work.

Having overcome such obstacles to reach its recipient, any letter from prison is exceptionally precious. Most prison letters nearly always contain an implicit or explicit imperative: send instructions or supplies, punish the informer, publicize our plight, continue the struggle, remember us. No one could ignore the letter from sixteen-year-old Grzegorz Zalewski, writing from Pawiak Prison in January 1942: "I envy you walking, talking, laughing, singing, reading, studying, going to church, eating dammit, eating and drinking goddammit to hell, cigarettes, caressing women, records, beer, everything you do."[21]

Though all prisoners, political or not, naturally desire to communicate with the world outside, not all incarcerating regimes have similar interests in preventing communication or apply the same rules equally to sending and receiving missives. Political prisoners are presumably under surveillance because the state wishes to know whether their activities continue and opposition is still a threat. The letters written, and to a lesser extent those received, are a part of the prisoner's exercise of politics. The act of writing, secretly or openly, asserts the author's claim to autonomy and right to narrate the prison experience. Even official writing—petitions and legal papers filed by the hundreds in more legalistic regimes—has such potential. The regime's determination to find and interpret prisoners' texts is an effort to curtail those who escape its control. Censoring or preventing mail in and out of prison seems however to have been scarce before 1900. Prison officials may not have believed that "gentlemen don't read each other's mail," as US Secretary of State Henry Stimson is reputed to have said in 1929, but in the nineteenth century and into the twentieth, political prisoners were for the most part still well-born, and prisons did not devote a great deal of time to controlling communication. As with so many other inventions of the repressive state, prison censorship bloomed in the prisons of the Boer War. British regulations for Tokai Prison in 1901 outline in great detail how letters could be written, concluding that "Letters not complying ... will be returned to the writers to be destroyed by them, in the presence of the Assistant Resident Magistrate." That official, for his part, worried that "requiring the writers to destroy their own letters may and probably will lead to trouble, at any rate it invites trouble."[22] Better, it seems, to leave prisoners unaware of their letters' fate.

The stakes of the communication between political prisoners and their movements grew significantly during and after World War I. Social movements in the decades leading up to the war became more public, more organized, and more determined to bring about political change. The socialist and communist movements, nationalist campaigns (like that led by Gandhi), and civil rights campaigners like the suffragettes presented a sustained challenge to the state apparatus, as was apparent in the increased use of prisons. Prisoners were important to the movement image; aware of this, they could not accept being cut off from the ideas and actions gestated outside. States also became more ideologically focused, more likely to care about the content of what prisoners and their supporters wrote. The wartime obsession with treason certainly facilitated this, while communism heightened interest in what prisoners said or wrote. Many states had developed and institutionalized technologies for spying domestically and internationally.[23] If censorship or interception of mail had once been an ad hoc operation, or limited to the easily managed trickle of international mail, it now became possible to read much more.

Political prisoners proved capable of circumventing control of communication with impressive regularity. On the other hand, the thousands of confiscated messages in Polish archives and the frequent miscommunications between Robben Island prisoners and their supporters indicate that imprisoning regimes could also boast plenty of success. Even when censorship is successful, though, there are ways around it. Republican Terence MacSwiney, in a British prison in 1916, bribed a prison official with two bottles of beer a day to get access to incoming letters before they went to the military censor. After prisoners read their mail it proceeded to the censors in London before being returned to the prisoners heavily blacked out.[24]

Censorship of outgoing mail aims at keeping the inner workings of the prison secret, just as soldiers' letters may be vetted in wartime for mentions of poor morale, poor conditions, or sensitive military information.[25] The state may care less about issues of prison morale but any mention of prison conditions might still fall victim to the censor's scissors. More important are references to the political cause contained in incoming mail. Prisoners frequently note that letters received, as well as newspapers (if allowed) and visitors, were closely monitored for any mention of ongoing political situations. Isolation from the movement could not succeed if the prisoner knew about protests, conflicts, or other developments outside. Movements, in turn, wanted to know what the prison apparatus had managed to discover. Thus there are frequent references in Polish and Irish prison messages to informers or to those who had buckled under interrogation. Some prisoners also endeavored to stay involved in the activities of their comrades still at liberty.[26] For the political prisoner, communication is politics, embodying the conspiracy with comrades outside.

The Politics of Prison Escape

Any prisoner, political or otherwise, thinks about freedom, and surely many daydream about escape. The social context of prison escape has changed in the modern era as political organizations have evolved. Absence of information can scuttle the most daring plans. Thus, in the bloody dynamiting of a wall of Clerkenwell Prison in 1867, not a single prisoner escaped. The prominent Fenian incarcerated there, Richard Burke, happened not to be in the exercise yard when the explosion occurred. Burke had been exchanging messages (in invisible ink) with Fenian comrades and had suggested they blow up that wall, but other details were left undeveloped.[27] A common feature of the premodern escape, through the nineteenth century, is that the escapee works alone, or at most with a cellmate. A visiting family member or lover might assist, but less often could prisoners rely on an organized group outside.

The modern political prisoner has many more resources at his or her disposal. The elaborate escapes from the Gestapo's Pawiak Prison discussed in Chapter 6 required the kind of planning and supplies that only a well-organized underground could supply. From the same prison thirty-five years earlier, some eighty Polish socialists failed to escape, yet the attempt shows a similar investment of resources. Socialist fighter Ludwik Śledziński proposed to the prison head Kalinin that his Polish Socialist Party comrades outside would collect 40,000 rubles, of which Kalinin would get 10,000 for enabling an escape. The party would also arrange for Kalinin to accompany the fugitives abroad, whereupon, Śledziński assured him, he would become a hero in the American newspapers. Though Kalinin agreed, the plan fizzled without enough funds.[28] That such an outlandish project even seemed plausible suggests a level of coordination unlikely in previous decades. Just a year earlier members of the same Fighting Organization of the Polish Socialist Party had freed ten men—all condemned to the gallows—from Pawiak by dressing up as Russian soldiers, driving up in a Russian police carriage, talking their way into the prison, and leading the men out under the nose of the guards. Coordination within the prison made this elaborate plan—immortalized in a 1931 film—possible.[29] The socialists used the attributes of the institution itself—guards, police transport, and prison routine—as well as tight coordination across the prison walls to effect the liberation.

The historical arc of the prison breakout stretches from an individual digging in the cell floor or a blind attack on the prison walls to a deft combination of force, subterfuge, and military order. As the prison fortress grew stronger, opposition groups developed sophisticated systems in response. The arms race between prisoners and prisons culminates in actions like the dramatic breakout from Mountjoy Prison in 1973, when an IRA team hijacked a helicopter and freed three of its comrades, including the chief of staff of the Provisional IRA, Seamus Twomey. Without a high level of coordination, though, a helicopter is no more effective a tool than a shovel. An escape attempt highlights the channels that link comrades in the same cause on either side of the prison wall. As a demonstration of organizational resources, deployed against a fearsome institution and for a relatively modest outcome, few actions surpass the prison breakout.

Escapes also illuminate the relative strength of the state and of prison institutions. The frequent stories of breakouts during Poland's 1905 revolution reveal Russia's weak control over its western territories. British control over Ireland, and over Irish prisoners on English soil, likewise declined precipitously during the War of Independence. Escapees left the impression that they had lingered in prison merely as a courtesy and left when they pleased. When Robert Barton, a Sinn Féin member of the British Parliament, placed a dummy in his bed and crawled out through sawn-off bars, he left a cheeky note to the prison governor. "I am about to make an escape from your hospitality. If I escape well and good, if not I am prepared to suffer the consequences." He praised the guards for their obedience, faulted the accommodations, and concluded: "I hope that we may shortly turn your prison to a useful national purpose."[30] Austin Stack, breaking out of Manchester Prison a few months later, was almost apologetic in his note to the prison governor: escape had become necessary because the British had broken their pledge not to transport captives to England. Not that English soil inhibited his Irish liberators, who wheeled a long ladder on bicycles through the city streets, then overpowered the guards to free Stack and four others.[31]

Of the dozens of escapes in 1919, none embarrassed the British more than that of Éamon de Valera in February. De Valera had been spared execution after the Easter Rising only because he could claim American citizenship. In Lincoln Prison he was closely monitored but had gained the trust of guards and administration. "I feel," the prison governor remarked, "that [senior IRA prisoners] and I understand one another." The governor may have imagined that Lincolnshire was far from the reach of the IRA, but a key smuggled inside a cake—based on a drawing that had been embedded in an outgoing Christmas card—let de Valera return to Dublin shortly before all internees were released. The inability of prisons to segregate leaders from their movement hastened the British recognition that detention of the Irish in Britain was futile.

These and other escapes demonstrated the reach and organizational ingenuity of the IRA. Michael Collins engineered both de Valera's and Stack's escapes, along with others. "Through hundreds of individual contacts," writes biographer Frank O'Connor, "Collins gradually reached the point at which he knew everything that happened to prisoners, and even when the job of freeing them proved impossible he could give the gaolers the uneasy feeling that everything they did was observed."[32] One could add that he gave prisoners the crucial feeling that

Fig. 4.2 Postcard, n.d. [c. March 1919], showing escape from Mountjoy Prison.
Courtesy of Aisling O'Neill; originally in the possession of her great-grandmother, Mary
O'Neill.

prison was merely a useful sabbatical between stints in the active service of the cause. The IRA escapes thus shifted the balance of power between regime and opposition; the prison ceased to be an expression of state power and instead became an easy target.

Control of the prison became almost illusory during the Irish Civil War. Even the Republican forces found they had to try to manage escapes by their men lest too many attempts overwhelm the organization. Early in 1923, Sean MacBride was en route in a prison van from Mountjoy Prison to Newbridge Camp some thirty miles outside the city. No sooner had the truck pulled away than the imprisoned Republicans discovered a packet of hacksaw blades, pre-sumably left there by a friendly soldier. They did not avail themselves of these tools and went on to join their comrades in Newbridge. In the camp, MacBride found utter chaos, as the staff made only halfhearted attempts to maintain order. But an oppositional army needed order even more. MacBride's IRA superiors appointed him intelligence officer among the 2,000 prisoners, in charge of moni-toring escape attempts. "Every group was running some tunnel or escape project of its own. These were badly planned, unsuccessful and brought on attention. And so, part of my job was to try to find out what escape projects were on so that we could try and pick the best ones."[33]

If the Irish Free State hoped to demonstrate that it was capable of contain-ing its opponents behind barbed wire, the Republicans managed to demonstrate that their organization was seamless. On July 27, 1922, as IRA commandant

Frank Aiken was reading instructions to his men assembled in the exercise yard of Dundalk Prison, their comrades dynamited the prison wall, allowing more than 100 men to escape. Unlike the Fenians, these attackers knew very well what they were doing. Less than three weeks later another group arrived in an armored car to take over the prison. They brought with them Free State soldiers they had captured, and they invited the prison staff to remain on duty: "They had been good enough to serve the Free State Government, and why not serve their Government."[34] The escape attempt or the prison takeover, whether with dynamite, an armored car or helicopter, by smuggled key, rope ladder, or elaborate tunnel, does not negate the prison so much as reclaim it for the opposition. Each of these acts asserts mastery over the guarded space, making the state institution a site for expression of freedom and control. The prison escape is about more than simply getting free.

Like the smuggled letter, the attempted escape imposed great costs on the movement and on individual prisoners. Alongside the bravura jailbreaks there still loomed the gallows or other punishment. When Patrick Moran decided not to join his comrades in an escape from Kilmainham Prison in February 1921, he expected to be released soon; instead, he was tried and hanged a month later. Still, escape was part of the repertoire of movement protest in periods when the state's control was somewhat shaky.

Over the next half-century, inmates of Irish prisons would not be so fortunate. As the stakes grew higher, so did the barriers, and escapes were infrequent until the Northern Irish Troubles in the 1970s. During the intervening years, movements and regimes varied in strength, yet with a few important exceptions escapes faded from view. They had been important to the Poles and the Irish in the first decades of the twentieth century, but not, it seems, to the communists of interwar Poland—perhaps in part because they dreamed of destroying, not assuming control over, the institutions of a bourgeois state. Neither the communist press of the time nor later memoirs make any mention of attempted escapes or rescues, so common before 1918. In part, this reflected weaker public support for the prisoners' cause and less sympathetic prison guards than during the fight for independence. To some extent, support for prisoners declined in Ireland after 1923 as well. But the communists' goals were different, too. Communism displayed its prisoners suffering together and in solidarity with the sufferings of the proletariat, not staging jailbreaks.

In Nazi-occupied Poland, the escape theme returned, though the chance of getting out was vastly smaller. The liberation of Stanisław Miedza-Tomaszewski from Pawiak in 1942, or the famous escape of Witold Pilecki from Auschwitz in April 1943, gave the Polish underground valuable information and recovered trusted comrades, but it also demonstrated the limits to Nazi control over Poland. Leon Wanat, the Pawiak scribe who helped so many prisoners survive and sometimes escape, realized he would have to get out, given how much he knew about the prison's workings. Only his neat handwriting, he thought, had kept him alive so long. Knowing that an escape from Pawiak would bring reprisals against comrades there, he arranged to escape instead from Gestapo headquarters, using German identity papers.[35]

In the immediate aftermath of the war, anti-communist partisans attacked regime-controlled prisons in Kraków, Hrubieszów, Kielce, and Radom, and many others. These attacks, which freed hundreds of prisoners, lacked any evident coordination with the inmates, though. Prisoners in Kraków, surprised by their sudden freedom, convened to discuss the consequences; some thought it a ruse and chose to stay.[36] Nor did the partisans free any political leaders equivalent in prominence to de Valera, Stack, or Aiken. But by undermining the regime's claim to institutions, they effectively challenged its assertion of control over Polish territory. Whoever controlled the prison thereby demonstrated the capability to master the state, something both sides understood. One day in 1947, the head of Rawicz Prison posed a seemingly idle question to Kazimierz Moczarski, a captain of the Home Army who had directed the Information Bureau during the Warsaw Uprising: how many men would Moczarski need to take over the prison? "Fifteen minimum, twenty-five maximum," replied Moczarski. "Surely that's too few? I've got eleven guard towers and a company of guards." But Moczarski was confident: "It's difficult to be precise, but twenty-five is enough to release the prisoners and slaughter you, sir." The prison chief gave Moczarski three days in the punishment cell for his candor.[37] By then Moczarski's comrades outside did not have the manpower or firepower, and the communist regime could commit sufficient resources to render escape all but impossible.

In apartheid South Africa, escapes were rare, though the African National Congress was capable of organizing armed attacks on government property, and there were many poorly staffed prisons in remote areas. Like the communists of interwar Poland, the opponents of apartheid did not wish to assert control over the institutions of the state they opposed. In the Gandhian tradition, South African prisoners fought for dignity within the prison cell; the option of escape rarely came to the fore. Of course, the prisoners whose release would have most helped the movement were held on Robben Island, from which escape would have been almost impossible without a naval invasion or an armored helicopter. The ANC chose to use its resources in other ways. The two significant escapes in the apartheid era, sixteen years apart and from urban prisons, are exceptions that prove this rule. In the first, four anti-apartheid activists (one Indian, one black, and two white prisoners, all detained while awaiting charges) fled the central police station in Johannesburg in 1963 by bribing a friendly warden. At this point in apartheid South Africa, many leading figures were still free, Robben Island had just received its first political inmates, and so the Communist Party found the necessary money to finance the plan.[38] In 1979, by contrast, the three white ANC activists who manufactured keys in the prison machine shop and escaped from Pretoria Central Prison did so without any assistance from outside. Though their comrades had not enabled the escape, the ANC took this as a publicity coup. Tim Jenkins and Stephen Lee, who had been making and setting off small "leaflet bombs" in Johannesburg and Cape Town before their imprisonment, made their way to freedom in Mozambique and soon posed in full battle gear at an ANC training camp in Zambia.[39] This embarrassed a regime whose legitimacy rested on order and control.

During Northern Ireland's Troubles, in contrast, the jailbreak was part of the repertoire. British state policy frequently swung from intense repression to relative liberalization and back again. Reports of prison abuse frequently led to parliamentary commissions or external human rights investigations. A guard who shot an escaping prisoner was likely to be reprimanded. IRA prisoners intimidated the guards and demonstrated control over the space of the prison and the terrain outside. Any evidence that the British had lost control over the prison might suggest they had lost Northern Ireland as well.

The official inquiry into the 1983 breakout from Maze Prison concluded that the environment there, and in Northern Ireland generally, was ideal for an escape. With the help of arms smuggled into the prison and homemade knives, IRA prisoners overwhelmed the guards in one block, took hostages, commandeered a delivery truck, and breached the gate; nearly forty prisoners took part, while others helped to divert attention.[40] A government report blamed prison staff, who had become inured to the danger of the men in their custody. Relations in the prison had turned upside down: "manipulation became possible, collusion could not be ruled out, intimidation could flourish, weapons could be smuggled in and messages passed out and [IRA] orderlies could move freely about."[41] In other words, an uncertain staff was overwhelmed by a highly disciplined and coordinated movement that placed a high value on escape. The press tended to depict prisoners as daring and clever, while prison administration looked incompetent, ill-prepared, and needlessly vicious. Popular culture celebrated prisoner ingenuity, too. The 1963 film *The Great Escape*, about British and American POWs escaping from a camp in 1944, was a generational touchstone.[42]

Republican prisoners were much more likely to escape than were Loyalists—who were by definition supporters of the British state and so felt less of a duty to break out of prison. IRA prisoners felt no such compunction, and were certain that they were needed in the struggle as much outside prison as in. The strong collective ethos of the Republicans also facilitated escape, while the movement's greater emphasis on ideas and culture—part of the training for eventually taking power and claiming one's land—meant that the average Republican prisoner was simply more sophisticated.[43]

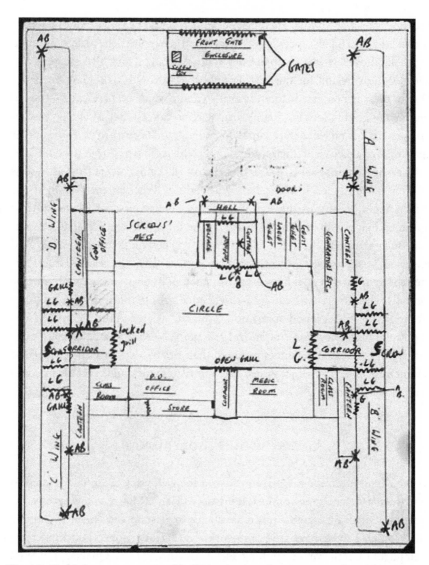

Fig. 4.3 Hand-drawn map prepared by IRA prisoners planning escape from Maze Prison (Long Kesh), 1983. Courtesy of Linenhall Library, Belfast.

The escaped prisoner—gleefully greeting his comrades at liberty, telling his tale at a clandestine press conference, his escape admitted to even by regime spokespeople—is the ultimate emissary of an underground movement ranged against a repressive state. Rejecting confinement seems a masculine role: though every movement since at least the 1890s has had female comrades in prison, hardly an example of a woman political escapee comes readily to mind.[44] Yet the escape also changes the role of the prisoner. He leaves behind not only the cell and his comrades there, but also the category—terrorist, criminal, nonperson—to which the state had assigned him. He then goes underground or abroad, since freedom is not really at hand. Escapees in Russian Poland generally tried to leave the country, as did those few who escaped from South African prisons. IRA escapees also left Northern Ireland for the Irish Republic. One could be holding forth at a Dublin press conference before the British knew what had happened—though the raucous celebrations in a Republican neighborhood in Belfast or Derry might tip them off.[45] Even when the escapee contributes to the cause in exile, the border crossing is of a piece with the escape, denying the regime its power to contain.

The released prisoner is still in the shadow of the regime, at least as long as the conflict continues. If release has come early, or if the sentence was light, the reason might be second-guessed. Whether or not the prisoner has become an informer, that possibility lingers. Early release might even be calculated to produce such an effect. The Polish Home Army was certain that the Gestapo used this tactic to sow uncertainty and conflict in the ranks of the released man's former comrades—that is, if he was foolish enough to try to return to them. The formally released prisoner cannot be welcomed back to the underground struggle, and even aboveground opposition is difficult as long as the regime remains in power. Polish television viewers in 1983 and 1984 were treated to some sorry spectacles as released detainees recanted their ties to Solidarity and pledged to refrain from oppositional activities. Thus imprisonment could sever the prisoner from the movement.

Gender in the Prisoner Cause

As men tried to escape the prison or faced the gallows, women endeavored to offer them assistance and comfort. If prison, as Hanna Sheehy-Skeffington acerbically noted, is a masculine place, assistance to prisoners has been a feminine role. Women activists have driven the work of caring for prisoners and publicizing their plight from the very beginning. Elizabeth Gurney Fry, a Quaker, pioneered prison assistance in Britain after visiting Newgate Women's Prison in 1811; she founded a women's society for reforming prisoners in 1817.[46] While her story is generally told as part of the middle-class zeal for imposing order upon the poor, it is no less an antecedent for the associations to help political prisoners. The constituency was different, but the dynamics of assistance and advocacy were similar. The Fenians, for example, were students, editors, teachers, and businessmen, neither noble nor poor. They had wives and mothers who could look after them and agitate on their behalf. The IRB Ladies Club was the first of many groups formed by female relatives of the men fighting or imprisoned.[47]

The Polish counterpart was a group of women socialists, active from the 1890s, among whom Stefania Sempołowska was most associated with advocacy on behalf of prisoners. For nearly half a century, as prisoner assistance moved from an individual passion to institutional form, Sempołowska advocated better prison conditions, especially but not only for her socialist comrades. Born to a noble family in 1869 in what was then Prussian Poland, she, together with lawyer Stanisław Patek and Maria Paszkowska of the Polish Socialist Party, created the General Fund for Assistance to Political Prisoners in 1903 (later renamed "Patronat"). The informal roots of this work stretched back at least a decade.[48] Patronat provided food and clothing to the prisoners of four successive regimes, until it was at last shut down by the Nazis.[49]

The women of Patronat did more than alleviate prisoners' suffering; they were, after all, Polish patriots, too. At the height of the Revolution of 1905, an arrested Warsaw socialist using the pseudonym Morawski was unmasked as a political by the prison's governor, Kurakin. A swift execution seemed likely until an emissary from Patronat arrived to warn Kurakin: "If Morawski is recognized by the Okhrana [that is, if the Russian secret police are told], you will be held personally responsible."[50] The threat of retaliation by the underground apparently worked. Reducing prisoners' isolation, Sempołowska and her Patronat comrades pursued work that was as much political as it was humanitarian.

Sempołowska's influence began to wane in independent Poland. At first the new state subsidized Patronat and responded with alacrity to its reports.[51] The emergence of a parallel aid group for communist prisoners soon muddied this relationship; the subsidy disappeared, and suspicion took its place. In the last years of the Second Republic, the Polish government declared that Sempołowska served communist ends, and decreed that all correspondence between Sempołowska or her colleagues and any prisoners should be confiscated and sent to the appropriate prosecutor's office. Any money or goods that Patronat sent to prisoners was to be confiscated and used to pay prisoners' fines and offset administrative costs.[52]

Patronat's isolation and persecution deepened during the Nazi occupation, though it was allowed to continue to distribute food and clothing and to provide care for the children of those arrested, as an organ of the officially tolerated Central Welfare Council. As in the Soviet Union, where a committee to assist political prisoners was tolerated until the 1930s, the Nazis may have seen prisoner assistance as a way of underscoring their ability to control the prisons.[53] Patronat raised funds by selling jewelry in the shape of handcuffs.[54] In some ways, nothing had changed: the same kind of discerning eye still measured the prison cells against the standards of the Polish national struggle, as in an anonymous report from 1942 on conditions in Kraków's Montelupich Prison. The writer, an older woman, reported that the guards had treated her well, while helping themselves to the packages Patronat sent in. At her request, she was sent to visit "the worst cell," where "seriously engaged politicals" dominated. One of the twenty-two women in the cell, "feral and lice-infested," was a prostitute, whom Patronat arranged to move elsewhere so the politicals could have the cell to themselves.[55] In defense of Patronat, there was little more that could be done, as prisons and camps were part of everyone's lives in occupied Poland. The ongoing guerrilla campaign left the Polish underground little energy for all but the most crucial prisoners of the Nazis' carceral system. Patronat could only ensure they were not forgotten, and perhaps survived.[56]

A generation younger than Sempołowska, Irish Republican activist Sighle Humphreys also came from the pro-independence provincial elite and moved to the capital, coming to Dublin shortly before World War I. She, too, acquired a deep commitment to socialism that bolstered her ferocious nationalism. In 1919, Humphreys joined Cumann na mBan, which began as an armed women's auxiliary during the Easter Uprising and the War of Independence before adopting prisoner assistance as a main activity.[57] Humphreys did not shy away from confrontation; in the early days of the Civil War she was captured in a shootout with Free State troops at her house. She spent the rest of the war in Mountjoy and Kilmainham prisons and was caught attempting to dig a tunnel from the latter. Subsequently, as a former prisoner, she centered her life's work on that institution, continuing to advocate better conditions for prisoners until the 1970s.[58]

Prison aid in Ireland was largely the domain of the wives and sisters of revolutionaries. The nationalist movement, whatever the strand of politics espoused, consciously kept women away from conflict.[59] No doubt radical women like Humphreys sometimes experienced this as marginalization, yet through their charitable work, their protests, and their own incarceration they forged deep connections between the movement and the cell. As Máire Comerford—herself on the road to prison—wrote to Humphreys in Mountjoy Prison in 1927: "You have the consolation of being very much in the fight at any rate and I am sure that will please you."[60] That, perhaps, was the point: prisoner aid work placed both donor and recipient "in the fight" and linked their experiences beyond what a flimsy smuggled letter could bear. The aid work confirmed that the prisoner was important; the prisoners confirmed that their benefactors were working for the cause.

Throughout the years of Anglo-Irish conflict and the Civil War, familiar names appear on both sides of the prison gates. Hanna Sheehy-Skeffington and Charlotte Despard, seasoned suffragettes, co-founded the Women's Prisoners' Defence League (WPDL) in 1922. Indeed, membership in the WPDL, which opposed the Anglo-Irish Treaty, required that one be related to a prisoner. Mary MacSwiney, who had coordinated assistance to the prisoners of Frongoch (including her brother Terence), was very active. Caitlin Brugha, widow of IRA Chief of Staff Cathal Brugha, arranged for prisoners released from Civil War camps to be met and helped home. The famous names linked nameless prisoners to the Republican cause and helped in the public appeals for funds and supplies.[61]

By the mid-1920s, Humphreys was Cumann na mBan's most vigorous Dublin activist, pushing it insistently toward prisoner assistance and remembrance. As the Civil War receded and the number of political prisoners shrank from the thousands to the tens (or less), Republican rhetoric grew more heated. When many of her comrades left the cause, Sighle Humphreys continued on; her advocacy brought her to prison again in the late 1920s and 1930s. In or out of prison, she aligned campaigns for attention and assistance to prisoners, released prisoners, and their families with the struggle for national freedom and unity.[62] A treasured ritual, in the years after the Civil War, was the greeting of those released. These open celebrations of martyrs to a marginalized cause may have been more important to the movement than the acts of protest that sent them to prison in the first place. Releases could be proudly announced in the press or heralded with a banner at the railway station, while the police and courts controlled the framing of arrests.[63] Humphreys and her colleagues used the mainstream press, especially during parliamentary election campaigns, to publicize "their" prisoners.[64]

Humphreys's work met the same stern response as did Sempołowska's, at about the same time. In 1936, the Ministry of Justice reclassified the Commission of Inquiry into the Treatment of Political Prisoners (a newly created sister organization to her Republican Political Prisoners Committee, with many of the same people involved), declaring it an unlawful organization, on the grounds that it had clearly been established "to hamper the Government in its efforts to deal with organizations responsible for acts of violence and thus to encourage the commission of such acts."[65] The Women's Prisoners' Defence League came under regular police surveillance.[66] From the vantage point of women like Sempołowska or Humphreys, states built by former comrades had betrayed the cause of freedom. But Poland and Ireland, like many interwar states, were trying to meet the challenges of governing a newly independent state with pretensions to democracy. Prisoner advocacy was a sore spot for governments whose pre-independence lineage included imprisoned freedom fighters, as it highlighted contradictions between the founders' ideals and the realities of governing.

South Africa's history of assistance to political prisoners is also dominated by one woman. Helen Suzman, unlike Humphreys and Sempołowska, was never imprisoned, nor did she form an aid society. Suzman used her position as Member of Parliament (MP) for Houghton, a Johannesburg suburb, for nearly forty years, most of them as the only opposition MP. A generation younger than Humphreys, she took up the cause of prisoners at the beginning of the apartheid state's incarceration campaign in the 1950s and pursued it to the end of the regime. Until the 1980s, she was one of the very few to champion prisoners and publicize their plight.[67]

Suzman first visited a prison in 1960, the only MP to take up the minister of justice's invitation to investigate the conditions of State of Emergency internees following the Sharpeville Massacre. That first encounter exposed the farce of prison order and showed Suzman what she could offer the prisoners. The guard accompanying Suzman instructed the detainees:

> "You're not allowed to talk about any of the conditions inside this place. You can talk to her and give messages for your family and so on, but no discussion about anything that's happening inside."
>
> A young [imprisoned] lawyer I knew well, Ernie Wentzel, a member of the Liberal Party, immediately said, "Commandant, you mean I can't tell Mrs Suzman we're on a hunger strike?"
>
> The Commandant said, "No man, you can't tell her that."
>
> Ernie then said, "And I can't tell Mrs Suzman that we haven't had any extra food in here from our relatives?"
>
> "No man, you can't tell her that either."
>
> "Can't I tell her we are not allowed any visitors?"
>
> "No man, you can't."
>
> This went on for about fifteen minutes with Ernie spilling the beans, while I remained absolutely deadpan.
>
> When I came out of the men's section I went across to the women's prison, and my opening gambit, out of the corner of my mouth, to the first detainee I met there was, "Are you women on a hunger strike too?"
>
> "No, but we're thinking about it."

Suzman could not address prisoner welfare in the same way that an aid society or a group of political supporters could, but she could reach the public more effectively. Facts that could not be reported in the press became accessible when voiced on the floor of Parliament.

In 1965, Suzman began regular prison visits, reporting after each of these to the minister of justice. Maintaining the façade of democracy, the state accommodated Suzman, the lone elected representative of an opposition party, an English-speaker, a woman, and a Jew—though the courtesies shown her came grudgingly. When the government increased the use of detention without trial in the late 1970s and early 1980s, neither Suzman nor anyone else could visit such detainees, though she frequently read letters from them aloud in Parliament.[68]

Suzman paid at least as much attention to the collective experience of prison—poor food, cold cells, lack of exercise—as she did to the specific complaints of individual prisoners. She did not, however, protest incarceration itself. Thus, reporting on the habit of keeping white political prisoners in Pretoria Local Prison in the C or D category, which allowed just one letter and a visit every six months, she commented: "Surely there can be no justification for not allowing them to serve their sentences under the same conditions as ordinary prisoners."[69] This naturally divided Suzman and the movements that these prisoners represented, whether the ANC, the PAC, or the South African Communist Party. Yet dozens of letters from prisoners around the country, some clearly political, over the course of a quarter century, were often addressed "Dear Mother" and fondly recalled a visit by Suzman. The letters trace the limits of what she could do: many could not be quoted, still less answered, without endangering the contact. Very few asked for Suzman's help in obtaining release; aside from food or sanitary conditions, the most frequent complaint was denial of access to grievance procedures after a warder's assault.[70]

The visit itself, on top of the official intervention that Suzman undertook via a letter to the minister or a speech in Parliament, accounted for Suzman's impact. Her interventions could be discounted as props to an illegitimate system, but they relieved the near-total isolation experienced by prisoners. Gladys Manzi, detained in Johannesburg Fort in 1978–79 under suspicion of terrorist acts, invited Suzman to visit. Soon after, she wrote in thanks: "Your visit relieved me, because I don't get visitors. Durban is too far from this place, and my sister has never been to this city before, she won't know which side to turn. Though I am missing my children and hear about them I wouldn't like them to come over. I always think about the moneys involved and the inconvenience, because visiting time is only 30 min. I don't think it is worth it! Thanks again Mrs. Suzman."[71] A visit could also resolve specific problems, most famously when, during her first visit to Robben Island in 1967, Suzman heard from prisoners about a sadistic warder with a swastika tattoo. Upon her formal complaint, the Ministry of Justice removed him.[72] She attended as well to the minutiae of prison existence: access to hot water, food, recreation facilities, clothing, and the right to keep family photographs. At the other end of the scale, she thought of South African incarceration in a global context, gathering documentation on detention procedures in Northern Ireland and Israel, for example.[73] The practical underscored the political, as a letter from an ANC member and former Robben Island inmate, at that time in Paarl Prison, indicates: "Firstly we political prisoners wish to thank you on behalf of the prisoners on Robben Island for the many changes brought about on your recommendation, we can truly say that because of you we are better treated now. Because of your suggestion many of us have been transferred to lighter prisons . . . . I am Progressive Party minded, as the majority of us are now."[74] Though Suzman could not have their votes, she certainly had their attention.

The Prisoner as Party Member

What could the prisoner offer to comrades outside? An especially senior or respected prisoner might continue to direct or advise the movement from behind bars, as did Nelson Mandela, Jacek Kuroń, and Gerry Adams. In these cases, or in that of the Polish Communist Party in the 1920s and 1930s, the movements inside and outside the prison were tightly integrated. Even when prisoners possess mainly symbolic value, their physical needs and actual suffering provide a framework around which the movements mobilize.

Political opposition movements use their prisoners to indict the regime, evoking ignoble carceral traditions. To Polish communists, it seemed self-evident that political repression had continued unabated since independence. Appealing "to the Polish proletariat" in March 1921, one group of prisoners portrayed an unchanging police state: "Independent and 'democratic' Poland no longer has the *Okhrana* or the *Feldpolizei* [the Russian and Prussian secret police, respectively], [... but] there is a powerful gendarme-police apparatus that hunts down and arrests workers. Those arrested are treated no worse than they were by the famed torturers of czarist times."[75] This idea of continuity helped to legitimize the sacrifices made by a new generation of prisoners and to fix them in the imagination of movement constituents.

Polish communists in the USSR grew alarmed at the stories of their comrades suffering in "bourgeois" Poland. Julian Marchlewski, a co-founder of Poland's Communist Party, responded to an appeal from comrades in Warsaw and pitched the idea of an International Organization for Aid to Revolutionaries. At the Fourth Congress of the Communist International (Comintern) in November 1922, Feliks Kon—who, like Marchlewski, knew Polish prisons well—announced the new organization. MOPR (the organization's Russian initials) was headed by Marchlewski until his death in 1925. Instead of helping imprisoned revolutionaries centrally from Moscow, MOPR adopted a federated model, through the communist parties of individual countries, which the Comintern exhorted "to assist in the creation of organizations to render material and moral aid to all captives of capitalism in prison."[76] The German section of MOPR took the name Rote Hilfe, and the Polish section similarly adopted the name "Red Help" (Czerwona Pomoc) to affirm a broad leftist appeal, albeit on the communists' terms. Red Help's statute promised "material, moral, and legal assistance . . . without regard to party affiliation."[77]

In Poland, Red Help worked alongside Sempołowska's Patronat, though their rhetorics were quite different. Sempołowska played upon the contrast between expectations of democratic Poland and the repressive reality, while Red Help assumed that capitalism and its state would naturally repress workers. An open letter from women in Łódź prison, styled as from "those who fight

Fig. 4.4 "Join the ranks of MOPR!," postcard, Moscow, 1930. In author's collection.

to those who once fought," put a revolutionary spin on Sempołowska's frustrations: "We appeal to you, comrades, former fighters, don't lay down your weapons, don't stop halfway down the road, return to our revolutionary ranks and continue the struggle along with us, until victory."[78] The target audience included Sempołowska, who addressed the Red Help Congress at which this letter was read. Where the 1921 appeal characterized an unchanging repressive state, and Sempołowska directed attention to cells still full, these women returned to the cause; passive observers could rejoin the struggle by embracing those in prison. A moderate socialist like Sempołowska might not want to fight shoulder-to-shoulder with the communists for revolutionary justice, but the prisoner alliance was different. The political activist in prison, in this view, sheds party affiliation and becomes eligible for support from all. Ceasing to represent the repression of his or her specific cause, the prisoner stands for the generalized struggle for freedom.

This position is the germ of the idea later advanced by international human rights advocates. MOPR advanced an international cause, helping activists to draw the connection between the victims of repression in their own country and those abroad. Prisoners thus dissociated from a particular struggle could then be understood as subjects of nascent human rights campaigns. The Polish League for Defense of Human and Civil Rights (LOPCziO), founded in 1921, embraced prisoner welfare and rights as well as addressing state repression more generally. It led national campaigns such as one for a general amnesty in 1926. Its board included supporters of Red Help and Patronat, as well as prominent left-wing writers from the period's oppositional landscape.[79] LOPCziO complemented the grassroots model adopted by Red Help, which encouraged the creation of dues-collecting local circles. Each circle then accepted sponsorship of one or more prisoners. Circles wrote to or visited their prisoners, provided them with legal and material assistance, and supported their families. They conducted street collections, held fundraising balls, organized lotteries, and staged welcoming banquets when their prisoners were released.[80],

Was this all grassroots activism, or was Red Help primarily an annex of the Polish Communist Party, as many in other parties and in the Ministry of Justice believed? Communists certainly dominated the activist ranks of Red Help and did their best to exclude others from decision making. Critics of Red Help pointed out that the Soviet Union also imprisoned opponents; MOPR responded that these deserved their fate: "One should realize who political prisoners in the USSR are and from what circles they are drawn." To avoid having to toe the Communist Party line on such matters, the Polish Socialist Party warned its members not to join MOPR.[81] At the same time, the constant discussion of money raised for the well-being of prisoners and their families indicates that Red Help activists believed strongly in the cause of helping prisoners. This broad coalition around a humanitarian issue helped to highlight the "fascist" character of the Polish state.

MOPR activists understood that the political prisoner's fate and the impact of the prisoner's sacrifice depended upon broad recognition of that sacrifice and shared anger at the way prisoners were treated. Thus, insufficient engagement of "the masses" in support of prisoners was a common refrain. There was no point in suffering torture and isolation if no one cared. In a moment of rebellion or revolution, the prisoner-martyr might be a flashpoint, but in a long struggle the connection could be lost. Prisoners could still build organizational skills and practice resistance techniques in the prison cell, but this gained value when political prisoners could claim to be vehicles for social indignation and activism. A 1935 MOPR analysis called for "mass anti-terror agitation, wide discussion, and persuasion of people who are neutrally disposed, or even hostile toward political prisoners and MOPR—and not mainly illegal, individual dues gathered clandestinely." The prospect of peasants delivering in-kind assistance by horsecart right to the prison gates particularly excited MOPR dreamers.[82]

Implicit in these appeals and plans for "mass" activities was a belief that the political prisoner uniquely conveyed the essence of the cause. Party propaganda condemning regime excesses or repressive measures might meet with a shrug, but the prisoner translated the cause into an irresistible language. Red Help's periodical *Więzień polityczny* [Political Prisoner] asserted in its inaugural issue:

Let the worker and the peasant discover what goes on behind the walls of the prisons and police dungeons, what his best brothers and sisters, fighters for his cause, suffer.

When those facts, covered up by the government and the entire Polish press, reach the worker's apartment and the peasant's hut, then the popular masses will speak out in their proletarian way, they will tear down the fortresses of oppression, break the chains that hold the prisoners, and crumble those detestable tools of class oppression, the state of the bourgoisie and the nobility.[83]

The average movement participant should feel the oppression of the dungeons, fortresses, and chains, and then take action to free these specific comrades. Such logic has pervaded the thinking of many who work to publicize the plight of political prisoners.

Red Help attempted to change the political role of prisoners and their families and to motivate the latter into active participation in the struggle against the bourgeois state. "Broader interconnections in the area of work with families" were needed, it concluded in the stiff communist vernacular of 1936. It resolved to dispatch prisoners' families, especially wives and mothers, to court, to the prosecutor's office, to the prisons, to public rallies; and to enlist them in Red Help administration. In short, they should be comrades in the struggle.[84]

Red Help's first major campaign was for a general amnesty of political prisoners, in summer 1926. Józef Piłsudski took power in a coup in May; since he and many of the new leaders had spent time behind bars or in Siberia, some hoped that they would free the previous government's opponents. Rather than petition the government, Red Help aimed to mobilize the masses with voices from within prison. "Our freedom is in your hands," proclaimed prisoners in Katowice in an open letter to the workers of Upper Silesia in early June. "Only under the pressure of the worker and peasant masses will the bars of prison break . . . . Remember that freedom cannot reign in Poland, and real improvement in the worker's life is impossible, so long as one political prisoner sits behind bars."[85] Thus the prisoner and the worker—who presumably shared the same politics—advanced hand in hand toward each other's freedom. Prisoners in Mysłowice reported in 1928 that they observed the anniversary of the Bolshevik Revolution to show "that political prisoners (behind bars) are linked with the working people who are free." The very term used here for being free, *na wolności* (literally "at liberty"), implies a possible state of being incarcerated; thus either worker or prisoner could be the other.[86] Each issue of Red Help's periodicals, each press release, featured reports from prisoners all over Poland, rendered into open letters addressed to workers either local or nationwide. They describe their activities and the repression they endure, including torture, discomfort, poor food, and deprivation of visits, always taking care to refer in general terms to the political cause for which they have been incarcerated. They usually ask for no specific assistance, only for support of their demands for better conditions.[87]

The prison report or open letter became an essential part of movement propaganda, though it did not help prisoners directly. To get out of prison, a letter to the court or the ministry should have greater effect; for material assistance, party comrades are surely a better bet. But as a symbolic gesture, the open letter intertwines the prisoners with their political community, including both the movement from which they came and their potential supporters, inviting them to engage with the prison as potential inmates and to adopt the politics of those who sacrifice for them. In August 1932, Red Help instructed prison comrades to help prepare for the Third International MOPR Congress: "Prisons should send resolutions, greetings, descriptions [of their conditions], correspondence, drawings, prison newspapers, speech outlines, theses, appeals and all kinds of materials which could be used for mass agitation and propaganda." In return, Red Help planned a day of demonstrations outside prisons nationwide.[88] While "mass propaganda" might have limited impact in Moscow, it would symbolize the unity of prisoners and their worldwide supporters.

The open letter was not a new genre, but those letters published by Red Help, addressed from one political collective to another, completed the incorporation of the political prisoner into the political struggle. This tactic underscored the value of the prisoner to the cause. "We are not victims," wrote a prisoner in Siedlce in 1928, "for we have consciously chosen this path. For us, battle-readiness is more important than mood. Where there is a struggle, there is life, and the joy of life. Desolation and doubt cannot be our themes, not even the themes of prison. We are the pioneers of a universal revolution. We are a part of that great worldwide force, even when we sit in prison."[89] The task of an organization like Red Help was to make this identification obvious both in and out of prison. Such coordination requires a determined, mobilized, and well-resourced movement. Red Help surely employed a bit of smoke and mirrors. Some letters may have been written by recently freed prisoners or by their associates outside, and demonstrations or collections may have fallen short of the "mass" appeal posited. Artificial or not, such coordination is a common element in the most powerful prison communities of the twentieth century.

The Polish Second Republic saw the effect of communist prisoners on the non-communist public as a serious threat. Government authorities monitored the activities of Red Help closely; this was, a top secret memo warned, "the starting point for a whole range of mass political activities . . . and also gives the party the possibility of getting into the broader political arena."[90] This fear explains why prisoner assistance could seem as threatening as ordinary Communist

Party activity, a political act punishable by the regime and honored by the movement. "Comrades Kamenc, Ołdak and others sat in prison for a year and a half for offering aid to prisoners," Red Help reported in early 1926. "Two non-party women workers were arrested a month ago in Łódź for possession of three ten-groschen subscription stamps supporting political prisoners. In Lwów, officials decided that prisoner aid was 'a danger to the state' and refused to legalize prisoner support."[91]

In regime materials, Red Help looked dangerous; in its own periodicals, heroic. On the ground, activists struggled to help prisoners they knew or felt solidarity with. Helena Michnik-Szechterowa, an activist in the Communist Party of Western Ukraine, recalled hearing that party members in Lwów "are disappearing, and probably being shipped to Łuck," a city she had never visited. She set out to Łuck to organize food packages for the prisoners, equipped only with the address of the mother of one of the prisoners, which Red Help in Lwów had given her. "She asked how many people I want to send packages to, and when she heard 40, she began to laugh out loud. This is Łuck, after all—here you give packages to three people and you're off to prison. But this woman organized a whole staff of people who prepared the packages, each one different so they would not look suspicious, and organized people to deliver the packages."[92] This prisoner's mother turned entrepreneurial social activist, and women like her, elicited the suspicion of the regime and the gratitude of the party.

Over the next few years, the letters and appeals from Polish prisons grew ever darker, reporting on comrades dying from torture, going insane, and losing all contact with comrades outside. Red Help was increasingly strapped for cash and unable to provide any support to prison. Struggling with the "sophisticated methods of slow murder," prisoners heard "the distant echo of heroic battles" outside.[93] Isolation could make them turn accusatory: "Kraków intelligentsia! You boast of your culture, beauty and honeyed words about nobility and justice are ever on your lips, but where is your voice of protest! Are you not ashamed that there are prisons a hundred times worse than the czarist torture chambers, here in Kraków?!?!"[94] Not only communists went to prison in the 1930s, as the dictatorship cracked down even on the parliamentary opposition. Shortly before the tortures of communists commenced in Łuck, nineteen members of Parliament, from various center-left parties, were arrested and interned at Brześć Fortress. In 1934, the remote and forbidding Bereza Kartuska concentration camp welcomed its first inmates, who came from both the right and the left. In 1938, the Communist Party of Poland, illegal for most of its existence, was dissolved by order of the Soviet Union. Party activists in Polish prisons were relatively fortunate, as it turned out; many of their comrades who had escaped to the USSR were executed on Stalin's orders. The confiscated letters from those years tell a story less of community than of isolation.

Still, the Polish interwar prison afforded its inmates and their supporters a field of political activity that would not be imaginable again for more than forty years. The memoirs of prisoners in Stalinist Poland never mention organized aid. After the spectacular attacks on prisons in 1944–46, the Polish underground no longer had the capability to publicize the plight of those incarcerated, let alone provide any assistance. Instead, much more modest gestures and anonymous demonstrations of moral support are remembered. Prisoners traveling under escort in passenger trains were slipped food and cigarettes, or could pass notes to their families.[95] A doctor at the women's prison in Inowrocław hired inmates, ostensibly to work in his garden, so that they could rest and recuperate from prison rigors for a few days.[96] Boy Scouts met released prisoners and helped them get home.[97] Many Poles, in the worst years, evidently felt obliged to at least look kindly upon political prisoners, as they had done during World War II. When Stalinism ended in 1956 and nearly all political prisoners were freed and rehabilitated, the occasional remaining inmate was far from public consciousness. Not until the formation of a new social assistance movement in 1976 would the political prisoner again become a figure in Polish consciousness.

The national and social movements of the century from the 1860s to the 1950s cannot be understood in isolation from their prisoners. Activists behind bars defined and ennobled the work both of their comrades who continued the struggle directly and those who performed more concrete humanitarian tasks. Assistance to the prisoners from earlier movements like the *satyagrahis* or the suffragettes had not been politically essential because the simple fact of being in prison was enough. In the interwar years, prisoner assistance entered the repertoire of contentious politics, until authoritarian regimes rendered it all but impossible. A new strategy of international aid developed to resituate the prisoner at the center of a broad humanitarian cause.

"How to Free Your Prisoner"

The Personal and the Political of International Prisoner Support

The political prisoner is not self-evidently an international actor. Political prisoners have nearly always been incarcerated for opposing the actions, policies, or ideology of their own state, not that of another state or of an international phenomenon.[1] The struggle between a regime and its opposition, today so clearly encoded in the expansive language of human rights, is first of all a local affair, the core of which—a strike, a restrictive law, a banned newspaper, a civil war—has forceful meaning only to the citizens of that country. Just as the domestic conflicts that lead to incarceration are not in and of themselves of international import, so too protests concerning events in other countries are less likely to provoke significant repression. The emergence of an international moral economy around political incarceration over the course of the twentieth century is thus remarkable.

Examining such transnational networks requires distinguishing support for international causes from support for prisoners. Early assistance efforts centered on struggles for socialism, feminism, or the freedom of minorities in a multinational empire. Freed prisoners from these movements could help to galvanize support for such causes, as in the case of Italian nationalists, British suffragettes, or Russian revolutionaries. The earliest international support came from diasporic communities identifying with those repressed in the homeland. Many a packed lecture hall in London or New York listened as freed "sons of liberty" told stories of brave sacrifice and terrible privations.

If some prisoners were fê in their freedom, others drew international support while imprisoned; in the nineteenth century, these were chiefly nationalists who inspired their countrymen abroad. For example, by the time of the Fenian Uprising, sizable Irish communities abroad had become well established and were linked to home through a robust diasporic press. Fenian supporters in the United States and Britain raised awareness of the movement's prisoners. Irish Revolutionary Brotherhood (IRB) men conducted speaking tours in

America, while others returned from Irish-American communities to join the fight. Charitable concerts, raffles, direct solicitation and advertisements in the Irish press at home and abroad raised money to be disbursed to Fenian prisoners and their families by the women active in prisoner assistance groups. As the prisons emptied toward the end of the 1860s, the fund then switched to support of released prisoners.[2]

The Irish model was replicated in other migrant communities. Italians in America raised money for their heroes, various Eastern Europeans for theirs. In Paris, Poles formed the Foreign Union of Assistance for Political Victims, which sent money to help prisoners in Russian Poland; a similar organization in Kraków raised money for those in Siberia.[3] While the plight of Irish prisoners might briefly attract the attention of the non-Irish press, the closed circuit of material support largely matched the circuit of potential fighters for the nation. The execution of the leaders of the Easter Rising (and the contemplated execution of American citizen Éamon de Valera) and the deaths in hunger strikes of Thomas Ashe, Terence MacSwiney, and others all kept prisoners and jails within the imagined geography of the Irish struggle. Diasporic organizations and prominent figures sent letters and telegrams, or picketed the British Embassy, while communities raised funds for prisoners.[4]

The circulation of funds in support of incarcerated socialists and suffragettes at the turn of the century followed a similar pattern. Men and women with experience in Russian, French, and German prisons were predominant among the delegates to gatherings of the Socialist Second International, for example.[5] Suffragettes, too, enjoyed international reach. English and Irish suffragettes coordinated their protests, with some crossing the Irish Sea to participate in both. Hanna Sheehy-Skeffington was one of these; she also toured the United States in 1916–17 to raise awareness and support for the Irish cause.[6] The *satyagraha* campaign against the Transvaal Asiatic Registration Act also attracted support beyond the Indian diaspora, though not as much as Gandhi's later campaigns in India.[7] Material support was not always the most important commodity: international awareness itself contributed to the pressure on an incarcerating regime.

Meanwhile, international conventions began to outline the rights of one particular type of international captive, the prisoner of war. The Brussels Conference of 1874, in the aftermath of the Franco-Prussian War of 1871, contained some first principles of appropriate treatment; the Hague Convention of 1899 (updated in 1907) extended these.[8] While the POW became a legally recognized category among all signatories, the political prisoner generally was not. At the same time, contentious politics in this era undermined the idea that state sovereignty could delimit what was acceptable warfare and what was not. The distinction between "prisoner of war" and "political prisoner" could thus seem arbitrary. Perhaps for this reason, political prisoners have used the "prisoner of war" category to frame their struggle and to measure their treatment.[9] The Hague Convention furnished a language through which protest could be recognized and made implicitly international.

For prisoners and their supporters, an international convention is of little use if states choose not to admit its applicability. The first international organization to work internationally with prisoners, beyond the call of ethnic or ideological ties, was the International Committee of the Red Cross (ICRC). The ICRC emerged in the same decade as the modern political prisoner. Founded in 1863, it worked at first to aid soldiers wounded in battle, expanded its mandate to prisoners of war, and began visiting prisons during World War I. But the division between international and domestic conflicts was difficult to maintain. For the first time during the Russian Revolution and Civil War, and the Hungarian Revolution in 1919—both part of an international campaign against Bolshevism—the ICRC visited those interned by their national opponents.[10] This was a significant step toward providing care for political prisoners. The soldier in a civil war, unlike one in an ordinary interstate conflict, fights for an alternative vision of the state. Caring for such prisoners therefore challenged the ICRC's role as a "neutral intermediary." Back in 1912, a Russian delegate to an International Conference of the Red Cross had argued that any assistance during a civil war would be a hostile act, since a country's laws "can only consider [such captives] as criminals."[11] Intervention challenged the ability of a regime to categorize its adversaries—an essential aspect of political incarceration.

World War I and international intervention in the Russian Civil War effectively destroyed these distinctions. In the Russian case, the ICRC at first limited itself to ministering to wounded and hospitalized insurgents, but a resolution passed at the 1921 International Conference declared that both prisoners and internees—presumably including noncombatants—"should be considered and treated in accordance with the principles which inspired those who drew up the 1907 Hague Convention."[12] In other words, such prisoners could lay claim to internationally mandated rights.

When Republican prisoners protested their conditions during the Irish Civil War, the ICRC dispatched a team of investigators to visit camps and prisons across the country. The IRA supplied a lengthy list of documented charges, including murders of prisoners, torture, and poor conditions. The ICRC's September 1923 report largely exonerated the Free State government, but the inquiry caused it some consternation.[13] As an advisor to President W. T. Cosgrave recognized, international attention could bring not only condemnation but also legitimacy. "I have a curious feeling myself that we are exposing the meanness and cruelty of our own people," he admitted in a memo, adding: "I am not sure that [the attention] will be an evil. In fact I think it will do much good."[14] Governments since have welcomed ICRC inspectors into their prisons, even when the conflict can no longer be described as a "civil war." The ICRC would not ordinarily advocate the release of political prisoners (except for the gravely ill) nor argue that their detention was unlawful or wrong. Nor would it publicize their plight. Attending to their physical well-being and to their living conditions, the ICRC left the politics of prisoners and regime aside. Nevertheless, the ICRC helped to make nationally bounded prisoners a potential subject of international politics.

Several strands, then, came together in the first half-century or so of the history of political prisoners. The liberal revolutions of 1848 made civic rights a cause as well as provided an international canvas on which that cause could be projected. National diasporas made use of developing technology to get news of their compatriots' persecution and to participate in a war of words. Civil wars and minor international conflicts in the 1850s–70s spurred the development of an international humanitarian public. The resultant organizations and legal frameworks furnished a rudimentary language of rights and status for prisoners.

"The Moral Effect of Even a Little Sympathy"

The foreign prisoner suffering for a universal cause turned out to be a surprisingly portable icon. The editor, the union activist, or the foot soldier of a movement becomes recognizable and accessible through incarceration, because the prison is a universal tool of repression. The celebrity ex-prisoners of the nineteenth and early twentieth centuries often framed their suffering as in the cause of liberty more generally.[15] In the interwar years, imprisonment offered a way for regimes to make political arguments about the international menace of Bolshevism, either through their own prisoners or those elsewhere. The Soviet press reported on the sufferings of communists; Western regimes imprisoned communists as agents of an international cause. The Soviet Union branded its imprisoned opponents as international threats, too, and stories of the travails of victims of Soviet rule circulated in other countries. Each regime critical of repression by others has had some prisoners of its own.

For advocacy movements, talking about prisoners abroad risked deflecting attention from the suffering of those at home. For example, when Irish newspapers began to carry stories of the persecution of Catholics in the Soviet Union, Sighle Humphreys's Republican Political Prisoners Committee perceived an effort by the Free State government to divert attention from domestic prisoners. A leaflet entitled "God Save Ireland" announced:

> A widespread appeal has been made for sympathy and prayers for those who are suffering persecution in Russia. As Christians it is our duty to pray for the oppressed of all nations. But should we not first pray

for the persecuted of our own country whose cause is our cause . . . .
IRISHMEN AND WOMEN. Take your eyes from the ends of the earth
and view dispassionately the wrongs and humiliations which are being
inflicted upon those who are working for the complete separation of
Ireland from the British Empire.[16]

Yet this same committee, just one year later, sent a letter to Gandhi, inviting him
to Dublin. Noting the similarity of their struggles and of their tactics, they hoped
he might speak at a public meeting in support of "our political prisoners."[17]
Gandhi could offer a convenient way to brand their struggle, as did the victim of
religious persecution. Neither regime nor movement could yet place the political prisoner in an international frame beyond that of the shared cause, however.

The international appeal was more than just a rhetorical tool. It could knit
together an opposition by giving local activists important tasks that raised
awareness of the cause for which they struggled. This would be the genius of
Amnesty International: solidarity through small tasks on behalf of strangers. An
early version of this strategy appears in the activities of Poland's chapter of Red
Help. First, local sections in the Soviet Union adopted individual communist
prisoners in Poland.[18] Similar linkages developed with other countries, so that
the Polish or Soviet or American worker could read of imprisoned leftists far
away and be moved to rally, to write letters, or to contribute money. The Polish
Red Help developed an analogous domestic program. Red Help circles could
adopt a local prison or a prison to which their comrades had been sent. But some
also tried to build ties to distant prisons across the country. Łódź circles adopted
the prison in Lwów, some 270 miles to the southeast; a Ukrainian circle in eastern Poland adopted Wronki Prison, near Poland's western border. These choices
seem to have been intended to bridge the ethnic divides of interwar Poland
as well. Locally, each circle might adopt one prisoner. "At circle meetings,"
explained an article in the *Political Prisoner* newspaper, "members learn about
the life of the comrade whom they look after. They read letters sent to them from
prison and thus strengthen the bonds between patrons and the comrades under
their care."[19] Interestingly, the circles did not appeal for their comrades' release.
Studying the suffering itself would deepen members' ideological commitment
and engage the prisoner in the movement, in a way that begging the regime for
leniency would not.

Oppositional movements faced a problem as they sought to make use of aid
to alleviate the suffering of their incarcerated comrades. Though national revolutionaries and communists were the captives of repressive states, outrage at their
suffering was not shared by those who did not share their politics. Even those
imprisonment campaigns aimed in part at awakening enthusiasm or provoking
horror in broader society, like those orchestrated by Gandhi or the suffragettes,

found it difficult to inspire condemnation of their imprisonment as such. It took extreme measures like hunger strikes and forced feeding to ensure sustained attention, and even then that attention came principally from the regime rather than the general population.

Prisoner assistance, then, followed divergent paths until well into the Cold War. One approach ministered to those who suffered, and it set aside the policies or practices that allowed states to incarcerate them in the first place. This humanitarian approach continued to flourish in the twentieth century as the ICRC entered the prisons. The other strand of prisoner assistance sought to alter the root causes of particular incarcerations through political victory.[20] For the revolutionaries in Red Help and MOPR, this meant sharing the goals of their imprisoned comrades who sought to destroy the bourgeois state. The Women's Prisoners' Defence League similarly called for the unification of Ireland, giving voice to the cause of the prisoners it championed. Others staked out middle ground, advocating prisoners' freedom and calling for the end of such repressive measures while not pressing for regime change. This stance, of increasing importance over the course of the twentieth century, was introduced by the International Committee for Political Prisoners (ICPP), the first international organization to speak for political prisoners beyond the bounds of comradeship. The ICPP, like the Soviet-sponsored MOPR, discovered that political prisoners could be vehicles for international solidarity; it did not, however, require ideological affinity.

Roger Baldwin, a co-founder of the American Civil Liberties Union (ACLU), created the ICPP in 1924 and described its work as "precisely similar in the international field as the Civil Liberties Union's work in the United States."[21] The founders, all writers and politicians prominent on the American left, were motivated most immediately by the Russian Civil War, when the Bolsheviks began to incarcerate not only the opponents of revolutionary change but also members of more moderate left-wing parties. During the years it was active, the ICPP published document collections about leftist prisoners in the Soviet Union, Poland, Italy, and elsewhere.[22] It also took up some collections to aid prisoners, but its chief activity was to lobby for prisoners in public meetings, in letters to the editor, and in letters to foreign governments.[23] In so doing, the ICPP experimented with the repertoire that would later be perfected by Amnesty International. Operating on the general, unspoken assumption that the prisoners it supported represented progressive forces, it was the first organization to protest political incarceration in a variety of regimes, and specifically the carceral practices of both fascist and communist regimes.

In other ways the ICPP departed significantly from the international model developed at the same time by the communists. Because the ICPP was situated at some distance from the prisoners it championed, there was no question of an ICPP-sponsored rally in front of a prison nor of meetings with the families of revolutionary inmates. Supporters would have to develop activities among themselves. Most important, the ICPP made a conscious effort to support representatives from a variety of movements. Its by-laws mandated that the committee "consist of representatives of foreign groups suffering imprisonment or persecution in any country, together with a greater number of persons interested in the general issue."[24] At the same time, in contrast to the International Committee of the Red Cross, it did "take into account the origins of the sufferings endured." It mattered that these prisoners were revolutionaries. Thus in its first publication, *Letters from Russian Prisons*, the ICPP pointed to the paradox of "a revolutionary government based on working-class and peasant power" incarcerating its "old comrades in the struggle," and proposed "to tell the story of these revolutionary political prisoners."[25] Subsequent books also deemed prisoners' plight to be significant in part for the cause they espoused.

The ICPP did open up a path toward a shared view of political prisoners. As Roger Baldwin explained in the introduction to *Letters from Russian Prisons*: "We have tried to exclude all references to prisoners who joined active counterrevolutionary movements of violence, as did a considerable number of those in the revolutionary parties opposed to the Soviet Government."[26] Baldwin here appears to accept the Bolsheviks' justifications for the Civil War, but he also admits the quandary any defender of prisoners encounters beyond the borders of one's own cause. What is more important, the nature of the prisoner's belief or the nature of the sentenced deed? The former is easier to defend, but absent an objectionable act, why would the content of the prisoner's thought matter? Baldwin's exclusion of violent prisoners leaves unmentioned the fate of those nonrevolutionaries who peacefully opposed the Soviets. The implied separation of nonviolent opponents into those whose thought deserved support and those whose ideas did not would eventually be cast aside.

Baldwin and his allies introduced an emphasis on facts into the cause of international prisoner assistance. If emotions were sufficient to support a comrade, only facts could ensure that one was supporting people who deserved assistance from a fair-minded organization. Founding ICPP Secretary Eleonore von Eltz urged Baldwin to place accuracy above all else, lest the public lose interest:

> Of course I could keep busy sending out bulletins to Committee members on conditions as indicated by the fragmentary bits that are coming our way . . . . But that's only valuable to keep up their interest – it's half-baked, unchecked stuff that cannot be used for public appeal . . . . If we try to interest the public now in the issues of imprisonment we'll get nowhere. We'll make a statement on the basis of some class or racial group in regard to Poland, for instance, and the Polish nationalists will

contradict it. The public will decide, correctly, that we don't know what we're talking about and refuse to get involved or to contribute. That leaves us in the "Letters to the Editor" class.[27]

In search of facts, Baldwin departed for Europe in early 1927 and spent nearly the whole year traveling all over the continent, as far as Moscow and Turkey, gathering data about prisoners and about European organizations that assisted political prisoners. The "disinterested" stance he continued to advocate nevertheless furthered a strong advocacy: "I cannot emphasize too strongly," he wrote in his last letter to ICPP supporters from Europe, "the moral effect here abroad of even a little sympathy and practical aid from a country regarded chiefly as a place of arrogant and unfeeling wealth."[28]

A decade after the Russian Revolution, Baldwin and the ICPP had shifted from support of revolutionaries to support of those who pursued nonviolent opposition.[29] This distinction would crumble in the face of fascism, which rendered the ICPP ineffectual. There were many nonviolent political victims of fascist or Nazi repression, but the conviction that great evil must be opposed by any means grew stronger in the 1930s. The imprisonment and torture of the suspected conspirators in the attempted assassination of Hitler in 1944 would have strained the ICPP's programmatic principles had it still been active.

The deep ideological divisions of the early years of the Cold War hindered any continuation of the ICPP's work. Advocacy on behalf of political allies seemed in any case inadequate after the Holocaust. The famous lament of Martin Niemoeller about the fatal consequences of supporting only one's own began to circulate widely in 1946–47. "First they came for the socialists," goes a popular version of his words, "and I did not speak out, because I was not a socialist." Niemoeller captured for many the perils of standing by in the face of a repressive dictatorship.[30] But his speech also critiques the sectarian approach to repression characteristic of the interwar years and served as a reminder that dictatorial regimes usually target opponents across a wide political spectrum.

The language of human rights began to appear more insistently in international politics after the war but mainly in elite discourse, such as that of the International League for the Rights of Man, founded by French exiles in New York in 1943.[31] As the Iron Curtain became more impenetrable, direct assistance gave way to long-distance advocacy. Meanwhile, Cold War rhetoric turned the focus away from the victim and toward the repressive—"totalitarian," in the language of the times—state. Where prisoner aid and advocacy had highlighted the suffering or martyrdom of groups of prisoners, Cold War political imperatives focused attention on states of the opposite camp as repressive agents and protagonists. In the American perspective, the victims of communism were as much the collective "captive nations" as they were individual people. Incarceration became just one of a variety of repressive measures not directed at one particular opponent, such as the closing of churches, persecution of minorities, censoring of the press, and confiscation of private property. This made it possible to talk about, for example, the Stalinist show trials without dwelling on the fact that many prominent victims were themselves communists. The prisoners who received the most attention in the West in the early Cold War were Catholic priests, in Eastern Europe, China, and Vietnam, for example. The left, in turn, championed the prisoners of Franco's Spain.

The array of organizations in the broad sphere of human rights reflected these shifts. The International Rescue Committee, founded in Europe in the 1930s to help refugees from Nazi Germany, expanded its postwar reach globally, seeking to aid those already on the move rather than those who were trapped behind borders.[32] The Workers' Defense League, founded in Detroit in 1936, which had previously campaigned on behalf of American workers imprisoned for union activities or strikes, prepared a report on global forced labor for the United Nations and investigated the situation of labor activists imprisoned in Spain and Latin America.[33] In Britain, an Appeal for Amnesty in Spain attracted brief attention on the left in 1959–61; a creation of the Communist Party of Great Britain, this campaign could be interpreted as an effort to deflect attention from prisoners of the left to those imprisoned by the right.[34]

Turning a human rights spotlight on prisoners themselves was difficult because it required moving against the division of the world into good and bad states (with deserving and undeserving captives, respectively). The efforts of the International League for the Rights of Man (later the International League for Human Rights) to highlight the abuses of left-wing and right-wing dictatorships, and colonial powers as well, met with a cool response in the United States, while its decision to work primarily through the United Nations weakened its visibility.[35] The international climate itself would have to change before political prisoners themselves could be the object of sustained advocacy and assistance.

Amnesty International Invents the Prisoner of Conscience

Amnesty International (AI) both changed the international climate and took advantage of the change it had helped to produce. The organization emerged about a decade before détente unfroze international human rights advocacy.[36] Though Nikita Khrushchev's 1956 revelations about Stalin's crimes had caused widespread disillusionment with discourses of left/right division, a neutral stance continued to be elusive. One way to achieve it was to focus narrowly on human suffering. After World War II, the International Committee of the Red Cross deepened its attention to the victims of internal political conflict without altering its creed. "The vocation of the Red Cross is to alleviate human suffering," affirmed a special Commission of Experts convened in Geneva in June 1953. "This role falls to it not only in the case of international warfare, but also in that of civil war or disturbances, and in all instances where men must suffer through international or national political causes." However, the commission continued, the ICRC "should not take into account the origin of the sufferings endured but merely record them and seek the means for their alleviation."[37] This position persuaded incarcerating states to continue to open their prisons to ICRC representatives. As important as this work is, it does not leave room for Baldwin's idea of "a little sympathy" that is rooted at least partly in political empathy. How can suffering that is the result of politics be separated from that politics? Amnesty International, founded in 1961, offered a way to embrace the political prisoner not only as a human being but as a political person, too.

The origins of Amnesty International are confused and contested. Historian Tom Buchanan casts doubt on the organization's oft-told origin story of British barrister Peter Benenson chancing upon a news report about the arrest of Portuguese students overheard drinking a toast to liberty in a Lisbon bar and resolving to do something for these "forgotten prisoners." No British newspapers, Buchanan reports, published an article about any such students (or similar Portuguese victims) in the fall of 1960. Whatever his epiphany really looked like, Benenson brought a new perspective to the cause. Schooled in left-wing politics, he had recently converted to Catholicism; this may have stimulated a broad interest in all prisoners. Perhaps because he found himself equidistant from traditional organizations, Benenson discarded both the partisan approach of the Spanish Amnesty campaign and the desk-bound advocacy of the International League for Human Rights. Instead, he proposed several innovations. The first was a rigorous balance in the advocacy for prisoners. The appeal that he published in the Observer in May 1961 placed the politics of the incarcerating states and their prisoners in the background. Second, incarceration itself, and not mistreatment (as in the work of the ICRC), became the focus. The term that Benenson proposed for these prisoners, "prisoners of conscience," underscored both of these points. The content of the prisoner's conscience did not matter, only the fact that this conscience had led to incarceration, the conditions of which were immaterial. The term erased the distinction between lawful and unlawful repression, between left and right, implied in more partisan approaches. In Benenson's words, "Any person who is physically restrained (by imprisonment or otherwise) from expressing (in any form of words or symbols) any opinion which he honestly holds and which does not advocate or condone personal violence" was a prisoner of conscience.[38]

Benenson adopted one distinction that had been important to Roger Baldwin as well. Acts of violence, or espousal of violence, placed a prisoner outside of Amnesty International's purview. Violence could not be reciprocal; states could legitimately use violence to protect themselves and their citizens or property and could appropriately imprison those who engaged in violence. Oppositional violence also threatened Amnesty International's carefully maintained political neutrality, as it challenged the very operation of the state to which Amnesty members petitioned. Support of prisoners who condoned or advocated violent acts implied acknowledging the justness of their cause. One could still protest the mistreatment of those associated with violence, and Amnesty would do so, but not their incarceration itself.[39] The violence exclusion kept AI off a slippery slope toward being seen as partisan by states or the public. AI recognized that nonpartisanship actually opened a space to act as an advocate for political prisoners.

The distinction that Amnesty drew necessitated an objective stance built on gathered facts, as it had for the ICPP. A prisoner's conscience was by definition subjective, but the content of the prisoner's mind or heart did not matter as much as the factual absence of violence. Violence or support of violence, by contrast, invited subjective judgments: What was the motive? How damaging was the violence? Was it justified? Amnesty's nonviolent prisoner of conscience, then, required the organization to have a particular kind of knowledge about the prisoner.

An Amnesty analyst drew the connection between nonviolence and accuracy in a 1966 report. "In the light of the general absence of information from East Pakistan it is also difficult to know how many of those arrested would be defined as 'Prisoners of Conscience' in the Amnesty sense," Elizabeth Gordon wrote.

> Violence is by no means unknown amongst Pakistanis and the difference between a peaceful demonstration inspired by wholly non-violent ideals and a full-scale riot is sometimes remarkably small. On the other hand, indiscriminate arrests may be expected to take place wherever a government has and uses widespread arbitrary powers of preventive detention. For this reason, and in view of the difficulty of obtaining reliable information and contacts in Pakistan the Investigation Department would particularly welcome the assistance of any members with specialist or up-to-date knowledge of this part of the world.[40]

Amnesty's distinction between a prisoner of conscience and a political prisoner who advocates violence has wielded great influence over the last half century. For many, the term "prisoner of conscience" has become synonymous with

Fig. 5.1 Joop Lieverst, poster for Amnesty International Netherlands, 1969. Courtesy of
Amnesty International Netherlands.

"political prisoner." In the preceding era, a political prisoner could be anyone
who fought for a cause and suffered the consequences. Now this subject of international support has been refigured as a man or woman of peace and thought (or
belief), subject to the violent will of a regime that fears the power of conscience.
Disposition has eclipsed opposition as the key criterion for inclusion and support. For the ICPP, nonviolence was implicitly the function of a broadly socialist philosophy. Amnesty discarded the specific politics to advocate for the soul
instead. Renouncing political difference while insisting on the right to political
belief, Amnesty has found success in transcending the dividing lines of the Cold
War and celebrating common human traits among people of disparate peaceful
beliefs.

Violence and conscience could not, however, be so neatly distinguished. Within a year of its founding, Amnesty International confronted the case of Nelson Mandela. Arrested in August 1962, he was sentenced to five years' imprisonment for standard political crimes, inciting strikes and violating travel restrictions. A lawyer and a passionate speaker, Mandela fit the prisoner of conscience category well; AI adopted him later that year. Yet the following year Mandela was put on trial again, this time for sabotage and conspiracy to overthrow the government; he was now linked to the armed wing of the African National Congress, Umkhonto we Sizwe ("Spear of the Nation"), of which he was the co-founder. At his trial and subsequently, Mandela conceded the first charge and refused to renounce violence against the apartheid state until the regime renounced its own violence.

The British circle that had adopted Mandela's case stopped calling for his release.[41] Yet Mandela was not a guerrilla fighter but a lawyer, albeit one who had founded a guerrilla group. The life sentence he received in early 1964 was disproportionate to his actions. An urgent poll of Amnesty members, the results of which were announced at a September 1964 membership meeting, revealed that an "overwhelming majority" of those who responded continued to support the nonviolence rule. Nelson Mandela could no longer be considered a prisoner of conscience. The meeting did agree, though, that Amnesty could continue to protest the sentence as well as the treatment meted out to any prisoner on humanitarian grounds.[42] Though the consequences of this decision would cause Amnesty some embarrassment, it did preserve the organization's hard-won pluralism. Only by depoliticizing the experience of political prisoners could Amnesty ensure that support for an imprisoned South African or a Latin American communist would not be the cause of a narrow band of British communists, or that the plight of a Catholic priest in Eastern Europe would not be ignored by those same communists and left to Catholic circles. Instead of competing stories of partisan repression, there developed a common story of humanity.

The common experience of incarceration would be no surprise to prisoners themselves. Transporting that solidarity outside the prison was not so easy, however. Prisoners' movements themselves could not embrace it without weakening their politics. Humanitarian organizations like the ICRC could, but at the cost of ignoring the injustice of incarceration itself. Amnesty International overcame these limitations by introducing a new distinction based not only upon the acts for which people had been convicted but also on their thoughts and words. This distinction, as unsatisfactory as it could be in individual cases, did enable incarceration for political reasons to become a worldwide human rights cause and offered recognition of the diversity of political prisoners.

Peter Benenson's announcement of the Appeal for Amnesty was in other respects quite traditional. He informed readers of a "London office" that was

gathering facts about prisoners, some of whom would be profiled in a forth-
coming book. He described the amnesty campaign as being "the result of an
initiative by a group of lawyers, writers and publishers in London."[43] The format
was very much like Baldwin's initiative nearly forty years earlier, but the outcome was something new: readers around Britain responded with enthusiasm to
Benenson's appeal, and local groups formed both in the UK and in several other
European countries. It appears that Benenson, who evoked in his 1961 essay
the newspaper reader's "sickening sense of impotence," believed that hands-on
participation could be transformative, while also doubting that it could have
any real effect. The work of these local groups—which at first researched and
adopted prisoners to campaign for and write to largely on their own, or in loose
coordination with a few dedicated volunteers in the main Amnesty office—soon
came to define AI.[44]

In the quarter century after Amnesty's consolidation around 1964, interest
in political prisoners as prisoners of conscience peaked. The period began with
several high-profile trials and imprisonments. In addition to Mandela, poet Josef
Brodsky was tried for "social parasitism" in Leningrad in 1964. Amnesty found
many other individuals to adopt, while coups in countries on three continents
signaled an ongoing rollback of democracy around the world. Charismatic
men like Brodsky and Mandela, with compelling stories, appealed to an emerging global human rights community and provided a template for the Amnesty
International campaigns over the next decades. Mandela's release from prison in
February 1990—close on the heels of the selection of Václav Havel, also recently
released, as Czechoslovakia's president—marked a symbolic end to this era.
Behind these headline-grabbing cases, the prisoner of conscience terminology
had fashioned hundreds of stories of courage and suffering from every continent. Despite their protagonists' ideological differences, these stories strongly
resemble one another. Each begins with an individual's conscience, including a
firm adherence to principles like truth and fairness. Each one features small acts
of courage, such as rendering legal or medical assistance to those in need, speaking out in public about injustice, or composing poetry and songs. Each figure
confronts a petty or vindictive state apparatus—for example, in a local police
station or in the dock at a public trial. Each then shows courage and resilience
by speaking out in court, writing letters from prison, or simply bearing up under
torture and in isolation.

Amnesty International publicized hundreds of such cases over this period.
Some individuals became well known long afterward, when they published
memoirs or letters from prison. Wei Jingsheng's essay on democracy plastered
on Beijing's "Democracy Wall" in 1978 earned him a sentence of fifteen years in
Chinese labor camps. Kim Dae-jung, a prominent opposition politician in South
Korea, was sentenced to death in 1980. Egyptian doctor and women's activist

Nawal el Saadawi wrote a short memoir and play about her incarceration for opposition to President Anwar Sadat. Mathematician Anatoly Shcharansky was imprisoned for his campaign for the right to emigrate from the Soviet Union. Argentine journalist Jacobo Timerman's 1981 memoir of imprisonment and torture, *Prisoner without a Name, Cell without a Number,* captured in its very title the essence of modern state repression. Countless other prisoners also benefited from publicity and from the work of local Amnesty groups over this period.[45]

Collectively, the stories publicized by Amnesty constitute at once a numbing litany of the intransigence of state repression and an inspiring message of perseverance and hope. At the same time, they could seem to flatten the cacophony of civil disobedience around the world and mine complicated political stories for their anodyne moral. Each struggle for justice becomes equal to every other, measured only in the person's number of years behind bars and the severity of torture endured. The complex ideas of the prisoner cease to matter. If for the Amnesty supporter some cases became personal, even intimate, thanks to the letters sent to prisoners of conscience and their captors, at a distance the accounts in Amnesty reports and newsletters blend together. A news release like that in 1974, listing no fewer than 171 writers imprisoned around the world, raises more questions than it answers: Why writers? Are they more deserving of freedom than priests, trade union activists, party leaders, or generals? Who is left off this list? For those on the list, does the quality of what they have written matter?[46]

Yet the category of prisoner of conscience worked because it created a global imagined community of prisoners and ex-prisoners.[47] Celebrating Human Rights Day, December 10, Amnesty International brought freed prisoners from distant parts of the world to London to light a ceremonial candle. Others addressed annual meetings or met with groups of their letter-writing supporters. Such encounters allowed former political prisoners to develop affinities and act as advocates for one another based upon shared experiences. They joined or created Amnesty circles in their own countries, raising awareness of the global contexts of their own persecution. Polish journalist Emil Morgiewicz, for example, sentenced to four years in prison in 1971 for conspiracy to burn down the Lenin Museum in Poronin, compiled a report on Polish prisons and sent it to Amnesty. He and several colleagues then joined Amnesty and gathered signatures on petitions and sent letters protesting imprisonment elsewhere; these activities occasionally resulted in further detention.[48]

Amnesty's campaigns individualized political prisoners who were persecuted for their adherence to an intellectual or spiritual cause. The acts that followed—editorials or poems written, a boycott or strike planned or urged—could be collective, but they were the product of introspection and individual will, not simply a political party's dictates. The prisoner of conscience is thus appealing

as a romantic figure, yet the freeing of a prisoner depends equally upon a rational process. Even more than did the ICPP, Amnesty International has emphasized the collection of accurate and sufficient information. In the early decades,
subscribers received background sheets on the countries holding the prisoners
in addition to extensive notes on the prisoners themselves. Sending out new
background sheets in 1967, the London office urged: "Where necessary, please
ensure that you insert the new sheets and destroy the old. We hope that this will
both lead to increased effectiveness in your writing on behalf of prisoners and
also make your work more interesting."[49]

With accuracy and objectivity came a determinedly nonconfrontational tone.
In its first newsletter issued to members, when introducing the cases of South
African Robert Sobukwe, a Yugoslav conscientious objector, and a Spanish
priest, Amnesty urged those members planning to send cards to "always bear
in mind that our purpose is not to aggravate the situation but to make the government concerned think about the prisoner and put them in a frame of mind
that will make it logical to release not only the prisoner you are writing about
but also others in similar circumstances."[50] A 1974 handbook issued to Amnesty
groups, entitled "How to Free Your Prisoner," offered practical advice about how
their symbolic actions yielded concrete results. Members could thus enjoy an
emotional connection to their work but also achieve satisfying outcomes. The
logic of public relations and international pressure based upon human decency
delivered results, unlike the petitions and letter-writing campaigns of the past.

Connecting the world's political prisoners, Amnesty International gave them
similar characteristics. It achieved the same effect with the incarcerating regimes.
These states all rely upon caprice—postponed trials, flouted rules, unexpected
punishment—and cruelty, such as lengthy sentences or physical labor out of
proportion to the alleged crime. Some regimes seem to imprison nearly anyone who expresses political disagreement, while others only detain, for example,
those who refuse army service. But state repression becomes a constant in the
Amnesty literature.

Each country studied here presented different challenges for AI and its supporters. Poland proved quite unproblematic for the prisoner of conscience
paradigm. Nearly all of the political prisoners in communist Poland were
immediately adopted. The first of these, Jacek Kuroń and Karol Modzelewski,
authors of a Marxist critique of communist rule, were recognized in the March
1967 "Postcards for Prisoners" campaign, alongside an American conscientious
objector and a Bolivian lawyer. Amnesty identified Modzelewski, a young his-
torian at Warsaw University, as a "Communist . . . who comes from a tradition-
ally Communist family . . . . Less is known about Kuroń's background, but it is
reported that he had been awarded the Polish Silver Medal for his political work
with young people." The story of the two Poles fit the Amnesty schema well: they

had been arrested for providing "false information" in their 1965 "Open Letter to the Party"; they had been convicted on the basis of a legal code introduced as a temporary measure in 1945; the trial was staged during the summer, yet "hundreds of Warsaw University students waited outside the Court" and sang the "Internationale," the anthem of the international communist movement; and they were required to perform physical labor in prison, where they were also denied writing materials. Thus, legal irregularities, civil disobedience grounded in political convictions (both among prisoners and their supporters), punishment for intellectual pursuits, and deprivation of such pursuits within prison were the key themes in this narrative, which was based upon two years' work by Amnesty groups in England and Italy. For those groups who wished to write postcards, the newsletter supplied the addresses of both men's prisons and of the Polish communist leader, Władysław Gomułka.[51]

Amnesty's focus on Poland followed this basic framework for the next twenty-two years. Research conducted by AI groups or contributed by in-country contacts established the bona fides of candidates for recognition. AI offered information about the political beliefs of prisoners to indicate the line connecting those beliefs to their imprisonment, and then invited members to send letters to prisoners, their families, and to government officials. Contexts discouraged placing any import on specific beliefs. Thus, for example, the report of Kuroń's release later in 1967 immediately preceded an account of an AI investigation into the incarceration of nine Roman Catholic priests in Czechoslovakia, with a view to adopting them as prisoners of conscience.

While balance was the core of the Amnesty method, AI groups and individual members were autonomous and free to pursue their own political convictions. No one was obligated, for example, to send postcards to all publicized prisoners of conscience. In any case, members seem not to have complained too loudly about the ideological distribution of adopted prisoners. Each newsletter presented a balanced group of prisoners—in the 1960s, this was typically a communist in a Third World country, a liberal intellectual imprisoned in a communist country, and a conscientious objector in a Western democracy—as a package. The passions that drew people to participate in AI might naturally incline them to write as if the recipient (a government official or prison administrator) was personally culpable for any discomfort their adopted prisoner might experience. The very first newsletter twice cautioned postcard writers not to be "impolitic." For example, members wanting to support an imprisoned Basque priest could direct their pleas to the Spanish minister of information and tourism. AI identified the minister as having been cooperative in the past and asked members to make their letters "non-aggressive and polite."[52] A prisoner whose cause one supported could be compromised by too much enthusiasm. A contact in South Africa reported that "some Groups use phrases in their letters to the wives or dependents of political prisoners which could cause difficulties for them with the police. Remarks which seem innocuous to most people can have a highly political connotation in a country like South Africa; phrases like 'liberation struggle' or 'fight for freedom' could put the very people Amnesty tried to help in a dangerous position if the letters were read by authorities."[53]

The contrast of the terms "innocuous" and "political" in this report is revealing. Amnesty was cultivating a respect for political conscience and expression separate from politics as such. Thus, cards could express concern about incarceration and urge early release, but reference to political content only endangered the prisoners, their families, and perhaps their cause. In addition, the phrases "liberation struggle" and "fight for freedom" implied violent resistance. The appropriate intervention left politics aside altogether. In this way, Amnesty International created a new model for affinity between political prisoner and supporter. The exemplary prisoner biographies presented each month differed in their beliefs and life paths, yet they shared deep convictions and the willingness to express them. One gave a sermon, another organized a boycott, a third wrote an editorial. Each word or deed by a prisoner of conscience advocated freedom for the rights of others, and AI members emulated them by sending a postcard that also advocated freedom. The global bond between prisoners and advocates became stronger than what divided them, and prisoners' acts could, in a way, be replicated outside prison.

The idea that ordinary citizens could do something about suffering around the world by meeting in their living rooms and writing letters lay at the heart of Amnesty International's longevity and success. From the beginning, Amnesty maintained a rule that groups could not be advocates for prisoners in their own countries. Thus Britain itself remained out of AI's purview during its first decade.[54] Northern Ireland's Border War of the late 1950s had nearly ended by the time Amnesty was founded, but Irish nationalism was bound to provoke a challenge at some point. Amnesty did investigate use of the Special Powers Act of 1922, even before the Troubles erupted in 1969. But not until 1973, when the Swiss chapter of Amnesty adopted Michael Tobin (sentenced for possession of pamphlets appealing to British soldiers to leave Northern Ireland), did the conflict yield a prisoner of conscience.[55]

In prophetic words in May 1971, Peter Benenson worried that the strict ban on domestic campaigns limited Amnesty's impact: "We should be looking at what goes on in Northern Ireland," he commented on the occasion of AI's tenth anniversary. "Then we'd have a bit more credibility when we criticize what goes on in Indonesia."[56] A few months later, the introduction of internment without trial posed a significant challenge. Compelling accounts of torture (discussed in Chapter 2) led to the formation of two investigative commissions by the British government and a separate investigation by Amnesty. The Amnesty report published one year later drew a careful distinction between imprisonment itself and the "ill treatment" in prison. It made no statement on the politics of either the prisoners or the British government, and it offered no biographical information about prisoners except age and, sometimes, home city or religion. "Conscience" is entirely absent.[57]

Yet for all its documentary distance from the conflict, Amnesty's report meant a great deal to the IRA prisoners themselves. It was proof that they were political, even if that word, in the report, is used mostly in contrast to "military," when describing the presumed aims of the British government. The report allowed detainees' experience to be discussed and recognized as a legal case, as a political problem, and as a human story. So did the case against torture brought before the European Court of Human Rights (ECHR), initiated

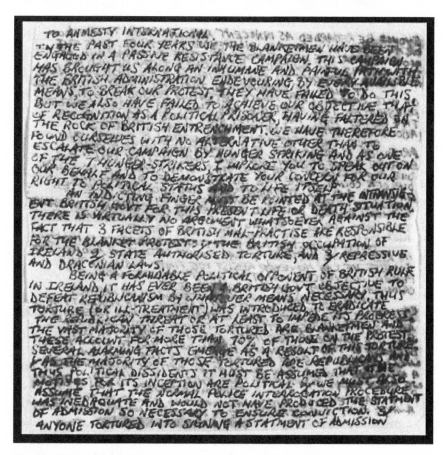

Fig. 5.2 "Comm" from IRA Prisoners to Amnesty International, c. 1980. Courtesy of Linenhall Library.

by the Republic of Ireland with the support of Amnesty International. While rhetoric about politics was absent, an investigation into human rights naturally synchronized with the cause espoused by those tortured.[58] The ECHR case placed the British government under an uncomfortable international spotlight. Local prison officials had to respond to inquiries from the court in Strasbourg and cope with increased protests from parliamentary opposition and local citizens.[59] Local civil rights groups organized around specific cases that gained international visibility.

Across the world, in quite disparate regimes, a variety of factors both global and local transformed the politics of prisoner advocacy in the 1970s and 1980s. Human rights advocates like Amnesty International (later joined by Human Rights Watch, formed in 1978) acquired new tools and allies that allowed them to publicize the cause of political prisoners more widely and forcefully.[60] Awareness of political prisoners, especially those behind the Iron Curtain and on Robben Island, contributed to and benefited from this changing climate. The emerging consciousness of political incarceration can be illustrated by the list of recipients of the Nobel Peace Prize. The first recipient who could be called a political prisoner was Martin Luther King Jr. in 1964; before that the vast majority of prizes had gone to diplomats or to humanitarians. But from 1974 (when Sean MacBride received the prize) to 2000, the prize in about half the years has acknowledged work on behalf of prisoners or gone to a person who had been a political prisoner. In addition, both governments and civic groups wielded sanctions or boycotts that cited political prisoners, such as the US sanctions of Poland in 1981, and the international campaign in the 1980s to force divestment from the South African economy.

Global and Local Prisoner Advocacy and Democratic Change

Prisoner advocacy transformed at the domestic level as well. In the decade after the general failure of the revolts of 1968, civic activism in Europe and the United States turned away from ideology and toward individual experiences. In this context, political incarceration was reframed as a story of unjust pain inflicted upon conscientious individuals. In Northern Ireland, in South Africa, and in Poland (as well as in Argentina, in Turkey, in the Soviet Union, and in other countries holding large numbers of political opponents), a growing susceptibility to international pressure coincided with and was fed by a thickening web of civic activism. Local prisoner advocacy shows that as prisoners had become globally recognized, the global story of imprisonment enriched and reinvigorated local efforts.

In the last years of the 1970s, prisoner advocacy in Poland almost disappeared for the lack of political prisoners. Workers arrested after the June 1976 revolt had nearly all been released by early 1978; occasional arrests of trade union activists warranted protests from the Workers' Defense Committee (KOR) and condemnation by Amnesty International or Helsinki Watch. Strikes in the summer of 1980 brought new repression, and demands for the release of dissidents helped to fuel the emergence of the huge social movement and trade union, Solidarity. Over the following year, civic organization in Poland reached a level and breadth unmatched anywhere in the world. While the regime conceded the formation of the trade union, crackdowns at the local level continued. Even as the jails emptied, protests of short-term detentions remained an important part of the repertoire, culminating in a nationwide campaign of protest marches in May 1981. Regardless of whether the regime was arresting its opponents, the demand to "release all political prisoners" became part of the language of contentious politics.[61]

The sudden imposition of martial law at midnight on December 13, 1981, began with the internment of some 6,000 Solidarity activists, followed by thousands more over the next few months. Their plight became the focal point of underground opposition activity and of aboveground work as well. Solidarity's prisoners became the face of the movement; ironically perhaps, those who remained free could not appear in public for fear of arrest, so those behind bars gained greater visibility. Many of them, including future prime minister Tadeusz Mazowiecki, smuggled out accounts of their internment; others, like Adam Michnik, issued a steady stream of passionate letters from prison.[62] Underground printers created postage stamps with images of prisoners.[63] Very quickly, Amnesty International adopted Polish prisoners of conscience. Although international pressure on behalf of prisoners brought results in a few cases, domestic pressures mattered more.[64]

In martial-law Poland, prisoner assistance quickly became the most attractive form of civic engagement, drawing upon the extensive social networks that Solidarity had built. The fact that mass internment took place just before Christmas resonated especially strongly. Four days into martial law, Cardinal Józef Glemp, head of the Catholic Church hierarchy in Poland, created the Primate's Committee in Support of Those Deprived of Freedom and Their Families, whose base in a church on Piwna Street gave it a more manageable nickname. The Piwna Committee involved some 200 people, both clergy and laypeople. They collected information about the location and needs of those interned; gathered and distributed food, clothing, and medicine; and offered legal assistance.[65] Similar committees formed under the auspices of archdioceses or in parish churches in Wrocław, Kraków, and other cities.[66] The engagement of the church hierarchy offered sufficient legal cover for Solidarity members who could no longer act in their workplaces. It also seems likely that many Polish clergy became engaged in politics for the first time, visiting interned Solidarity activists who had become candidates for material and spiritual assistance. The largest political incarceration in Poland since the end of Stalinism twenty-five years earlier provided a cause around which grassroots activism, dramatically curtailed by martial law, could endure. For many in Poland, providing help to others was the only possible form of politics.

In late 1984, after the murder of Jerzy Popiełuszko, a priest active in the Piwna Street network, underground Solidarity took the next step, again around the problem of political incarceration. "I intend to act openly," wrote Zbigniew Romaszewski in an editorial in an underground newspaper, announcing a civic initiative to provide legal help and material support to those arrested, fined, and otherwise targeted by the regime. Over the next five years his Commission for Intervention and Legality, more confrontational than the church groups, became an engine of civil society around which Solidarity reemerged as a political force in 1989.[67]

Bogdan Ciszak's diary of internment in small-town prisons suggests that the presence of political internees initially energized communities that had been quiescent during Solidarity's legal phase. He mentions waving and signaling to people in nearby buildings, friendly contact in a local hospital, letters from strangers, and even a sympathy strike visible in a factory across the street. A worker in the town circulated a petition to free the internees, earning himself internment as well. Though the underground as such did not exist in small towns, martial law awakened wartime models of solidarity.[68] The intense communal activity of the martial law prison was matched by a surprisingly resilient civil society outside. However, a series of amnesties in 1984–86 not only emptied the prisons again but also showed that civic activism was defined and limited by the prison.

Like Poland, South Africa in the apartheid era boasted a rich tradition of civic opposition. The relationship between the local opposition and the global was complicated by Amnesty International's ambivalence. Nelson Mandela was not the only convicted ANC leader whose connections made him ineligible to be a prisoner of conscience. In the early 1970s, less than 20 percent of Robben Island prisoners had been so designated.[69] South African exiles in London and elsewhere compensated for this omission, raising the visibility of their comrades back home.

Of particular importance was the International Defence and Aid Fund (IDAF), established by Canon John Collins in 1956 in response to an attempt by the apartheid regime to convict Mandela and more than 100 others of treason. In its early years, the fund was based in Johannesburg, before being forced out and relocated to London. By the 1980s, the IDAF was by its own estimation one of the largest nongovernmental organizations in Britain.[70] The IDAF resembled traditional prisoner-aid groups, raising funds which it smuggled into South Africa through a "multilayered system of legal firms" for legal support and for prisoners' dependents. Families who received aid got it ostensibly from individuals who, like Amnesty letter writers, were cautioned not to mention politics.[71] Also like Amnesty, the IDAF focused on gathering and supplying detailed data on the victims of oppression. In 1978, it produced a 180-page encyclopedia of prisoners and banned persons.[72]

The IDAF's growth in Britain during the 1970s coincided with Amnesty International's shift to a broader critique of prison conditions and torture.[73] Meanwhile, the Soweto Uprising in June 1976 revolutionized South African opposition politics. The Uprising was sparked by a protest over school curricula, specifically a mandate increasing the use of Afrikaans. While the regime began developing plans to entrench racial segregation more thoroughly into the constitution, its crackdown reenergized politics in the communities and in prison. The Black Consciousness Movement (BCM), which grew to prominence after Soweto, contrasted itself to the older opposition that, it contended, was alienated from the community. The BCM emphasized self-education, strikes, and community projects over national politics. Thanks to the regime, the BCM quickly established itself in prisons as well. Its activists fit the "prisoner of conscience" profile better than did those of the ANC.[74]

The regime's mass detentions in the 1980s made it difficult for international organizations to respond effectively to individual cases, even as prisoners of apartheid became the most recognized political prisoners in the world. Locally, civic associations blossomed in many cities; increasingly, they focused on political incarceration. One such grassroots initiative was the Detainees' Parents Support Committee (DPSC), founded in late 1981 by the parents of a detained student.[75] The DPSC was the first civic organization in South Africa focused on prisoners since the banning of the IDAF in 1966, and it quickly grew into the most important source of information and support for detainees. South African detention presented particular problems as it was used to circumvent the legal requirements of normal imprisonment. Detainees were not charged, but they also had no visitation rights; families might not even know where a relative had been placed. The DPSC studied the psychological effects and legal ramifications of detention and tried to publicize the lonely plight of detainees—for example, picketing churches at Christmas with signs about those behind bars at the holiday.[76] A second group, the Ad Hoc Detention Action Committee (ADAC), formed in Cape Town a few months later, adopted a more aggressive stance.[77] Both groups contributed to the emergence of a national opposition network, the United Democratic Front, in 1983. The declaration of a state of emergency in 1985 (lasting until 1989) meant thousands of detentions. The DPSC and ADAC both endeavored to make detention a broad social issue. They reached out to students who faced detention, supported their families, protested conditions and the legal frameworks of detention, and assisted ex-detainees readjusting to life outside. Unlike in Poland, civic organizations were not illegal, though restrictions and risks were significant for those who participated in them.[78]

Prisoner assistance groups had multiplied across the country by the end of the 1980s. Observance of National Detainees' Day each March brought activists together in street demonstrations. The state continued to take measures against the DPSC and other groups: participants were themselves detained, and security police raided and closed DPSC offices. In April 1987, the regime attempted to ban campaigns on behalf of detainees entirely.[79] As in Poland, prison suffering was an issue both palpable and beyond politics; it thus supplied a framework for civil society.

Fig. 5.3 National Detainees' Day poster. Produced by Call of Islam/Community Arts Project, Cape Town, 1986. Courtesy of South African History Archives.

Conditions for civic activism were of course dramatically different in Northern Ireland, which lacked any formal barriers to prisoner support. Yet coincidentally, in the same year as Poland's martial law imposition and South Africa's detention campaign, a hunger strike in the H-Blocks of Long Kesh/Maze Prison changed the landscape of civic-prisoner relations in Northern Ireland as well. As transformative as the strike was within the prison, it also helped to reshape politics outside.

The prisoners of the 1970s were already ubiquitous in Northern Irish culture, but distant. They led almost mythical lives, moving between the secret world of the paramilitary groups (whether Republican or Loyalist) and the enclosed space of the prison. Civil society, meanwhile, focused its attention on the broader issues of peace and reconciliation. A Nobel Peace Prize for Betty Williams and Mairead Corrigan, founders of the Community of Peace People, in 1976, was emblematic of this emphasis.

Early in the 1981 hunger strike campaign, an opportunity arose for a different kind of public campaign. The death of Frank Maguire, a moderate nationalist Member of Parliament for Fermanagh-South Tyrone, necessitated a special election to fill his seat. Republican prisoner leader Bobby Sands, already several weeks into his hunger strike, was put forward for election. This gave Catholics in Northern Ireland a new way to interact with their heroes behind bars. While neither illegal—Sands could run, thanks to a 1967 law allowing convicted persons to stand for Parliament—nor unprecedented, the plan was fraught.[80] Much of the story of this brief campaign centers around maneuvers to ensure that Sands would not have to compete for votes with other pro-Republican candidates. But a good turnout and respectable support for an imprisoned candidate voters had never met and could not even hear speak was hardly guaranteed. Northern Ireland Catholics, especially in a rural district far from Belfast, had been thus far reserved in their support for the hunger strike. Many nationalist voters were expected to spoil their ballots in protest of IRA violence.[81] And the tradition of standing for Parliament from behind bars had faded since 1916–22, when imprisoned men and women won seats in the British Parliament and the Irish Dail, and then refused to serve. Two IRA prisoners, Thomas Mitchell and Philip Clarke, had won seats from Northern Ireland during the Border War of the 1950s.[82] Sands was the first IRA candidate of the Troubles, and the campaign would last just nine days. Sands was denied contact with journalists, leaving his campaign to be managed by a twenty-six-year-old local activist.

The British authorities walked a delicate line: "We must avoid allowing Sands to exploit his position as a valid candidate," wrote Northern Ireland Secretary of State Humphrey Atkins to Prime Minister Margaret Thatcher on April 3, "while at the same time avoiding the trap of so constraining his campaign as to make him a political martyr."[83] This amounted to the same problem prison administrators faced, only on a much larger scale. Sands himself issued what must be the most downbeat campaign message ever: "I place my life and the lives of my three [hunger striking] comrades in the hands of the people of Fermanagh-South Tyrone. I ask you to . . . keep the seat in Anti-Unionist hands. I am confident that the people of Fermanagh-South Tyrone will not let the prisoners down. I can be your MP for approximately two weeks. Better that than Harry West [his unionist opponent] for two years."[84] Would forecasting his imminent death make him more sympathetic to voters, or less?

Supporters from the Republic of Ireland campaigned on his behalf, and the nationalist press made the case that a victory would prove that the armed struggle was indeed political. The belief that a vote for Sands might keep him alive, and respect for his willingness to die, outweighed voters' antipathy.[85] Campaign strategy and voter preferences aside, the episode brought prisoners and the Northern Ireland public together in a way the parades and commemorations of the previous half-decade had never done. As Sands's biographer Denis O'Hearn puts it, the campaign volunteers "gave grassroots Nationalists the same sense of agency and possibility of victory that the prisoners had already experienced through their struggles in Long Kesh and Armagh Jail."[86] A turnout greater than 85 percent bears out this observation.

Sands's victory preceded his death by less than a month; the IRA was thus able to contest the same seat again during the hunger strike. The Parliament had hurriedly passed a law disqualifying prisoners from candidacy, but Owen Carron, Sands's campaign manager, retained the seat in a six-way race.[87] The hunger strike seemed to have made the prisoners more popular than the IRA itself. Sands in particular became an international figure after his death, and global opinion became more inclined to see the IRA prisoners in a positive light.[88]

The funerals of hunger strikers and of victims of the Troubles continued to dominate through the next decade of conflict, but underneath lay a current transforming the prison community. As during the election campaigns, IRA public relations reached out to the community instead of assuming all Catholics should be supporters. For example, prisoners were encouraged to write "spare letters"—that is, any left in their quota after writing to family—to local newspapers, simply commenting on local issues and community work.[89] As prisoners were released in the mid-1980s, some returned to their communities as campaigners for cultural rights—for example, organizing language classes to share the Irish they had mastered in prison.[90] Perhaps there were few other skills from the prison cell that could be useful outside; this one made prison life a community experience as well.

In each of these cases, prison and community connected in new and powerful ways, particularly in the 1970s and 1980s. The prisoner or detainee/internee in Poland, South Africa, and Ireland reached beyond the relatively limited circle of political activists. In all three countries, although society at large was distant from the radical experience of the prison cell and that distance potentially diluted the impact of the prisoners' sacrifice and martyrdom, majority approval nevertheless surrounded small islands of active support. Decades of prisoner advocacy had helped to make the political prisoner a central figure in the contest between incarcerating regimes and their opponents. Thanks to the work of Amnesty

International and others, the prisoner became a figure in human rights discourse as well. One could support Nelson Mandela or Jacek Kuroń without knowing much about his politics (IRA prisoners could not be regarded so impartially). The 1980s brought prisoner support full circle: in societies where fear or apathy or the power of myth may have put prisons at some remove from passive supporters, that distance now lessened and prisoners became real again.

"A Close-Knit Group, Chosen with Care"

Community and Order in the Political Camp and Prison

"The cell doors closed behind me," recalled Adam Grzymała-Siedlecki, "as I returned from the Gestapo, and I entered that prison fetor, that squalor and degradation—all that—as if into my own home, my place of salvation. Finally I am not *there*."[1] Violet Weinberg confessed—to a South African court, no less—a similar desire to return home. She would not testify and be a traitor. Instead, "she wanted to be sentenced to imprisonment in order to be with other prisoners, in that way to escape from the misery of solitary detention."[2] "There were times," adds Zdzisław Jędrzejewicz from a Stalinist prison, "when in that tiny space, no more than 26 square meters [for eight men], I felt myself a truly free man."[3]

Even in the most repressive regimes the prisoner's place in a social network matters. The familiar story of heroic individual struggle against injustice falls short in capturing the prisoner experience. Alone with their thoughts and a glimpse of sky, individual prisoners work out ideas of honor, responsibility, and identity that embed them firmly in their political movements, but the politics of the prison emerges most powerfully out of a cell community. That community sometimes comes ready-made from outside, as the leaders of political movements rejoin their incarcerated comrades and make the cell an extension of the fight outside. Conversely, the prison could be the place to return to the movement. A lawyer for IRA prisoners explained to Kieran McEvoy why men who had given information to the British would not face punishment from their comrades: "Once a prisoner moves to [Long] Kesh the key thing is to get him onto the wings, make him feel that he is still part of the struggle, included, still part of the collective movement."[4]

The prison offers a human environment that might even be stronger than that in the often stressful conditions of freedom left behind. In the underground, or in the harried world of semi-legal opposition, social ties could be fragmented and uncertain, fraught by suspicions and squabbles over tactics. The cell brought its own suspicions but also simplified social networks. Generations of Polish political prisoners called this social world the *komuna*, or commune. Unlike an ordinary community of individuals, the prison *komuna* is based upon both voluntary and forced sharing. A cell community cannot avoid having rules governing interpersonal relations and the management of assets; these rules, passed along in oral tradition, can become quite elaborate.[5] Understanding how prison communities form and function leads back to the movements outside, for the cell community can be at once a product of what goes on beyond prison walls and a catalyst for activity there. The prison might be more diverse politically— and that too can be a lesson for the outside world.

This chapter reconstructs the cell community, mapping the practices that make it function as a home. How do movements shattered by arrests and interrogations reconstruct social ties? The forms of community changed significantly from the late nineteenth century through the 1930s, the period that set the patterns that have continued since. Even as prisoners recreated community, they have also tried to bridge the gap that separated them from the outside. This chapter explores the ways that political prisoners build relationships, with particular attention to communal structures that produce and sustain opposition politics.

Technologies of the Cell

The rules of prison society have depended in part on whether the institution places inmates in communal cells and open-door wards, where complex social rules are essential to maintaining order, or in single cells, which greatly inhibit communities. Linking such cells in a tenuous network of desperately lonely and suspicious individuals, under guards' watchful eyes, demands great ingenuity. In early 1945, the Soviet Army summoned sixteen Polish military and civilian leaders to a meeting, arrested them, and deported them to Moscow, where the subsequent trial ended with the execution of most of them. During his trial testimony, labor leader Kazimierz Pużak remarked offhandedly: "I concluded, after communicating with my fellow prisoners . . ." The prosecutor interrupted, demanding an explanation: Lubyanka Prison made it impossible for prisoners to communicate. Pużak's response, according to legend: "I've been imprisoned in czarist Russia, I was a prisoner of the *sanacja* [the interwar dictatorship], the Germans arrested me, and now the Soviets. I'm an old criminal, and have no intention to lecture the prosecutor on how one establishes communication."[6]

Prisoner memoirs tend to hold to this reticence, since those techniques might well come in handy again after a new political upheaval.[7] Methods of communication naturally depended upon the level of isolation. The essential building block of prison community was a note smuggled within the prison or to the outside, a *kite*, or, in British slang, a *stiff*; in Irish usage a *comm*; and in Polish, a *gryps*. When Bronisław Pluciński, a socialist worker, spotted a familiar face nearby in Pawiak Prison in 1902, he sent a laboriously composed *gryps* in simple Polish, revealing—naively, as the note was intercepted—the tricks and uses of prison communication.

> Dear comrade! I wanted to write to you but I didn't know if you read Polish, and anyway now it is so hard to send notes. It used to be that one could send notes and books and food, but now they watch . . . . My name is Bronisław Pluciński. Bookbinder. I know you from somewhere, were you at the demonstration? I got nothing here, no money already 10 weeks and I have nothing to read . . . . I'm terribly bored. If you have books here give me them and I will give you mine, but since it is hard to send them, well I have a thick rope, so in the evening when it is dark I will throw it at your window, and you grab it, so I can send you books . . . .
> Goodbye.
> Destroy this note because they search here.[8]

The most severely isolated prisoners could only leave hasty, desperate graffiti for their successors, with no hope of receiving a reply. For prisoners who at least had comrades behind a thick cell wall, there were two common codes one could use to knock out a message: Morse code (dashes indicated by louder knocks or by two knocks close together) and the 5x5 system, in which letters corresponded to numbers on a grid coordinates (A=1,1, etc.). Neither of these would be obvious to a newcomer. Józef Kłosowicz found a guide to Morse code on the underside of his chair; Zygmunt Heryng knocked randomly on the wall to show he didn't know the code and soon received a *gryps* with the 5x5 system.[9] Prison languages, like other languages, not only unite isolated prisoners, but also separate the experienced from the neophytes. Walery Sławek thus failed to communicate with a newcomer in the Citadel in 1917:

> Someone started knocking in the prison alphabet on the ceiling above us. Medard Downarowicz and I, old hands in the art of spending time in prison, quieted our colleagues and started an attempt to communicate . . . with this person. Knocking without sense or order. Downarowicz was furious that someone so clueless could be in prison,

not knowing even the most primitive principles of communication. Meanwhile the knocking—or rather the rapping with a bootheel— continued. Whatever, foolishness not worth paying attention to until whoever it is gets wise.[10]

The newcomer's boots sent a message that he did not belong to the community in the Citadel, whatever contributions he may have made outside.

Other technologies came to the prisoners' rescue. The cell toilet or plumbing, for example, if there was one: prisoners could scoop out the water and speak into the bowl, or tap on the pipes. A toilet down the corridor becomes a post office, with messages stuck in chinks in the wall or underneath the fixtures. Here, the need for privacy ironically overlaps with emotional and social needs, and the unpleasant, unavoidable sharing of the sights, sounds, and smells of others is compensated for by the promise of social intimacy. Naturally, guards attempted to control access to the toilet, placing it under surveillance or limiting access to an impossible few minutes or seconds.[11] The prisoner's body too is a vehicle for contraband information. Written messages hidden in the mouth, the anus, the genitals, and the lining of clothing force guards into heightened vigilance.[12]

As Pluciński knew, messages and larger packages could also pass overhead. For example, IRA prisoners created the Ho Chi Minh Trail, an intricate system of pulleys and wires to reach comrades in more isolated parts of Long Kesh prison. This communication required not only that the prison authorities turn a blind eye but also that rival factions over whose territory the goods passed be placated. Wires from cell to cell in some Stalinist-era prisons in Poland were "horses." Other prisoners developed elaborate systems of strings to deliver flints and tobacco from cell to cell.[13]

Prison communication seems impersonal, with commercial exchange and letters in code sent to an unseen partner. Yet it could also be intimate, as prisoners could recognize each others' knocking styles. When a guard at the keyhole or in the corridor made conversation impossible, then for a greeting or simply to wish good night, "we just scraped the wall lightly with a fingernail. Seemingly nothing, but how much was contained in that movement, how much love for another person."[14] Jerzy Śmiechowski and Wiesława Pajdak met in adjacent cells in Mokotów Prison in late 1947; caught knocking, they were moved to opposite cells, where they adapted the Morse Code to light, blocking gaps in the doorframe in dots and dashes. Thus they carried on a courtship until they were married in prison in 1953.[15] When Marek Kulczyk finally moved from that same prison almost thirty years later, he wondered if he and his comrades were heading to Siberia. But more important was that he could finally see the faces of Solidarity comrades whom he knew only "from conversations conducted

Fig. 6.1 Communication techniques in prison, drawn by Mirosław Andrzejewski, a Solidarity detainee in Poland in 1982–83. Courtesy of the artist and of Princeton University Press. Thanks also to Marek M. Kaminski.

through the window or the pipes." "You could tell at once," he recalled, "that we were blood brothers."[16]

Codes and conversations comprehensible to prisoners could of course be understood by guards. The IRA men in Long Kesh used Irish not just to ground their cause in national culture but to keep plans from the "screws," yet many of these guards claimed to have acquired a working knowledge of "Jailic," as they derisively called it.[17] More than one Robben Island guard learned some Xhosa for the same reason.[18] Communists imprisoned in Katowice invented a new code, apparently to signal to supporters outside but presumably for use between cells or in the exercise yard, too. An index finger by the eye was the letter A, right hand grasping the chin meant B, and so on. The police and prison authorities certainly learned the system, though, as a *gryps* explaining it ended up in their hands.[19] Marian Metelski and his fiancee, Walburga Urszula Prange, used a more intimate, personal sign language to reach across the courtyard in Pawiak in 1940. But again, it is striking how much had to be committed to paper. "The window in which you saw me," wrote Metelski,

> is in the latrine, and my cell looks out on 24 Dzielna Street, as I wrote before . . . . If you have received my *gryps*, then as you approach stroke your hair and I will do the same. If you have sent one, stroke your chin. If you are in danger (God forbid) put your hands to your eyes. Never wave your hand, it's enough that you smile and nod your head slightly. If you've had an interrogation, grab your wrist. If I am going to the doctor I will let you know by wrapping a kerchief around my hand. A hand by the ear signals sleep, meaning tomorrow.[20]

The simple coded gesture subverted the watchful Polish prison. How could a guard interpret or forbid the gentle scrape of a fingernail or hands clapped to one's eyes? These codes retained their ambiguity, too. When Władysław Śliwiński received his sentence in 1951, he signaled the news to his also-imprisoned wife Myra as she passed near his cell. But the sign he made that day, a circle traced in the air, signified a life sentence. He in fact had learned he would be executed, but offered false news as a comfort instead.[21] Andrzej Sołdrowski recorded a remarkable exchange of information in a silent exercise yard:

> At the command "about face" the circle reverses direction. One of the prisoners places his right hand on his chest and bows his head. Another prisoner on the other side of the circle sees this. At the next "about face" this second prisoner makes a negligible sign of the cross and whispers "*ego te absolvo.*" At the moment of turning their eyes meet; the first one bows his head lower in reflection, while a guard pulls the second one from the ranks and stands him face to the wall.

Father Tomasz Rostworowski had just heard confession and would be punished for not revealing his partner in this ritual. So much and so little has transpired: a litany of sins unspoken but acknowledged and forgiven, as well as a simple acknowledgement of shared beliefs.[22] Not dissimilar is this exchange recorded by Jan Weremowicz in a prison corridor in 1905. Coming around a corner, he met Stanisław Okrzeja, whom he knew only by sight; both men were under heavy escort. Okrzeja called out "Long live socialism!"; Weremowicz responded in kind. To the guards, this was simple insubordination, but to Weremowicz and Okrzeja it conveyed much more than a common greeting.[23]

With tunnels in the walls, signs at the window, whispers in the exercise yard, and shouts in the plumbing, even the most isolated prison seems a veritable hive of interactivity. Still, without the ties of the movement or of shared identity, communication could seem pointless. Stanisława Sowińska bitterly confided to her diary in 1949 or 1950 that while she knew the prison alphabet well from pre-war experience, "Then things were different. Then I 'conversed' with comrades who, like me, considered it an honor to be imprisoned for the cause. And now? . . . With whom exactly would I be trying to make contact? With the enemy? So what, that they are my neighbors behind bars. They are first of all the enemy." It did not seem to her possible that other Communist Party comrades could have met the same fate, until one day she recognized the shouts of a party comrade in the next cell.[24] Communication—even an anguished cry or a curse at a guard—was not only an end in itself but also a means to re-create the ties of the cause within prison.

The running of the prison always requires some prisoners to circulate freely, and these go-betweens play a crucial role in prisoner communities. Aleksander Ringman convinced the chief in the Warsaw Citadel to give him the job of making and delivering tea to the hundred or so prisoners in 1907. He spent all day tending the fire at two huge samovars and could move freely about the fort, talking with every inmate and befriending the soldiers who made the rounds with him. He brought no particular message along with the tea but clearly felt that he did much to lessen prisoners' isolation.[25] Similarly, a university education got Canzibe Ngxiki assigned to the Robben Island library, distributing books to his comrades. When in March 1966 the prisoners' Disciplinary Committee decided on a hunger strike, Ngxiki spread the word on his afternoon rounds. The next morning no one took breakfast, and guards fingered Ngxiki as the culprit. Yet the web continued to work: the prisoner delivering food to Ngxiki's punishment cell also brought a message from Mandela, demanding information. The wing housing Mandela and other leaders had not struck because Ngxiki had no access to those cells. The next day they too joined the strike and Ngxiki lost his library job.[26]

An enterprising prisoner could collect tiny pieces of visual and aural information to build a comprehensive picture of the prison and its community. Father Rostworowski claims that in 1952 there were 120 priests in Wronki Prison, but even decades later such figures remained well hidden in the archives, and church networks could not yield such data. Rather, months and years of patient knocking, of whispers in the yard and corridors, of stories shared in each new cell, and of guards' indiscreet comments or interrogators' boasts gradually yielded data, and a three-dimensional portrait of a community of priests emerged.[27]

As improbable as was communication in the Stalinist dungeon or in the "Robben Island Hell-Hole," no prison environment was less conducive to community than the Nazi prison. Relatively few prisoners even survived Pawiak; perhaps 90 percent died there or in the camps to which they were sent. Moreover, Pawiak was the destination for most Poles suspected of underground activity, so the Gestapo kept a close eye on everyone within its walls. And yet the prisoners built astoundingly complex networks, using at least three separate though related nodes. One of these was the "black laundry," staffed by women prisoners, to which male prisoners brought their underwear to exchange for clean sets. They had often tucked *grypsy* into the seams; laundry staff removed the messages and sent them on to their destination inside or (sometimes) outside the prison. The laundry was as much under surveillance as anywhere in Pawiak, so the women distracted their German minders by playing on expectations of Eastern exoticism. One offered palm-reading, another told fortunes with a deck of cards, while others flirted with the guards.[28]

Another node, surprisingly enough, was the clerk's office, where new prisoners were processed and records were kept. For over four years the clerk was a Polish prisoner, Leon Wanat, a teacher who knew German. A new arrestee would first encounter Wanat, who would endeavor to convey solidarity with a tiny gesture or whispered word. He then passed word to the cells about the new arrival—for example, whether the registry indicated that he or she was an informer. He could alter the registry, which for the Gestapo and prison administration decided everything. A criminal prisoner given a coveted task in the kitchen could be demoted in favor of a political. "All kinds of run-ins with such criminal prisoners were not uncommon; we tried to get rid of them, sending them back to their cells and putting in their place someone more appropriate and reliable—someone through whom one could get things done." Thus, when a hated *Volksdeutsch* was given a job in the clerk's office, Wanat had him quickly demoted.[29]

Wanat used his position to track incarcerations and interrogations, sometimes alerting the underground outside about imminent transports to Auschwitz and Ravensbrück. In one case, he learned that two prisoners were to confront one another during interrogation. Duly warned, they pretended not to recognize each other and thus prevented their cases from implicating others. When anonymous denunciations came to the prison, Wanat destroyed them.[30] With the help of the third node, the doctors, nurses, and dentists of the prison hospital, he could even arrange to remove a valuable prisoner from transport to a camp. As Wanat puts it laconically, most prisoners "did not realize that there existed in Pawiak an organized, close-knit group, chosen with care, who communicated with one another and attended to all matters through trusted individuals."[31]

The hospital—which at first had just thirty beds, increased to over 100 in late 1940—became an object of desire for every prisoner. "We pined for the chance to go there even for a week, to rest for a little," recalls Wanat.[32] To survive, one needed a break from torture and the Gestapo's watchful eye, in a decent bed in a room with good ventilation, and to eat regular meals and talk with a staff much friendlier than the prison guards. Even the mere existence of a hospital, with a surgery, an X-ray machine, and a dentist's office, offered prisoners a signal that they had a chance to survive. Though the hospital presumably served the prison's goals by keeping valuable prisoners alive, it was also a security risk, giving a select few prisoners a means of escape. Stanisław Miedza-Tomaszewski, a painter who gathered photographic evidence of Nazi crimes, was captured in 1941 and taken to Pawiak. His underground work merited an effort to free him, and so a *gryps* from the underground opposition told him he could expect help, without offering any details. Next Wanat told Miedza-Tomaszewski he needed to visit the dentist, who deliberately infected him with typhus. This got him a coveted bed in the hospital, where he lay in fear that the patient in the next bed was eavesdropping on his fevered mumbling, probably for the Gestapo. Eventually, Miedza-Tomaszewski was transferred to a hospital outside the prison from which—with the help of faked appendicitis and a borrowed corpse—he was able to escape.[33] Józef Suliński escaped in the same way—though it took special lice harvested from a dead typhus victim to properly infect him.[34] Roman Kizny-Gaczyński slipped out through a barred window after the prison dentist helped him contact friends outside; one of the prison doctors cleaned up any clues to his escape.[35]

The Gestapo knew that messages passed through the hospital and that some prisoners had escaped. The prison hospital must only have reinforced their suspicion of the Poles. Meanwhile, Polish doctors could play on Nazi beliefs about disease-ridden Poles, delaying an entire Auschwitz transport simply by declaring prisoners "unfit for transport." Prison guards referred to the hospital staff as the *Spital-bande* (the hospital gang) or the *politische Clique*.[36] It is therefore remarkable that the hospital was maintained—though no doubt executing all the staff and prisoners would not only damage information-gathering efforts but also leave prison administrators and Gestapo agents without a job in relatively cushy Warsaw and make them available to be sent to the Russian front. The Gestapo had no interest in prisoners' health; in fact, recovering prisoners were often summoned directly from the hospital for execution or for deportation to a camp. But to control Polish resistance and render prisoners immobile and illegible, the

Nazis were dependent on local assistance. Since Pawiak was in foreign territory for the Germans, go-betweens like Wanat and the hospital staff were essential. Their work underscores that though a total institution, the prison contains hundreds of people constantly moving about and performing tasks under human, and thus fallible, supervision.

From the POW Camp to the Political

Among political prisoners, social networks do not just meet basic human needs but can also reinforce political communities and re-create movements inside the prison. They can in this way sustain the movement outside as well. "Each *gryps*," writes Regina Domańska about Pawiak, "strengthened the solidarity of both communities—that in prison and that in freedom." Analyzing these documents, she notes that while early ones contained mainly news about family, later messages focused more and more on the "cause"—in this case, of Polish freedom.[37]

The prison community does not form automatically. In the first half century of the phenomenon of political prisoners—roughly 1865–1915—links among prisoners were on the whole weaker and more temporary than later connections. Often, they were built upon ostensibly nonpolitical forms, perhaps chosen without any intent to expand into political activity. The prayer meetings staged by Fenian brothers in Portland Prison in the 1860s, for example, may have been feisty but not long-lasting. Perhaps exasperated by similar antics, British authorities in the Cape Provinces responded testily to Boer prisoner and Calvinist minister P. J. Perold's request to hold "divine service" in Tokai Prison in 1901. Assistant Resident Magistrate Orpen allowed him to minister to individuals but warned him that "he was distinctly to understand that he was not to endeavour to establish a position of authority for himself among the prisoners."[38] Perold expanded his ministry to prayer meetings anyway; these, complained a fellow prisoner who turned state's evidence, had become political meetings, in which Perold and others offered prayers for the Boers against the "barbarous enemy." Whether Perold was merely guiding the faithful, "counsel[ing] them to obedience and submission," as he claimed, or inciting the boisterous cheers that sometimes accompanied prayer, administrators and prisoners alike recognized that any gathering offered a way to reconstitute the struggle.[39]

Almost until World War I, the prison building or fortress was the only state institution holding political prisoners, and forms of prisoner organization reflected this mode of confinement. In moments of revolution, such as in Poland in the years 1905–07, the political prisons became chaotic opposition centers, barely controlled by state authorities. They were not yet schools for opposition but freewheeling havens of freedom under lock and key.[40] To understand how political prisons became organized, we must consider the history of the prisoner of war camp and its offspring, the concentration camp. The POW camp predates other carceral institutions; at least since the Napoleonic era, states have needed to find some place to put captured enemy combatants. Quick release might only strengthen the ranks of the enemy anew, while mass execution invited retribution against one's own soldiers in enemy hands. Relatively small numbers of captives could be exchanged or paroled, released in such a way that they might not return to fighting. A POW camp, in turn, makes sense only in the age of mass, trained armies. Beginning in roughly the 1890s, regimes introduced a new carceral institution for their opponents: the concentration camp. The concentration camp emerged as a way both to sequester captured combatants and to pacify the population that sustained the enemy.[41] Like the POW camp, concentration camps held many "prisoners of politics," people who had not themselves engaged in political behavior but were interned as the result of political decisions. Camps of either type are thus not necessarily a site of politics, yet they play a key role in the history of political incarceration.

As an ad hoc institution for large populations, a camp (whether for soldiers or civilians) cannot be run like a prison. The sheer size of camps, which might consist of dozens of buildings or temporary shelters dispersed amid parade grounds or work sites, necessitates that inmates organize themselves. Captured military officers, no less than their counterpart captors, need to create order in the place they inhabit and to rebuild social hierarchies and communities among the interned masses. They have some leeway in doing so, for unlike in a prison, the administration typically leaves the distribution of food, the maintenance of hygiene, and the management of minor personal conflicts and grievances to the interned, taking advantage of the extant hierarchy among them. They may or may not formally delegate such tasks to men with recognized authority among the interned, but class affinities lead camp commanders to favor those whom they could recognize as their peers, trusting in soldierly values of honor and hierarchy to relieve the captor of an inconvenient burden.[42] Of course, following the orders of their officers, soldiers might stage a revolt or a mass escape; this risk, endemic to POW camps, helps explain why some regimes eventually decided upon a much stricter system.[43]

Until World War I, concentration camps generally arose out of insurrectionary, colonial struggles, in which administrators representing the empire confined soldiers and civilians of another nation. They therefore were a space in which national politics, or at least a national consciousness, might be cultivated among the officers of a defeated army or among educated civilians. They not only began to incubate politics, just as prisons do, but also provided an environment in which new forms of prisoner organization and hierarchy developed. Among the inhabitants of these camps were men who would lead their armies and governments in subsequent decades, as well as many who would return to prison under subsequent regimes. The Great War intensified and accelerated innovations in incarceration as well as in warfare.[44] The heightened prison organization of the interwar years in Poland and Ireland in particular originated in the camps of World War I.

This transformation in the prisons occurred rapidly. In February 1919, Senior Warden Bunting of Reading Prison took the unusual step of writing a complaint, with the backing of the prison governor. He, and his fellow guards who contributed similar letters, had never seen such collective insubordination, even though he had guarded senior Sinn Féin men after the Easter Rising. "I had a good deal to do with the previous batch who were here in 1916 and though there were double the number at that time, there is no comparison regarding the difference between the two parties, the former were on the whole decent and reasonable men to deal with, whereas the present lot 16 in number are most unreasonable and selfish and do all that is possible to give trouble." They made constant demands and sought to provoke guards to say or do anything that might warrant a complaint; meanwhile, they contrived to gum up the workings of the prison, making the guards, for all practical purposes, their servants.[45] These were more or less men of the same background and political outlook as in 1916, but an intervening incarceration had changed their approach to prison.

World War I was the first major war after the Geneva and Hague conventions had clarified international standards on the treatment of captives. The stalemate of the Western Front yielded millions of captured soldiers, for which the major powers were unprepared. The belligerent states quickly abandoned the Hague Convention's system of prisoner parole, choosing instead to hold on to the enemy soldiers they captured.[46] Britain transported thousands of Germans to camps across the English Channel, unwittingly creating spaces for a new type of prisoner. The disused Frongoch whisky distillery near the Welsh village of Cwm Celyn housed several hundred German POWs in the spring of 1916. When the Easter Rising in Dublin seemed to pose a serious threat closer to home, the British authorities simply evacuated the Germans and replaced them with nearly 2,000 captured Irish fighters. These men may not have been the first political internees in a camp, but the rapid transformation of Frongoch is nevertheless a landmark in the history of political incarceration.[47]

Though the situation was novel, in 1916 both the British captors and their Irish charges had models upon which they could draw. In the Boer War, the British shipped some 25,000 captured soldiers to POW camps overseas; locally, they also interned soldiers' families and tens of thousands of other rural residents. Besides the soldiers and the unfortunate "prisoners of politics," the British also held men whom they suspected of treasonous activity largely because of their prominent position in Boer society.[48] In the Great War, these practices of control became commonplace: the internment of German-born civilians in Britain, and of British POWs and civilians on the Continent, were widely publicized. For their part, the rebels of 1916 included some who had fought in the Boer War alongside many who were recent volunteers or even mere bystanders to the Rising. The internment helped the rebels to feel they were still fighting a war. As if to reinforce the connection, the rebels' first days in Frongoch were shared with a few remaining German POWs. The British may have given little thought to what effect internment would have on the rebels, other than cooling their ardor in dreary isolation.

Categories that have since acquired stronger legal connotations here became confused. Clear policy was absent, and mid-level officers simply reached for a recognized term that fit the circumstances. Some, such as Frongoch Commandant Colonel Heygate-Lambert, for a few weeks referred to their Irish charges as "Prisoners of War" and allowed the men to send letters home in envelopes marked "Prisoner of War—no stamp required."[49] Other officials denied any such appellation, and the privilege of free letters was revoked in early July. By treating the men as POWs in all but name, they gave the Irish rebels the opportunity to build a new form of political imprisonment in a military setting.

The Frongoch captives immediately organized a General Council of fifty-four members, which then elected officers and an executive committee, a structure more extensive than among their predecessors in the Irish cause. Although most of the men had taken part in the Uprising, they opted at the outset for civilian forms of decision making, while creating a parallel command structure,

Fig. 6.2 Republican prisoners arrive at Frongoch Camp, 1916. Courtesy of Gwynedd Archives Service, Caernarfon, Wales.

naming a commandant, captains, and lieutenants. The effort to separate civilian and military duties may have reflected an uncertainty about their status as political prisoners or prisoners of war. The case for being called a POW, writes W. J. Brennan-Whitmore, a member of the civilian leadership, was weak as long as the civilian council advocated on their behalf. He and others among the senior IRA officers instead called for a system in which each dormitory and camp would choose officers. As Brennan-Whitmore put it, "No civil institution, however excellent and desirable its constitution might be, could enforce the disciplinary and other measures necessary for the proper and efficient control of the camp . . . . Not many days passed until it was patent to the most obtuse that the 'Civil Government' could not maintain the necessary discipline."

The Irish prisoners were searching for a solution to the most basic problem that political incarceration poses to a movement: how to maintain cohesion and identity with a cause. A small, tightly knit secretive group with a strong ideology might have less trouble facing this challenge, but a mass internment of men from all over Ireland and from varied political and social backgrounds might as easily undermine the struggle for independence as strengthen it. In the aftermath of a failed uprising, prisoner organization was crucial to maintaining the allegiance of a fresh generation of volunteers. Military leadership addressed an organizational problem even as it promised the comfort of familiar military forms. "We decided," writes Brennan-Whitmore—allying himself with the noncivilian solution—"to accept responsibility for the control of the Camp."[50]

Some prisoners—perhaps influenced by Gandhi's *satyagraha* movement—advocated passive resistance instead. Refusing to maintain order and discipline would require the British to deploy more manpower and resources and might incline them quickly toward prisoner release. The internment order had specified that men could appeal their detention to a special advisory committee within seven days. For the General Council, the appropriate tactical response was clear: all prisoners should lodge appeals so as to gum up the bureaucracy; if they were successful in gaining release, the struggle outside could be resumed more quickly. Those whom Brennan-Whitmore calls "the military chiefs of the prisoners" articulated a more aggressive politics of the prison: internment would be used to train prisoners for the struggle after eventual release. Thus the military staff opposed the appeals as "cringing and slavish," and injurious to the cause. The men were needed in prison, where they could deepen their collective bond and their commitment to the revolutionary struggle.[51]

The difference in tactics illuminates the progress of prisoner politics toward more collective forms. The appeal process was by definition individual, as each man would use his own cunning, resources, and life story to win his own freedom. The military leaders, though, conceived of the prisoners as engaged in a common struggle for Irish freedom. Hierarchy, organization, and sacrifice for

the collective good were hardly new in political movements, but the conditions of World War I made them applicable in prison, too. While the Gandhian
approach to prison served well in some circumstances, the environment of
Frongoch yielded a fused military-political organization.

The subversive genius of this organization was that it appeared to also serve
the interests of the prison authorities. Each morning, after the British guards
unlocked the dormitories, the Irish were in control. It "became the duty of the
[prisoners'] Staff Officers and Company Commanders in each dormitory to
see that all men quitted bed and got ready for the morning inspection. By 6.10
a.m. we had the men drawn up in columns of fours in the inner yard, with our
Camp Commandant at the head and the Adjutant and Aide-de-Camp on the
flank."[52] This saved the British a lot of work, but the point of this discipline was
to demonstrate that only the imprisoned Irish officers could maintain order.
Brennan-Whitmore records an instance when a prisoner began coughing during
the morning count. The British officer counting yelled for the coughing to stop,
whereupon "every prisoner in the yard was seized with a violent fit of coughing.
For the best part of ten minutes pandemonium reigned supreme," until the officer gave up and stalked off, "shaking his fist at us." In similar fashion, Sinn Féin
badges confiscated during inspection multiplied on prisoner lapels at the next
inspection.[53]

Work generated similar opportunities to build collective discipline and to
express resistance. When prisoners refused to empty the guards' latrines, they
were banished to a distant part of the camp. Prisoner leaders then chose men to
be delegated each day to report for and refuse to carry out this duty. In this way,
they took control over placement of men in the camp, ensuring that the British
could not thus disaggregate community. Indeed, military forms of incarceration
provoked responses that were at their heart political, as they advanced the cause
for which the interned had been fighting. The interned men sharpened morale
and discipline, making protest more effective while protecting the individual
prisoner from divisive or discouraging punishment.

The Irish case was not unique among the camps of World War I.[54] Poles
fought in the Russian, Austrian, and German armies, and ended up in the
POW camps of nearly all the belligerents, sometimes in significant numbers.[55]
The key moment in the Polish struggle for independence came in July 1917,
when German General Hans Hartwig von Beseler, commander of German-
occupied Poland, decreed that the Polish Legion should swear an oath of allegiance to an unnamed future Polish king while pledging to fight alongside the
German and Austrian armies. Most soldiers and officers of the Legion's First
Brigade refused, and suddenly the military campaign acquired a clear political cast. The Legion's commander, Józef Piłsudski, was interned in Magdeburg
Fortress, a lonely captivity that cleansed him of any hint of collaboration with

Germany and allowed him to return in 1918 as the de facto leader of interwar Poland.[56]

The German authorities disarmed the Polish Legion's rank and file and interned them at Szczypiorno, a camp outside the city of Kalisz; officers were sent to another camp hundreds of kilometers away. Having first allowed the Poles to build a hierarchical military structure, the Germans attempted to dismantle that hierarchy, fundamentally misunderstanding how nationalism worked. The internees of Szczypiorno were expected to return to their pre-legionnaire state as ordinary imperial subjects, but Polish nationalism had developed much too far for that. The British had faced the same problem: they attempted to weaken the community at Frongoch by removing the more aggressive leaders to a different prison, yet the Frongoch community flourished despite their efforts.

As a POW camp, Szczypiorno made the same demands upon the authorities as any other such camp would have. The internees needed to organize their living space themselves; for example, two legionnaire doctors operated a sick bay, staffed by interned soldiers. However, one of those doctors, Jan Kołłątaj-Szrednicki, was in fact a captain of the 4th Infantry Regiment, who had "voluntarily exchanged his captain's insignia for a simple soldier's shirt," wrote eighteen-year-old legionnaire Ludwik Dudziński in his diary, "to bring us comfort, to keep our spirits up and to share our fate."[57] More than a dozen other officers also changed their names and discarded their insignia to stay with the troops in Szczypiorno. Over the summer, as the Germans endeavored to convince soldiers to take the oath, they worked even harder to uncover these hidden officers.[58] Dudziński delights in their mostly fruitless efforts to pick out the real officers from among "so many intelligent, roguishly smiling guys. At least half the NCOs look good enough for an officer's uniform, but could just as easily be a genuine corporal or sergeant."[59] Eventually the Germans tried segregating even the NCOs from the rank and file, in the hope that the men would descend into anarchy and offer to the world proof of the "revolutionary subversive tendencies of the Piłsudski gang."[60]

Soldiers and officers alike recognized that hierarchy and order were as crucial to this political struggle as they had been to the military campaign. For imprisoned men and women in previous campaigns, such as the Polish socialists imprisoned by Russia during the Revolution of 1905, a certain amount of disorder sufficed and might even benefit the prisoners. In the much larger camps of the Great War, the prisoners' order triumphed. Thus, for example, on October 14, 1917, the soldiers of Szczypiorno observed the 100th anniversary of the death of General Tadeusz Kościuszko, whose uprising of peasant soldiers against the Russian Army in 1794 symbolized the struggle against a powerful foreign occupation. At precisely 9:30 in the morning, barrack leaders read out a special address to the men in their daily orders. The men then marched outside to an altar to hear a full Mass with choir. In the afternoon there were speeches, poetry, and more. Commented Dudziński: "It's a lie to say that the bubble burst long ago and that Legionnaires have no guts."[61]

Guts alone could not create such drilled pageantry. Such ceremony, an expression of the political cause in military form, was possible thanks to the camp's Soldiers' Council, whose leader—typically a twenty-something NCO, chosen camp commander with the tacit approval of the camp authorities—wore a white and red band on his arm. The actions of the council, and even of the membership, emerge only indirectly in the sources.[62] Its leaders quickly attracted the suspicion of the Germans and were arrested and deported to other camps. But for soldiers like Dudziński, real authority rested with those senior officers in disguise who presumably could not join the council for fear of unmasking themselves. The figure of Second Lieutenant Leon Koc, for example, surfaces again and again at the margins of camp memoirs, never taking an active role but respected for the sacrifice and risk he took by staying with the soldiers. Dr. Kołłątaj-Szrednicki commanded authority through his work in the sick bay. This diversification of authority, uncharacteristic of the military, indicates how far the POW camp at Szczypiorno had altered to become a camp of political prisoners.

When the German authorities decided in November 1917 that all inmates must wear a number affixed to their clothing instead of soldiers' insignia, they aimed clearly to demilitarize their captives. Michał Brzęk-Osiński, twenty-five years old and newly chosen camp commanding officer by his fellow internees,

Fig. 6.3 Szczypiorno, 1917. Polish prisoners assembled to have numbers sewn on their uniforms. Courtesy of Muzeum Wojska Polskiego, Warsaw.

recognized that he could not counter this move with military authority alone. As he recalled the scene late in life, his barrack stood in formation in the yard, facing armed German infantry across barbed wire, while some twenty Russian prisoners waited, needle and thread in hand, for the order to sew on the numbers.

> As commandant, I stood first on the right flank; they would have to begin with me. It was a truly dramatic moment. The responsibility crashed onto my shoulders: what does one do in this situation? I decided to take the risk that the Germans would not open fire. So when the prisoner approached, I didn't object and, with my left hand on my hip I watched with feigned interest as he began to sew the number on the right sleeve of my uniform. All the cavalry and gunners watched me and followed my example, allowing their numbers to be sewn on.
>
> Thus, to the evident triumph of [Lt. Col. Baron von Oeynhausen], the whole operation went off without the expected disruptions. But at the moment his adjutant reported that the operation had been completed, I launched my plan.
>
> "Does everyone have their numbers sewn on?" I boomed. "Well, then it is possible to rip them off!" And with one tug I ripped mine off and threw it on the ground. My statement was not a command, because I used an impersonal construction—"it is possible"—but the cavalry did the same, as if on an expected command.[63]

Brzęk-Osiński was sent into isolation. His successor as prisoners' commanding officer called a hunger strike; it ended in four days without having won concessions but succeeded in publicizing the legionnaires' struggle beyond the camp fences.[64]

"The Prison Has Become a Political Battlefield"

What legacy could these new, hybrid POW camps like Szczypiorno and Frongoch leave for the next generation of political prisoners? In both societies, political prisoners had already figured prominently in the public imagination for several decades. There were obvious continuities between the earlier struggles and these camps: Jeremiah O'Donovan Rossa's funeral, which included a procession through the streets of Dublin, preceded the Easter Rising by just a few months, for example. In Poland, Józef Piłsudski was only the most prominent of many once-imprisoned socialists who served proudly in the Polish Legion. During the war, both Frongoch and Szczypiorno, isolated as they were by distance and by wartime censorship, nevertheless remained in the public eye.

Already in a July 1916 speech to the British House of Commons, Tim Healy, Irish nationalist and Member of Parliament for Cork Northeast, needled the British home secretary for giving new life to the political cause of Irish freedom:

> There was no Sinn Fein organisation. He has created it. He has started a Sinn Fein academy, a Sinn Fein university at Frongoch in Wales, where he has brought together some 2,000 . . . men, guilty and innocent, and instead of these men being left at home in their little farms and cottages, scattered and dispersed as they were from one end of Ireland to another, he has congregated them together . . . and has enabled them to exchange ideas. I regard the right hon. gentleman the Home Secretary as the father of the Sinn Fein movement.[65]

Szczypiorno was no less the focus of attention. On December 9, 1917, students demonstrated in the streets of Warsaw, demanding the release of the Szczypiorno internees. Both in Kalisz and in Łomża, where most of the men were moved in mid-December, local citizens formed assistance committees, sending food and other necessities. The best-known song of the Polish Legion, "We, the First Brigade," was composed on a train to Szczypiorno and first sung in the camp.[66] The ways of Szczypiorno reached future political prisoners through popular culture and the press. Few if any prisoners of the 1920s and 1930s would have been earlier POWs; men of the First Brigade were unlikely to become communists, for example. Yet the struggle at Szczypiorno was widely celebrated. Józef Piłsudski often referred to the camp in his speeches as a model of organization and perseverance.[67] While there is no record of communists or other regime opponents specifically studying the lessons of Szczypiorno, they would have been unlikely to miss them. A number of prominent communists, including Marian Buczek, arguably the most famous of all communist prisoners of the interwar years, had fought in Piłsudski's Legions.[68]

For Polish prisoners in World War II, prison's transformative potential remained rooted in its military likeness. One has to envy the mental prowess of young Eugeniusz Widlicki, who smuggled a note to his family from Pawiak Prison in January 1942: "I told myself that I am not in prison, but in army barracks . . . . During gymnastics I imagined that we are soldiers exercising, when we were marching it seemed to me this was parade practice, and when we were ordered to do burpees in the mud I thought of it as ordinary military exercises, not prison ones. Generally I have tried to find something military in everything," he concluded, "and thanks to this I feel like I have just received an officer's rank."[69] Prison offered Widlicki the opportunity to connect with a military tradition that was inseparable from the politics of national resistance.

Memory of incarceration, however, becomes brittle without movement continuity, unless it becomes enshrined in popular tradition. Thus the prisoners of the Boer War left little trace in national carceral tradition. The concentration camps for civilians are a focal point of Afrikaaner culture; the POW camps, which the British established for their captives in far-off Ceylon, India, Bermuda, and St. Helena, faded from history quickly. The prison campaign of Gandhi's *satyagrahis* have had much greater impact—but in India, where Gandhi relocated in 1915. Until at least World War II, there would be no comparable prisoner communities. That war did, however, leave a similar legacy. A reporter for the *Johannesburg Star* noticed this in the detentions that followed the Sharpesville Massacre in 1960. The detainees "did the same sort of things and 'organized' themselves in much the same way," reported the *Johannesburg Star*, as did those interned in camps in World War II. "Discipline among themselves was strict. There was no unilateral action. Each group of detainees operated as a unit and punishment, if any, offered to any one member of the unit would be demanded for all."[70] Just a few years later, Baruch Hirson reported the same kind of order prevailing among white political prisoners in Pretoria Local Prison: "Despite sharp differences, we all agreed to accept the directions of a secret three-man committee which was re-elected every three months to consider policies when confronted by the police and the prison admin and to pool all items of news, which were redistributed through specified contacts. The committee continued to function through most of my time in prison and its decisions were rarely challenged. It was this body that decided what demands could be made of the authorities, which issues should be pursued or dropped and, in individual cases, what courses of action should be followed."[71] Thus, even before such structures became famous on Robben Island they had emerged in a variety of contexts elsewhere in the country.

One recognized antecedent, for white prisoners at least, would have been the camps for pro-German Afrikaaner nationalists established in World War II. Beginning in 1942, the South African government interned thousands of activists of the Ossewabrandwag (Oxwagon Sentinel) and its paramilitary wing the Stormjaers. The camps engendered a rich cultural, educational, and organizational life; many of the inmates would later be the jailers of the anti-apartheid opposition.[72] But their experience was well known to the South African opposition. In 1973, Nelson Mandela was allowed to meet with Chief George Mzivubu Matanzima of Transkei, as the authorities evidently hoped he could induce Mandela to soften his position. Mandela took the opportunity to compare the situation of political prisoners like him to that of Robey Liebbrandt, a Nazi convicted of conspiring to overthrow the South African government in 1943.[73]

The road from Frongoch is lit more clearly. Many of the Frongoch captives returned to prison over the next seven years, during the War of Independence and then the Civil War. Several were among those causing so much difficulty at Reading in 1919. Renowned hunger striker Terence MacSwiney was among the early leaders in Frongoch. Another was Patrick Moran, who famously declined a chance at a jailbreak from Kilmainham Jail in February 1921. During the Civil War, Frongoch prisoners could be found on both sides of the conflict. Among supporters of the Anglo-Irish Treaty, Michael Collins, chairman of the Provisional Government, and Minister of Defense Richard Mulcahy had both been in Frongoch, as had Paudeen O'Keeffe, deputy governor of Mountjoy Prison. On the other side were inmates of half a dozen internment camps, including James Ryan, Collins's hut mate in Frongoch; Thomas Malone (who was also imprisoned in 1917 and in 1920–21), and Séamus Fitzgerald.

The constant presence of the camps in published memoirs and commemorations helped to transmit patterns of camp organization. Szczypiorno became "a symbol of the Legionnaires' steadfastness and will to persevere, and of their martyrdom," while Frongoch became a cornerstone of modern Irish mythology, both as a place of suffering and as the "university" that gave birth to the IRA.[74] Both camps exemplify the centrality of political internment in the national-heroic pantheon, but the way they transformed the practices of political incarceration merits equal attention. The politico-military order that the belligerent powers shared with their captives transformed the loose pre-war forms of collective behavior into highly organized political communities in the prisons and camps of interwar Poland and Ireland. These forms fit perfectly in an age in which both states and oppositions espoused uncompromising ideologies.

Six years of war in Ireland so ingrained the Frongoch model into the prison that future prison generations did not trouble to distinguish the categories "prisoner of war" and "political prisoner."[75] During the War of Independence, in prisons across the United Kingdom and Ireland, Irish internees tested whether organizational forms suited to barracks and parade grounds would also work in prison corridors. In 1920 in London's Wormwood Scrubs, a prison that received seventy Irish leaders, the British authorities were unprepared for the tightly organized protests that ensued once Joseph McGrath, a veteran of British prisons, arrived. He mobilized prisoners to make frequent demands and to resist punishment for violating regulations. Tellingly, the prison governor complained that such men were not suited for prison and ought to be interned in an army camp.[76] At Pentonville Prison in 1921, prison authorities facilitated prisoner hierarchy simply by arranging for the few dozen Irish politicals to go to confession each Saturday. Locked in chapel for an hour, the prisoners had the opportunity to consult with their commanding officer, Tom Hales (whose brother had been in Frongoch). Over the autumn of 1921, Hales gradually convinced his comrades to join in a clothing protest, in which the men threw off their prison jackets.[77] In these cases and others like them, the regime attempted to impose upon politicals the familiar discipline of a state institution. Instead, Irish prisoners who knew about the freedom and the organizational potential of the camp found they could transform the prison in the same ways.[78]

The organization of Irish prisoners reached its full extent during the Civil War. Unlike their British counterparts, Irish prison authorities like Paudeen O'Keeffe could not be surprised by what the prisoners were capable of, having themselves participated in the same kinds of parades and protests. They allowed for open cells and relatively lax supervision, and may have expected the good-natured disorder of the pre-war prison. Instead, civil war internees militarized. In Mountjoy Prison in January 1923, for example, Frank Gallagher became frustrated with attendance at Mass. As commanding officer, he summoned his fellow prisoners to a special parade—a "Church Parade," the prisoners' newspaper called it. "Volunteers must remember," he told them,

> that they have a duty to God as well as to their country and if they endure their present sufferings gladly for love of country they should submit to some inconvenience for love of God. Tomorrow all volunteers will parade for Mass under their company officers who will report absentees. Callers have been appointed and will call all men half-an-hour before Mass begins.

The next day, fewer than half a dozen skipped Mass.[79]

That same week in Mountjoy, women prisoners called for new elections to the prisoner council, as one member had "defie[d] majority rule." "We summon prisoners to meeting," council member Lily O'Brennan jotted in her pocket diary. "Propose concerted action + a fresh C[ouncil] election . . . . Question put to each member does she wish a prisoners C[ouncil] or act on her own. 31 for—12 against." Under the council's direction, the women began a violent, coordinated campaign of cell destruction, smashing crockery and furniture and throwing it into the corridor and prying the locks from the doors.[80]

When prisoners at Newbridge Barracks insulted a guard in November 1922, the military governor cracked down on letter-writing privileges. J. J. Layng responded on behalf of the prisoners in disarming detail: "The [prisoners'] Camp Council had ordered every prisoner to desist from hurling remarks at the guard, officers and privates, either inside or outside the Compound . . . . We assure you such offenders if found and proved guilty will be suitably punished for a breach of the disciplinary rules laid down by us." Nine days later, Layng reported that a prisoner-run court martial had tried a man for this offense and found him guilty. Yet he hastened to put the governor in his place: "The Camp Council has complete control of management and discipline within the Camp."[81] The prisoners' commanding officer also asserted the authority of prisoner organization, claiming in stilted tones his right to post notices:

These notices were issued by me to facilitate the smooth running of the camp, and to make relations between you and me more harmonious and systematic. When issuing these notices, I considered them as essential to the health and orderliness of the camp. I am still of the same opinion. If, however, you take exception to these notices, you are at liberty to take them down, but I, as responsible for the well-being of the men in camp, cannot as a thing which I consider would be detrimental to such.[82]

In each case, prisoner cohesion and organization speak to the military experience most of these prisoners, male and female, would have had, and to their greater capacity for order. The prisoners acted as if they governed the camp, issuing orders and posting rules in the name of "health and orderliness." As for the regime, the bumbling, sometimes hesitant prison officers disappeared. No longer did concepts of honor and class fog the regime's evaluation of its prisoners. The concomitant arbitrary cruelty of imperial control gave way to a tighter control rooted in state security and ideology.

The Irish regime was determined to keep its prisoners, former comrades, under close surveillance, but also to win their submission. During the war, the British captors had felt more ambivalence. They went to great trouble and expense to haul Frongoch inmates to London to induce them to renounce their role in the Easter Rising. Yet they wanted principally to be rid of the prisoners and released most of them back to Ireland as soon as possible, in fact before the end of 1916. The Free State's imperatives were quite different and mandated keeping a more watchful eye on its prisoners. Paudeen O'Keeffe was only the most dramatic example, using his knowledge of prisoner habits to keep a tight hold on Mountjoy Prison. Far above him was Richard Mulcahy, who had been a military lieutenant among the Frongoch internees, then became chief of staff in the IRA during the War of Independence, and then minister of defense in the Free State.

The Polish transformation was no less dramatic. The Russian Empire's confused and erratic punishment regime was gone. The Germans had been both cruel and yielding; like the British, they placed high value on getting prisoners to pledge loyalty, yet at the same time sought to find some common ground with their former allies. After the war came a government no less nationalist than the Irish one, and ferociously anti-communist as well. Here, too, the prisoners of the early interwar years were the countrymen of those in power, and they opposed the new state's very existence. One early minister of justice, Bronisław Sobolewski, had made his name as a member of the Political Defenders' Circle, taking on cases in political trials during the 1905–07 revolution.[83]

In early 1922, Minister Sobolewski received an impassioned memo from his former colleague in the Defenders' Circle, Stefania Sempołowska. She reminded him that he bore moral and legal responsibility for the thousands of political prisoners in independent Poland, and teased him about the sheer impossibility of controlling prisoners' communication. She noted that the first state prosecutor, Jerzy Skokowski, a colleague of Sobolewski's from the 1905 era, had honored the traditions of political incarceration, including the right to choose delegates to negotiate with prison authorities and the right to a separate section in the prison both for living and exercise. Skokowski, wrote Sempołowska, had also "dramatically, in a formal announcement, ordered metal blinds to be removed from Pawiak cell windows," having called them "'a barbarian cruelty that shall not remain in a Polish prison.'" Sobolewski's efforts to crack down on the prisoners was doomed to failure, Sempołowska continued. Placing politicals in individual cells had not broken their community, as recent coordinated hunger strikes attested. If the purpose of shielded windows was to prevent prisoners from communicating, they had failed. Sempołowska explained that no one could throw a *gryps* from a cell to the street outside the prison unless one used a rubber band—in which case the metal blinds were ineffective. In any case, she added, "I personally know of more than twenty *grypsy* from [Pawiak] during the last hunger strike."[84]

As in Ireland, the prisoners were already too well organized and prepared for prison authorities, even as the latter, at first sympathetic to former comrades in the struggle against empire, turned against them with unprecedented severity. An element of hyperbole runs through accounts like these of interwar prisons, so punishment may have in fact been lighter than claimed in both countries. Still, punishment at the hands of those who knew incarceration left a bitter taste. As Sempołowska concluded: "The prison has become a political battlefield." This veteran of thirty years of prisoner advocacy did not say prison was still a battlefield, but that the new regime had made it one. Sempołowska—who almost certainly would have been involved in assisting legionnaire prisoners in 1917—knew that her erstwhile comrade would also understand how things had changed since they had fought the Russian Empire together.

The *Komuna*

The prisoners of interwar Poland produced the most sophisticated and sustained form of prisoner organization to date and it remained unsurpassed in its intricacy and ambition for decades. The commune can be found in pre-war prisons as well, though it was then really just a loose expression of prisoner solidarity. Gustaw Daniłowski recalls that while all politicals in a czarist prison belonged to the *komuna*, it mainly served to share food donated from outside (mostly from Sempołowska's prisoner assistance operation) among those who had no food from home.[85] Despite its name, the *komuna* was not Marxist; in some prisons like that in Łomża, it was divided along class lines, separating the better-off intellectuals from workers.[86] Still in its infancy, the prison community lacked the ideological backbone and organizational structure that would be essential to survival in the interwar prison. Nor was it necessary, as long as prisons freely permitted food parcels and books to be sent in from outside.

At best, the prewar *komuna* helped the administration keep the prison operating smoothly. Guards and administrators learned to use its leader, the *starosta*, to quell disturbances and to handle the goods sent in from the outside. Ludwik Śledziński reports that from time to time the guard would come and let him out into the corridor so he could deal with some problem—a minor complaint, or an ill prisoner—in another cell. In exchange, he could bring prisoner concerns to the prison chief.[87] In independent Poland, the *komuna* developed much more advanced structures and no longer assisted in the management of the prison. It was structured to distribute foods and power fairly, attending to physical survival and to political principles. The Prison Committee in Białystok, elected from among 170 prisoners dispersed around the prison in January 1927, developed five separate *komuny* to manage food; a chart distributed in the prison listed the number of prisoners in each, the amount of food received weekly, and a per-prisoner estimate. The committee asked the better-off groups to send food to those with smaller allotments.[88]

Communists outside prison endeavored to create a unified system via a set of instructions for political prisoners, issued in November 1933 by Red Help. The *komuna*, stated point 1 of 39, serves to "defend one's interests, to make positive use of the time spent involuntarily within prison walls, and to assist one another both materially and ideologically." While membership was voluntary, the instructions advised that the most effective means to achieve this goal is the "unanimous action of all comrade political prisoners, members of the collective, in accordance with the guidelines and tasks set by the collective's current leadership."[89]

The language of international communism is striking, and indeed, Communist Party discipline bound prisoners who were members. At the same time, prison posed serious obstacles to party leadership and party solidarity. The document acknowledged this, leaving open the means by which prisoners would choose their leaders, as it would "depend upon technical conditions" (point 5). Similarly, *komuna* leaders were to be chosen for six-month terms, but longer if conditions necessitated this (point 7). Prisoners generally lived in individual cells, meeting only during exercise walks; thus, the regulations proposed that each "walk" also elect a troika to oversee each "exercise collective" (point 10). The regulations recommended only that the elections be conducted by an ad hoc group of "the most serious comrades, most experienced in revolution," which would collect nominations and also make its own (point 13).

Perhaps those "most experienced" prisoners recalled with some nostalgia the more informal organization in the prisons of the Russian Empire. Once upon a time, there were hampers of food from relatives or concerned citizens; the cell doors stayed open all day; a guard would look the other way or even carry messages himself. The prison experience of the 1930s in other ways required greater discipline and party accountability. The exercise troika, explained the regulations, should report to its constituents monthly about the distribution of goods and more generally on its activity at the end of its three-month term. Control of goods, as envisioned by the instructions, would have seemed fantastical to comrades of the previous era: "No comrade who is a member of the collective may make any independent purchase or request for any kind of food, books, newspapers, medicines or other goods anywhere without the knowledge and permission of the chief of the collective's troika" (point 18). Each member of the collective had to inform the troika of any money received, so that it could be used for the benefit of all. Organization penetrated even below the level of the exercise collective: "In order to conduct work during exercise in a rational way," reads point 21, "all comrades shall be divided into groups of 5–6, which will choose a secretary whose task is to convene and to lead [the group], and sometimes to announce resolutions of the collective's troika."

This document (which was probably never followed strictly) is as much a record of fear as of solidarity. So many things could break the collective—new repressive measures, a recalcitrant or informing comrade, an intercepted message. The collective identity that emerged as an attribute of political prisoners in the late nineteenth century became a vital component of the politics of incarceration. The range of self-imposed punishments as well as the system of courts, arbitration, and appeals enshrined in the document blend those of a military unit and those of a communist self-criticism session. Possible sanctions (point 34) ranged from private reprimand through expulsion from the collective and even to severing all contact with a boycotted individual. The "most experienced comrades" in the 1930s prison knew all the ways in which the repressive efforts of a hostile administration, ideological disputes both within and beyond the prison, or mere status differences could divide prisoners and make the experience both miserable and deleterious to movement unity. A military-style political structure helped prisoners to control the mass politics of the prison.

The *komuna*, indeed, accomplished two tasks. First, it provided a reliable way for politicals to manage conflict among themselves. The degree to which this could be achieved depended upon the authority of prisoner leadership. When a comrade named Bohun quit the Białystok Prison *komuna* sometime in

1927 or 1928, he felt compelled to explain to his comrades (see figure 4.1, p. 94; the paper on which he wrote is marked by a row of holes, suggesting it was sewn into the hem of clothing to be sent out for laundering) why he left. His complaint reveals just how important prisoner structures had become as reflections of leftist politics, as well as their economic significance. "I am forced," he wrote, "to shed some light on my actions, what specifically caused me to break with the distributionary-communal hypocrisy practiced by *komuna* members and by the P[rison] C[ommittee]." Bohun's reasoning is complicated and confusing, including a careful tallying of packages received from home and evidence that some of his cellmates were well-to-do peasants. He called for new elections and for the creation of a new department to manage goods. The solution, in other words, was not to leave everyone to his or her own devices but to add more committees in the hopes that the collective could better manage itself. Indeed, Bohun clearly recognized that leaving the *komuna* was a drastic step that placed him at some risk.[90]

Even as it might fail to distribute food to everyone's satisfaction, the *komuna* remained the structure through which the boundaries of the political community were worked out. "Life in the *komuna*," reads one *gryps* from Kielce, "is the fundamental principle for the political prisoner . . . . He who departs from this principle becomes a traitor." Another ex-member of the Białystok *komuna* found out how serious these words were:

> Dear comrades! Wasylij Sawczyński has voluntarily quit the *komuna* . . . cutting off all contact with his comrades. Sawcz[yński's] actions and behavior do not accord with the political prisoner ethos and such behavior can not be tolerated under any circumstances . . . . Wasyl[ij] Sawczyński is suspended from all rights of membership in the prison org[anization] and may not be accepted into the *komuna* until the matter is resolved. Sawcz[yński] is on the list of those 16 comrades in cell 7 belonging to the *komuna*. Sawcz[yński] must be crossed off that list . . . . We are sending this letter on the Sawczyński matter to the senior prisoner in cell 7 to be read aloud in the cell.[91]

Whatever Comrade Sawczyński's problems were, the prisoners' leadership treated this as a collective concern. His actions threatened the very ethos of prison life, and so he was publicly punished by exclusion.

The seriousness with which these documents treat membership in the *komuna* reflects a changing understanding of the prison experience. Sawczyński or Bohun may have felt that the laborious politics of the *komuna*—the careful division of meager rations, the elaborate voting rules, and the maintenance of arbitrary schedules—were not worth the trouble. But the *komuna* had in a way

become the purpose of imprisonment. In prison, one could work through practices that were important to the political movement as a whole, but that might
be more inconvenient outside. When voting, prisoners had the leisurely opportunity to discuss and evaluate candidates, to learn techniques of vote counting,
and to consider and debate whether comrades of different political perspectives
could be won over.[92] Food distribution might not have reminded every comrade
of the principles of socialism, but it still necessitated intimate cooperation.

Above all, the *komuna* taught communication and demarcated the boundaries of political incarceration. Whether it was a plea for justice or extensive
instructions from leaders, the medium was the message. To be a political prisoner in interwar Poland meant to send and receive communiqués, missives,
notes, and letters from one's comrades. In May 1927, one "Bim-Bom" wrote to
assure his comrade "Karol" that they had both been politically correct when they
sang the "Internationale" on May 1. On that day, a parade of railroad workers had
marched by the prison singing. "When the opposition in Cell 16 heard this, they
spontaneously began shouting 'Long Live Mayday!' and sang the Internationale
and other songs. Other cells joined 16 and the singing spread . . . . Number 16
did well, capturing our thoughts and feelings . . . . That is to their credit, and so
you were not breaking the rules."[93] Bim-Bom's *gryps* illuminates many commu-
nicative circles. The story began with a message from outside prison, as railway
workers sang to be heard by imprisoned comrades. Immediately some prisoners
responded, presumably so their marching comrades could hear. They also communicated to neighboring cells this way, summoning a moment of community
in the prison wing but inadvertently running afoul of some political directive
which labeled the men in Cell 16 heretics. Or perhaps Cell 16 held prisoners of a
different political stripe, so joining them was heretical. This necessitated a more
direct communication to debate the politics of comradeship. Offering Karol an
answer, Bim-Bom admits the excluded group into the community on his own
terms. Of all these communications, the *gryps* might have been the most important—and yet it wound up intercepted by the prison administration.

The signposts of political community could change rapidly. In 1927–28 the
Polish Communist Party was entering a phase in which other leftist parties
would be as much the enemy as were the fascists. Instructions from the Red
Help Central Committee put the *komuna* in the hands of party troikas who were
to ensure that *komuna* leadership "met the demands of the time" and emphasized politics over economics. Such maintenance of ideological purity clearly
underlay some of the communications in Białystok Prison.[94] But by the mid-
1930s politics had shifted again. Red Help instructed that the *komuna* should
welcome all non-fascists, regardless of party. Dissenters should not be excluded,
and "one should convince comrades of alternative views and not pin on them
labels like 'anti-Bolshevik' or 'counterrevolutionary.' "[95]

The *komuna* of interwar Poland, like the structures in Civil War Ireland, took shape in difficult circumstances. Many officials in both regimes knew that prison experience or work with prisoners could be steps on the road to political power. From the perspective of their captives, though, the prisons offered less freedom than had those of the preceding imperial regimes. At the same time, the ideological terrain was more hazardous.

The Russian Revolution, on the one hand, and the toxic atmosphere of small-state nationalism, on the other, together produced oppositional groups sufficiently revolutionary to land their members in prison. The Polish *komuna*—and the entire prison organization, from the cell elder to the prison committee—was integral to oppositional politics. And yet the *komuna* differed from underground political units as it advanced the social cohesion and the well-being of its members as much as it advanced the party line. It thus mirrored the development of post-POW organizational forms in the Irish prison. There too a highly disciplined structure outside the prison helped to shape the organization of incarcerated men and women. There too hierarchy and order within the prison served to maintain the prisoners' general sense of mission in the face of an occasionally vindictive regime. "Mission"—the political cause, but also the defense of the human bonds and social structures that formed in prison—was inseparable from the daily life of prison.[96]

Over the several decades after World War I, two innovations took root in the contest between states and their political opponents. States increasingly turned to camps as a means to contain larger numbers of opponents. Camps like Frongoch or Szczypiorno would seem quaint compared to the Polish camp at Bereza Kartuska in the late 1930s, which in turn was tiny in relation to the vast camps of the Soviet Gulag or the Nazi system. Camps offered greater capacity and potential for social engineering, in exchange for a measure of autonomy for the residents. While camps often hold political prisoners, their most frequent residents are ordinary civilians interned during wartime or other exceptional periods. To associate camps with openness seems cruel, yet inmates moving from prison to a camp often experienced a tiny sense of liberation. Alexander Solzhenitsyn makes this point in discussing the Gulag, for example; as in czarist Russia, Siberia promised an exchange of the damp cell and ever-vigilant guard for relative unaccountability, albeit in a brutal environment bereft of familiar society.[97]

States do not create concentration camps to give prisoners greater freedom; most camps were in any case large and complex institutions that usually contained prison-like zones of confinement.[98] To say that "Auschwitz was not a prison" is not to say that it was better or worse, but only to say that it was different in the possibility for some to move about with somewhat less restraint than in a prison. Nor have camps been the exclusive domain of the harshest ideological regimes. Robben Island Prison certainly had camp-like features, as prisoners gained increasing ability to move around its territory and organize aspects of their lives. Within any hut or barrack, prisoners enjoyed less privacy from one another, but endured less scrutiny from without. No one guard could monitor hundreds of men scattered across a large, semi-furnished space the way that he could survey a cell. For the same reason, authorities managing the former spaces had to cede some level of cell organization and even control to the prisoners themselves; this enabled prisoners to refashion their political lives.

Despite its connotations, the camp has continued to be used by a variety of regimes—including the United States, at Guantanamo Bay. When in the early years of the Troubles the British prison authorities found themselves overwhelmed by detainees, their solution was to erect Quonset hut compounds at a former Royal Air Force base at Long Kesh, outside Belfast. The Long Kesh camp, which opened in September 1971, was quite unlike other places of incarceration in Northern Ireland. The separate huts, each with its own yard, evoked a military training camp, inviting prisoners to segregate themselves and to construct their own hierarchies. This was hardly the British intention; within a few years, work began on imposing prison buildings with the evocative name "Her Majesty's Prison Maze," after a nearby village; the shape of the buildings gave them the informal name "the H-Blocks." This transformation of the camp into a prison coincided with the termination of the Special Category (essentially equivalent to political prisoner status) for new prisoners. The camp turned out to be a privilege, as those already incarcerated retained this status and remained in the huts. The construction of the cell blocks, housing fewer people per square meter than the huts, could not keep up with the oversupply of prisoners, and thus the Long Kesh camp survived for several more years.

Prisoners' organizational forms in camps and prisons were in part the product of experience and memory, adapted to test the limits of particular prison environments. The structures that Leon Wanat managed in the Nazi prison look very different from those before the war, but it is likely that some prisoners at least knew of both. The "bourgeois" prisoners whom Stanisława Sowińska scorned would develop other forms of sociability, but their communist captors made a real *komuna* impossible until the 1980s. In South Africa, political prisoners as a group disappeared with Gandhi's departure for India in 1915. It took enormous effort on Robben Island to produce anew elaborate forms of prison organization (to be discussed in Chapter 9). There, as in Long Kesh and the H-Blocks, prison organization in the last third of the twentieth century would produce forms of control and protest beyond the ability of the regime to contain them.

"I Was Confusing the Prison"

The Contest in the Cell

Sixty years after Marx and Engels exhorted the proletariat to cast aside their chains, a group of Polish socialists in Łomża Prison in 1908, awaiting transport to Siberia, found an opportunity to do just that. They had figured out how to loosen their manacles and slip them off when the guards were not looking by slightly flattening the circular bracelets with a stone. In the Russian system, prisoners were ordinarily kept chained only for a certain period at the beginning of their imprisonment. When one of the prisoners reached this time and the prison head refused to remove his manacles lest he escape, "we pulled off quite a ruckus," recalled Jan Kwapiński. "At an agreed-upon day and hour, we all on cue threw our manacles through the cell windows."[1] The rain of metal crashing into the prison yard surely brought some consequences, yet the prisoners had neatly upended the very idea that they were imprisoned. The regime still held them but could not be certain of its instruments of incarceration. The public nature of the act confounded their guards, as prisoners had not unchained themselves to plot an escape; instead, they had revealed just how little their guards knew of them.

"Resistance" is a poor term to describe actions like this one. The men were no closer to freedom, after all. Destroying an instrument of their captivity, they did not resist prison. The prisoners in Łomża instead signaled their control over the chains that held them as well as their ability to act in unpredictable ways regardless of the consequences. Thus, this chapter considers prisoners' actions as efforts to control information, their political relationships, and their bodies and selves. Political incarceration is by its nature full of ambiguity, embodying the contradictions between what the regime says it is and what it does. Regimes insist that they hold only criminals or terrorists; prisoners' actions, however, question the nature of crime and incarceration. The regime may assume their political inmates to be incorrigible and unchanging, but then it is forced to see politics in every action. For prisoners, the situation is much clearer. By acting collectively, they harness the ambiguities of prison to equalize, slightly, the prisoner-regime relationship. As prisoners endeavor to assert such control, they deny to the regimes their ability to recognize and predict what prisoners will do; in this way, prisoners take control over their incarceration.

Knowledge in the Prison

From arrival to departure the political's sojourn in prison is defined by conflicts over information that amount to more than mere surveillance of a captive. Prisoners are often quite aware of regulations and laws and seek to use them to their advantage; they also endeavor to form communities with their own rules. Knowledge of the rules conveyed mastery of the place even when those rules were fictional. Regina Mikulska sardonically recalls her first days in solitary in Mokotów Prison in 1949: "a bare, iron bed, and on the wall hangs the rules and prisoners' rights. I grabbed this, enchanted by print and began to read; it felt like I was carrying on a conversation. I read this document several times a day while I was there, until I knew it by heart. When I was brought to a normal cell I recited to my cellmates the rights they enjoyed, thus bringing a little humor."[2] Prisoners were unlikely to invoke these rules successfully, but knowledge that such a document existed bolstered their understanding of their situation.

This struggle to retrieve and preserve information is two-sided, as the regime requires prisoners' participation. Even when the rules are illusory and the categories arbitrary, they are made real when the prisoners acknowledge them. The Gestapo needed Polish prisoner-clerk Leon Wanat to run Pawiak Prison; most regimes make use of prisoner organizations not only to maintain order but to help manage information—through morning roll-call, for example. This participation in the management of information allowed prisoners to protect each other. One day Wanat encountered Zofia Kossak-Szczucka, leader of the underground Council to Aid Jews, unexpectedly returning from Auschwitz in 1944—and, catching a worried look on her face, realized she had forgotten the false identity that had kept her alive. He quickly grabbed the prison ledger he maintained and read that information aloud before the German guards could question her.[3] The Irish rebels held at Frongoch in 1916 went to great lengths to remain anonymous, even at the morning count in the presence of British officers. They neither answered to their names nor represented themselves individually to the authorities except through their officers. The consequences of protecting identity were as great as for Kossak-Szczucka, for by refusing to be treated as British citizens they avoided conscription into the army and dispatch to the Western Front.[4]

Even the expectation that inmates would want to know their fate gave them a tiny advantage. Sighle Humphreys refused to look at the trial papers she was handed, citing in her journal "my principles." While she did eventually peek at them, she nonetheless felt a small victory.[5] The individual prisoner face to face with the regime, and either needing information or required to supply it, knew this quandary well, though the rules of behavior always shifted. To speak at trial meant upholding the honor of one's movement, perhaps at the cost of a more severe sentence; to speak in interrogation might save one's life, but perhaps at the cost of one's honor. It might be better not to acknowledge any concession from the regime. Shortly after Stalin's death, a slight thaw touched Polish prisons. The prison head at Inowrocław visited all the cells to ask women whom they would like as a cellmate. Irena "The Mouse" Cieślińska-Skrzypiec calculated that this was a trap and answered that she preferred to remain alone. "I knew that if I say whom I'd like the result will actually be the opposite."[6]

Prison regimes of all kinds need prisoners' cooperation to understand relations inside and outside prison and to distinguish the threatening from the trivial. A security officer once asked Hugh Lewin to interpret a letter Lewin had received. It was nothing more than a friendly, chatty letter from a female acquaintance, but the officer saw "passages he couldn't understand. They seemed to mean other things." Lewin cooperated lest his acquaintance's mention of air travel be understood as code for a planned hijacking.[7] A more dangerous letter arrived for Eliza Lamert-Mianowska in Pawiak Prison: a list entitled "Courier Equipment" that she had left in the pocket of a bathrobe which came in a package from home. As a guard began to shout that illegal correspondence had been found, a Polish prisoner working in the mailroom grabbed the note, announced it was a list of items contained in the package and ripped it up.[8] It is remarkable she was believed. Their total lack of power and privacy, with jail snitches, spyholes, and interrogations ranged against them, still left prisoners with much that was out of the regime's sight, whether personal information like that Lewin provided about his correspondent, or the cultural knowledge required to reframe Lamert-Mianowska's note.

The urge to control, protect, and disseminate information becomes particularly stark when the regime chooses to execute its prisoners. Execution is an opportunity for a regime to demonstrate its resolve and might, so it is remarkable how often prison regimes carefully guard information about carrying out death sentences. The Irish Free State exhibited some ambivalence about executions; while it needed to show that it was clearly in charge, prisoners were former comrades and often widely respected men. Thus, some executions were ordered or carried out in secrecy.[9] The Nazis saw an opportunity to manipulate knowledge by letting it be known that certain prisoners had been executed when they had not; other prisoners then felt free to speak about them under interrogation.[10] Executions in the Stalinist era were not announced—and yet prisoners recall knowing when they would occur. They watched through spyholes or cracks in the window shades as victims were led away; aware that what they saw would not reach the outside world, they scrupulously gathered data on time of death and place of burial.[11] Czarist prisons were little different in this regard, though Feliks Kon was glad that he and his comrades did not realize they could view executions from their windows. "They did everything," he writes, "so that we could see. Unsuspecting of the possibility of such bestial taunting, we were spared the sight."[12] Kon's ambivalence about something later prisoners regarded as a duty stems from awareness that the regime wanted him to watch.

Making what was hidden legible or refusing to acknowledge the regime's version, prisoners sought to control information. As in the case of the Stalinist executions, they might gather and assimilate information even if only for themselves, if there was no hope of conveying it outside. The story of a newspaper composed by white political prisoners in Pretoria Central in 1967 illustrates how writing makes community. Whereas some such newspapers were quickly smuggled outside as proof that the movement was alive and well, this was less possible for the tiny political community in Pretoria Central. *The Gleek* was really a diary of the year, refashioning the monotony of incarceration into something to recall with pleasure and "reaffirming that, in reality, there had been some 'events,' some changes even whereby we could measure our spoonfuls of life." The text, Hugh Lewin admitted, "was essentially frivolous and inexplicable to anyone not privy to our arcane intimacies." The most interesting thing about *The Gleek*, though, was its fate: the complete edition was passed around to be read by all—and then ripped up and thrown in the chamber pots.[13] The gathered knowledge of their communal experience disappeared beyond the reach of the prison.

Perhaps nothing these men and women possessed would be guarded as carefully as their political relations with one another. The regime would assume that easily legible political connections like participation in a demonstration or membership in a party obscured more conspiratorial ties. Setting aside the fevered imaginations of interrogators and prosecutors, a political is assumed always to be linked with like-minded others both outside and inside the prison. Informers thus often begin their acquaintance with cellmates with a mention of mutual acquaintances outside. Interrogators build their attack on the slightest hint of familiarity. The only correct response is not to recognize one's comrades at all, whether one encountered them in an arranged "confrontation" or in a chance meeting in some prison space.[14]

Having refused the categories that the prison offered them, political prisoners can then choose to assert their own responsibility. Jan Krzesławski, a socialist, recalls the moment when he and his comrades were to be transferred to another Warsaw prison, and he had to sacrifice his claim to innocence in order to assert leadership. "The move took place, of course, amid heightened emotions. I was asked to speak. I agreed, somewhat unwillingly, because I was certain that the

Okhrana [Russian secret police]—to whom I pretended I was the victim of a mistake—would soon know the content of my speech. I spoke forcefully, like a revolutionary, and the prisoners in the hall where we awaited the prison carriages responded with various cheers. The turnkeys remained passive. And then the carriages rolled up."[15] Krzesławski and his comrades reframed an administrative transfer as a stage in the revolution, but at the cost of revealing his political self. The cause, he decided, was worth the price. In a provincial prison a few years earlier, Ludwik Śledziński had no opportunity for speechmaking. One after another, his comrades were tortured, then dragged to his cell to identify him. Śledziński also chose to unmask himself, but did so in a way that laid the regime bare as well: he began banging on his cell door, alerting the whole prison and awakening, so he claimed, the sympathy of criminal prisoners. The head guard threatened to shoot him if he didn't stop, to which Śledziński screamed: "Shoot me, you scoundrel, you bandit, you killer."[16] This galvanizing moment exposed Śledziński, but also demonstrated the limits of the regime's power: he was not shot, and he showed that prisoners can cooperate to protect one another.

Śledziński's outburst recalled, perhaps deliberately, a legendary protest of a generation earlier; Michał Mancewicz, of the *Proletaryat* socialists, avenged an insulted female comrade by striking Lieutenant Fursa, the head of the Warsaw Citadel, in the face. Mancewicz was sent to an isolation cell, where Fursa visited him, still enraged. Waving his broadsword, he yelled "I could have killed you!" "So kill me," retorted Mancewicz, and threw himself on the blade. The general backed away, and Mancewicz lived a long life. The narrator of this tale evoked the "spirit" that, he avers, forged links among prisoners and spread its power "by imperceptible routes" across the country.[17] Challenging the prison to live up to its threats, Mancewicz exposed it, catching his tormenter off guard with a random, apparently spontaneous act of solitary protest. Wiesław Chrzanowski recalls running the notorious gantlet upon arrival at Wronki Prison in 1950. As the guards beat the naked prisoners with truncheons and bunches of keys, an older priest suddenly threw down the bundle of clothes he was clutching and yelled at one guard "Apage Satanas!" [from the exorcism rite, Greek for "Begone, Satan!"]—and the flustered guard helped the priest gather up his things.[18]

The violent confrontations of that revolutionary era find their counterpart decades later in cool ostracism. Prisoners could behave like prisoners and gain an edge in this way. Northern Ireland prison governors, for example, voiced the same complaint over and over at their semi-monthly meetings in the 1970s: their prisons were "quiet—perhaps too quiet!" or even "Unnervingly quiet."[19] Well-organized prisoners, with the help of that "spirit" of the prisons, need not do anything at all to unbalance their jailers. In South Africa, John Nkadimeng described how an encounter with a magistrate in 1963 taught him a new tactic:

He helped me a great deal—he didn't know that—because, you see, I have decided that I'm not going to die anyway, I'm going to resist it, and I'm prepared, if they kill me I must fight before I die . . . . this magistrate insulted me, you know, before he spoke to me he just looked at me and started . . . you know, insulting me in Afrikaans . . . and then I was very furious with him. [He] started telling me that he's a magistrate, he has come to see me—I said: Look here, I think I don't want to waste my time . . . with people like you, what do you want—and he said: "No, I'm a magistrate, I came to see you." I said: "Nonsense, . . . I know magistrates, I don't expect a magistrate to behave like you."[20]

The magistrate retreated in the face of this indifference. Internees of Solidarity used similar tactics. Marek Kulczyk says that after martial law, some guards at Hrubieszów Prison had to be sent to other prisons to be resocialized: they had grown used to following the lead of the internees, who insisted on treating them as state servants. A cell would respond, for example, to the beating of a comrade with a boycott of the offending guard: "We treated them like air. We didn't react when they opened the cell door, we didn't put our dishes out for dinner." These trivial actions forced the administration to remove guards until, Kulczyk claims, they became more compliant.[21]

Though the regimes vary widely, in each case the prisoner gained some control of the prison relationship simply by renaming things: the accidental inmate is really a revolutionary, the guard is an executioner, the magistrate is not a magistrate, a violent guard no longer exists. The customs and rituals of the prison cell invite transgression, and if the regime used those rules to confound prisoners, so too could prisoners violate them to confuse prison order. Jacek Kuroń spent many of his years behind bars, in the 1960s and 1970s, working on a doctorate in sociology; though prison was not his subject, he often treated the cell as a sociological experiment. Once his two-man cell was joined by a third inmate who "looked around and said: 'There's a snitch here, and maybe even two.'" Kuroń quickly replied "Let's agree that there are three."[22] He played here with the paranoia that accompanies political imprisonment and rendered the very idea of an informant absurd by implicating both himself and his accuser.

Kuroń was acutely aware that the prison regime probed constantly for any weakness. A major crisis in the Polish opposition began in prison in the summer of 1968, among students arrested after demonstrations that March; Kuroń, in his mid-thirties, was among the oldest in the group. For about two months, nearly all refused to make any statements in interrogation. Then quite unexpectedly, Kuroń was shown very detailed confessions from a number of the students. A minor slip in a *gryps* to him, in which a prison staffer promised to deliver letters to any prisoner he wanted but used the wrong slang term for cigarettes, led

Kuroń to realize suddenly his comrades had been duped into writing. He leaped to the window and yelled to the courtyard: "It's a provocation, don't get tricked into writing *grypsy*." For this he was packed off to a distant, windowless cell.[23]

Kuroń's call to the courtyard echoes a much more lonely struggle in the Stalinist prisons, in which the cell window provided the only means of saving a prisoner community. In 1946, the secret police arrested Captain Barbara Sadowska, a key figure in the intelligence unit of the underground Home Army. Over the following year, she wrestled with her interrogators over how much information she would share with them. Silence was not an option, for she hoped to protect both comrades already in prison and those not yet arrested by taking more blame on herself. Her relationship with other prisoners was crucial to the interrogations, and her captors deployed a powerful weapon: "someone named Barbara Sadowska (a snitch, set up by the Security Police), who claimed to be me. She conducted conversations through the walls, both by tapping and whispering, and elicited confessions; she also gave out information according to instructions from the Security Police. My comrades were disoriented."[24] The regime tactic to make prison leadership illegible by planting a false version of Sadowska both gained useful information from confused prisoners and, when prisoners became aware of the deception, weakened the bonds of community. To restore her comrades' trust, Sadowska began to sing, which was presumably harder to imitate. When others recognized her, she could then shout out instructions.[25]

Sadowska tried to get her comrades released or at least to spare them the execution she expected for herself. Confessing and assuming all responsibility was not enough, so she began a remarkable series of hunger strikes. The regime responded at first by releasing a few women, but when the regime reneged on later promises, she developed a new tactic: for the first week of her fourth hunger strike, she hid her protest from the authorities: "I wanted to get myself in serious condition before they began force-feeding me," she writes. "I managed this with the help of many cellmates." Though she landed in the hospital and was force fed, several of her comrades were freed. Two years later, in the infamous Fordon Prison, Sadowska discovered that many had been arrested again. She began her last strike, again informing the authorities of her protest only after a week had passed. They sent her to solitary and force fed her; however, after three weeks, she got a visit from the ministry, and then from her father, who informed her that those arrested had been freed.[26]

Though she herself would not be released until 1953, Sadowska's individual protests worked because she countered the regime by putting herself out of its reach. When she tried to accept the charges against her and claim to be the only guilty figure, she failed to help her comrades. In the hunger strikes, the regime discovered it could not know when Barbara Sadowska was on strike or not, or predict when she would stop eating. Becoming at least partially illegible to the Stalinist regime, she gained some control over herself and over her political relationships.

Sadowska and Kuroń faced regimes willing to isolate and manipulate their captives and responded by shifting the realm of available knowledge while also shaping how other prisoners thought about that knowledge. So too in the Irish War of Independence. The British executed sixteen of Éamon de Valera's comrades in 1916; he proved to be a formidable foe behind bars. During his imprisonment, de Valera used British legal bureaucracy against itself. While in Dartmoor Prison, for example, he tossed a small loaf of bread to a hungry comrade. Punished with solitary confinement, he refused to eat and promised to do the same again given the opportunity. He was transferred in shackles to another prison, where he kept up a barrage of protests and petitions. As Seán McConville comments: "A great deal of effective publicity had flowed from the throwing of the 8 oz loaf; a battle of attrition was being waged against the most immediately available representative of British authority; the morale, solidarity and standing of the convicts had all been substantially strengthened: a rebel success."[27] The IRA prisoners of the 1970s and 1980s realized the same thing. "We were getting legal aid," one recalled. "It was a pain in the arse for management in the prisons, it tied up judges and cost them money and sometimes you might get a result." Concluded another: "If you make it hard to impose prison discipline, you make it very hard to run the prison."[28] The results of protest, legal or otherwise, were secondary to the main goal, which was to subvert the prison system, inhibiting control of the prisoners and knowledge about how they might act.

The master of unsettling knowledge and authority was Nelson Mandela. His letters do not demand respect but assume it. Lawyerly in tone, they are neither plaintive nor intemperate; instead, they are written as if prisoners and authorities had the same goal. In a 1970 letter to the commissioner of prisoners, he detailed a number of serious complaints about prison conditions, including assaults by warders. He framed these complaints on the prison's terms: "We have always accepted that firmness of discipline is a necessary instrument for the preservation of law and order in prison, but it is our firm belief that human beings are more likely to be influenced by exemplary conduct on the part of the officials than by brute force, and by mutual respect between officials and prisoners." In this context, detailed charges against various prison staff and careful reference to previous letters acquired greater weight, as did his ominous concluding remark: "I sense rising tensions and growing impatience with the policy of a department which is clearly incompatible with our welfare, and I urge you to act with speed and to take appropriate measures to relieve the situation before matters go out of control."[29] Mandela thus rebalanced prison relations. He, not the administration, possessed knowledge about the situation on Robben Island

and controlled prisoners' exposure to the regime. The regime, not the prisoners, was responsible for disorder in the prison.

Of course, the authorities could have responded by throwing Mandela into solitary confinement or simply ignoring his letters. Mandela gained control by acting as if he had the upper hand, outside ordinary prison categories. He displayed his mastery of the prison in full during a 1973 meeting with a delegation headed by George Matanzima, a member of the puppet government of the Transkei Bantustan whom the apartheid regime hoped would have some influence on Mandela. In the presence of several other ANC prisoners and the prison's commanding officer, Mandela launched into a comparison of conditions on Robben Island with those experienced by South African prisoners in the past. Recalling the lenient regime imposed on the rebels of 1914, for example, he opined that their crimes were more serious: they took up arms though they had parliamentary representation to air their grievances, while the ANC lacked this and so "had all justification to resort to violence."[30] Mandela had admitted as much in his famous trial speech in 1964, but here he compared his actions to those of the regime. He made the commanding officer his mouthpiece, knowing that what he said would be conveyed to Pretoria, where some officials, as Mandela knew, had themselves been political internees in the 1940s.

Refusing the Prison

By taking control of their own emotions, behaviors, and reactions, prisoners rejected the way the regime sought to categorize them and asserted control over relations within the cell and the prison. Mac Maharaj explains how he learned this lesson from Mandela:

> There was a period in prison when I became "ratty." Any provocation by a warder would incite me to backchat. I began to accumulate prison charges for cutting remarks and intemperate language. Mandela called me aside. My reactions, he explained, were correct and we ought to challenge the warders. The warders were at fault and were being provocative. The problem was that an injudicious word by me was picked on by the authorities to charge me. Prison rules and regulations were stacked against the prisoner. Patiently he advised me to change my stance; but instead of erupting spontaneously, I should pause, count to ten, measure my response, and choose my words. That way, he said, the anger would still charge my response, but I would be in control; my anger would not control me. Rather simulate the anger needed to give effect to the response, he counselled.[31]

A code of honor, whether enforced by a prisoner community or by the prisoner's own sense of self, creates a platform on which one can decline to participate in the routines and the rules upon which prison power relations are built. One of the first guides to prison life for politicals, published in Kraków in 1903, instructs future inmates in the virtues of restraint:

> At 6 in the evening the so-called "duty officer" visits all the cells to ask *"pros'bu imiejetie?"* (do you have any requests?). Considering that no request is ever fulfilled, the prisoner who has any self-respect never "asks" for anything, but "compels" them to give him what is legally his. Ludwik Waryński, for example—and many others as well—<u>never once made a "request" to the officers.</u>"[32]

Invoking a legendary prisoner, this pamphlet makes the prison experience a daily performance of honor and self-respect. The code implies respect from the guards as well; this was still a period when prisoners, even those headed for the gallows, might expect their rights to be recognized and enforced by gentlemen. Each refusal was a small reminder of that expectation.

Embedded in a political movement, the individual could resist the regime's categorization in myriad ways: refusing to provide name or prisoner number, obstructing the counting of prisoners, sending letters under the wrong name.[33] Even where the prisoners' identity was in no doubt, the meaning of "prisoner" could still be denied. In most cases, political prisoners objected to prison-issued clothing because it made them indistinguishable from ordinary prisoners. Yet clothing that set them apart was also a sensitive issue. After a few years, Robben Island authorities realized that the mandatory "African" uniform of short pants and sandals was inadequate for propaganda purposes; they requested of Nelson Mandela that since he frequently had contact with official visitors (such as the Red Cross or members of Parliament), he accept more respectable "non-African" clothing. Mandela refused; this was no more his choice than were the humiliating short pants.[34] Halina Wohlfarth would have understood the need to refuse privilege granted by the prison. As she led gymnastics one day in Pawiak Prison, a senior guard took his cap off and placed it on her head. This would have branded her a collaborator, so she threw the cap on the ground and got several days in an isolation cell.[35]

Perhaps the hardest thing to refuse was the visit from one's family, which provided to the prisoner succor and a conduit for communication. IRA prisoners in two Free State prisons in the 1930s refused visits, as an affront to their dignity, when they were required to meet in a large, partitioned room in which private conversation was impossible. Michael O'Leary suddenly announced to his visiting mother, "I am sorry to bring you down [to Curragh prison] Mother—I can't take this visit as they are trying to make criminals of us here."[36] The family visit, as O'Leary understood, required prisoners to perform their assigned role dutifully, dressing in prison-issued clothes and presenting themselves to visitors as inmates, restricted in their speech and actions. O'Leary and his mother turned this visit instead into a performance of dignity, conveying a message that O'Leary, as he was led away, urged his mother to pass on.

The choice of language offered a way for prisoners to confound or evade the regime. Polish prisoners might refuse to speak Russian or German, depending on their captors; South African prisoners used African languages to their benefit, otherwise preferring English (using the guards' Afrikaans strategically); Irish prisoners deployed Irish, though they often underestimated their guards' facility with that language.[37] A cell informer's encounter with Adam Stanowski, a Catholic intellectual in Mokotów in 1951, suggests the many ways a prisoner could use language as a cover and to fashion an image. Stanowski had the habit, his cellmate reported, of standing by the cell door listening to the prison staff—often drawn, in those years, from among Poles born in mining communities in Western Europe—conversing in French. His cellmate wondered if Stanowski knew French. No, Stanowski replied, just English and German. Well, but one could pick it up? Not in this case, came the reply, because they use some kind of slang. But then Stanowski began humming a French song to himself, and several times dropped the phrase "c'est la vie." His minder (who rendered this last phrase "selawi") was frustrated: "One has the impression that he is either pretending not to know French or actually doesn't know it but wants to pose as a mysterious, cryptic individual, not wanting to let on all he knows."[38] More likely Stanowski took his perhaps shallow familiarity with French and made it into an object of desire for his cellmate—and thus, whether Stanowski knew it or not, for his interrogator. Enduring long interrogations (which resulted in a seven-year sentence), Stanowski could at least manipulate how he was perceived, creating the impression that he could not be fully knowable.

One final example of the power of solitary refusal comes from an extreme human experience: the torture of Jacobo Timerman in Argentina. Timerman was sitting blindfolded, hands tied behind his back, soaking wet in the rain, in the courtyard of a clandestine prison. He expected his execution to come soon. Suddenly he was brought inside to a warm kitchen, and the blindfold was removed. "Weapons are everywhere. The men are drinking coffee, and one of them offers me some in a tin cup. He keeps smiling. Tells me to sip it slowly, asks if I want a blanket, invites me to come close to the stove, to eat something." It seemed an end to the pain of the previous months, but Timerman understood it differently, and declined. He refused the offer of a bed and of a female prisoner to sleep with, too. Now the "torturer" became angry. Timerman explains: "In some way he needs to demonstrate to me and to himself his capacity to grant things, to alter my world, my situation. To demonstrate to me that I need things that are inaccessible to me and which only he can provide."[39]

Refusing to cooperate brings Timerman particular satisfaction. He describes here the power relations of any prison: the prisoner is both denied dignity and then offered relief, often with a pretense of magnanimity. The presence of the torturer makes this political, and so too does Timerman's reaction. Timerman's conclusion is that he provokes the torturer's "incomprehension"—a response he can only sense, as he was again blindfolded and returned to his chair in the cold drizzle. Timerman's scope for control was vanishingly narrow. All he could use to confound his captors was an unreachable dignity, and with it he made himself inscrutable, illegible to his torturers.

Mixing It Up

Collective action among political prisoners, in which they assert that prison space is a place of political relations, is no less volatile and confounding than individual actions. As the regime confines them in forced inactivity, prisoners know that any action they undertake is unpredictable and thus increases their control over their lives. "Between the hunger strike and passive submission to the regulatory yoke," declared Red Help in a circular sent to all *komuny* in Poland in August 1932, "there is a whole range of forms which, properly applied, will ensure victory in this campaign."[40] The campaign in question was waged against new repressive prison regulations. Victory would elude the communists until after World War II, but the circular offers a good introduction to the strategy of the *przeplatanka*—literally the "weave," a creative mix of methods and tactics of protest. The strategy had two goals: to keep the prison regime off balance, unable to predict what prisoners might do on any given day; and to ease the impact of any one protest method on the prisoners themselves. The *przeplatanka* also widened the space for other community activities.

The Polish communists did not invent this approach. Both the Fenian prisoners and the early Polish socialists protested or made themselves a nuisance in a variety of ways, often with the apparent goal of causing a diversion.[41] Éamon de Valera figured out, as his biographers put it, that "there were fewer punishments than there were ways of breaking up prison discipline."[42] Marched from cell to cell all over Britain in 1916–17, de Valera aimed to take control of the prison by subverting its order. As a rule confronted him, he would break it and accept the consequences, betting that the regime would tire of inflicting punishment. The actions of Sighle Humphreys and her comrades during the Irish Civil War must have been similarly vexing. While some embarked on a hunger strike, others refused to enter their cells; still others kept a Rosary vigil through the day. The relentless, multifaceted protest, lacking clear purpose, seems to have stymied prison administration. The male prisoners were no less difficult, but the women could play additionally upon the discomfort that their gender imposed upon the men who jailed them.[43]

In much larger numbers, the Polish communists took on the Polish prison system. As in Ireland, the regime that imprisoned them knew the prisons from the inside and was often able to anticipate prisoner actions. Thus on important holidays—such as the anniversary of the Bolshevik Revolution in early November, or May 1—communists would predictably sing songs and pin red ribbons to their jackets during exercise. The administration could decide to allow this harmless ritual or plan to block it. The latter choice could divide the prisoners over whether to boycott exercise in response.[44] As the prison administration showed it could take control of the politicals' agenda, the communists developed new tactics.

Red Help frequently offered prisoner *komuny* instruction on protest methods. A lengthy memo in June 1928, for example, envisioned a nationally coordinated campaign in which prison communities in industrial areas and in the east, where local support was most reliable, would take the lead in opposing changes in prison regulations. In more isolated prisons, like Wronki or Rawicz in western Poland, "the struggle should be conducted at a slower pace," aimed at "disorganizing the order of prison life." Prison communities should "conserve strength and prepare for a long struggle. As we raise the temperature and move toward open protest, we must allow for rest breaks and time to confer on the next action." Each action, Red Help instructed, should be focused on concrete issues, especially "questions of hygiene and basic human relations," and commensurate to the demands. Thus, a hunger strike was not always the best choice.[45] In this holistic approach, prisoners forged and maintained links to comrades outside and in other prisons, while trying to anticipate administration tactics and plan for the long haul. Communist prisoners, highly organized and politically conscious, had recognized the need to control the narrative and the pace of prison protest, yet their plan was essentially defensive, as the needs of the movement outside took precedence. The protests in this period could be quite impressive, but they essentially copied the politics outside.

The crackdown in 1931 isolated prisoners and forced them to think about what prison protest was for. The *przeplatanka* emerged as the basic strategy; the prison community would juggle the protest repertoire to keep the administration guessing. Red Help continued to urge "passive resistance," a middle ground between surrendering to "fascist prison regulations" and a fight to the death.[46] In fall 1933, prisoners in Grudziądz, one of the most notorious prisons of the time, requested advice from Red Help on how to react to a series of repressions they had endured. "We have given serious thought to the situation in your *komuna,*

the new attacks, and the tactics that should be applied in this situation," came
the reply. "We have come to the conclusion that considering the totally exceptional conditions your struggle should not be adapted to fit any general schema."
It was paramount to ensure that the prisoners kept their mental and physical health and that the *komuna* maintained its battle fitness. Red Help offered
innovative suggestions: to resist prison clothing, for example, prisoners could
request a visit from prison officers, whom they would greet "provocatively, in
deshabille (for example, without prisoner jackets)"; they might also throw aside
clothing articles during morning review. In response to other restrictions, Red
Help recommended a "brief *przeplatanka,*" including verbal protests and refusal
to exercise.[47] The key was variety: the administration would not know what the
prisoners would do, while protest itself would no longer be a test of wills that the
prison was all too likely to win. Instead, prisoners regained control of the protest
agenda.

Komuny around Poland adopted similar tactics. Smuggled instructions for a
week of protest in Sandomierz Prison are almost comical in their detail: their
protest would begin on a Thursday, when a "chorus" would demand a visit from
the prosecutor and a main course at lunch. The next day, the prisoner chorus
would call for return of writing materials. Saturday's demand would be for more
butter, as well as a full exercise period. Sunday the prisoners would call for the
prosecutor again, but also refuse to eat the inedible beets at dinner. On Monday,
books and newspapers would be the focus, but during exercise prisoners would
leave the yard after three circuits, shouting "Down with isolation!" The prisoners
planned to escalate their actions if the administration withheld food.[48]

Protest consisting of refusing to eat one's vegetables or marching just three
times around the exercise yard seems pathetic—and yet it apparently brought
results. A prisoner moved to Kielce Prison boasted that although his new prison
comrades mocked his stories of "utopia," the *komuna* had "partly defended dinner's main course" and won a ninety-minute exercise period, common space for
pre- and post-trial prisoners, a complete end to isolation, access to newspapers
and Marxist literature, permission to share food, recognition of the *komuna*
leader, and much more. One might wonder whether the communist revolution
for which these prisoners had sacrificed their freedom amounted to a hot mid-
day meal. But this prisoner recognized that much more was at stake: "This is not
demeaning; prison clothing is demeaning . . . . [W]e keep our political spine
straight." He rejected insinuations that nothing would be achieved. "Is it madness
to demand one's own clothing and a two-hour exercise? . . . Our Communist tactic is to adapt to circumstances, but only as much as our backbone can endure—
and so never to give up for temporary gain. The tradition of prison struggles
enjoins us to put forward [such] demands, though they may temporarily be
unattainable." This, he concluded, separated politicals from ordinary criminal

convicts.[49] Immediate goals, no matter how trivial, mattered less than did the struggle itself. And the struggle was both coordinated and unpredictable.

The apotheosis of the *przeplatanka*, a five-month campaign waged in a Warsaw prison in 1933, came with its own activity-packed appointment calendar. Every day from the beginning of June into November, prisoners would have something to do as they fought against regulations and for their dignity and that of their movement. Daily tasks included

- morning roll call: sitting without reporting
- morning roll call: standing in a crowd by the door
- morning roll call: walking around
- shouting slogans, once or three times/daily
- singing *sotto voce*
- speeches to criminal convicts

Meanwhile, each week brought a longer-term protest action as well, such as these:

- during exercise, randomly switching walking partners and conversing loudly in the stairwell
- blockading the toilet area, singing, then going to and from exercise normally
- boycotting exercise: coming down to the gate and then returning upstairs
- engaging in a hunger strike
- and, finally, "Week of intensified relaxation of prison discipline: a) talking loudly in the corridors; b) blockade of the toilet area; c) banging on cell door; d) getting up late; etc."[50]

Inventive as they are, the actions are mostly small-bore. The prisoners could anticipate that some would elude scrutiny but that collectively they would amount to a campaign that was recognizable yet difficult to stamp out. The "weave" required a high level of organizational discipline and aimed at maintaining internal unity. It gave prisoners something to do that did not necessarily impose high risk. How much punishment could a prisoner incur simply for being disorderly during exercise? The key to the weave's success, among prisoners and against the regime, was variety. Prisoners always had something to do, and the administration was constantly caught off guard, even if, as in this case, it had intercepted prisoner communication.

Some version of the weave can often be found wherever there is a long tradition of incarceration. Caesarina Makhoere was by her own account absolutely indefatigable in her search for new ways to object to certain restrictions in South African prisons and to unite her fellow prisoners. She filed constant complaints about food, clothing, and the cell; refused to parade or work; and even taunted visiting officials.⁵¹ Marek Kulczyk regretted the lack of success in flouting the rules of martial-law internment because different groups of prisoners did not coordinate. His efforts to ignore absurd regulations (such as standing when a guard entered) met with his cellmates' distrust, not solidarity. Still, incessant minor acts of insubordination wore down the rigors of the prison.⁵² The principle is the same as that for movement organizing outside prison: people who have found themselves engaged in a movement, whether they have merely shown up for a demonstration or in fact ended up in prison, need constant activity to keep them engaged.

In any history of prison protest, the actions of the IRA during the Troubles must loom large. Yet each action, including the hunger strikes considered in the next chapter as well as prison destruction, protests over clothing and food, intimidation of guards and other prisoners, and more, should be considered in the context of all the others. IRA prisoner leadership employed a wide and shifting array of protest methods. The sheer range of possible actions, some with the direct involvement of the movement outside prison (such as escapes, or the killing of prison guards at home), endowed any individual act, even the most innocuous, with uncertain portent. A sudden lull in prisoner activity, a boisterous soccer game, a captured communication, or a joke told in Irish might hold a clue to the next prisoner move, or it might not. The prison authorities in Northern Ireland nearly always played defense, or at least talked that way.⁵³ These prisoners, like the Polish communists and many others, kept their opponents guessing.

"It Does Your Heart and Soul Right": Overwhelming the Prison

On October 21, 1958, some 1,000 women marched to the pass office in Sophiatown, Johannesburg, to protest the laws that required them to carry a pass at all times. Over the previous six years, beginning with the Defiance Campaign of 1952–53, thousands of men and women had sent letters, burned their passcards, and demonstrated, and thousands had gone to prison. Influenced by Gandhi's *satyagraha*, they had protested in an orderly manner, hoping to force the apartheid regime to recognize the unjustness of its laws.⁵⁴ The women's campaign of 1958 turned attention to the prisons themselves, as a means of confounding rather than simply embarrassing the state. The police arrested several hundred marchers, sparking further demonstrations. But where demonstrations at prisons in 1952 had called for those detained to be released, these protesters demanded to be arrested. The police refused, implicitly conceding the limited capacity of the state. The next morning, another 250 women crowded into a pass office and refused to register. When the police threatened to arrest them, "the women broke into loud cheering, followed by boisterous singing and dancing until the police vans came. Then they cheerfully assisted the police by opening the doors of the vans." At another pass office that week, "latecomers tried to climb voluntarily into the police vans but were pulled out by the police and told that there had not been enough of them to cause an obstruction." A week later, 600 women in Alexandra followed suit, taking hired buses to the city center, where the police were waiting for them. "Wild cheers greeted the police warning that they might all be arrested, and the women kept up their singing and dancing for the next hour and a half while the police vans loaded up. In high spirits, the women eagerly jumped aboard the vans and trucks as fast as they rolled up, composing new songs on the spot to fit the occasion."[55]

The women of Sophiatown and Alexandra accomplished several things. For one, they irritated the African National Congress, which hurried to pay the women's bail against the latter's wishes.[56] More important, these protests, by focusing on the prison in an unconventional way, exposed the mismatch between the state's laws and its institutions, at least when some resistance was applied: the police and prisons simply could not handle hundreds of protesters eager to flout the law. They reversed the natural order of power: what did an arrest mean if it provoked dancing and singing rather than anger and flight, and if police had to pull protesters out of their vans rather than force them in? The campaign would be echoed a few years later in Nashville, Tennessee, when hundreds of students protesting for civil rights experienced "a sense of jubilation," as participant John Lewis put it. There too arrestees sang songs and were released within six hours.[57] The great gap in power between mostly white police and black protesters made a demonstrative version of Gandhian passive resistance more effective. In Wrocław, Poland in 1987–88, the guerrilla performance art collective Orange Alternative used the same tactics very successfully, provoking arrest for acts like dancing on the streets in elf costumes. Once detained, participants gave candy to or kissed the police, waved merrily from police vans, and then danced and sang children's songs in the jail until exasperated police released them.[58]

Once inside prison, extraordinary collective effort is required to seize the initiative and influence the institution. Individually, upending the prison order is unlikely. One could try disinformation, as communists in Poland appear to have done. In one instance, Herzel Lang, the leader of the Rawicz *komuna*, was heard to claim after his 1936 release that life in Rawicz was pretty good and that communists were treated well there. This necessitated a lengthy rebuttal from the prison head, Andrzej Junczys, who suggested that Lang hoped to "provoke and mislead the authorities, so that they would not send prisoners of that type to Rawicz. Life here for them is really quite wretched." Perhaps so, but Junczys fell for another line himself, passing on information from a cell informer that communist Marian Buczek had boasted of winning the support of guards in his previous prison, Wronki.[59] As charges flew between the two feared prisons, communists had reason to cheer, even if no concrete changes resulted.

Refusing the rules of the prison, such as who could arrest whom and who could decide whether a prison was fearsome, prisoners make up their own rules. To officials at Pretoria Central in 1981, the four women who filed complaints about being held in individual cells were obstreperous and uncontrollable. Caesarina Makhoere "elects to sing and to make noise at a time when this is disturbing to fellow prisoners and always ignores orders to remain silent"; Kate Serokolo "refuses to bath" [sic] and "voluntarily attends religious gatherings and then disrupts them by mocking behavior"; Elizabeth Nhlapo "has a habit of laughing at any person who gives her a lawful order"; and Thandi Modise "attempts to exercise in her night clothes."[60] All these women frequently initiated hunger strikes. One almost feels sympathy for the prison authorities, who are reduced to whining about petty behavior and begging Makhoere, after her transfer to a regular cell in Klerksdorp Prison, "not [to] try to make [her cellmates] clever."[61] Prison officials were hardly helpless, no matter how many court proceedings their charges initiated. Nor were the prisoners' actions likely to advance their date of release. Yet Makhoere entitled her memoir *No Child's Play*, and though the title refers to regime treatment, she and her comrades were certainly "confusing the prison" with every game they played.[62]

Their frivolous actions had parallels in other prisons. Gerry Adams's tales of Long Kesh made prison life seem like an endless stream of sophomoric jokes: this prisoner hands a guard a ten-pound note, instructing him to pick up a newspaper and a sandwich at a corner shop; that one pretends to be a priest, hearing confession; another parades around naked, leading an imaginary dog on a leash.[63] Even in the Stalinist prison, Jerzy Stokowski recalls poking fun at the restrictions on prisoner recreation: "Two guys would sit opposite each other and with great seriousness make moves with invisible pawns on an invisible chessboard. This drove the guards particularly crazy, because they weren't sure if they were being made fools of or if the chess game was quickly hidden when they entered the cell."[64] Tired of being constantly observed in a Pretoria cell in 1963 (having been summoned from Robben Island to testify at another trial), Mandela, Govan Mbeki, and Ahmed Kathrada devised an elaborate stunt. Noticing that a particularly suspicious guard, Lieutenant Swanepoel, was observing them, Mbeki composed a note, then ostentatiously handed it to Mandela, who nodded and passed it to Kathrada. As Kathrada pulled out matches to burn the note, Swanepoel swooped in and grabbed the note in triumph; it read "Isn't Swanepoel a fine-looking chap?"[65] The real message in the note was clear: leave us alone to pass the time as we see fit.

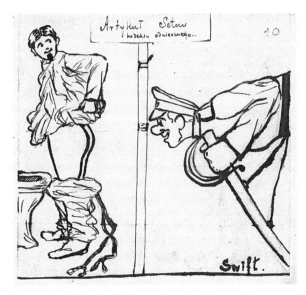

Fig. 7.1 Tadeusz Długoszowski, a Polish socialist, drew this cartoon in his diary
in the Warsaw Citadel c. 1912, recounting a prank he played on a snooping guard.
Caption: "Article 100 of the Eternal Law Code." Courtesy of Muzeum Niepodległości,
Warsaw.

Every feature of a prison conveys a message that its inmates are denied the
comforts they take for granted outside. Subject to its rules, they can only enjoy
the limited amenities that the regime chooses to give them; indeed, states often
boast about the hardships that the incarcerated must endure. But these bare
comforts—warmth, a bed and other furnishings, and even clothing and food—
also provide the political prisoner with a means to confuse prison relations.
Thus, for example, destroying the cell allows the prisoner not only a means to
reject the terms of incarceration but also to demonstrate indifference to the rigors the state imposes.

The pioneers in property destruction were the British suffragettes, imprisoned for blowing up mailboxes and breaking windows of government buildings.
In prison, they had to surrender their umbrellas, a most reliable implement, but
still managed to break more windows and other glass fixtures.[66] Irish prisoners in
the War of Independence and the Civil War turned systematic destruction into
a vocation. They smashed their furniture, broke doors off their hinges (a Bible
stuck in the doorjamb provided leverage to unhinge even the stoutest door),
and hacked through cell walls. Their actions made the space uninhabitable and
themselves ungovernable.[67]

One might wonder whether the space prisoners demonstrated control
over—a pile of kindling and broken glass open to the cold and rain—was worth
the trouble. But that space was not really theirs, inmates knew; cell destruction

both preempted guards' invasion of prisoners' privacy and unified prisoners in intense physical activity. "The Cell Search," a song composed by Polish communists and apparently sung in a number of prisons, made this clear:

> Oh, it does your heart and your soul right
> When you pound on your door with all your might.
> Boom-tra-ra, Boom-tra-ra, Boom-tra-ra!
> We've smashed the trashcan, the broom, the table and chairs,
> Over in "Serbia" the women are smashing up theirs . . . .[68]

Cell destruction put the regime in reactive mode, forced either to make the cell more secure or to move prisoners to new locations. It usually was unaccompanied by concrete demands.[69]

The burning of the IRA huts at Long Kesh Prison in October 1974 may be the most extreme example of prison destruction by political inmates in history.[70] Notwithstanding contemporary accounts, the prisoners staged neither an uprising nor a riot. They did not seek to take over the prison, and their actions were disciplined, not anarchic. Most prisoners lived in the barrack-like compounds they called cages, separated from prisoners of other political groupings by chain-link fences. Each group interacted with the prison administration only through their own commanding officers, who were permitted to visit other cages as if they were themselves in charge of the prison.[71] Over the summer and fall of 1974, Republican prisoners engaged the administration in constant disputes over privileges, food, and various minor grievances. Control of prison space was crucial to these morale-building disputes.

By early October, IRA Special Category prisoners had been refusing prison food for several weeks, dumping it over compound fences and eating only provisions sent in by their families. They had also taken to draping bedsheets over the fences, supposedly in protest of the poor laundering of prison linens, but in effect restricting guards' view of the compounds.[72] A spark was lit on October 15: the prisoners' commander in Compound 13 demanded that a prison guard assigned to the compound be removed for having made offensive remarks to a prisoner. The prison governor refused, the compound's prisoners forcibly ejected all guards, and the governor demanded that responsible prisoners be surrendered to the punishment cells. When David Morley, the Republican prisoners' campwide commanding officer, was denied permission to visit the offending compound to evaluate the complaint (and to deliver prisoners for punishment if he deemed it appropriate), Republican prisoner leaders issued an order to burn the camp.[73]

Nearly the entire camp was destroyed; unsentenced internees joined their sentenced comrades as the walls between cages were breached, arming themselves with wooden boards and the like to hold off guards and soldiers. Both sides sustained dozens of casualties. Meanwhile, Republicans in three other prisons staged solidarity actions; the Northern Ireland Prison Service estimated two million pounds in damage.[74] The compounds' days were numbered: the British built the H-Blocks and, in 1976, eliminated Special Category status for new prisoners. Significantly, no coordinated escape attempt took place, perhaps because a major breakout was planned for three weeks later.[75] Just the day before the fire, reports Adams, some argued that any burning must be accompanied by an escape; otherwise, the destruction would have minimal impact. Instead, prisoners congregated in a safe area during the blaze and then asserted their authority when soldiers approached. The prisoners refused to surrender anyone named by the army but did submit to searches and accepted food.[76] By demonstrating their ability to destroy the camp, they showed that they controlled it; in addition, they rejected the administration's separation of prisoners by legal category as opposed to political allegiance.

Each of these prisoners, at some risk of retaliation, disturbed the rigid certainty of the prison. Retelling stories of these exploits or finding humor in their interrogations lightens a bleak experience. The prison experience becomes their own, impenetrable to guards and other authorities. These actions and inactions, small and large, occupy a halfway point between conforming to the prison and creating alternative structures and collective experiences. The irony for incarcerating regimes, however harsh or liberal they are, is that they can themselves become confused about what is political and what is not. Was Adam Stanowski merely humming French tunes he had heard on the radio or revealing his ties to some West European network? Were the books prisoners read or—in more lenient times—the music they listened to subversive or a harmless diversion? Why would anyone destroy the furnishings that made incarceration bearable? The asymmetry between captor and captive is thus destabilized. Even the extreme act of cell destruction accomplishes this, questioning the ability of the regime to house and care for its inmates.

"Dear Mother, You Will Be Quite Surprised...": The Strip Strike

Prisoners risk a great deal as they endeavor to confuse or subvert the prison in defense of their identity and their cause: they might receive extra punishment or a beating. The stories of feigned chess and shared loaves of bread seem like mere games, compared to the struggle over clothing, in which prisoners risked their very sanity. "Convict" clothing has been a central point of contention throughout the modern era of political incarceration. Regimes affix a double mark on their political captives by forcing them into institutional garb that identifies them clearly as wards of the criminal prison. The regime makes prisoners indistinguishable from one another and from nonpolitical inmates.

The demand to wear one's own clothing is entirely logical and clear, but the political prisoner who refuses prison clothing must overcome shame and great discomfort. While powerful and universal taboos concerning nakedness benefit the authorities, they can become the asset of the prisoner who dares to flout them. Much of the prison routine, beginning with the examination upon admittance, revolves around the denial of normal clothing. The earliest political prisoners, like Gandhi and his colleagues in Johannesburg, made much of this debasement. They confronted the shame they felt upon standing naked for inspection, a shame compounded by class and religion, and used it as a point of contention in their stories of incarceration. O'Donovan Rossa too made forcible stripping—of his "Irish clothes," he takes care to point out—at Pentonville and Chatham prisons emblematic of the cruelties visited upon him.[77]

The earliest "strip strike" in Poland was recorded by Antoni Lange in the summer of 1907, when "the prisoners staged a so-called naked revolt, which means they walked around without their shirts and made unbearably loud noise and screamed in their cells, with the result that prisoner leaders were able to win almost complete freedom of movement for prisoners in the prison corridors."[78] The authorities probably preferred to negotiate with heretofore unrecognized leaders than to deal with semi-naked howling men. Embracing the taboo against nakedness by adding inhuman behavior, Lange's comrades inflicted further unease on their captors.

Patrick Fleming, one of the most obstinate of Sinn Féin prisoners in the years between the Easter Rising and the War of Independence, sought to discomfit his guards in a similar fashion. A report in the *Irish Independent*, November 1917, described Fleming and two other prisoners going to Holy Communion one Sunday in "rugs." This, commented the chair of the General Prisons Board, was "presumably to cover their nakedness." The prison's governor denounced this "falsehood," adding: "In a country where such high religious feeling prevails statements of this nature can but only be put forward with the object of making the life of the responsible official unbearable and subjecting him to social ostracism . . . . To my own personal knowledge the statement referred to has had a disquieting effect in families of Catholic officials." Fleming would have relished this exchange. He and his comrades had in previous weeks at least dressed themselves for Mass, throwing aside the gray flannels upon returning to their cells. Fleming in particular perplexed his captors, who worried constantly that he was about to launch a hunger strike. During a second stint in prison in 1918, he escalated his strip strike to Houdiniesque levels. Guards forcibly dressed him each day and then placed him in iron restraints lest he remove the convict garb. Somehow, Fleming managed to tear off his clothing each day—or so reported

Piaras Béaslaí in a pamphlet celebrating Fleming's struggle—and "at the first opportunity he flung [it] in shreds contemptuously out of the cell. This entailed a new suit each day for the process of forcible dressing."[79]

Republican prisoners in British, Irish, and Northern Ireland prisons continued to employ the strip strike tactic, singly or in groups. Prisoners willing to choose nakedness over prison clothing may or may not have offended the sensibilities of those who saw them, but they made a mockery of prison discipline. When Kieran Nugent appeared at the H-Blocks in September 1976, as the first IRA man to be sentenced after the ending of Special Category status, the greatest strip strike in history commenced. Just nineteen years old, Nugent famously vowed, "If they want me to wear a uniform they'll have to nail it on my back."[80] He had been in the compounds before; one of the guards who knew him suggested that he could compromise and wear a prison shirt over his own pants. He laughed—and spent his first night alone in a cell without blanket, clothing, or even a mattress. From the beginning, the "blanket protest" raised insistent questions of control. Did Nugent, and the more than 200 men and women who eventually joined him in this and other prisons, command the situation with their laughter, their firm resolve to refuse any prison clothing, and their willingness to shiver through a Belfast winter? Or did they surrender total control of their lives and bodies to the prison? Clothed prisoners avoided the incessant physical punishments from warders and even the prison governor, who slapped Nugent in the face and watched warders beat him.[81] But they conceded the regime's right to mark them as prison residents and convicts. Naked, they displayed their suffering and their mettle. Yet their protest worked only as the administration responded.

Concerns about offending Catholic sensibilities were long gone by 1976. For a time, the protesters were allowed to exercise outside in their blankets; then they were told to leave the blankets in the cells and exercise naked. The guards reveled in increasing their embarrassment, making prisoners go to the canteen, the doctor, and other blocks naked.[82] "Not once did I try and cover my nakedness with my hands," recalls Ned Flynn. "They had taken so much from us already but they could never take away our dignity or self-respect." Jackie McMullen and Sleepy Devine accepted exercise in the December sleet "as if there were nothing unusual . . . . We knew we were being watched in the hope that we would give up, so we didn't."[83] Even as they recalled the campaign more than a decade later, in interviews compiled by their prison comrades, the utter loneliness of these men threatens to overwhelm their story of resistance.

Two prison spaces defied prisoner efforts: the chapel and the visiting room. Most blanket protesters donned prison trousers to attend Mass.[84] While in chapel, political prisoners saw only themselves and criminals, distinguished by the fact that the latter wore shirts. The visiting room, where clothing was also required, was more fraught as a space where the outside world could see the prisoner clothed as a convict, adapted to the institution. Kieran Nugent wore the uniform once, in his first days in the H-Blocks, in order to tell his mother: "You will not be seeing me for three years," the length of his sentence.[85] Only the occasional visit from a lawyer, a priest or, more rarely, a journalist would offer a break in the routine. Like the prisoners of Robben Island, the blanket protesters of the H-Blocks existed only in smuggled photographs and in legend.

A brief protest in late 1976 won prisoners the right to wear a towel outside the cell. Throughout the next year, tense struggles over these rectangles of cloth continued, until a March 1978 crisis in prisoner leadership precipitated a dramatic new protest over space and legibility. Brendan "The Dark" Hughes had just been transferred to the H-Blocks from the Special Category barracks. The blanketmen received him warily; proud to have defied the prison regime for as long as a year and a half, they had come to think of the Special Category men as not up to the real challenges of prison. Some even placed bets as to how quickly men like Hughes would turn "squeaky boots"—giving up the blanket for prison clothing and bare feet for a new pair of prison-issue shoes. The previous year the blanketmen's commanding officer had himself "squeaky-booted," deserting his men for the comforts of junk food and television, as the warders taunted. Meanwhile, the blanketmen had become trapped in a cycle of small violent confrontations with guards. Hurrying to the toilet or the showers in their towels, they found that the prison had adapted to them. "We were in a rut," recalled one. "The screws and the administration appeared to accept the protest; what set H3 and H5, the Blanket Blocks, out from the rest of the Blocks was merely that there was a different routine. The different routine . . . was becoming institutionalised and so was giving the administration no real cause for concern." Hughes floated the idea of accepting the uniform so as to fight within the system—perhaps then trying to burn down parts of the H-Blocks. But "wearing the prison clothes was an obvious mental block that no one wanted to step over."[86]

Hughes proposed an escalation instead, taking their protest beyond what any political prisoners had ever attempted.[87] The path they followed had been lit by one of their heroes, Terence MacSwiney, in 1920: victory would go to those who could show that they could "endure the most." The new phase of protest began innocuously enough: prisoners refused to leave the cell for showers and the toilet, on the grounds that they were frequently beaten or humiliated in the corridors en route, and demanded that they be allowed to wash in their cells. They refused to make do with the washbasins in their cells and ceased washing altogether; they also refused to sweep out their cells. Guards withheld clean linens; prisoners refused to accept dirty sheets. Next, guards began "accidentally" spilling the contents of chamberpots on cell floors. Prisoners tossed the contents of their pots out their windows or under the cell doors; the guards squeegeed it

Fig. 7.2 IRA prisoner daubing cell wall with feces, c. 1981. This picture was taken with a clandestine camera and smuggled out of the prison. Courtesy of Pacemaker Press International.

back in. Rotten food and maggots accumulated in the cells, too; though prisoners were eating, the food they did not finish was not collected. Guards came periodically with high-pressure hoses and disinfectant to wash cells. Prisoners smashed all their furniture; prison administration removed everything except chamberpots and mattresses. Finally, the blanketmen resorted to smearing their feces on the walls of the cells.

The campaign in retrospect seems logical enough, strike and counterstrike to the limits of human endurance. Even the smearing of the walls made sense, so that the excrement would dry on the walls (and stink less) instead of rotting with the food. The campaign's power lay in its unpredictability, breaking the routine that the administration had gained mastery over in the previous two years. The prisoners felt they had regained control and were even—despite the foul conditions—elated. "Morale was at its highest," recalled one blanketman; "there was a sense of purpose which was missing beforehand," added another. A third asserted, "We felt that we were winning and for a change we, not the screws, had control over our lives because we dictated the pace of events. The screws for their part were demoralised because they had no control over what happened next. They dreaded Mondays because that was the day that we kept upping the protest by introducing something new."[88] Prevously, prisoners had lived with uncertainty, wondering if the next trip to the toilet would end in a beating; the uncertainty had been thrown back at the guards.

To make themselves unrecognizable to the prison regime, the blanketmen transformed themselves into something that not even a prison uniform could normalize. Some still made an exception and donned clothes to receive visitors. But when they went to the visiting room to meet their families, in prison-issue trousers and boots, they presented to all a spectacle at once terrifying—sallow skin, wild hair and beard, glassy eyes, in clumsy oversized clothes—and attributable to the warders standing guard over the conversation. Control over the narrative of their treatment, though, came at quite a cost. The no-wash protest blurred the public and private beyond the prisoners' control. Peadar Whelan explains: "Despite the inevitability of putting shit on the walls, it wasn't any less a conflict of conscience; after getting over the taboos we still had to come to terms with living and eating in a small cell covered in shit." The wall-painting was inevitable, he explains, because the act of dumping the chamber pot into a bucket brought around by the warders made a very personal act public. Smearing it on the walls was thus an act of control. But Whelan observes that how people outside reacted mattered greatly: "While we worried about our health, we worried too about how people would see our going against everything we had been taught and if they understand it." Only by recovering the political context could Whelan come to terms with his actions:

> When it came to it, I saw putting shit on the wall as an aspect of the struggle I was part of. At the time words and ideas about pride, dignity and principles were a large part of our vocabulary and thinking. I believe we were influenced by the images of past Republican heroes but as our struggle was going on in different circumstances, we had to use what methods we had. Putting shit on the walls was one such method and we had to come to terms with it in that light.[89]

Draped in blankets and sporting long beards, the no-wash men looked Christlike. They reveled in the physical contest with the "screws" and overcame their squeamishness and shame by boasting about their excretive prowess.[90] Two years after the no-wash protest began in the H-Blocks, Republican women prisoners in Armagh joined in, provoked by a bloody set-to with male guards over a parade march. The dynamics of their confrontation differed significantly, and indeed the IRA outside had tried to prevent the women from protesting. They wore their own clothing and could exercise outside, but now refused to accept clean linens or clothing and smeared their feces on the walls as well.[91] Since the days of Sighle Humphreys and Hanna Sheehy-Skeffington, Irish prison protest had become a masculine enterprise, responding to the carceral apparatus on increasingly violent terms. The Armagh women re-expanded the discourse of protest.

The prisoners' scope for control of their image, though, narrowed as the stakes grew higher. In the no-wash protest, the Republican prisoners reached an extreme at which their actions became illegible not only to the prison staff and administration but also to the world. They wanted to shock observers and to demonstrate that they were resolute men forced into appalling conditions by an unfeeling state, but they also desired empathy and support. Kieran McEvoy quotes one former prisoner who admits the protest was "naïve," as it allowed the authorities to "argue that it was all self-inflicted, say it was being directed by the Godfathers of the IRA or that we were the sort of animals who liked living in our own excrement and so on. With nobody other than Republicans appearing to care about the beatings and so on, it was self-defeating I suppose."[92] The European Court of Human Rights, hearing the prisoners' case against the United Kingdom in 1980, indeed ruled that while the British authorities ought to find a way to resolve the situation, the conditions in which prisoners found themselves were "self-imposed" and could improve immediately if the prisoners chose.[93] Bobby Sands hinted that the experience had driven "many men to the verge of insanity"; one suspects that some in fact crossed that line.[94]

The protest had the desired impact on prison authorities. In September 1977, they met to discuss a worrying trend: prisoners were "beginning to feign deterioration in such faculties as depth perception," and the blanketmen might begin to claim psychiatric problems resulting from long confinement.[95] About eighteen months later Kieran Nugent, the first blanketman, approached his release, spurring much hand-wringing about his appearance. Would it be advisable, management wondered, to wash and shave him and arrange for a medical inspection first? Nugent would have laughed to hear this, considering the brutal treatment and beatings that accompanied periodic bathing of the blanketmen, as well as the callous indifference of prison medical personnel.[96]

The H-Block protest exposes the forbidding intimacy of a protest against prison clothing, difficult to imagine in other contexts. South African prisons, for example, contain no mention of strip strikes through most of the twentieth century. White prison officials showed no compunction in stripping their black charges naked, so a strip strike would only have underscored the prisoners' powerlessness and perhaps allowed the regime to further liken them to animals.[97] Some black prisoners apparently did adopt the tactic in 1985, in order to draw attention to other grievances.[98] Still, the complicated cultural associations of nudity would have made this tactic difficult.

The limits of the clothing protest are clearest in the case of a long-forgotten strip strike in a Polish prison on the eve of World War II. An unknown number of communist women of Fordon Prison began the protest in spring 1937. Six different women mention the strike, and since they appear to have started at slightly different times, it may have begun in one cell and then passed on. "Dear Mother," wrote Klara Schillinger in a postcard that never reached her home in Drohobycz, "you will be quite surprised when you learn in what state I now write to you. But it's really true! I am sitting here completely nude (even without underwear), almost two weeks now (since the 14th). There is nothing in my cell but the bare furnishings—not a scrap of cloth. Despite this I feel good so far, both in body and especially in morale. I know it is hard to stay calm hearing this, but please do not worry about me!"[99] Schillinger tried to frame her extreme actions as normal.

"R" explains the outset this way: "On March 2 the prison administration tore our own clothing off by force, wanting us to wear prison uniforms . . . . We went into action: we will put on no prison uniforms. We are sitting in nothing but underwear, fighting for the most primitive rights of a political prisoner." Rywa Kac wrote to a friend, in late May: "Already 17 days I am completely naked. I have in the cell only a menstruation pad and . . . a towel. That is all I possess. I am a little weak, but that's nothing. Everything will work out and it will be OK." Anastazja Kuresza wrote to her parents: "I am returning to those days when I first saw the sun shine on the world . . . . Like the day Mama gave birth to me, and she had to borrow pillows and comforters from the neighbors. Thus completely naked, without a shirt and on a hard bare bed since the 13th [of May], you can imagine how this affects one's health."[100] For five months or more these women braved the chilly stone walls of Fordon Prison. Little of their protest reached outside; most letters exist now because the prison administration confiscated them, while one that made it to Red Help did not appear in print. On October 10, party leaders apparently directed the women to end their protest and accept uniforms.[101] A Polish winter was probably the ultimate argument, but the protest was also surely as difficult for party activists to frame for their public as was the no-wash protest in the H-Blocks. A more lonely protest is difficult to imagine, and the impact may well have been unsatisfying. A letter from Zisla Ciller upon her return home to Łuck hints at some concessions won.[102] More important, the extant letters reveal pride and a strengthened camaraderie. Whether that compensated for the hardship they endured in their nearly secret protest cannot be measured.

From Caprice to Madness and Beyond

The Polish legal term for insanity, *niepoczytalny*, literally means "not readable." The effort to make oneself completely illegible to the prison institution by destroying the cell or refusing clothing indeed touches the edge of madness. Separating with certainty the prisoner who might simulate madness in order to become unknowable to the regime from another whose mind has been destroyed by the immense strains of confinement, torture, and deformed social relationships is nearly impossible. The evidence of prisoner resistance through madness can be quite misleading, even to the researcher. A document in the archives of the General Prison Board in Ireland yielded an intriguing story about suffragette prisoners in Mountjoy: "The Governor stated that he did not think it likely the prisoners would resort to a 'hunger strike' but that it was very difficult to prophesy what their action might be as two of them Miss Margaret and Miss Jane Murphy appeared to have neurotic tendencies."[103] The picture of befuddled British authorities leaped from the page, vaulting the Murphy sisters into the ranks of this book's heroes, until a reading, just five days later in the National Library of Ireland, of Hanna Sheehy-Skeffington's unpublished journal. There, she recorded a series of concessions from the prison authorities and added, in an apparent note to her husband Francis: "The Murphys are a plague—please let [the Irish Women's Franchise] League know." Margaret, Sheehy-Skeffington added, is "not all there. They may easily go mad here . . . . They have threatened the Hunger Strike tomorrow if no reply re exercise comes and we haven't actu-ally been <u>refused</u> that even!"[104] So much for the wily Murphys. Not every politi-cal prisoner withstands the pressures of prison and pulls the strings effectively, and individual tragedies can in a political context appear to be something else entirely.

Still, there are occasional examples of the calculated use of insanity or erratic behavior. The Long Kesh prisoner walking his "dog" in the nude is one who clearly hoped to unsettle the authorities—while no doubt having some fun as well. Ludwik Śledziński recalls another: a socialist comrade who successfully styled himself "Ferdzio Pu," a painter en route to Italy, and talked of nothing else. In the recreation area one day, he handed his coat to a guard and leaped into a bucket of water and lime, which burned his skin. Eventually the doctors sent him out to a hospital, and with Śledziński's help he escaped from the train.[105] He was fortunate, for Śledziński notes other comrades' gambits that were less successful. The line between feigned madness and the real thing might easily be crossed. Stanisław Skalski was sent to an isolation cell for two weeks in Rawicz Prison. When the guards came to release him he refused to come out, cowering in a corner.

> Hidden in that grave, I could see them in the [corridor's] light. They began
>   to search for me in the darkness, cautiously, as one would look for a dog
>   in its kennel, uncertain if it had expired or might yet pounce and bite.
>   Finally their gaze fell upon me.
> "OK, come out, Skalski."
> I shrank into the corner.

"Come out!"

"None of you sons of bitches would last an hour in here. I like it here. Scram!"

Skalski realized later he was lucky: the guards could easily have slammed the door and left him to die instead of deciding he had lost his mind and sending him to the prison hospital.[106] His behavior was all too real in this first human contact in two weeks; Skalski does not hint that he had plotted a path to a comfortable respite. But he had made the guards wary of him, and that may well have paid further dividends later.

A sane mind could create an alternate reality to relieve the grim surroundings and use that to come to terms with the prison and gain a measure of control, but so might a mind that had lost its moorings. No place could be as conducive to paranoia as a small room with a spyhole in the door. Cell informers often recount the naked fears of their subjects.[107] And few prison stories can be as heartbreaking as the disintegration of Robert Sobukwe in the late 1960s. A deeply erudite man and powerful leader who clearly frightened the South African regime and his Robben Island captors, by 1969 he was writing rambling letters about a hidden machine in his prison hut that, he believed, was aiming jets of air at his body. In a final cruelty, regime psychologists assured Sobukwe that he was fine, thus denying him even the opportunity to accept his illness.[108]

Prison memoirs rarely speak of suicide; the dark topic undercuts stories of survival and collective resistance. But certainly some prisoners manipulated the end of their lives toward political ends. The hunger strike, the subject of the next chapter, can be understood as a harnessing of the potential of suicide through collective protest. Not all political prisoners are fortunate enough to be part of a collective and to stage prisonwide protests together. Alone, the prisoner who would confound the prison might only destroy himself. The solitary inmate has far fewer assets, but even an individual can strive, sometimes at great cost, to be unknowable to or unreachable by the regime, and thus contribute to the struggle for a political cause.

In May 1980, journalist Tim Pat Coogan applied to visit the H-Blocks and received permission to meet IRA "blanketmen" in their cells. The government had clearly rehearsed a spectacle for Coogan, beginning with tea at the Northern Ireland Office, followed by lunch at a golf glub. Finally reaching the H-Blocks, Coogan was first taken to see "conforming" prisoners, those who accepted prison rules and prison clothing. He was shown the best of a modern British institution—television, cafeteria food, model boat-building, and other crafts— yet Governor Stanley Hilditch portrayed the smiling inhabitants as monsters held in check by the progressive carceral apparatus and hinted at their evil deeds. About one, he remarked: "I could tell you a story about him and things about him but it would be a breach of professional integrity."[109]

Approaching the blocks where the protesting prisoners were housed, Coogan felt his guides' certainty ebb away. How would this Dublin journalist react upon seeing the cells and their occupants who lived among piles of rotting food and their own excrement? They allowed Coogan to pick a cell at random, but not to speak to the inmates. Gazing at a scene which a previous visitor, Cardinal Tomás O Fiaich, had likened to "the spectacle of . . . homeless people living in sewer-pipes in the slums of Calcutta," Coogan felt "helpless and angry . . . prevented by bureaucracy and by history from talking to two of my fellow human beings who had brought themselves and been brought to this condition of self-abnegation." The prisoners, for their part, could only stare in fear and defiance, unable to articulate their goals, their hopes, and indeed their humanity. Coogan asked to see the cell of Martin Meehan, an IRA leader. The tour party found Meehan, similarly attired in a towel, using a piece of his foam-rubber mattress to trace palm-tree patterns with his feces on the wall. The governor, clearly ill at ease, asked Meehan brusquely just what he was doing. Meehan replied: "I don't know, but it's well beneath me anyhow."[110]

Meehan knew very well what he was doing—and knew it was beyond the imagining of any respectable, well-dressed visitor. Everything about the encounter was unreadable to his guests: the foul cell; the haggard, almost primitive appearance of some prisoners; the patterns on the wall; the shouts across the courtyard in Irish. From the position he had created, Meehan could confound simply by offering Coogan a genial parting handshake. He had reversed, or at least equalized, the relations of power in the cell. The governor was not at home, but Meehan was. Even as he sparred with the governor about the wrongfulness of his sentence, he demonstrated that the cell was under his control, and that the prison tour could not be as easily orchestrated as a visit to a golf club.

The blanketmen's actions were extreme, but they were also a logical development of the politics of the prison developed over the previous century. Confusing the prison and making themselves illegible, prisoners like the blanketmen endeavored to make it unworkable. This chapter has highlighted ways that individual actions can destabilize prison relations and carve out some autonomous space. It does not illuminate much to call actions like refusing clothes "resistance," because the term obscures the creative power such an action contained. Prisoners retain or claim control in the face of the regime's efforts to know and to categorize them and to leave them in uncertainty by making themselves illegible, beyond the regime's understanding. Extreme and unpredictable actions give prisoners control over their lives, the space they inhabit, and the political relationships they maintain and build in the cell. They prove that these inmates are still human—and still political.

"Why Wouldn't I Laugh, When I Win Either Way?"

The Hunger Strike

Angered by endless petty rules and eager for a fight, some 100 Solidarity activists interned in Hrubieszów Prison staged a hunger strike in September 1982. Hunger fasts among Polish internees were staged on the thirteenth of every month to mark the imposition of martial law the previous December, but this one was intended to last "until victory." The prisoners subsisted on tea, vitamins, and salt water for two and a half weeks, enduring beatings and force-feeding.[1] In the end, the prison administration relaxed some of the offending regulations and practices. But this small victory weakened the prisoner community and turned it against itself, observed Marek Kulczyk: "To some extent the prison authorities acted deliberately, deepening the absurdity and senselessness [of internment]. When the prison ceases to be a stereotypical dungeon, all resistance seems to be senseless. After all, things are good, the guards don't pick on you, sometimes they let you visit others' cells, you can do what you want. So what is there to protest against, and what, in this situation, does protest mean?" Kulczyk eventually reached a different conclusion: resistance could not be for "specific goals, but to defend one's dignity and identity, threatened by the prison system .... Resistance does not cease to be resistance when the guards no longer react, because it is not just a battle with the guards."[2] Whether treatment was harsh or liberal should not determine prisoner actions. The great challenge for prisoners—one that the term "resistance" papers over, Kulczyk realized—was to disentangle prisoners' actions from those of the regime.

Through the lens of the political prisoners' supreme protest tactic, the hunger strike, this chapter examines the dynamics, the potential, and the pitfalls of collective protest, culminating in the eight-month strike in 1981 in which ten Irish Republicans starved to death in bleak succession. The hunger strike attracts more attention than any other form of prisoner protest precisely because the outcome of the drama is so uncertain. Prisoners usually declare or at least imply their readiness to die, yet the protest is sufficiently protracted as to allow them to negotiate with the administration or the government. At the same time, the hunger strike is a terrible act of self-abnegation. The regime can only guess whether the prisoners' inner resolve matches their outward defiance, and cannot know what the strikers will do nor how they might respond to any repression or concession. Strike participants face challenges as well in maintaining unity and clarity in the face of physical and mental hardship.[3]

The Irrational Logic of the Hunger Strike

The course and outcome of a prison hunger strike depend upon three disparate factors. First, the goal must be one prisoners can recognize, and the politics clear and compelling to strike participants; cultural, religious, or political traditions by themselves will not suffice. To refuse food for days and weeks, facing death by degrees, is so much more exacting an exercise than any other protest that prisoners need a clear frame for the experience before they begin. Second, a hunger strike requires strong coordination, as any dissent in the ranks can make the sacrifice too much to bear. Firm leadership and durable networks clarify demands, alleviate doubts, and gain buy-in for strike tactics. Finally, much depends upon the regime and its institution. Prisoners locked in single cells have to work much harder to agree upon their grievances and to coordinate tactics. A regime that is determined to let all strikers die, or which has the resources to force-feed them all, may be able to outlast the strikers or defeat them early. And if strikers are unable to alert supporters outside, the challenge of their protest is that much greater.

Even so, it is difficult to gauge what constitutes success. Must the regime change, or at least agree to release the strikers? Do concessions on the way prisoners are treated amount to a victory or merely reconfirm their subjection to the will of the regime? A key factor in strike success is whether the strikers are able to use the unpredictable nature of the tactic in their favor. In this almost inhuman act of self-denial, the will and the intentions of the individual prisoner become unknowable to the regime. Until the striker dies or takes food, she or he frustrates the jailers. Insisting that their irrational act is in fact rational, born not of individual madness but of a collective purpose, hunger strikers build a unity that confounds the regime, each inmate encouraging the others in their resolve. Their goals, no matter how clear the demands laid out in communiqués, remain beyond the grasp of the prison and the regime. Asserting control over their bodies and their lives, prisoners deny the same to the authorities.

Though prisoners and administrators alike often regard it as an ultimate weapon, the hunger strike in some ways resembles other forms of prison protest. The Polish communists' *przeplatanka* usually included a protest fast, and the potential of a hunger strike has loomed over most political incarceration at least since the suffragettes' campaigns. For their part, prison authorities often suspected an imminent hunger strike in inmates' protests. They were not far wrong, since the discipline and dedication required to stage a hunger strike are essential to other protest tactics. The hunger strike, though, is a tool best used by those with a strong commitment to a cause, for once the physical effects become palpable it becomes a deadly serious affair that excludes all other actions.

On one thing, prisoners and their jailers agreed: the hunger strike was a weapon of irrationality. In September 1917, on the day that hunger striker Thomas Ashe died in Dublin, the Irish General Prison Board issued instructions to all prison governors on "cases of prisoners who abstain from food," suggesting that such men were likely mad: "In the case of the insane or doubtfully sane, artificial feeding is an ordinary procedure to be carried out in cases where it is necessary, at the discretion of the Medical Officer. In cases of voluntary starvation by sane prisoners for the purpose of obtaining their release or other privileges, artificial feeding is a necessary duty of the Medical Officer."[4] The administration thus contrasted its rational, medical/psychiatric response to the questionable mental health of the striker. Compare this to Marek Kulczyk's account of a one-day hunger strike in Łęczyca Prison in May 1982. The prison social worker summoned each prisoner individually to ask him to explain his action.

> Each of us answered for himself, and each said something different. One said it was to remember the first anniversary of the assassination attempt on the Pope; another, that it was for a private matter; a third, that it was to improve his health; etc. Our answers deepened their confusion. If only everyone fasted for the same thing, and here who the hell knows what's going on! They began to threaten us in any way they could, demanding our real motives.... They only calmed down the next day when we took our breakfast. They key thing here is that we countered absurdity with absurdity. We demonstrated to them—perhaps more unwittingly—that in the absurd world that prison is for us we are capable of breaking out of the categories recognized by a prison officer, even as we respect the outward logic: if they want motives we'll give them motives.[5]

The prisoners' charade worked because they appeared to be serious. Even a one-day fast returns attention to the cause for which the prisoner has been fighting, because it so clearly is not "about" food. If the clothing strike is primarily about the signs of prisoner status and the destruction of a cell could be simply a visceral reaction to deplorable living conditions, the hunger strike is almost certainly not about the quality of the food. As Maud Ellmann observes in *The Hunger Artists*, "hunger strikers tend to underplay the motives for their gamble with mortality. The hunger strikers of Long Kesh claimed that they were fasting to resist the prison uniform; but it is scarcely plausible that anyone would starve to death in order to wear civilian clothes."[6] While she underestimates the significance of civilian clothing, the basic point holds: the hunger strike is about more than any one demand.

Not all prisoners consider the hunger strike to be an ideal form of prisoner protest. Nelson Mandela called it "quixotic," as it relies on publicity lest prisoners "simply starve themselves to death and no one will know." He offered a second, deeper objection: hunger strikes are

> altogether too passive. We who were already suffering were threatening our health, even courting death. I have always favoured a more active, militant style of protest such as work strikes, go-slow strikes or refusing to clean up; actions that punished the authorities, not ourselves. They wanted gravel and we produced no gravel. They wanted the prison yard clean, and it was untidy. This kind of behaviour distressed and exasperated them, whereas I think they secretly enjoyed watching us go hungry.[7]

Despite his doubts, Mandela supported and participated in hunger strikes when outvoted by his comrades. As he recognized, mutual sacrifice demanded solidarity.

Does the hunger strike in fact depend upon reaching the outside world, and does self-punishment otherwise merely provide entertainment for the regime? Mandela argued that there were always alternatives to a hunger strike, which proved surprisingly true on Robben Island. Not so in the Stalinist prison. Recalling his time in the police dungeons in the cellar of Warsaw's Mostowski Palace, Jerzy Stokowski asserted that "the prisoner's only weapon that can reach the authorities is the refusal to eat." Even the cause does not matter, only the expression of extreme adversity. "We announced a hunger strike one time, I don't remember exactly what for, but it was probably because for supper and breakfast we got cold, undrinkable coffee and bread later. The reason didn't matter as much as the fact that those whom we could contact, in a dozen or more cells, joined the strike." When the prisoners refused supper, a prison officer came downstairs and tried to persuade them to eat. Meeting silence, the officer tried to divide the prisoners: he turned to an older prisoner and appealed to reason. Failing this, he threatened to send them to the isolation cells, but "we knew," writes Stokowski, "that they won't stuff half the Palace into two rooms. The next day we got hot coffee and bread."[8] This brief hunger strike succeeded because the principles were the same as in other strikes: solidarity among prisoners deprived the guards of their power to divide and thus limited their ability to punish. Stokowski's older cellmate, informally recognized as their leader, could compel the regime to give in and to acknowledge prisoners' self-organization.

The hunger strike has inspired competing legends of its origins. W. B. Yeats's retelling of an Irish legend in which a poet fasts for justice at the king's doorstep struck a chord as the hunger strike became a ubiquitous weapon of the Irish struggle for independence in 1917. It cemented an idea that self-sacrifice for justice against tyranny was both noble and uniquely Irish.[9] Parallels to the self-sacrifice of soldiers on the field of battle suggested themselves, too, so it was easy to believe that Sinn Féin prisoners had been first to put their lives on the line.[10] The hunger strike, though, furnishes compelling stories that travel across borders and between quite disparate movements. The first modern Irish hunger strikers were the suffragettes, in 1912–1914, borrowing from English suffragettes who had, in turn, learned from Russian revolutionary emigres in London; the suffragettes called it the "Russian method."[11] The first modern hunger striker may have been Russian socialist philosopher Nikolai Chernyshevskii, who staged a strike during his time in Petropavlovsk Fortress in 1862 in an effort to force his freedom; sixteen years later, detained socialists in that same prison also went on strike. Chernyshevskii was by this time a revered figure thanks to his novel of revolution, *What Is to Be Done?*, and so his solitary struggle in prison had an outsize impact.[12]

Polish radicals were very much of this milieu, striking a number of times in the decades before World War I, usually in protest of the interminable wait for justice.[13] Hunger strikes in the Kama penal colony in Siberia received much publicity in Russia and abroad. It seems likely that the tactic gained popularity because it resembled a religious fast while also evoking the idea that starvation reflected badly on one's master. Early hunger strikes, from the 1860s in Russia through the 1910s in England, Ireland, and the Transvaal tended to last just a few days before authorities either gave in to demands or began force-feeding. Neither strikers nor their custodians knew how long the human body could hold out without food.

To Irish suffragettes, the hunger strike seemed at first a dubious tactic. Much smaller than the English movement, they couldn't spare anyone to undertake such a radical protest.[14] The first hunger strikers in Ireland, in fact, came over to Dublin from England to protest during an appearance by British prime minister Herbert Asquith. They—and Irish comrades like Hanna Sheehy-Skeffington, who quickly joined them—deployed the same combination of inscrutability and stubbornness that had served so well in England. When an official from the

General Prisons Board, Dr. Edgar Flinn, visited Mary Leigh in Mountjoy, he enticed her with an array of privileges—newspapers, letters, her own clothing—that could be hers if she would take food. Leigh retorted, "Why were these terms not offered to us at once as political prisoners?" and reminded Flinn that her demands—"the Vote or a pledge"—were well known. In other words, she placed the resolution of her protest beyond the power of the Prison Board. Flinn remonstrated that she was doing herself harm. "That's not my affair," came the disingenuous reply. "My health is in your hands." Flinn hoped at least to exonerate the prison: "Everything possible is being done for you by all the officials here." Her response made it no easier for him: "Agreed. I am perfectly happy."[15]

This vexing exchange conveys the power of the hunger strike. Maud Gonne elaborated further on this theme a few years later: "Why wouldn't I laugh, when I win either way?" she responded to a British official who thought she was taking her hunger strike too lightly.[16] Laughter disarmed: instead of demanding something the administration could give her, Leigh and Gonne made negotiation impossible. Leigh even refused to lodge a complaint against the prison, and so Flinn could only wonder how she could be "perfectly happy." Her condition was to him both absurd and illegible. The prison embarked upon forcefeeding, which only made the regime and its medical personnel look sadistic. So the authorities proposed instead to isolate the hunger strikers (and other imprisoned suffragettes) in Tullamore Prison, where it would treat them like "borderline insane cases," giving them quite lenient conditions while "solemnly warn[ing] them they will be allowed to starve themselves if they so desire."[17] The result, wrote striker Margaret Cousins in 1913, was "a straight fight between granting of treatment and our fasting powers"—and by "treatment," Cousins meant both the conditions in prison and "sex equality in political treatment as in everything else."[18] The suffragettes in Ireland and England believed that by going to prison and then refusing food they could win votes for women. The first step toward that victory, though, was to confound the authorities. Thus they laughed at exercise, wrote slogans ("No surrender") instead of complaints in the daily registry, resisted photographs and fingerprinting, and tore up their conditions of release.[19] All those things could be done on a full stomach, but hunger strikes won them even quicker release and made the authorities hesitant to imprison them again.

Why Endure the Most? Ireland, 1917–1920

Regimes grappled with three challenges in the face of a hunger strike: the management problem of a prisoner who would endanger his or her own health; a moral problem, as the regime considered its responsibility for a person's health and survival; and a political problem, as the drama played out in public. None of these could be addressed by any policy that assumed a static situation. A prison staff could adjust to a strip strike, counting on cold weather or the promise of visits to bring the protest to an end. Physical actions like cell destruction or marching during exercise might be either accommodated or prevented. But the hunger strike eludes any consistent response. As Governor Munro of Mountjoy Prison plaintively remarked to Frank Gallagher on the ninth day of the hunger strike there in April 1920: "Why do you do this thing? When you smash the prison cells, everything, we know what to do. You remember when you were here last? But this hunger-striking makes it so difficult for us." Gallagher's retort: "That is why we hunger-strike."[20] Like Maud Gonne, Gallagher knew the strikers would win either way.

Thanks to the confluence of a "hunger-strike mania" that persisted, off and on, for six years, and a regime willing to hash out arguments and strategies both in private correspondence and public rhetoric, revolutionary Ireland provides an excellent window into the various bad options available to a regime and its prison authorities.[21] If the suffragist protests had caught the British government off guard, making officials look alternately foolish and heartless, by 1917 it presumably had learned from experience. Yet time and again—in the September 1917 strike that resulted in the death of Thomas Ashe, in the strike of April 1920, and in the deaths of Terence MacSwiney in Brixton Prison in London and two other prisoners in Cork that autumn—early official intransigence was exposed and nullified by later concessions.

Force-feeding had at times eclipsed all other aspects of incarceration of the suffragettes. Days before Ashe's strike began, Undersecretary of State for Ireland William Byrne affirmed that force-feeding was "shocking only to those to whom the routine of asylum, prison & workhouse infirmary life is unfamiliar."[22] Civilization itself, he implied, had become foreign to such inmates, and the institution had no choice but to adapt. Force-feeding began on the third day of the strike and soon claimed Ashe as a victim when an orderly conducted the procedure improperly. However, just after Ashe's death, the Irish Privy Council approved granting to prisoners the very concessions that Ashe and his Sinn Féin comrades had demanded.[23] While prison authorities admitted no mistakes, Dublin's lord mayor allowed Ashe's body to lie in state for public viewing and veneration at city hall. Such mixed messages of torture and respect seemed to vindicate the armed version of republicanism that Ashe had represented and only encouraged more such protests.[24]

In futile hopes of stemming the tide, Dublin authorities prepared the following card to be placed in each cell: "NOTICE. All persons committed to prison are informed that they will not be able by wilful injury to their bodily health caused by refusal of food or in any other way, to procure their release before their

discharge in due course of law."[25] This warning assumed that prisoners calculated
a balance between the damage they might do to themselves and the probability
of early release. Yet what if release was not the prisoners' goal? The policy made
no mention of enforcement—by force-feeding or otherwise—which, given a
free press and a parliament, inevitably placed the government on the defensive.

Despite their best efforts, the British authorities proved helpless against the
hunger strike, as Frank Gallagher and his comrades in Mountjoy knew when
they struck to demand recognition. On Easter Monday, April 5, 1920, they
gathered in the exercise yard to swear a solemn oath "to the honour of Ireland
and to the lives of my comrades not to eat food or drink anything but water,
until all here have been given prisoner-of-war treatment or are released."[26] By
this time the British had but nominal control of the prison; moreover, having
halted force-feeding after Ashe's death, they could not control the narrative of
incarceration, either. Officials feared any damage to the prisoners' health, even
releasing one prisoner who had earlier threatened a hunger strike.[27] They offered
instead half-measures, such as prisoner-of-war status if prisoners would move
to English prisons. The prisoners in turn found these overtures easy to reject,
leaving the authorities to humbly ask what exactly the prisoners wanted.[28] On
the tenth day the strikers escalated their demands from status change to release.
Both strikers and authorities believed that some prisoners were near death; the
medical officer at Mountjoy signed certificates stating that lives were in danger.
This capitulation would further invigorate the independence fight.[29]

Even in victory, the prisoners raised the stakes further. When the prison governor agreed, finally, to release hunger strikers, there remained the problem of
how they would depart the prison. The governor insisted they could all leave
simply by acknowledging parole, but the prisoners' commanding officer, Peadar
Clancy, insisted that the prisoners would sign nothing. Even a tacit acceptance
of parole would mean conceding guilt. "Will you inform your authorities," he
instructed the harried governor, "that we refuse to give any written, verbal, or
implied parole; that we are not coming back at the end of six weeks or any other
time; and if, in spite of this declaration, your authorities still release us, we shall
accept that release as absolutely unconditional?"[30] This refusal even to negotiate denied the governor's authority. While the prison still staged a cumbersome
reading of a statement to each individual prisoner, the prisoners (many of them
on stretchers after ten days on strike) had gained control over their release and
negated the ability of the institution to frame them and their behavior.

The Irish prisoners of this period perhaps had unusual power to shape their
incarceration since they were highly organized and knew their captors well. They
could have simply demanded to be treated like gentlemen; instead they showed
themselves uninterested in the terms of imprisonment. About one group, Visiting
Justice John Irwin reported with evident frustration in spring 1918: they "went

Fig. 8.1 Cumann na mBan (The Irishwomen's Council) procession outside Mountjoy Prison during prisoners' hunger strike, July 23, 1921. Photographer W.D. Hogan. Courtesy of National Library of Ireland.

on hunger strike immediately [after] they were admitted to Mountjoy and before they could possibly experience the privileges granted under the new rules." This revealed, Irwin was sure, "a preconceived plan" that made further concessions pointless. As he recognized, these prisoners were not protesting any set of rules but the right of their captors to make rules at all.[31]

When Terence MacSwiney was arrested in Cork in August 1920, he immediately announced that within a month he would be "free, alive or dead." His speech to the court made clear that a hunger strike would defeat any sentence: "I will put a limit to any term of imprisonment you may impose . . . . I have decided the terms of my detention whatever your government may do."[32] At first reading, MacSwiney seems to be confident in gaining release from his hospital bed, but he seems to have been indifferent as to which version of freedom he would gain. He was immediately transported to Brixton Prison, but unlike other transported prisoners he did not cease his strike once out of Ireland; a number of his comrades, meanwhile, continued the strike in Cork. Having thus given MacSwiney a very public stage, the British authorities were stuck. The Home Office debated whether MacSwiney's prominence—he had just been named lord mayor of Cork—made him the right vehicle for demonstrating the government's resolve. If he died, authorities realized, it would weaken the prisons and embolden the IRA.

Their response was instead erratic and defensive. The doctor talked of sneaking food into his patient; leader of the House of Commons Andrew Bonar Law suggested dosing his water with vitamins; MacSwiney was urged to accept juice. Questions were raised about his communion wafers. Rumors of smuggled nutrition, either with or without MacSwiney's consent, accompanied nearly the entire seventy-four days of his strike.[33] The whole performance made MacSwiney's death as much a consequence of British actions as if he had been force-fed. At the same time, the many weeks he lay in the hospital, attended by clergy, doctors, and relatives, made him exactly the figure he had anticipated at the outset: "Knowing the revolution of opinion that will be thereby caused throughout the civilised world and the consequent accession of support to Ireland in her hour of trial," he informed the public in the first week of the strike, "I am reconciled to a premature grave. I am prepared to die."[34] MacSwiney's funeral indeed magnified the Republican movement at a crucial moment in the War of Independence. Yet his death also cast a shadow over the very tactic he used. MacSwiney had set the bar very high: his near saintly status, cultivated by his sister, and the competitive frame he gave his strike—proclaiming that victory went to him who "endured the most"—enticed many but won few followers. He had discomfited the church and chastened the movement, whose center of gravity moved back outside the prison. Fellow revolutionary Piaras Béaslaí concluded that MacSwiney had "kill[ed] the effectiveness of the hunger strike as a weapon. The worldwide sympathy which the heroic martyrdom of MacSwiney evoked was no doubt a valuable asset to Sinn Fein, but not a very tangible weapon in our warfare."[35] Indeed, three years would pass before a well-publicized hunger strike again occurred.

Yet MacSwiney had shown that prisoners themselves, not the authorities, controlled the hunger strike and could determine its outcome. Only death confirms that the striker intended to go that far. But even a fast for a limited period does not necessarily let the regime off the hook, given the deep basis of such a fast in many religious traditions. McConville's observation that death or victory are the only outcomes that do not diminish the "moral capital" of the striker connotes certainty,[36] yet it is precisely uncertainty that is the prisoner's greatest weapon. The hunger striker does not have to be willing to die as long as the guards and administrators and ministry officials cannot be sure he is not.

"We Were Back Conducting Political Struggle": South Africa, 1966

Each hunger strike, though it begins with a specific issue or an articulated principle, is ultimately waged in the prisoner's mind and body. Even without a strike, prison heightens awareness of the body and of food. With little to occupy their time, prisoners talk about food, share food, hoard food, devise rules about eating and about using the toilet. The hunger strike, though, places food external to the body: the tray left untouched by the door, or the rotting food piled up in the corner. On Sunday morning at the end of the first week of the April 1920 Mountjoy strike, the administration distributed porridge to the cells. Prison porridge seemed to the weakened prisoners to deepen their agony—until the order came to send it back. Returning from Mass, Frank Gallagher heard men cheering, calling out to one another, laughing as they spooned porridge and splashed milk through the cell-door aperture into the passageway. "The gloom," he saw, "has melted away under the hot joy of spooning clammy porridge out through a small hole in an iron door."[37]

And yet with the food removed, the worry remained: did brandy count? vitamins? a mustard plaster? a communion wafer?[38] Questions about food dog every hunger strike, as the body becomes the measure of one's honor. Mandela said that steps in the corridor in the night betray who has been sneaking food, since hunger strikers no longer need to use the toilet.[39] Body and mind separate, the former subordinate to the latter's control. "I feel vaguely sorry for [my body]," mused Hanna Sheehy-Skeffington in her journal in 1912, "as if I had passed sentence on an unknowing and innocent victim."[40] As a battle of the mind, the hunger strike is emblematically a tactic for the political prisoner.

The prison administration, in the modern hunger strike, is usually confident that the collective discipline this protest requires is beyond their charges' will. In South Africa, that assumption was civilizational. "I know the Bantus," Lieutenant Bosch, the officer in charge of food on Robben Island, supposedly remarked when men at the quarry refused to take their lunch one day in April 1966. "That's how they behave when their stomachs are full. As soon as they become hungry, they'll outrun each other to collect their porridge."[41] Though South African prisoners could draw upon the *satyagraha* fasting tradition, that offered little guidance. For Gandhi and his comrades, cultural traditions blurred the political outlines of the hunger strike, as some *satyagrahi* refused to eat inappropriate food or observed religious fasts.[42] The first collective strike, in Diepkloof Penal Settlement, accompanied a demand that either an abusive guard be removed or the prisoners themselves be moved to Johannesburg Prison. The regime seems never to have considered force-feeding, and acceded to the transfer within a week.[43] More recent history furnished few precedents. There had been an action by some Pan Africanist Congress (PAC) prisoners on Robben Island in 1965; white women prisoners had briefly refused food in Pretoria in 1960. Lieutenant Bosch's comment, overheard by prisoners and perhaps inflated in the retelling, provided a powerful incentive for the strike. He could not imagine that black prisoners had the discipline required. The 1966 strike, which appeared to be spontaneous but was in fact a collective, planned effort, countered these racist assumptions.[44]

Moses Dlamini of the PAC explained the strike's origins: long-term political prisoners realized that conditions had to improve before short-termers (those with sentences under five years) were released, cutting the community in half and reducing its leverage. Dlamini and his comrades thus conducted "mass mobilisation . . . preparing all the comrades in all the cells." But the strike was organized on the spot, when those first in line at the quarry simply declined to take lunch, and the word went down the line. The 900 men on the crew that day would have included criminal prisoners, though how many of either group participated is unknown. More than most such strikes, this had to be a performance. "After lunch," Dlamini continues, "we went back to work on hungry stomachs, pretending as though our stomachs were full. After work we returned to prison, went for tauza [the body inspection in which prisoners danced naked before the guards] and from there went past the kitchen to sit on our haunches or flat on our buttocks to go to our cells and be counted in."[45] They could not simply fast in their cells, nor could they shirk labor. They would have to carry on as usual, showing indifference to food. They would use guards' ideas about their physical and mental capabilities to gain advantage. Martyrdom and sacrifice were not available to them; their lives were expendable and their deaths might go unremarked.

The 1966 strike needed to appear spontaneous in order to preserve and strengthen the Robben Island prisoner community. The regime had gone to great lengths to isolate both African National Congress (ANC) and PAC leaders from the rank and file. Any hint of coordination by these leaders would surely have brought serious reprisals. ANC-PAC relations, meanwhile, had been strained from the first days on the island, reflecting the distrust between them on the outside. This had probably doomed the previous PAC strike. This time, young prisoners from both groups met and planned to sidestep their leaders.

> The hunger strike had to drag on indefinitely until prisoners started to collapse. We would continue going to work every day and do whatever we could manage. The hunger strike would not be championed, guided, or directed by either the PAC or the ANC. It had to assume spontaneity . . . . When the enemy was prepared to negotiate, there would be one representative from the PAC, one from the ANC and one independent . . . . No organisation or group of individuals would be allowed to conduct negotiations on our behalf. All the above conditions were propagated throughout our cells by our secret group as spontaneous decisions not coming from either the PAC or the ANC.[46]

As many other prisoners had discovered before, a hunger strike could splinter a community. A generation gap on the island reinforced the political division: most PAC prisoners were quite young compared to those from the ANC. At meal times that April, "PAC youths ran to be in front so as to dissuade others from taking the food." This maintained the performance of spontaneity, but led some to suspect that the PAC was in fact directing the strike.[47] An ANC memoirist, Indres Naidoo, recalled that it was ANC men who took the lead, suggesting that the strike outcome helped to erode rumors of PAC dominance.[48] The strike did indeed spread: to the hospital; to the B-Section prisoners, including Mandela; and even to Robert Sobukwe's hut. The administration demonstrated that it was quite willing to let strikers die: at the hospital, guards retaliated by denying patients medicine and marching them out to the quarry to work, while those who collapsed at the quarry were loaded into vans and dumped back in solitary confinement to be fed. Yet the prisoners managed to alert the outside, thanks to a friendly warder who smuggled a letter. And the scope of the hunger strike overwhelmed the prison apparatus, especially as guards ceased forcing prisoners to work.[49]

The 1966 hunger strike succeeded precisely because prisoners acted in ways the regime could not expect nor understand. Instead of savages bent on self-preservation, good only for working and eating, they were political beings, acting in concert against their short-term interests. "With the hunger strike," recalled Natoo Babenia, "we were back conducting political struggle."[50] But political, to a regime that assumed black prisoners could not entertain and develop complex ideas involving long-range planning, meant unreadable. Thus when Lieutenant Bosch arrived at the quarry on the afternoon of the strike's fifth day, he found it impossible to reason with the prisoners, who berated him instead of recognizing his authority. Eventually, he acknowledged that the prisoners controlled the situation, and he allowed them to elect three representatives to discuss grievances. Bosch and these representatives then visited other work groups, the B Section, and Sobukwe's hut to inform them of the development, thus imprinting prisoner organization all across Robben Island.[51] The strikers negotiated a wide range of concessions on food quality, clothing, hygiene, and relations with criminal prisoners. The regime nevertheless found ways to punish many of the participants. Protest alone would not transform the relations in the prison on Robben Island, but it would create conditions that allowed the prisoners to organize. The strike's signal accomplishment was to reignite politics in a broader community, forging links between previously hostile (and still rival) organizations. Called into being by prisoners acting politically, the strike thus built a framework for further political activity.

A Double-Edged Sword: Poland's Hunger Strikes

The hunger strike as a collective protest is not easy to orchestrate, for it is entirely subject to individual calculations or emotions, easily swayed by the actions of those in the next cell or the moves of a guard or prosecutor. The political movement is as likely to be reacting to the twists and turns of a hunger strike as it is to be shaping it. Yet in the retelling, the personal dilemmas often disappear in the collective story. Many men who began the Mountjoy strike in April 1920 did not last a week before quitting, but memoirs draw a veil over such personal failings.[52] Irish Republican prisoners could believe that the entire nation fasted with them in active support of their struggle. Not so in interwar Poland. Like Republicans in Ireland, Polish communists believed that erstwhile comrades had stolen and mishandled a newly independent state. Their prison struggles, though, were built on the idea of a society divided by class conflict, not united against one external, alien enemy.

When communists in Warsaw's Mokotów Prison collaborated on a clandestine newsletter in 1928, they had among them enough experience in confinement across the country to compile a history of hunger strikes in the first decade of Poland's Second Republic. They framed that history starkly: the bourgeois state revealed its true cruelty in its treatment of "defenseless captives," deploying methods it inherited from its imperial forebears. Fighting for their lives and their cause, political prisoners had to "take up the ultimate weapon, slow dying by hunger strike."[53] Without the reassuring frame of national or religious tradition, the communists could not easily reconcile a passive tactic with a violent narrative of class struggle. The Mokotów chroniclers recall dozens of hunger strikes, generally the products of extreme despair. In the earliest years, sheer hunger was the catalyst: "political prisoners often are deprived of any help from outside, because of the general destitution of the working class. So they prefer to go hungry for days on end rather than to let that *Wasserzuppe* [watery soup; the German word evoked imperial subjugation] made from rotten turnips and carrots touch their lips." Similar emotions surround a grim strike in Pawiak Prison in 1922: "pushed to their limits they prepare for the struggle, having decided to die or to win for themselves and other political prisoners humane living conditions. The hunger strike is unusually hard-fought. The administration and the prosecutor try everything to break the solidarity of the strikers. But the heroic bearing of the strikers, their fervor and enthusiasm for the fight wins out, though many of them are already coughing up blood." These strikers are weak from the outset, yet they summon their strength to defeat the regime from their deathbed—only to see the regime renege on its concessions.[54]

No MacSwiney-like martyrs appear in the prisoners' history. The bourgeois regime breaks its "half-alive" victims with force-feeding and orgies of beatings, often after just four or five days.[55] Strike reports from the time convey a slightly less heroic picture of the prison struggle. Strikers advanced a variety of demands specific to political prisoners, such as clearer distinctions between them and criminal prisoners and acknowledgment of prisoner leaders, as well as more mundane concessions like educational materials, health care, and swifter resolution of prisoners' cases. For example, an "incredibly fierce and unified" hunger strike of eighty-four prisoners in Wronki Prison in March 1927 protested separate-cell isolation and the division of prisoners by national groups, while demanding the right to wear their own clothing and the right to form a *komuna*. They also sought a longer recreation period; access to books, letters, and writing materials; better food and health care; no more forced haircuts; a separate room for science lectures; and an end to imposed fees for prison utilities. This pulling together of every possible grievance is hardly the stuff of which fights to the death are made. Ignacy Wrzos, the strikers' spokesman, assured comrades outside on the ninth day that, although many were near death, no one had broken.[56]

While Wrzos does not mention force-feeding, this was the usual ending to a strike. The authorities might not even have to resort to the practice but merely threaten each prisoner alone. A Katowice prosecutor explained how he broke a November 1923 strike of forty unsentenced communists who were demanding immediate release:

> I went to the prison where, with the help of guards and soldiers I gathered all the communists in the corridor. I did not allow them to submit a collective petition, but listened to each of them one after another, explaining to them the fruitlessness and pointlessness of a hunger strike
> .... Prandzioch and Wieczorek tried to influence the other prisoners by addressing them, but I got around this by ordering that agitators and troublemakers should be separated from the others in individual cells, forbidden to communicate with one another.

He ordered dinner to be served and claimed that most prisoners accepted it. The strike dwindled quickly, with just a handful still striking after a couple of days.[57]

The relative ubiquity of the hunger strike in the 1920s most likely contributed to its lack of effectiveness and led to the development of the *przeplatanka* a few years later. Instead of one tactic to achieve many goals, the *przeplatanka* focused on one general goal, amplifying its demands through a variety of protest tactics. Though the hunger strike might still be a local affair with multiple articulated demands,[58] the communist leadership tried to impose more coordination from above in order to make the hunger strike more unpredictable. In September 1931, communists in over thirty prisons across Poland protested new prison regulations, with most of them fasting for three days. In Grodno, where the comrades had only recently staged an eight-day fast, the new strike was "conducted in a very organized way." The administration tried to break it after four days by offering some concessions and permitted the *komuna* leader to visit all the cells to convey the news and bring the strike to an end. Instead, he "entirely correctly enjoined them to continue the strike, and several comrades who had accepted breakfast now refused lunch." The administration offered further concessions and the strike ended successfully that day.[59] But in the end, hunger strikes cannot be measured only by concessions gained. A hunger strike aimed at multiple targets succeeds depending upon the ability of the movement, inside and outside prison, to transform any results—whether they are concessions, or newfound camaraderie, or martyrdom—into lasting signposts for other prisoners and activists.

The twists and turns of Poland's political fortunes in the twentieth century erased many valuable prison memories. During the two years of martial law, 1981–83, some 10,000 members of Solidarity spent time in any of nearly fifty camps or prisons. They had no native models of hunger striking to draw upon. The battles of Polish socialists in czarist prisons had faded into obscurity. Jan Krzesławski observed in 1911 that "the hunger strike is a double-edged tool and is used only as a last resort, when prisoners are under attack. One can rely upon this means of broadening prisoners' rights only when the revolutionary movement is growing rapidly."[60] This observation—by no means a universal truth, but at least some guidance from Polish history—would not have been self-evident in 1981. Nor would the strategic lessons of the Polish Communist Party, which urged (through Red Help) that an "ultimate" tactic like a hunger strike could only be undertaken in coordination with other prisons and with the party organization outside, have had any echo for those imprisoned by the communists fifty years later.[61] Auschwitz, Pawiak, and other places of Nazi cruelty were far more familiar to the Solidarity internees, and there had been no hunger strikes in those prisons and camps.

In the hunger strikes of martial law, at a time when underground Solidarity had neither the inclination nor the ability to direct its members' actions, the tactic played out in unexpected ways. As had the rightist dictatorship before, the communist regime often interned people far from their homes and tried to isolate prominent leaders from rank-and-file activists. Those activists still at large focused on keeping up the spirits of the frightened and immobilized general public. A key part of that campaign, as seen in Chapter 5, was assistance for prisoners. But if Poles were supporting their countrymen and women by sending them food, would a hunger strike make any sense at all? Protest itself was of course a given; all had learned a lot about organized civil disobedience during the union's legal existence and had nothing better to do behind bars. Polish hunger strikers also knew about the recent campaigns in Northern Ireland.

A comprehensive survey of martial-law internment identifies over a dozen hunger strikes. Many of these were individual protests that advanced very specific demands like a family visit; anniversaries of martial law also provided occasion for protest.[62] Solidarity hunger strikers most often framed their actions as a protest fast, whose participants gather in a church for a set period of time to call attention to some problem, receive visitors, and issue statements. This type of fast, such as one staged by members of the Workers' Defense Committee in a Warsaw church in May 1977, could unite and energize the opposition.[63] The hunger strike of seventeen Solidarity leaders, some of whom had fasted in 1977, in Białołęka Prison in Warsaw in May 1982 adopted a similar style. In a message to the nation they called their action "a protest against martial law and a demonstration in favor of societal reconciliation according to principles proposed by the Polish Episcopate."[64]

Another group of Solidarity leaders, formally arrested and awaiting trial in Warsaw's central prison, staged a one-week fast in summer 1983, in celebration of a visit to Poland by Pope John Paul II. The underground leadership sent word that it opposed the strike, so Henryk Wujec shouted this communiqué from his cell window. Another prisoner, who like Wujec had fasted five years before, shouted back that the prisoners should decide for themselves, and so it began. Wujec recalled mixed feelings: "a person gets used to certain comforts that he's created for himself, he's made himself at home. A hunger strike means cell searches and confiscation of one's things. So it requires determination. I also think that one should not squander one's health in prison."[65] Wujec thus clearly doubted that personal sacrifice by prisoners could contribute adequately to the larger anti-communist struggle outside.

A symbolic protest is in some ways a more difficult challenge to prisoners' willpower than a struggle to the death. About forty internees in Ostrów Wielkopolski announced a hunger strike on March 8, 1982, "against martial law, against lawlessness and the violation of both human rights and the rights of the nation." Bogdan Ciszak explained in his diary: "We want in this way to shake up the national conscience." Ciszak, who quit the strike on its sixth day, worried that his comrades had begun to talk of "striking to the end," though that had not been the initial plan. His diary traces growing obstinacy: prisoners found that as the days passed and their hunger pangs subsided, the lack of regime response hardened them. "More and more want to hunger strike without an endpoint," he wrote on the tenth day. But the security police threatened force-feeding two days later, and the remaining strikers ended their protest on the fourteenth day, after Mass. "Did such a protest form make any sense," Ciszak wondered. "Have we attained any goals with this sacrifice? No doubt it has improved so-called 'morale' among the interned. People who were, after all, extremely active when the union was in operation could do something in prison, fight for the cause that has lost them their freedom . . . . Personally, I am against this form of struggle, which I consider passive and suicidal." But Ciszak finds himself drawn to an opposite conclusion, too: the hunger strike is "the only possible protest for prisoners in the Polish People's Republic."[66]

Ciszak's ambivalence likely stemmed from the fact that even a modest hunger strike can quickly turn into a grand romantic sacrifice. A similar dynamic unfolded in the Hrubieszów strike six months later. "Curiosity" about a fabled weapon inspired Marek Kulczyk's comrades when one of them was sent to an isolation cell. They quickly agreed they had to oppose this punishment as a matter of principle and stage a hunger strike to win political prisoner status. But behind this principled stance was also, Kulczyk saw, a physical and mental test, in which the prisoners proved themselves as men and as citizens. He foresaw failure: "The dominant mood then was that this was a cause in which one fights for oneself and also, as it were, for future generations. Yes, people said such things." Initially, the strike produced the desired reaction, as prison administration was "stunned." A judge came to remonstrate with the strikers and asked what concrete demands they had—open cells? books? visits? "But we were striking for a principle, for status, and not to have the Prison Administrator grant us some favor by gracious decree because he can afford it—and then if his mood changes he can annul that order."[67] The administration's indulgence indeed proved to be limited: force-feeding and beatings began on day seven. Families were allowed visits so they could beg the strikers to stop. Many did, though Kulczyk notes with pride that even these rejoined the strike so that nearly all ended it together. But their achievement turned out to be short-lived; Kulczyk felt they had fundamentally misunderstood the hunger strike. "After seventeen days it turned out that this form of protest has outlived its value and was cheapened. After all, what could we do now except hunger strike again . . . . We thought that they would fear a hunger strike more than anything, but that isn't how it turned out. We thought it was the ultimate weapon—but it wasn't."[68] They were a long way from the more self-assured one-day symbolic fasts of previous months. The principles of the men in Hrubieszów Prison proved no match for the hard reality of an existential conflict.

Ireland 1923: "A Wilful Waste of National Strength"

The expectations surrounding a hunger strike shape its outcome. Rituals like a monthly protest fast may strengthen a strike or raise participants' assessment of their capabilities. The threat of force-feeding may dissuade prisoners who have only skipped a meal, or they may welcome the chance to force the regime's hand. The community of prisoners' supporters may accept the need for martyrs or try to get the strikers to accept food. Analysis of an utterly failed strike in Ireland illuminates how leadership strategies, regime resources, and social dynamics shape prisoner choices.

Much had changed in Ireland by 1923. MacSwiney's death in 1920 had, as noted earlier, made hunger striking much more daunting. The signing of the Anglo-Irish Treaty in December 1921 also complicated the political cause as it created an Irish Free State, without six counties of the north, that many did not want to accept. In place of a more-or-less united struggle against the British Empire came a confused conflict among erstwhile comrades. Those who rejected the treaty, fighting and going to prison, had to ponder anew what victory or defeat could mean. Equally uncertain was the strength of bonds of comradeship against a fraternal enemy.[69] The prisons of the Irish Civil War, therefore, could no longer be the engine of the struggle they had been a few years earlier. Many of the same men and women felt cut off from the real action, forced to languish in humiliating captivity—humiliating because the captors were no longer the hated British.

Arriving once again in Mountjoy Prison from Gormanstown Camp in October 1922, Frank Gallagher tried to organize the men in his wing, but it seemed hopeless. "Discipline non ex[istent]. Awful parades. Empty conversations. Blather all day. Went to a cell here and there." In Gormanstown, military discipline still kept inmates focused on the struggle—the men had just commemorated MacSwiney with a one-day fast, complete with a recital of the rosary and a concert. Now, Gallagher heard stories of a violent clash with guards in which several prisoners died—and when order had been restored, prisoners took up a chant: "We want our breakfast." Gallagher "nearly died of shame. Yet that type here is plenty. Rosary said so nobody can hear"—in contrast to the camp, where the men, "shaven and clean," said the rosary on their knees so all could see. In Mountjoy, Gallagher aimed not just to relieve boredom and combat indolence but to retrain men who were "leading a worthless life . . . and prepared for nothing."[70]

Discipline and determination did return to Mountjoy as the regime cracked down. Over the course of 1923, the prisoners' council looked for an occasion to lead the men of Mountjoy back into the fight. IRA leadership, which had long advised against a hunger strike, changed its position after Civil War hostilities ended in May 1923 but cautioned that prisoners should decide for themselves, as they would be "entering on a life and death struggle with the Free State, [which] will fight to the end for its mastery."[71] When the Mountjoy administration embarked on a drive to "normalize" the prison, stiffening rules and ceasing to recognize prisoner representatives, the prisoner's commanding officer Michael Kilroy announced that one wing would begin a hunger strike—"the last weapon of passive resistance," he called it—for "unconditional release."[72] Dumbfounded, Gallagher fired off a long memo remonstrating with Kilroy. Gallagher's wing had just voted by a three-to-one margin against a strike, yet all would surely be "stampeded" into one by peer pressure though they were unprepared. This was nothing but a trick, he charged, "and like all tricks it will surely fail."[73] But discipline came first, and he and his comrades all fell into line. After a "bumper" last meal, "luscious to the eye and taste," nearly all IRA prisoners in Mountjoy refused breakfast on Sunday, October 14, 1923.[74]

The strike reawakened the Republican struggle, growing rapidly into what was likely among the largest hunger strikes of the twentieth century. At least 8,000 men and women, in every camp and prison in the Free State, fasted at the strike's height; several hundred more prisoners in Belfast joined as well. Perhaps only such an ambitious, bold undertaking could give these rebels-turned-spectators a new feeling of having rejoined the fight. With the Civil War formally over, the Free State government had lost its rationale for internment, so opinion was believed to be on the strikers' side. Anna O'Rahilly reported a crowd "cheering and singing hymns" outside North Dublin Union one evening while she and fifty other women fasted inside.[75] As camp after camp joined, the force of the wave seemed unstoppable. Mountjoy prisoner leaders reported that "hundreds of public boards and other representative bodies throughout Ireland" supported the strikers. Finally, after months of confusion and inaction, the cause was just and the battle was joined.

Republican leadership outside prison quickly raised the stakes beyond sheer morale. Sinn Féin called for the public to show commitment worthy of the brave hunger strikers: it urged civil bodies to suspend all but the most necessary activities and proposed a rigorous schedule of public fasting, solemn processions, and recitations of the rosary. Thus, for example, processions on Friday, October 26, would circle each jail or camp seven times while reciting the rosary.[76] IRA Chief of Staff Frank Aiken framed the strike as a battle "in defence of the rights of Irish citizens to be free to set up their own Government and live their own lives without yielding a voluntary allegiance to any power or authority hostile or inimical to the Republic of Ireland." Articulating the cause for which these women and men had gone to prison, he overstated the original aims of the strike and whitewashed the strike's tense beginning, asserting that each prisoner had made the individual decision to strike. The strike, he continued, "has the support and approval of the [Republican] Government and GHQ and under no circumstances will it be called off by them, because they believe it will be valiantly carried through to the end by all the loyal volunteers who commenced, and because they believe also that it will finally prove that the IRA 'can suffer most' and that their sufferings will not be in vain."[77] This was an internal communication, so the warnings were not to the Free State but to the strikers themselves. And yet with his confident assertion of an unspecified "end," Aiken undercut the cause. Evoking MacSwiney's dictum, he made the strike a competition that would redeem the defeated army.

Internal divisions and external indifference worked against the strike from the beginning. On October 28, the same day of Aiken's communiqué, Kit Byrne, the Republican prisoners' commander at the Curragh Camp, among the largest internment centers, wrote "the saddest letter I have ever written in my life" to his wife. Over the previous twenty-four hours he had seen the strike collapse. Despite a hostile chaplain and the constant temptations of warm food, more than 95 percent had still been striking on October 26. Then it all fell apart, and a trickle of defections became a flood, even as the administration made men sign a "Form of Undertaking" before they got food. Byrne could see that to continue the strike would break his prisoner community into factions, "so what in God's name had I to do to save the movement as those wretches were all going to sign the form . . . . I would rather have faced the firing squad than call it off, but there was Divisional Officers ordering their men off."[78] The strike at Newbridge Camp ended in similar disarray, according to the self-satisfied report of the camp's governor: "Many of those who were on strike made no secret of the fact that they believed they were doing wrong, that they were acting against their better judgement. They also stated quite frankly that they had no option but to go on strike, that they were afraid to do otherwise." Strikers' initial "truculence," he claimed, faded as the protest entered its second week. When the administration took control of one cookhouse and prepared food, strikers' resolve weakened. By November 1, he asserted hundreds of prisoners were storming their own food stores and "clamouring for something to eat."[79]

Aiken responded with a communiqué much less confident than the one of the previous week. Talk of comparative suffering disappeared, replaced by "the depression that must overtake you when you lie, cold and uncared for, suffering agonies of body and mind. We know that men who are ordinarily good soldiers will fail to face death in this most horrible form, if they have not fully made up their minds and weighed the consequences to themselves and to their country before commencing." Aiken acknowledged the effect of the regime's "lies, brutality, and cunning." And yet the campaign continued, claiming two deaths. Those who took food were "defectors," and Aiken called it victory "if one volunteer, officer or private, succeeds in setting the example to his fellow citizens, by voluntarily suffering long drawn out tortures of flesh and mind and offering his life and suffering to God for the Republic of Ireland."[80] Ernie O'Malley, fasting in Kilmainham, added military metaphor, urging his fellow officers to "go over the top." He called the strike "a spiritual and mental test, not a physical one, so my message to the lads is 'Keep your hearts up; so long as you are not beaten in your heart you win.' The Honour of God and the Glory of Ireland is worth untold suffering. It is a fight for the individual, each must fight his little battle in his own heart and win."[81] Like Aiken's message, this left little room for any other outcomes.

The Free State government took its captives' anger seriously, monitoring the strike's daily progress.[82] It waged a war of propaganda and temptation—like the warm food at Newbridge—and found that a "fight for the individual" provided it thousands of individual targets. Some succumbed to pressure from their chaplain, others responded to offered comforts, while others simply regretted the campaign from the first moment. Republican grousing that the government had tricked the prisoners or that the clergy had betrayed them did not help the cause, and initial public support for the strike seems to have waned rapidly.[83] The rhetoric had flown too high, the demands on prisoners and the public alike had been too steep, and the government was more than willing to break the strike, perceiving an existential threat. To concede and release so many thousands of recently armed men would seem to invite a rekindling of the Civil War. "We are going to break the hunger strike at whatever cost," wrote Provisional Government Chairman W. T. Cosgrave to Minister of Defence Richard Mulcahy. "We regret the sufferings, . . . but they are not of our making."[84] In the end, with national elections approaching, the strike exposed society's exhaustion rather than the unquenchable fire of Irish republicanism. On the afternoon of November 22, Michael Kilroy requested and was granted by the Kilmainham governor a motorcar for two strikers to visit all prisons and camps. They met with their comrades and informed them that the strike was really over.[85]

Mary MacSwiney, who since Terence's death had continued to campaign for sacrifice and had herself been a hunger striker the previous year, traced the failure to its being a "sympathetic strike," without any "great injustice" to fight for; still, she was sure that the debacle "means nothing at all as far as the big fight goes."[86] Sighle Humphreys saw it differently: "We were flattened. We felt the Irish public had forgotten us. The tinted trappings of our fight were hanging like rags about us."[87] Others shared her sense of desolation: their less-resolute comrades had "dirtied their bibs" while they starved; camp organization had been "shattered" by the strike.[88] Thousands had fasted for up to forty days, achieving nothing. Michael Kilroy, who had initiated the strike in Mountjoy, recast the strike's end as itself a "sacrifice," thus equivalent to its beginning. This time, Republican men and women had agreed to lay down their powerful weapon "for the sake of Ireland, and for the future."[89] This was the best that could be said about the strike of 1923. Frank Aiken, reflecting on the strike a few weeks later, saw it differently: it had been "a wilful waste of national strength."[90]

Apotheosis: The H-Block Hunger Strikes

Hunger strikes accompanied the Troubles from the very beginning, when IRA Commanding Officer Billy McKee and a few other prisoners in the Crumlin

Road Prison (soon joined by comrades in Long Kesh and Armagh) struck for political recognition in May 1972. The strike provided an impetus for the introduction of Special Category status for Republican and Loyalist prisoners, both sentenced and interned.[91] Though the British had reasons to grant the status even without the strike—prisons were overcrowded, and at this early stage there was some hope of bringing a swift end to the conflict—the idea that endurance had brought victory would not fade.[92] There were many inconclusive hunger strikes in prisons in England, Ireland, and Northern Ireland in the 1970s—most famously the strike that resulted in the death of Frank Stagg in Wakefield Prison in early 1976, less than a month before the British ended Special Category status—but each burnished complementary narratives of struggle and martyrdom.[93]

As Republican men and women moved in and out of prison, and among the different prisons and wings, the stories of all these hunger strikes became part of the prison canon. By the late 1970s, prisons in Northern Ireland held some 1,500–2,000 conflict participants, of which members of the Provisional IRA (founded in 1969 and generally referred to as the IRA) was the largest group. Strict military discipline and adherence to message typified the IRA in this period; it explicitly hearkened back to Civil War heroes like Ernie O'Malley. The demarcation between the IRA and its political party, Sinn Féin, allowed the former to stay away from political debate and to focus on organization. Discipline, organization, and historical consciousness indeed tailored the IRA for prison, which favors a controlled message and a practiced repertoire of actions.

The blanket/no-wash protest would seem to have left little room for further escalation, especially considering the violence of the H-Block staff response. At the same time, the British government was quite susceptible to public opinion and unable to make prisoners and their protests disappear. A democratic government with civil-servant prison administrators must work through many of the same arguments for and against forced-feeding and other measures as an authoritarian one. But the fallout from the torture investigation of 1972 and the negative publicity around the no-wash protest offered plenty of room for a well-organized, collective protest based on shared sacrifice. Perhaps the final piece that needed to fall into place before the hunger strikes was a realization of the limits of negotiation. The no-wash protest, precisely because it was so shocking and offensive and imposed such heavy costs on the institution and its employees, appeared to open a space for negotiation, as both Republicans and the government hoped to find a way to bring the ugly spectacle to an end. But talks between church leaders and Margaret Thatcher's government broke down in the late summer of 1980. The current protest could go no further, and so to break the stasis only a hunger strike was left. Brendan "The Dark" Hughes and Bobby Sands compiled a list of volunteers for a hunger strike and chose seven men including Hughes to begin on October 27, 1980.[94]

The seven strikers chosen represented the six counties of Northern Ireland, plus an additional striker from an allied non-IRA group; the number seven also evoked for some the seven signers of the Easter Proclamation of 1916. The strike was thus framed as one for the nation, not just for the prisoners; symbolism weighed it down from the outset.[95] The collective organization of the strike also presented a problem that had dogged the strike of 1923: seven men could not be equally committed to the same terrible goal, as each would understand and experience the approach of death in a different way. Indeed, one of the strikers, whom Hughes recalls being the most persistent in getting chosen for the protest, turned out to be the weakest physically and mentally. Before he slipped into a coma, Sean McKenna extracted a promise from Hughes that he would not be allowed to die. The group was too small to absorb one defector; Hughes suspects that others in the group calculated that McKenna's death would end the strike and let them off the hook.[96]

The British government found that it could manipulate the strikers as their demands encompassed both the specific (such as clothing) and the general (status). Hints of a compromise on specific demands tantalized the strikers. On the day McKenna was fed, a nonbinding proposal did indeed arrive; the promises it contained, though, would be fulfilled only if the prisoners first conformed to prison clothing and prison work. These concessions may have been significant from the regime's perspective; indeed, the British authorities argued in a December 4 statement that the prisoners already enjoyed most of what they sought.[97] That Margaret Thatcher paid a visit to Dublin at this time encouraged some in Northern Ireland to believe a breakthrough was imminent, as did a visit to the strikers by a senior British official. The prisoners would not get the status they sought, but the government created enough ambiguity that ending the strike seemed sensible. The end of the strike, on December 18, threw the nature of "success" into sharp relief. Seven weeks of starvation had won nothing except attention and promises. The 1980 hunger strike was nearly forgotten in the shadow of the epic campaign of the following spring, but its failure made its successor possible.

The hunger strike of 1981 began to take shape immediately upon the end of the first one, against formidable odds. The Republican prisoners had sent to the battlefront some of their strongest and most determined men; their long road back to health would be a daily reminder to all of the enormous difficulty of a hunger strike. Yet the leadership could draw on deep reserves and confidently plan another. Remarkably, the spectacle of their comrades wasting away had not daunted the men.[98] At the same time, the hunger strike had become predictable, and the authorities had proven able to manage the situation. And so the prisoners responded with a devastating innovation. Bobby Sands began the new hunger strike alone, on Sunday March 1, 1981—the fifth anniversary of

the end of prisoners' eligibility for Special Category status. By setting out apparently alone—among dozens of men who would willingly have joined him—
Sands remade a familiar protest form, adding to it another layer of inscrutability.
A single striker, if sufficiently well known and supported, delivered a powerful impact: that was the real message of MacSwiney's fast in Brixton Prison in
1920. On the day after the strike began, the prisoners ended the no-wash protest
(though continuing to refuse prison clothing). This further focused all attention
on the lone striker.

Yet Sands, unlike MacSwiney, was not alone. The strike announcement
offered mystery: "a number of our comrades, beginning today with Bobby
Sands, will hunger strike to the death unless the British government abandons
its criminalisation policy and meets our demands for political status."⁹⁹ But who
were those other comrades, and when would they strike? Since prison authorities never took any measures to isolate suspected strikers, they likely never knew
who would be next. Two weeks after Sands began, Francis Hughes announced he
was not taking breakfast. The next Sunday, two more men, Raymond McCreesh
and Patsy O'Hara, joined the strike. Each remained an individual striker, their
protest independent of the actions of their comrades. No more joined before
Sands's death on May 5, but then Joe McDonnell took Sands's place on the
strike; each subsequent death then summoned a replacement from the ranks.
So too when an early striker took food; the authorities might have hoped that
this signaled a weakening of the protest, but a replacement just two days later
dashed that prospect. In all, twenty-three men went on this hunger strike, the
last in September.

Over the last two months of the protest, family members became more desperate, and some parents intervened to take their sons off the strike. Six men
were still fasting when the protest ended on October 3. The relay format perhaps
made it inevitable that death and survival would be mixed together, diffusing
the actions of individual prisoners for better or worse. Nor was the end itself
clear. On the one hand, there was no official signal that could allow the prisoners to celebrate victory; on the other, no individual emergency, as in the first
strike, precipitated the end. Bik McFarlane, the prisoners' commanding officer,
explained that the family interventions threatened to recast the strike as an act
of personal defiance, "and that's not what the whole thing was about. So it was
decided that we needed to end it and that we would be in control of the ending
of it."¹⁰⁰ As it had begun, so it ended at a time the prisoners determined.

Since prisoners did not win clear concessions, the strike could seem a failure
in the short term. But the relentless, unpredictable pace of striking and dying
rattled British politics in a way that the previous strike had not. Bobby Sands
became a figure recognizable around the world, thanks in part to his successful campaign for Parliament. The strike pushed the prisoners themselves into

national politics, no matter how much Prime Minister Thatcher might deny that there was anything political in their incarceration. The individual deaths had made the British appear inflexible and undermined the government's ability to name and categorize the prisoners. As journalist Padraig O'Malley concludes: "the British government's obsession with not appearing to be beaten consumed its more clever intentions. It won the contest of wills but little else. It lost the propaganda war, resuscitated an ailing IRA, and politicized militant Republicanism."[101] Just a few days after the end of the strike, the British conceded to prisoners the right to wear their own clothes and promised a review of rules on prison work.[102]

The strike had the greatest impact on the prisoners themselves. Ten valued comrades had died, five years of bitter protest were over, and only a few demands had been met. However, they had staged a protest like no other, and the guards could only wonder what they might do next. The challenge was to find ways of demonstrating resolve and endurance, building upon the reputation for unpredictability that the strike had given the prisoners. Laurence McKeown, a scholar and one of the 1981 hunger strikers, illustrates how protest experience paid off. In one case, a guard attempted to enforce a rule limiting prisoners to two showers a week, charging a showering prisoner for disobeying an order to stop washing. Pat Sheehan, a hunger strike veteran, witnessed the confrontation and "promptly undressed and stepped into a shower also." Both men were taken to the punishment cells, but the rule was shortly removed.[103]

The prisoners next fought for segregation from Loyalist prisoners, an indirect way of forcing the authorities to acknowledge their organizational status. The "non-conforming" prisoners who had been on the no-wash protest and continued to protest prison work were already segregated, as no Loyalist prisoners had joined them. But many had left the protest and been moved to "conforming" wings, where they were in the minority among Loyalist prisoners and communicated with their comrades only by shouting across the courtyards. To rebuild the Republican community and achieve segregation, protesters would have to "go into the system," accepting in full the liberalized prison rules on offer.[104]

The weapon of choice in the campaign for segregation was rumor, explains Séanna Walsh, the Republican prisoners' new commanding officer. The leadership delegated men to accept the rules and move to where they could unsettle "the comfortable life in the nice, quiet, mixed conforming wings." Walsh gives an example: "One of our lads came back [from the metal workshop] with a story that 70 makeshift knives had been discovered there and we put the word out that they didn't belong to us. The loyalists knew that they hadn't made 70 knives so they became paranoid." As more and more men came over, pretending that they had given up protest, neither Loyalist prisoners nor the administration could read prisoner relations and predict what could happen. "The loyalists realised," continues Walsh, "that they were soon going to be outnumbered and, worse still, by ex-blanket-men, 'crazies' who had lain locked up in their own shit for years, and who were now preparing to move into their wings and disrupt their lives." They asked prison officials in vain for protection and then joined the demand for segregation. With confrontations escalating and the H-Blocks descending into chaos, the administration gave in, uniting prisoners by organization in October 1982.[105] Exploiting the inscrutability that the no-wash protest and the hunger strike had given them, the Republican prisoners achieved de facto recognition. They regained the community that the blanket protest itself had aimed to recuperate: the one enjoyed in the cages, long before.

The paradox of political incarceration is that in an institution made necessary by legal codes and sentencing guidelines, in which time and space are strictly allotted, and in which there is no doubt who guards whom, uncertainty is both a central problem and a goal, on both sides of the locked cell doors. The prison authorities seek to know their inmates thoroughly, interrogating, observing, examining their bodies intimately. At the same time, they leave the political prisoner in constant uncertainty as to her or his fate. The hunger strike both dispels that uncertainty and generates new uncertainties for the regime, which must respond without knowing what exactly the prisoners are doing. As for themselves, prisoners experience the moment of beginning a protest as clarifying, even liberating. The less the regime is able to predict and manage prisoner actions, the more control prisoners can claim. The success of a hunger strike defies measurement, but even the attempt changes prison relationships. The state and the prison usually control physical discomfort and death, deciding when and where to incarcerate, what restrictions to impose, when and how to torture, and whether to execute. Through these inviolable powers the regime demonstrates its ability to repress its opponents. By targeting this central function with an unpredictable weapon, the hunger strike undermines that power.

9

"This Purgatory Is Useful"

How Prison Forges Politics

Costly, cumbersome, and cruel though it may be, regimes continue to turn to prison as a means of undermining and fracturing opposition. And yet prison is often less a deterrent to political activity than a forge of that activity. "Life in prison is a prayer all day long," wrote Helena Sieradzka, who considered her experience in Fordon Prison in the Stalinist years "essential. A person has to live through a lot to become someone. So prison was also necessary—this was not time wasted." Her husband Makary had also done time in Mokotów Prison; they agreed that prison was "work—a kind of active love for one's fellow person."[1] Baruch Hirson similarly recalled the small group of white anti-apartheid activists in Pretoria Central. "Prison was the most concentrated form of political activity I ever experienced," he said. "Every day, in every way, we were a political forum. Our discussions and arguments, our alliances and our differences, were all formed inside a political arena from which there was no escape."[2] As Hirson saw, the social formations and habits of the prison community mattered as much as the ideas themselves.

How, given the debilitating experience of prison, does it produce both individual activists and entire movements prepared for further political contest? Many political prisoners come to understand their experience inside to be complementary to what they did outside prison, as they are forced to find new forms of activity. For example, where books are not altogether banned, prisoners prize being able to read in their cells, the experience mattering as much as the content. Some read favorite texts from the prison library or sent by friends; these might be read aloud in the cell or passed around the prison. Others make do with the random selections thrown them by the guards; even the dullest technical or ideological literature offers some diversion. Some discover the opportunity to overcome intellectual or experiential barriers. Marian Płochocki, an uneducated baker, felt he truly became a communist as he struggled through the Russian edition of Marx's *Kapital* that comrades sent to the Warsaw Citadel. "Alone, I could think and digest in complete peace the mass of information I got from reading books," he wrote.[3]

Where books are forbidden, a cellmate who knows classic novels by heart might retell them or make up compelling stories.[4] Zygmunt Walter-Janke, an officer in the Home Army, discovered his talent as a teacher and an organizer in Mokotów Prison in 1949. He and his comrades enjoyed needling an illiterate cellmate until one day a prominent politician Walter-Janke called the "chairman" announced they would all educate him instead. Walter-Janke taught arithmetic.

> As a reward for good grades, I began to retell Sienkiewicz's Trilogy. I began just for Józio, but after a few minutes the whole cell was listening. After three hours, I wanted to take a break. But the chairman called Józio over and gave him a sugar cube. The chairman was in charge of all food reserves from packages we'd received. Józio gave me the sugar with a silent plea. I ate the sugar and continued my tale. I retold the Trilogy for two weeks, several hours a day.... [After this] in every cell to which I was transferred I proposed organizing our time and offered myself as the organizer. I found out what each inmate could do and obliged him to deliver some kind of lecture.[5]

The cells in Mokotów, like those in many other prisons, brought together prisoners who might never have met outside but who grew together as they studied and shared knowledge. Disparities of knowledge and political experience made communal education possible. Everything from mathematics to foreign languages to the basics of ideology brought prisoners together in a common activity. Aleksander Szetlich claimed that the only comrades he needed in his solitary cell were books. But he and his neighbors in the Citadel eagerly developed a plan to study together, holding a long debate about which subject they would choose. Finally they picked basic grammar and spelling; the classes were "held daily through the keyhole."[6]

Prison education inspires unexpected emotions. When Genia Ustrońska left Fordon Prison in September 1951, she looked back with genuine longing, even despair, at what she lost. Though already twenty-four years old when she was arrested, she had finished only six grades in her village school before World War II. Boarding a train home, she writes: "I could not rejoice. I missed all the women I left behind, and I missed school, because that was the one chance I had to fill in the holes in my basic education."[7] The only regret Frank Gallagher expressed in a letter to his wife as he embarked upon the disastrous hunger strike of October 1923 was feeling "sad for my poor old German class" that he had just started teaching.[8] Prison, then, is anything but time lost. Ustrońska, who entered Fordon as a semi-literate village partisan, felt herself becoming part of a conscious, nationwide community; her memoir contrasts the warmth of the cell community with the difficult years that followed her release. In many other cases, the lessons of prison contributed directly to political engagement outside. Exchange of knowledge and experience builds a prison community into something more than an extension of the political movement, with its own understanding of the program and the ideas that link the two worlds.

The first part of this chapter considers how prison forges the political individual. The relative luxury of time behind bars brings informal lessons about purpose, dignity, and honor. Not only fellow prisoners but the prison and the regime as well have much to teach. Every beating, every arbitrary rule in the institution conveys a lesson about political relations, about the enemy's resources and will, and about one's own capabilities. Taken from a life spent hurtling from one demonstration to the next or absorbed in the minutiae of underground work, the political prisoner has time during incarceration to examine the foundations and assumptions that have shaped that work.

Fig. 9.1 Sketch by Hilda Bernstein from Johannesburg Central Prison, 1960. Courtesy of University of the Witwatersrand Historical Papers and Toni Strasburg, the artist's daughter.

The chapter then explores the work of the "prison university," an evocative if imprecise image that its participants frequently invoke to describe a structured sharing of knowledge and training to produce informed graduates committed to fight for the cause. From seeing prison as a site of politics to seizing an opportunity to transform the prison community was a significant leap that required the extensive resources, organized structures, and solidarity across classes that developed in the interwar period. Five cases of concentrated preparatory education among political prisoners, in the Irish prisons and camps of the Civil War; among Polish communists in the interwar prisons; on Robben Island; in the detention centers of Poland's martial law; and in the H-Blocks during Northern Ireland's Troubles, will show when a prison university works, how success can be measured, and what conditions contribute to its impact on politics beyond the prison. The sources are for the most the graduates and beneficiaries of these universities as they evaluated their prison education and placed it in the context of the cause for which they suffered.

"A Great X-ray": Individual Transformations

In the assessment of former prisoners the institution reforges the self, stripping away what is unnecessary and uncovering or creating core values. Many have a sense that character revealed in prison is more real than that adopted and displayed outside. Stanisława Sowińska recorded in her prison memoir the image of prison as a fiery forge. "Prison is a hell, I know. But in this hell something happens inside a person—a reevaluation of values. What is bad is burned off, falls away. What is good remains, strengthened in the fire of suffering." Disturbingly enough, these stirring words were whispered in Sowińska's ear by her interrogator at the close of one session. She observes bitterly that "Major Ludwik" probably beat those same words into prisoners' heads on more than one occasion. Still, as she struggled with her communist commitment, she wondered whether prison would purify her as it had other comrades over the decades of struggle.[9]

Andrzej Sołdrowski was not one of Sowińska's party comrades but an enemy of the communists, whether jailers or prisoners. Yet he too knew that prison sorted people by moral and cultural categories. "The elites are in Wronki Prison," he explained, "and one must try to improve to their level." The "asceticism" of prison, he thought, did the work, giving some people a "sixth sense" that allowed them to see more clearly the political forces at play and to develop a consistent, bold strategy. Such people "rise above their surroundings not so much by force of intellect as by the force of their actions and the perseverance of the powerful."[10] Sołdrowski's eccentric theory of leadership reflects a common idea that only from prison can one truly understand the regime. So too qualities that

might lie dormant in ordinary life come to the fore in a kind of prison meri-
tocracy. "Jail . . . is a great X-ray," writes Frank Gallagher, quoting his comrade
Peadar O'Donnell. The operator of this X-ray is not the regime, but the prisoners' choice of a commanding officer from among themselves. The experience
of prison reveals men's character; "the men who come well out of jail trials,"
Gallagher concludes, "have much in them."[11]

As the prison forges some into leaders, it exposes others as being made of
lesser material. Thus runs the uncompromising logic of prisoner politics, a
source of much of the bitterness that often characterizes prisoner memoirs.
Marek Kulczyk evaluates his martial-law imprisonment in terms not unlike
Sołdrowski's. Prison was "a school of life. I came to know myself, and I know
how I will react in different situations . . . . I got to know people on whom I can
rely and who can rely on me. In this sense prison sorted people."[12] This characterization of prison as a test of personal character echoes what is said about
the battlefield or the trenches of warfare. Personal trust and moral clarity have
greater value than rhetorical or intellectual ability. Kulczyk deepens the analogy
to war, as prison offers the test of fear. While for him "prison ceased to be something fearsome," others give in to the fear and lose value in their comrades' eyes.

As the outside world disappears from view, prisoners come to think of the
institution that holds them as one that builds essential character and values.
A typical political prisoner enters as a young man or woman; they, and those
who share their experience, develop an idea of growing up behind bars. "I
came out of prison a mature person," writes Irena "Little Mouse" Cieślińska-
Skrzypiec, "much stronger psychologically and spiritually, thanks to these arduous ordeals and torments that I survived with the help of wonderful comrades in
misery."[13] The key factor here is a community of sufferers in close daily contact
with one another—Cieślińska-Skrzypiec also calls it a "school of life"—that self-
consciously develops values and attitudes that are more difficult to build outside.

Solidarity and loyalty are necessary products of the prison community.
Prisoners also cultivated both political and personal respect for one another.
ANC prisoners on Robben Island, for example, treated swearing or hitting a
comrade as "an insult to the organization," writes Galelikile Sitho; transgressors
could be punished by "boycott," ignored completely until they repented.[14] The
tactic—which could drive a prisoner close to insanity—made sense not so much
as a policing method but as a way of defending the political cause that could be
weakened by one wayward member. The political prison is a stage on which participants perform their allegiance to a political cause by espousing behaviors and
values that do it credit.

As they perform on that stage, experiencing together with their comrades
the travails in prison inflicted by political power, political prisoners also engage
with models from the past. When Polish students were jailed by the communist

regime after protests in March 1968, many were quite unprepared for the experience. Some of the imprisoned students came from prominent political families in which suffering for a cause was not unfamiliar. One of these was Marta Petrusewicz. Her father had been a communist since before the war, as well as a distinguished biologist. Her grandfather was a lawyer who spent two years in prison and two more in exile in northern Russia at the turn of the century. When the students received a letter offering them freedom in exchange for a statement renouncing their actions, Marta's father visited her and told her of receiving a similar offer in prison in the 1930s. He, too, had then received a parental visit. As he recalled it, his father's message was this: "As you know, I am not a Communist and I do not agree with you. But as for mercy—we do not plead for it."[15] Either of the senior Petrusewiczes would likely have offered very different advice concerning a dilemma outside prison. But prison rendered political differences subordinate to principles, although those very principles were then expressed in explicitly political actions, like refusing to renounce one's political activity or to accede to regime pressure.

The Petrusewiczes are here talking about honor, a way of thinking that was learned and reinforced during incarceration. Facing the challenges of prison with one's head held high, showing respect for one's comrades, sharing one's possessions, and refraining from swearing all express a sense of honor. Thus too when politicals express repugnance toward criminal convicts and ascribe actions they deem immoral (like homosexual activity) only to them, the class biases they have brought from outside interlace with ideas about the prisoner's code of honor. Some parts of the code are subject to debate, such as whether or not to work, to accept amnesty, or to protest. In each case, both sides accept that the political prisoner's honor is at stake.

In prisoners' memoirs, honor shines most brightly in those who face death. When socialist Edward Majewski received a death sentence in 1912, his wife Kama wrote to him that she was "sort of satisfied with such a severe punishment, since it proves that you were not an informer—and I was very much afraid of that. As long as you now don't try to purchase your freedom at that price—but I think you won't do that if you still love me even a little . . . . Just be honest and don't forget about honor."[16] Whether because Russian interrogators offered deals more frequently than did those in other regimes, or because Polish socialism was deeply romantic, steeped in the culture of failed national uprisings, memoirs and letters often circle around honor.[17] As a similar tradition of romantic struggle existed in British-controlled Ireland, ideas of honor (and death) look similar as well. Thus Terence MacSwiney from his hospital bed in Brixton Prison thought not only that his death could energize the national struggle but also that it would redeem his honor, sullied by his failure to join the fight in 1916. "Ah Cathal," he wrote to his comrade Cathal Brugha in the second month of his hunger strike,

"the pain of Easter Week is properly dead at last!"[18] The theme of honor and
death returned with redoubled strength in Nazi-occupied Poland. "Jasiu," wrote
a partisan to his brother after receiving a death sentence in 1943, "remember that
I will not stain the name. I depart with honor. I kiss you. Tad."[19] Stories of those
executed in Stalinist prisons also invoke honor in the face of death.[20] The deaths
of Steve Biko in 1977 and Bobby Sands in 1981 are framed by honor and dignity
as they are retold within the movement.[21]

To improve and to prove oneself in prison did not require death. Mandela
coaching Maharaj on how to control his emotions, or any political prisoner
drawing a comparison with criminals, took it for granted that their very principles were under attack. Those principles—in the broadest terms, fealty to a
cause or idea greater than the individual and a willingness to sacrifice ordinary
comforts for its benefit—no matter how dimly or even wrongly understood, had
led to this place. Whether the regime expressed any interest in rehabilitating its
captives or simply aimed to show them the futility of their opposition, incarceration increased the costs of those principles.

"Honor" is a daunting term for the rank and file. Thus when Władysław
Bartoszewski addressed his fellow Solidarity members detained in Jaworze on
Christmas Eve 1981, he offered a more accessible concept: decency. His message
was no less rigorous: "This is the ninth time I am spending Christmas in prison.
Maybe it is tactless to tell you that—but I do so to give you reassurance. One can get
through this and remain oneself." He then celebrated the Polish tradition of making formal wishes at Christmas: "I do not wish for you just a speedy return home,
though each of us would like that very much. My wish for you is that we return
home able to look our wives, children, and all our friends in the eye. We don't know
when we will all be freed. But more important than freedom is the external and
internal attitude which we carry with us from this place."[22] Bartoszewski entitles
his memoir "It is worthwhile to be decent," and his word choice decouples honor
from death, but the idea remains the same. Prison becomes a place not merely to
pursue oppositional politics but also to remake oneself in the service of the ideals
espoused by that opposition. Reclaiming and defending values like honor, loyalty,
respect, and decency, the political prisoner becomes a better member and representative of a political community. This transformation, in which values are rein-
scribed and members of the community prepare to bring their prison experience
back into society, is the basis of the prison university.

"We Must Educate Them to Be Revolutionaries"

In a memo to his fellow opponents of the Anglo-Irish Treaty in May 1923, one
week after the cessation of the Irish Civil War hostilities, Éamon de Valera spoke

enthusiastically about the "wonderful opportunity for a political discussion and reorganisation offered by the present concentration of some of our best men and women in jails and camps." He proposed an elaborate political structure, grouping internees by electoral constituencies to choose representatives who would in turn meet to elect a "general secretary" and agree on "a programme of policy and reorganisation to be put into effect immediately whenever they are released." De Valera's top-down scheme fit poorly with the mood in the camps, however, where residents showed no signs of submission to central authority; after all, they had all refused to accept the treaty negotiated by their erstwhile leaders such as Michael Collins.

De Valera, who circulated his memo to all camps and prisons, was addressing men and women with long experience under lock and key.[23] After seven years of political mobilization, Civil War internees were from all across Ireland, and could meet together with greater ease "than anything that could be attempted by organisers travelling through the country afterwards."[24] Two months after his first proposal, de Valera again urged coordination:

> The Camps should be converted into miniature Universities—the language, the history, the economics of our country can be taught and studied. Every problem that should interest us as Irishmen and women can be discussed and debated. The future is with the party that is most intelligent and of the most value to the nation and economic questions come foremost; the desire of everyone is to see Ireland completely free being largely allowed to go without saying. But all the intelligence in the world will not be sufficient unless we organise thoroughly.[25]

The fighting men and women behind the locked gates of camps and prisons could become a political force; de Valera was already looking ahead to the ballot box struggle and he intended to build a new type of cadre.

Leaders inside prison echoed de Valera's call, in the first and only issue of the Mountjoy newspaper *The Book of Cells*, in November 1922:

> It is the duty of all Republican prisoners to keep up morale, and to prevent their principles and their faith being sapped by jail surroundings. It is likewise their duty to use their enforced leisure hours to the best advantage for the cause they are being persecuted for upholding. This can best be done by studying hard to fit themselves to be better soldiers and more enlightened citizens of the Republic to whose services their lives and liberties are committed. It is with the idea of stimulating thought and preventing mental apathy that the "Book of Cells" is presented to the cellmates of Mountjoy.[26]

Yet no educational program followed. Nearly a year would pass before Frank Gallagher was elected president of the Mountjoy prisoners' education board. Only in August 1923, in the wake of a national election, would Gallagher "decide to run classes in Irish, mathematics, business subjects, English as a start."[27] Political education then got off the ground, but the subsequent hunger strike absorbed all energies. Irish prisoners knew the value of political education very well, but they no longer had the will to pursue it. Of course, the hunger strike itself was a powerful moment of collective self-education, albeit one that over-whelmed any effort at self-improvement. More clearly than any election or mili-tary campaign, the hunger strike offered a cold reply to the unreality of prison politics and brought an end, for most, to the "prison mentality" of the "prisoner organisation" that the Republicans had become.[28]

As might be expected given their common origins in the camps of the Great War as well as in imperial prisons, the imperatives of the interwar prison community in Poland bear resemblance to the Irish case, despite very differ-ent political goals. Education is integral to becoming a communist. Certainly, schooling can make one a better nationalist, yet whether the enemy was sec-tarian (as in Northern Ireland's Troubles), an occupier (as during World War II), or an anti-democratic and repressive government (such as apartheid South Africa or communist Poland), self-improvement was not obligatory. One could understand the evils of those regimes sufficiently through emotion and experi-ence. Communist doctrine requires understanding of the struggle against the united forces of the bourgeoisie, the nobility, and the fascists, concurrent with the struggle to enlighten the ignorant and backward masses. Its adherents strive to understand class relations and to recognize political forces, using canonical texts as guides. Study of these texts, in turn, requires literacy, understanding of economics, and knowledge of foreign languages.

All this one could learn in prison. One can feel the beads of sweat as Piotr Górczyński writes to his mother from Sandomierz Prison in 1931. He wants very much to see her, but he explains the party decision that as long as visits are through a screen and are limited to twenty minutes he must refuse. He takes the opportunity to flex his newly polished atheism for perhaps the first time: "I was very glad to hear that mother is well, but on the other hand it made me sad that mother is so backward and writes first of all about God, what do I care about some God, anyway no one has seen him and generally mother hasn't seen him and won't see him and mother writes that she is well by his grace so I ask mother not to write to me any more about some god and so I won't have to blush before my comrades because mother is so backwards."[29]

Communists like Górczyński had to learn that their enemies resided in prison as well, not just as employees of the regime. When the Piłsudski government began to arrest and imprison politicians from across the political spectrum in

1930, Communist Party leadership felt obliged to instruct its imprisoned comrades that this was merely a minor conflict within the "fascist camp." Under no circumstances, therefore, should communists welcome the "lackeys of fascism and capitalism who find themselves in momentary disfavor." The prison *komuna* could welcome rank-and-file workers and peasants of the "social fascist" parties, for "they are our not-yet-conscious class brothers. We must persuade them in discussion, enlighten them, make them aware that only in our ranks can they really fight fascism . . . . We must educate them to be revolutionaries, so that they will leave the prison cage as conscious revolutionaries, as our comrades."[30] This is the essence of the communist prison university: it is closed to those who do not qualify by reason of their class position. At the same time, it can transform the neophyte and the unenlightened alike into conscious revolutionaries able to deploy party doctrine. How does this university work? Here is Będzin Prison, 1925:

> We rise at half-past six in the morning, and at 8, after breakfast, we get to our studies. Until our first exercise at 10 we have political economy. These classes take place in the morning because of the importance of the subject. Today we are finishing Karyshev's textbook, which is supposed to be an introduction to Bogdanov and to the "Economic Science" of Karl Marx and of Kautsky. We had an exam on Karyshev when we got to [his discussion] of *Kapital*; exam results were above average. Now we are preparing a second exam on the whole text. How do we study economics? Lectures are divided up among all comrades. Each is obliged to prepare a lecture, and in consultation with the Education Commission to prepare questions and answers based upon the text.[31]

In Białystok Prison, 1927, where education was not possible in the cells and so took place in the exercise yard, a five-member "Cultural-Educational Commission" offered walking lectures on the revolutionary movement, materialism, economics, the party's social agenda, and current affairs.[32] By 1932, basic education had taken a back seat to proper communist practice, but the idea of self-improvement within the collective remained, as in Sieradz Prison. Comrades there met monthly to "examine the level of comprehension and acceptance of the political line of the whole *komuna* and overcome on the spot all deviations to the left or right from that correct line." The *gryps* quoted here concludes with notes on pedagogical practice. Method mattered a great deal, since each cell engaged in socialist competition (presumably in lectures delivered and other measures of political knowledge) and aimed to fulfill goals set by the *komuna* leadership. Formal self-criticism accompanied "each shortcoming or lapse in the fulfillment of the plan."[33]

The ideology of the communist prison community, isolated and combative as it was, gave rise to this peculiar educational system. Surrounded by real and imagined enemies, the collective educated and policed itself at the same time. Study among one's comrades built consciousness and pride in being a communist and a prisoner, but failure to keep up with the rigorous demands could bring the collective's condemnation. Thus honor and education are linked. Saul Hersz Weindling, for example, attempted to characterize the true revolutionary in a 1932 message from Mokotów Prison. A coward, he wrote, "without glory or honor buckles under at any misfortune. There is no one like that here.... A revolutionary, in my opinion, does not recognize defeat and prison for him is a school of hard knocks where his steel will to victory is forged. This purgatory is useful, and it does not hurt to take this course."[34] Ideas of honor and belonging are for the communist rooted not in the self but in pedagogical and written authority. One knew what a communist was and who the enemy was because one read and attempted to master both classic writings and current directives.[35]

The women of Piotrków Prison illuminate the workings of political education at its rawest. These women had no access to books because they were boycotting the prison library. They were cut off from the (male) *komuna* leadership, which failed to answer their messages. So the nine organized their education as well as they could. They divided into two teams: "Alliance," which took on the assignment of developing a program for agitation in the prison, and "Combat," which took as its subject the Rozenblat Factory in Łódź. Though the chances of reaching their free comrades were nil, these prisoners treated their assignments like real-world training: "Each of the teams is tasked with organizing and conducting all kinds of actions relevant to our [political] work outside on their assigned territory. The relation between the two teams is like that between a factory [party] cell and a *komuna* of political prisoners. In this way the comrades get practical training, both in organizational and political terms, for work outside." Soon after they formed their teams, the members of "Alliance" and "Combat" received a copy of a "bourgeois" newspaper, in which they read a brief mention of a "Day of the Hungry," most likely a campaign sponsored by a left-wing organization. They recognized a call to put their training into action, and so the teams scripted the following simulated protests:

1. a "mass rally" at the Rozenblat Factory;
2. a "flying rally" for the unemployed;
3. a "mass rally" in front of the Piotrków Prison;
4. a response from the imprisoned comrades.

They also composed "a special appeal to the unemployed and working proletariat, to peasants, and to soldiers."[36]

Have any political prisoners ever slipped the bonds of oppression so ingeniously as to imagine that they are staging rallies back in their home factory and in the street outside their prison? The women of Alliance and Combat were not just wishing themselves free; they were using their cells to hone their protest skills. This tiny prison university in Piotrków not only prepared them to continue the fight upon their release but also allowed them to recreate the revolutionary struggle at the scale of the cells they inhabited.

In Sieradz Prison, meanwhile, comrades were busy filling up dozens of notebooks with analyses of current politics and producing drafts of resolutions, appeals, and theses. Unlike the members of Alliance and Combat, the women in Sieradz had a demanding instructor, Teofila Zylbersztajn, who provided detailed criticism of each manuscript submitted by her students. Zylbersztajn faulted Sala's assignment, an appeal to workers, for being "poorly linked to the factory. It does not unmask social fascism and populist fascism and their role in war." Hela had submitted an appeal in the style of an illegal text, when the assignment was to write one that could appear legally, and thus with allusions instead of direct attacks on the regime. Bolka's was "good" in form and content, but lacked a connection to "universal aspects."[37] Like their comrades in Piotrków, the students of the Sieradz prison university were being trained to agitate among their fellow workers and to master the dictates of party doctrine. Before entering prison, they had probably been active party members, but they were too immersed in the daily grind of factory and home life to have time for the theoretical and practical training that Zylbersztajn offered.

Assessing the effect of prison education among the communists is hard, given the events that would intervene before their hour of triumph in 1944–45, when the Soviet Army crossed into Polish territory and the Polish Workers' Party (as the Communist Party was renamed) began its swift ascent to power. In Polish prisons, these communists avoided the fate of their comrades executed on suspicion of treason in the Soviet Union in 1937–38. Many would not survive the Holocaust and the war; those who did would probably have considered the years in the anti-Nazi underground or in relative safety in the Soviet Union, rather than their prison years, to be formative. Nevertheless, given the relatively small size—just a few thousand members—of the Polish Workers' Party in 1944, the months and years many had spent together scribbling in notebooks and delivering practice speeches in prison cells surely shaped the future of Polish communism.

"When We Get Out of Prison, We'll Liberate Poland"

Many of the men and women rounded up all across Poland in the wee hours of December 13, 1981, like Władysław Bartoszewski, had been in prison before and knew how to organize prison life and to draw lessons from the experience. Those who had not could learn from cellmates. Barely eight years later, the communist regime then gave way to a governing coalition dominated by former prisoners. Prime Minister Tadeusz Mazowiecki and most of the 260 members of the Solidarity faction in Parliament remembered internment well. Prison credentials were an easy way to verify commitment to opposition.

Yet the internment of 1981–83 lacked the coordination and direction visible in other periods of mass incarceration. The prisons and detention centers of martial law did not produce the next generation of political leaders in the way that Frongoch did, or in the way that Teofila Zylbersztajn's classes in Sieradz were intended to. The regime of General Wojciech Jaruzelski swept up the intellectual and political elites of the country at a scale comparable to the worst modern dictatorships. But the deep transformation of Polish opposition had already begun outside prison. Underground education had become crucially important to Polish opposition well before 1981, and the sixteen months of Solidarity's legal existence preceding martial law were a carnival of self-education: in thousands of meetings, rallies, and strikes; in informal education programs; and in hundreds of different independent periodicals and books. Lectures on political and historical topics drew great crowds, to factories as well as university halls. People came to prison already changed, and so the prison did not necessarily provide a perspective they could not have gained outside.[38]

Given the arguable centrality of the prison experience to Polish oppositional culture, though, the absence of a full-fledged prison education system in the 1980s suggests that the prison university fills a particular need for unity and conscious commitment that an opposition tradition might address by different means. The circumstances of the opposition in Poland in 1981 did not require a prison university. To the extent that martial law exposed the need for a new opposition strategy, it was not clear that prison communities would provide a better incubator for ideas than would underground political circles. The prisons did produce some very important texts, such as Jacek Kuroń's "Theses on Getting Out of a Situation with No Exit" or Adam Michnik's "Why You Are Not Signing" (both issued in March 1982), which took uncompromising positions and rejected any dialogue with the regime. But the surviving underground outside prison was no less prolific and reflective in the same period. Prison discourse naturally critiqued the strategies adopted in the period before martial law; in Strzebielinek, where many of Solidarity's leading figures spent the winter and spring of 1982, a series of lectures questioned the opposition strategies of the previous years.[39] These did not lead, however, to new political strategies outside prison, nor enlighten a new generation of activists.

The prisons of martial law were no less lively for all that. Marek Żukowski's comprehensive study of martial law internment mentions study groups and lectures in fifteen of the largest internment centers; no doubt many others were active as well. Some of them published their own clandestine newspapers.[40] The internees eagerly drew upon past models of prison education. "I recalled," says Adam Szostkiewicz, then a small-town high school teacher, "that in political prison self-education courses are always important. Especially when there is a large group of people, there are always differences in education or background. So it was an ideal opportunity. Gorkii's *My Universities* and all that."[41]

Solidarity prisoners were unlikely to submit to an educational regimen like that imposed by interwar communists. There would be no working through of canonical texts or exams on key elements of movement doctrine. They conceived of Solidarity as fundamentally democratic; in a country where the regime controlled knowledge, Solidarity offered not an alternative truth but broad access to knowledge, however construed. Lectures in prison were as likely to address topics like advances in genetics or physics as the history of Polish opposition or the psychology of communism. Anything could slake the Polish political's thirst for knowledge. While in preceding years this thirst had transformed many into dedicated opposition activists, education might not take the prisoner any further. Bogdan Ciszak complained to his diary in May 1982 that his comrades were using education as an "escape from prison life," burrowing into their books instead of contributing to community.[42]

The idea of community appears in nearly every memoir, as writers seek a way to express the values of the Solidarity movement. Władysław Bartoszewski avers, "We lived in a tolerant community, cultivating different individual or group interests and talents."[43] Jan Mur noticed that those interned in Potulice Prison tried to distinguish themselves from ordinary criminals by operating like the trade union had before martial law, maintaining "the structures of union hierarchy, organizing collective actions communally, working out common positions on various issues, and institutionalizing some traditions and camp rituals."[44] In Hrubieszów Prison, internees drafted a code of behavior, recalls Marek Kulczyk: "It contained many statements about dignity, about morality, and about the fact that we form a community, and also laid out the means by which decisions would be made."[45] Solidarity was by some measures the largest opposition movement in world history, and the rigors and rhetoric of martial law aimed to splinter that remarkable and aptly named movement.[46] Facing pressures to emigrate or to cease political activity, eyeing small but widening cracks in the movement, and wondering whether Solidarity still meant something to Polish society, internees kept the flame of a common purpose alive. They noted difference but celebrated community through protest, ritual, organization, and education.[47] The payoff would be victory. In the words of a well-known song composed in Kwidzyń Prison: "People remember: don't trust the Commies/They are strong when everyone's in prison./Nation, do not fear, we'll get there yet/When we get out of prison, we'll liberate Poland."[48]

The level of political awareness among detainees was probably higher than in most cases of mass incarceration. Martial law Poland had no examples of hapless bystanders swept up in the repression and held for years, as in South Africa or in Stalinist or Nazi regimes. Incautious presence at a demonstration might land a casual supporter in jail for a day or two, hardly enough time to develop a new commitment to the cause.[49] Yet despite the impression given in their memoirs, not every internee entered prison a conscious political. Certainly the average Solidarity member had less familiarity with the political debates than intellectuals and trade union leaders had; some of the rank-and-file could finally have an opportunity to learn politics in prison. Here's one example of how a prison educational community could transform such a person.

An officer's vacation home in Gołdap, in the Mazurian lakes region of northeast Poland, close to the Soviet border, was chosen as the destination for most women interned in the early months of martial law. Nearly 200 were moved there in January 1982, with another hundred or so joining them over the next few months. These women included the most prominent labor leaders and intellectuals, gathered together in one place. They found themselves in a "golden cage," whose comfortable conditions allowed the regime to depict Solidarity as having chosen to escape the drudgery of everyday life for a government-sponsored vacation.[50]

Krystyna Ziółkowska arrived in this community in May 1982. High school educated, she had been a popular trade union representative in her factory and had worked on the Solidarity newspaper there. When her senior colleagues were interned the previous December, she had taken their place in the underground until her turn came. With two school-age children, however, she had not had time to learn about Solidarity; she was a woman of action. So Gołdap was something new for her; the few weeks she spent in the "cage" transformed her politically and personally. There were lectures in Polish history, discussions of opposition strategy, and lessons in yoga—among elite women she could never otherwise have met. She had discovered a community, led by women from Solidarity leadership, that was also a network. "After Gołdap," she recalls, "there came together a women's network, all across Poland . . . women who knew what they have to do . . . . We know where to meet, where we can contact each other, how to communicate information . . . . We had training, we learned." The network Ziółkowska describes sounds like a vast sleeper cell, but she means it in a more prosaic, practical sense: she, and others like her, had been energized and activated by their encounter. In the summer of 1982, she threw herself into the work of underground Solidarity with redoubled vigor.[51] Prison had had an effect opposite to that intended by the regime. While many were worn down by the experience, those who encountered a community like this were retrained for the opposition movement.

"Yours in Sport": A University on the Soccer Field

There are two contrasting versions of Robben Island. In one, it was a hellhole where the bravest and the brightest South Africans wasted years of their lives, years that could have been dedicated to their country and their people. In the other, Robben Island created the new, democratic South Africa and gave it many leaders. To lock away the most prominent activists, thinkers, and eager young men of the African National Congress (ANC), the Pan Africanist Congress (PAC), the Black Consciousness Movement (BCM), and other groups in one place was surely the most foolish move the apartheid regime could have dreamed up. Every new wave of inmates, every crackdown, and every concession deepened the solidarity among hundreds of men. Both versions are true, because the prisoners made one into the other, turning the carceral weapons of a repressive state into the mobilizational tools of an organized opposition. As they developed a common identity as political prisoners, organized themselves as a community, responded to classification schemes, and engaged in collective protest, the prisoners of Robben Island created a space resistant to the regime and an alternative society. This transformation of identity was occurring in other places in South Africa (and in exile), too, but everywhere the opposition thought of Robben Island as the core of anti-apartheid politics. Its prison university, broad and innovative, produced the most impressive graduates.

Prisoner education of any kind challenged the racial hierarchy of the apartheid state. Many prisoners were much more educated and credentialed than their jailers. They understood education as empowerment in a state predicated on inequality. Memoirs often measure prisoners' success in terms of degrees (high school, university, and post-graduate) pursued or earned. The regime (whose laws encouraged all prisoners to study) had not, however, incarcerated its opponents to allow them to acquire still more knowledge. Prison authorities retaliated against real or perceived infractions of any kind by revoking study rights and devised numerous obstacles to formal study. Books purchased or ordered for coursework and research, for example, had to be vetted by prison or ministry censors, who often banned them.[52]

The steady pulse of informal education should have concerned the prison authorities even more. The ANC prisoners' Disciplinary Committee took the position that everyone must either study or teach; very early on, rest periods after work in the quarries became "study periods," in which everyone was expected to participate.[53] "We took people from the lowest level, who came to the island illiterate, and they had to be taught," says Govan Mbeki, the acknowledged leader among communists on the island. "We encouraged people to study. It is good for them. It is good for our discipline, too. It is good for them to improve their qualifications. It is also good for their parents."[54] Through their parents, education of prisoners would benefit the nation. Prison education shaped how prisoners saw the regime, the world, and their future role in the struggle against apartheid. In a prison whose inmates came from divergent opposition backgrounds, education was also a tool in political competition. This was especially true in the late 1970s and early 1980s, when a generation of younger activists from the Black Consciousness Movement arrived. Teaching the newcomers about the ANC and its program, Mbeki and others aimed to win them before they were caught up in the more racially divisive rhetoric of the PAC. Political and ideological discussions that had lain dormant since 1963, when ANC and PAC members decided they could not convince their rivals and so would coexist in prison, were relaunched for the benefit of the new wave of inmates, "a political force that could fall either way."[55]

Whether or not the ANC actively worked to recruit Black Consciousness activists, there is no doubt that politics sprang to life. Some senior comrades gave lectures, while others wrote letters to newcomers, offering insight into the tenets of the ANC or PAC. With all other distractions cut away, Robben Island must have felt like an endless seminar occasionally interrupted by back-breaking labor and other punishments, rather than the reverse. "It was as if we couldn't get enough," recalls one. "There were those who wanted to discuss politics every day. They discussed politics at lunch hour in the quarry, they discussed politics in the evening."[56] Throughout the 1970s and 1980s, discussions in the cells produced copious notes on economics, political theory, history, current events, and more. Before their incarceration most prisoners would not have had the time to study, let alone learn the kinds of things they did on Robben Island.

Even a devoted enthusiast could no doubt tire of listening to political theory during lunch break. The real innovation of the prison university on Robben Island came in its extracurricular pursuits. The authorities neither mandated nor organized prisoner recreation, while the camplike organization of the prison left time and space for nonwork activities. Sports seemed a safe ground for prisoner energies, relieving the administration of some of its supervisory duties. This left a significant opening for self-organization that prisoners exploited, creating an extensive and complex leadership training program in the guise of cultural and sporting clubs.

Sports offered more than exercise and physical exhilaration: organizational discipline and experience were political assets. Close up, the system they developed was indistinguishable from political organization: there were committees, meetings (often recorded in detailed minutes), and formal procedures.[57] The Island Football Association—renamed the Makana Football Association (MFA) to honor a Xhosa leader who died escaping from Robben Island in 1819—received official permission to begin operating in 1967. The MFA oversaw football clubs, maintained rules, and disciplined players and referees. But the prisoners' capacity for organization appeared limitless. Over the years, similar bodies formed to govern rugby, tennis, athletics, and more. There was even a Summer Olympics. By the mid-1970s, a Recreational and Cultural Committee oversaw all these, along with similar bodies devoted to film, music, and other activities.

For a community whose office supplies were rationed by the administration, the prisoners of Robben Island produced an impressive stream of communications as they managed their sports. Always conscious of the perception that blacks were less civilized than whites, they documented, with each formal motion, request, or directive, that they could organize a community as well as or better than their captors. Formality in tone and discipline in action were the rule. A sample logbook entry of March 5, 1978, reads: "The Directorate met to discuss the Org. Chart, interviews with the Comptroller"; in January 1977, responding to a complaint about misuse of power, that same directorate "decided to appoint a Provost under the Dept. of Planning to deal with future matters of discipline."[58]

The Robben Island sports bureaucracy built legal structures as well. Disciplinary matters were addressed with recourse to courts, with witnesses and prosecutors, ending with judgments, sentences, and appeals. Indeed, sports was among other things a way to enforce internal collective discipline, supplanting the discipline of the institution itself. The style of this discipline, purged of ideology, contrasts with the party discipline of the Polish communists or that of the Irish Republican Army (IRA). Formality took precedence over displays of power. Transfers of offices were marked by formal memoranda and the conveying of rule books and files. The job titles, acronyms, and procedures would have fit any organizational bureaucracy—and that was the point. The terminology itself was intentionally drained of politics, as prison authorities had access to all documents.[59] The administration worried about the meetings but found it easier to deal with its charges this way.[60] The political value was clear enough to the men themselves. Ernest Dikgang Moseneke, who went on to a business career and then a judgeship after apartheid, claimed, "I acquired my leadership skills by administering soccer."[61] Steve Tshwete, who would become the first minister of sport and recreation after apartheid, began as one of the organizers of recreation on Robben Island, though he claimed he had never played soccer before his imprisonment.

Respect for one another and for the rules of the community were key values. "Any organised group performs better and harmoniously if the procedural aspect of its affairs is strictly adhered to," wrote MFA chairman John Ramoshaba in his annual report for 1974. "Random and loose handling of affairs can never be a blessing."[62] Disciplinary matters were safely packaged in the discourse of procedure and community control. The "Naidoo Affair" of March 1971 addressed the fact that Indres Naidoo had accused members of

Fig. 9.2 Prisoners playing soccer on Robben Island, 1960s. The South African Prison Service blacked out all prisoners' faces in this and other photos it published. Courtesy of UWC-Robben Island Mayibuye Archives.

his team of "killing the club." An "executive meeting"—at 7:35 AM, presumably the only time these prisoners could meet—decided that Naidoo would write an apology, which was then read at a subsequent meeting.[63] Don Matta broke protocol by making a suggestion to the prison governor regarding use of funds given by the International Committee of the Red Cross (ICRC); in this way he breached prisoners' autonomy. Advocating respect for the community above the individual, a Federal Council meeting in August 1974 voted to censure him for his "unilateralist tendency."[64] Lungile Dwaba summed up the purpose of discipline during a heated discussion of the Matta affair, explicitly pointing out the benefit of civilized behavior: "We are an organised society, we don't come out of the jungle, we cannot accept creation of fronts where we will fight for no purpose. All these delegates represent the same community. This word <u>community</u> should be used with care—no one has the right to whip up emotions."[65]

Discipline, then, did not bind prisoners to a party or to an ideology, nor even to a nation; it bound them to a community. In the very earliest days, teams naturally formed by political affiliation; participants quickly realized, though, that this worsened relations between them, precisely what they hoped to avoid as they put aside overt political rivalry. Allegiance to community then became paramount. Emotions ran high and competition was fierce on the soccer pitch, the rugby field, or the tennis court. But through sports the prisoners reoriented their politics onto shared ground. Correspondence among sports clubs frequently included the salutation "Yours in sport," replacing "comrade."[66]

The figure most emblematic of this ethos of rules and respect was, surely, the referee. The members of the Referees Union are the unsung heroes of Robben Island.[67] Of course they were frequently objects of vituperation on the field, and their decisions could animate community discussion for weeks. But the Robben Island Prison itself represented injustice and disrespect of law; referees, like prisoner representatives, offered the opposite. For this reason, misconduct by referees, or by players toward them, was hashed out in great detail at prisoners' meetings and brought severe reprimand. In turn, referees asserted their right to speak about fairness. A plaintive letter from the Referees Union in 1990 reminded all that they were not professionals and aimed only to avoid bias— and yet "a comradely spirit is increasingly absent between some of us inmates. We conduct games to improve our relations among ourselves as comrades," the letter claimed, appealing for the "negative attitude from comrades" toward referees to stop.[68] While the exasperation they expressed would be familiar to sports officials anywhere, the idea of comradeship points toward a role that is political as well.

As on the field, so in the conference room. The officials whom prisoners chose to represent them frequently urged their comrades to take prisoner governance seriously. The prisoner leadership in 1974 felt particularly embattled by a series of minor scandals. Finally it pleaded to all prisoners: "some of our delegates come to meetings, resolve and are subsequently found to be ignorant or feign ignorance when their decisions are put into effect. 'Let Sincerity Be Your Watchword!'"[69] In truth, they were seeking not sincerity but for prisoners to recognize the consequences of their actions and thus their obligations to the community: if one votes, then the decision becomes one's responsibility. But "sincerity" implied that one's personal values were also owed to the community, indeed were what bound the community together. The rhetoric of Robben Island often implicated personal values in achieving a higher cause. Complaints that prisoners with kitchen duty missed after-dinner film showings necessitated a special meeting, at which it was agreed that the "kitchen must be prepared to sacrifice."[70] Thus an inconvenience became something one did for one's comrades. The language became a part of prisoner discourse, encouraging them to elevate ordinary actions with higher meaning. Preparing to leave Robben Island, one prisoner decided he would leave behind his trumpet. He was, he explained, mindful of prisoners' "need for recreational and cultural advancement," and so would give the instrument to the Directorate, "in your trust for the benefit of all."[71]

The values inculcated within the community, of course, would facilitate relations with the authorities. The introduction of sports and films came in the wake of the 1966 hunger strike. Having rejected the subhuman labels the regime attempted to pin on them, and having shown that their behavior was neither predictable nor controllable, prisoners engaging in transparent self-government recast themselves as potential equal partners to the prison administration. For example, as secretary of the MFA in 1968, Indres Naidoo attempted to acclimate the prison head to the community prisoners were forming. Naidoo had to straddle a line, portraying prisoner activity as both organized and unthreatening. "Sir, I request you to come and watch our soccer matches played, which I may say would be of great entertainment for you. The soccer standard is becoming so high that it is spoken of for days on end. Because of this high spirit in the game spectators like to come out and see the matches played. I would be very pleased if you would allow spectators from each section. The spectators who have managed to come out are very disciplined." He also needed to accustom the administration to the fact of prisoner organization. Having made some mild requests, he continued: "Sir, I have used the plural in many places but I would like to make an apology for it. I am not making complaints for other people, but as I am the Secretary of the Football Association I have to raise these questions in this manner. In the present I am making these requests in my individual capacity."[72] Naidoo's tone is so mild that he hardly seems like the dangerous saboteur the regime sentenced in 1963. His letter was also a lesson in manners for the prison administration, teaching them how to behave toward their captives.

Sports and the other activities that made up the Robben Island university could of course be suspended arbitrarily, reminding prisoners of the limits to the latitude they enjoyed. But the point of all these formal structures was to make tangible the idea that prisoners were a negotiating partner. This emerged, in fits and starts, from the late 1960s through the early 1980s. When activities were suspended in 1972, an "Ad Hoc Committee" stepped in to announce a strike. "We had no other course to pursue as prisoners but to suspend our sporting activity," they wrote, asking "where does sport stand in relation to the implementation of discipline in the prison. We are not unaware of the fact that under abnormal conditions when the [prisoners] have gone out of hand the Officer Commanding has all the powers to suspend all privileges in the interest of restoring Order [and] discipline. But do such conditions exist presently?"[73] Five years later Commanding Officer Lieutenant Prins informed prisoner representatives who had asked that punishment not include the suspension of sports that "Sport is . . . not even a privilege but merely an indulgence." On this occasion, the Executive Committee proposed an alternate punishment, which Prins agreed to: confinement to cells on Sundays in the case of an infraction.[74]

As they negotiated over equipment, funds, match schedules, rules, participants, spectators, punishments, and more, these men would be constantly reminded of the power relations on which their incarceration was built. At the same time, beyond the immediate desire to be playing soccer or showing a film on a particular day lay the larger goal of acting as if they were free and already equal before the law with the men who held them. Yet they had little leverage; for example, the prison administration had little to fear from the prisoners' comrades outside. Guards were not menaced as in Northern Ireland, and there could be no demonstrations outside an inaccessible island prison. International pressure and the tireless efforts of supporters like Helen Suzman eased life on Robben Island considerably. By the 1980s, the days of swastika-tattooed guards and sadistic work details were long gone, and prisoners were ordering and receiving exercise bicycles and electric guitars. Yet they were still frustrated in their most basic requests for prisoners from different sections to be able to mingle or even to watch sports together.[75] The education of the administration continued. During one of the lower ebbs in prisoner-administration relations, in the early 1980s, prison governor Major Badenhorst imposed a series of petty restrictions on sports. When his deputy tried to shift blame for restrictions to the commissioner of prisons, the prisoners' Directorate retorted: "It is unwise for authorities here to reduce their own jurisdiction and authority by referring issues to Pretoria—particularly issues which over the years had come to be accepted to work according to a clear and definite pattern. Referring to Pretoria reduces their own freedom of action to resolve issues locally, to which they will be more sensitive and responsive than Pretoria."[76] Nelson Mandela was by this time off the island, but these men used his trademark combination of respect and cold rationality to argue from equal footing, schooling the administration to be both decisive and fair.

Both prisoners and jailers knew very well that Robben Island was a focal point of apartheid politics. Prisoners here took up the mantle of struggle against apartheid from inside and came to believe that their every action as individuals and as a community could further that struggle. The rhetoric of the anti-apartheid struggle lay just below the surface even in the most mundane situations. A 1983 disciplinary hearing for a player who had tackled and used abusive language in a soccer match included the frank observation that "Boers should not take us as ordinary people, but as people deserving of great respect."[77] Prisoners could disagree over the means of gaining or asserting that right to respect: after all, attacking a guard or staging a hunger strike or speaking boldly to an official visitor had made it possible for prisoner representatives to meet with administrators. But education always remained a core task of the whole prisoner community on Robben Island. During a 1985 crisis in prisoner-administration relations, a general meeting of prisoners chastised the Directorate for losing touch with its mission. Those present decided to adjourn the meeting so that Directorate members could go interview "veterans of this community" who could teach them about the history of the Robben Island Prison. When the meeting resumed, the minutes of the founding meeting in 1976 were read to the assembly, after which veteran Isaac Mthimunye was "called upon by the chairman to elaborate" on what he had told the Directorate.[78] Relearning their accountability to tradition and to the community then allowed prisoner representatives to deal more effectively with the administration.

By 1990, as the ANC and the South African Communist Party regained legal status, and Nelson Mandela was finally freed from what was at the end barely house arrest, the men of Robben Island looked back almost nostalgically to a time when "comrades did not have much access to so much political material as we have today. There were fewer distractions like TV, videos, films, etc. Life was hard. Despite these conditions, Robben Island was transformed into a formidable workshop for revolutionary political training." Now, prison leaders worried about keeping focused: "Some comrades' thoughts are only dominated by the thought of being released and to catch up with the nice times outside. What is required here in the ANC is a seriousness and a singleness of purpose—the destruction of the apartheid state and the establishment of a non-racial united democratic state based on the Freedom Charter."[79] Political education reached a new level of discipline, with detailed supervised lectures—enshrined in a document called "The Mrabulo Syllabus"—and structured discussions. No longer relying upon scraps of newspaper fished from latrines for knowledge of the world, Robben Island prisoners could attend lectures on topics like "The Crisis in Poland." Increasingly, they could pay attention to developing communal methods of education, not just focus on content.[80]

The campus, faculty, and curriculum of the Robben Island Prison university look quite different from others in this book. Only Frongoch in 1916 was comparable for concentrating most of the leading figures of a nationwide movement in one place, but it graduated all its students in just a few months. The decades on Robben Island allowed many students to themselves become teachers, not only in the semi-formal discussions staged in the lunchroom, at the quarry, or in the exercise yard, but also on the soccer pitch and the athletics field. The history of apartheid and the goals of the struggle were always part of the curriculum, but so were comportment and respect, business practices, accountability, and leadership. Whether or not graduates returned directly to the struggle, they would be able to stand up as equals to the representatives of the apartheid state.

In May 1980, the South African National Intelligence Service commissioned a substantial intelligence review that included a survey of the impact of prisons on South African society. Robben Island, the report concluded, was a problem: "The Security Service of the Prisons Department," it advised, "should do an analysis on the effectiveness of keeping political prisoners under one roof. It is quite clear from this investigation that prisoners leaving Robben Island are more politically motivated once they have left the Island as a direct result of their prison sentence, and the fact that they form a political community where various plans are discussed, and then later applied after the release from prison."[81] The analysis was not wrong, yet it failed to grasp that the lessons learned on Robben Island were both more benign and more dangerous than the regime could have imagined.

"Push the Walls Back...": The H-Blocks after the Hunger Strikes

Hardened by clandestine warfare's severe demands, locked up together as the putative leaders of an uncompromising armed movement, the men of the H-Blocks, and of the Long Kesh barracks before that, were exceptionally self-aware. They had no difficulty seeing the campaign in prison as part of the conflict outside; for one thing, they easily identified the guards with the Royal Ulster Constabulary and the British Army, since the "screws" were often former police-men or soldiers. Nor could they doubt that the community from which they had come recognized them as participants in that same struggle. So there was never any question that Northern Ireland prisons, and especially the cages and cells that furnished the great prison battles, would be a central site of Republican self-education. History, language, culture, and ideology were all required subjects for IRA inmates. Yet at a crucial moment, the students reshaped the curriculum in a way that affected the struggle outside as well. Such a rethinking may have been possible only in prison, and because of prison.

In the 1970s, the task of the prison community in Northern Ireland was to train fighters; as a camp education committee in the Long Kesh cages put it, they were "educating for revolution."[82] The emphasis was on military topics, complementing the culture of roll calls and parades that built community in that decade. Tight discipline helped to build revolutionary cadres, so lectures were formal and mandatory. Complicated factional disputes within the IRA inside and outside prison certainly affected political education, which varied even between cages. Proponents of traditional Irish republicanism clashed with those who took the term "revolution" seriously and were investigating Marxism and the writings of Irish socialist James Connolly. At one point an IRA order went out to burn all Marxist books.[83] But the common idea was to train cadres. Gerry Adams began an "officer training class" in Cage 11, preparing his men to assume leadership roles after prison.[84] The IRA's system also aimed to supplant the prison education offered by the British regime. Prisoners who studied and got degrees, some Republican leaders felt, were being pulled away from the conflict to develop careers instead.[85] To their opponents, of course, the cages of Long Kesh were a "University of Terrorism."[86]

The end of Special Category status and the blanket protest changed prison-ers' thinking on education, however. "Non-conforming" prisoners had much more time on their hands, being unable to exercise or work, but the concomitant retreat to cells and the sheer physical intensity of the protest made formal classes of any kind impossible. So they improvised, yelling their Irish lessons up and down the corridor, for example. Then the hunger strikes of 1980–81 marginalized education even further. When the strikes ended, everything in the movement was up for discussion and reflection. No doubt, Republican prisoners had proven that they could endure the most. They had won the regime's attention and gained a few concessions. Were the deaths of ten men, the ruined health of many others, and the mental torment of the last five years worth it? The answer could only be worked out in conversations in each cell; out of this came a new approach to education. As they thought about the outcome of the protests and parsed scraps of information about how the community outside had reacted, prisoners' feelings were also colored by perceptions of leadership. Bobby Sands, an undisputed authority figure not only in protest but in education as well, was gone. No other leader came unscathed through the searing test of the last hunger strike; subtle differences in participation and support would filter through deep and often unacknowledged feelings of shame and guilt. The hunger strike both divided and united the prisoners as they returned to a semblance of normal life, wearing their own clothes and no longer waging daily battles with the "screws."

Normal life in the cell gave rise to a new form of the prison university. As new paths toward peace negotiations slowly emerged outside prison in the 1980s, hundreds of men and women remained in prison, both subjects of and contributors to the political process. One of them, 1981 hunger striker Laurence McKeown, provides a detailed study of the social and political transformation of the prison after 1981. McKeown begins by contrasting the hierarchical culture of the special category cages, in which prisoners shared food parcels only among their friends, with the more communal, horizontal culture of the blanket protest. The blanket protest had been, thought participant Jackie McMullan, "the Great Leveller."[87] No man could force another to put aside his clothes, wreck his cell, battle the guards, and smear his excrement on his wall. Each had to reach these decisions himself, and then reaffirm them, year after year, on his own, among others who did the same. As in the trenches of a war, this experience gave rise to intense feelings of comradeship and mutual support.[88]

The blanketmen were denied any goods from outside and had only tobacco, which they shared to stretch between the monthly visits when it was smuggled in. When the protesters were gradually dispersed among the prisoners who had been conforming to prison rules, the relative abundance of goods they found there seemed "selfish" to them.[89] The blanketmen came armed with the moral authority of the front line of the prison conflict and tried to impose their shared experience on others. Thus were born the "communes." Groups of prisoners, perhaps a dozen men or so, decided to "collectivise" the food parcels each received.

In some of the wings, these communes then consolidated into larger ones, which also pooled books and money.[90] These efforts toward self-sufficiency and cooperation were the prelude to rethinking political relations themselves. The community of prisoners had changed over the last five or six years, as had the political context. Amid the return to relatively normal life in 1982–83, some of the Republican prisoners' leaders resumed the standard lecture-based education, but others saw the "need for a radical overhaul of... out-dated and morally wrong militaristic lines of command."[91] This strong language reflects the blanketmen's sense that they had gained authority as they passed through a trial of character.

The ex-blanketmen did not just demand change but created the conditions for it to occur. They sabotaged the administration's efforts to force them to return to work, using go-slow tactics, pilfering tools, and ridiculing guards to render work regimes hopeless. Forcing Republican prisoners to behave like "ordinary decent criminals" became increasingly difficult for the regime. Work came to a definitive end in the aftermath of a mass escape in September 1983, followed by a period of violent repression and total lockdown. With so much time for themselves, the prisoners began to talk.

It is a bit jarring to encounter philosophical debates among men and women who, whatever their intellectual capacity, followed a path to prison that was active if not armed. These are not classic "prisoners of conscience," yet they began to behave like them when they had both the time and the distance to reflect on the cause. Sometime in 1982, Jackie McMullan received a copy of Paolo Freire's *Pedagogy of the Oppressed*; he and a few others quickly recognized that Freire's argument for education as a revolutionary tool of the marginalized fit their situation perfectly. It resonated with prisoners who had felt silenced by the military-political lectures of their commanding officers, reduced to passive receptors of "official" knowledge. McMullan offers a harsh description of old-style education: "It was compulsory. The wing would have been split into half a dozen groups with a section leader who would have got the men together and read out the lecture and ask did anyone have questions. No one asked questions. The attitude was get in and out as quick as you can."[92] Freire's concept of praxis encouraged the men to make their own education through reflection and focused dialogue among equals.[93] Such methods had already emerged organically, says McKeown: "We could clearly identify similarities with what had been happening educationally in our wings during the blanket protest."[94] Freire offered a way to recover the passion of those discussions. McMullan, who had been "on the blanket" from the beginning and who had also participated in the 1981 hunger strike, proposed what he called a "pragmatic programme." Having gotten the nod from H-Block leadership, he recruited a "nucleus" of four or five enthusiasts in each wing.

We asked them to get together and thrash things out and to discuss
their own needs, the strengths and weaknesses of their own wings and
how they were going to go about it . . . . They would be intense discussions and would be followed up on over a course of days. They would
cover things like the history of the jail, the situation at that time, how
we saw our roles within the prison, our relationship with the Movement
outside and so on. The line we pushed was that we were going to be
inside for some time and that we owed it to ourselves, to the struggle
and to the protest that had given us the conditions.[95]

The "pragmatic programme" was nothing if not ambitious. The prisoners reveled in their renewed access to books and devoured history, politics, international affairs, and literature. They had plenty of time, so they commissioned from
knowledgable comrades a study of republicanism over the last two centuries.
These texts were copied by hand, circulated to other blocks, copied again, then
discussed in small groups, chapter by chapter. Next, they turned their attention
to political theory and strategy, finding inspiration in Third World revolutionary movements like Mozambique's Frelimo. Reading Lenin, British and Irish
Marxists, and more, they aimed to transform the republican movement. In consequence, the movement inside began to diverge from the movement outside.
While leaders outside pursued a tandem strategy of negotiation within official
structures and a continued campaign of violence, prisoners had neither option.
A vision of socialist revolution made sense within prison because it built on
communal practices in the H-Blocks. It reflected the prisoners' desire to understand the radical change that they believed the impoverished Catholic population of Northern Ireland really desired.[96]

The Freirist dialogues became the basis for a democratization of camp politics. The education activists came to the conclusion that "education would only
be any good if we can make it relevant to our lives every day of the week. If we
were going to become involved in political education then we were going to
have to be able to put it into practice in the wings, the way we structured the
wings and that."[97] Thus was born the *coiste* (committee), a "civilian" collective
structure in each wing taking its place alongside the extant military hierarchy.
Individual *coiste* members had responsibility for education and cultural activities; the wing's Commanding Officer also sat on the *coiste* as first among equals.
The coexistence was deceptive, though; as historian Richard English puts it, now
"collectivization and collective self-regulation began to compete with a formal
chain of command."[98]

The *coiste* enthusiasts in effect reversed the direction taken in Frongoch seventy years earlier. Irish prisoners ever since 1916 had welcomed, indeed celebrated, a military culture of political imprisonment. Camps and prisons had

allowed them the time to perfect the hierarchy and the rituals of an armed force, even when the cadres outside were weak. Prison, indeed, had honed the IRA in ways the armed underground never could. But the ten-year campaign stretching from the Long Kesh fire of 1974 (discussed in Chapter 7) through to the 1983 escape had in a way completed the paramilitary mission of the imprisoned. Republican prisoners continued to follow the chain of command in protest actions, but their scope for political activity simply expanded. Prisoners participated, for example, in formal academic study (usually through the Open University), no longer viewing it as conformist. Instead, some used it to build their revolutionary knowledge and organizational skills.[99]

The pedagogical and organizational remaking of prison life in the H-Blocks added a new dimension to prison politics and movement politics as well. Even as the inside and outside worlds diverged, the H-Block debates furnished lessons that prisoners would try to apply. "It was one massive learning process for us all," recalls Seán Murray, who became vice commanding officer for political education in the H-Blocks in 1985. "Republicans became confident in their own ability . . . . One of the major lessons learned was that if we stand together no one can defeat us, whether it's in jail or outside." Murray, who became a neighborhood activist after leaving prison, believes the lessons extended beyond prison: "It would be great if we could transfer that from the jail community to the wider community outside . . . because that's what it's all about, the quality of life, people's advancement on a personal level and collective level. That's what freedom's about."[100]

With the focus taken off protest actions, many prisoners threw themselves into the intellectual ferment, honing their ideas and their debating skills with their comrades in the wing. Study was a way, recalled one, "to push the walls back, to gain a semblance of self-determination in what was an extremely controlled environment."[101] Another recalled the sections where only Irish was spoken as "the best wings I've ever been on . . . . They have, to me, generated a whole new level of dynamism and activism within the republican movement." Crucially, he links study of Irish to political work: "Those people who have come out are Irish language activists to the core, some of them, and they are also political activists to the core." The language itself, he claims, encourages a particular kind of *coiste* politics: "It's very difficult to lose your temper in Irish because the concepts don't exist, the words don't exist for it."[102] The search for knowledge could go well beyond the usual curriculum of military tactics and Marxist theory. When McKeown and McMullan persuaded a feminist scholar to offer a women's studies course for the H-Blocks through Open University, over 200 Republican prisoners enrolled in two years. Some men saw parallels between the egalitarian impulse of feminism and their own life at the margins; others wanted to engage with a politics they knew of through girlfriends or wives outside.[103]

The Republican experience dominates the history of political imprisonment in Northern Ireland. Loyalist prisoners have fewer dramatic stories to
tell, and perhaps as a result, they have written fewer memoirs and have fewer
chroniclers. The two opposing communities, whether mixed or segregated,
created very different prison cultures. Where the Republicans moved from
POW-style discipline through protest toward communal self-education,
Loyalists for a long time assumed they were the favored elite of the prison
and that their politics aligned with that of the regime. Loyal to the same
authority as their jailers, they found it harder to create a separate and positive
prison identity. Instead of structured protest and political debate, they chose
drugs and pumping iron.[104] In the words of a former prison guard, Loyalist
structures had "too many chiefs, not enough Indians." A prison governor contrasted the Loyalists' threats of violence to the "much cleverer game" of the
Republicans.[105] In 1987, IRA prisoners drew up a detailed list of demands,
some of them quite mundane. To prison officials, requests for Sony Walkmen
appeared a welcome depoliticization, but this was just a further example of
using the quotidian to build leadership, winning small victories on which they
could build. Making themselves the easier negotiation partners opened a path
toward eventual release.[106]

Rapprochements between Republicans and Loyalists happened first in
prison, in practical negotiations over everyday matters. Nowhere else in
Northern Ireland did large groups from both sides spend time in close contact with one another. It became obvious to some prisoner leaders that anni-
hilation of the other side was impossible, and so one would have to at least
acknowledge one's opponents. A key figure was the Ulster Volunteer Force
(UVF) leader Gusty Spence, a Loyalist folk hero with professional military
credentials who began, in the late 1970s, to call for a universal ceasefire and
power sharing in Northern Ireland. He did not advocate capitulation but coexistence in a British Northern Ireland. In prison, he studied the Irish language
and history, and even taught the latter.[107] David Ervine recalls the shock some
felt when Spence tried to build up negotiations between prison factions, tor-
pedoed eventually by the Republicans, who felt themselves in the stronger
position:

> I mean, you had just come into Long Kesh and the basis of your life
> was hatred for the Republicans [and] the next thing you know there's a
> Camp Council in which every faction, an unheard-of thing, [were] all
> pulled together by Spence to [engage in] dialogue about the conditions
> in jail, to challenge the jail regime about our conditions and circum-
> stances. But that's not what his real reason was; it was to talk politics
> among all of the factions, and he nearly pulled it off.[108]

The evolution of prisoner strategies helped to make the prisons what journalist Chris Ryder calls "a powerhouse of peace."[109] To some extent this became possible as prisoners learned that they might be left behind by transformations outside. A letter by an IRA prisoner to a Belfast newspaper circa 1990 suggests that violence was easier to renounce within prison. "Why is it," he wrote, "that the rest of Europe is settling its differences with flowers and the [IRA is] still using Semtex?"[110] The confluence of distinct processes of negotiation, both among those in prison and among those seeking power outside, made an agreement possible.

Prison empowered Republicans in a number of parallel ways: discipline, shared protest, and communal education. Laurence McKeown reflected on this process of self-discovery in his 1998 PhD dissertation:

> I feel that my time spent in prison was a very positive experience . . . .
> Most important for me, in terms of personal development, was the engagement in struggle, of both an intellectual and practical nature with comrades and adversaries alike. Through those struggles I came to have a better understanding of myself, of the social world I occupy and of the social forces that impact upon me. My time spent in prison was therefore a time of struggle in all its forms, a time of learning, a time of personal growth.[111]

The language of the peace process required conversion narratives, in which men and women sentenced for violent crimes accepted the end of conflict, but prisoners like McKeown and his comrades determined what their conversion would look like.[112] Experience of the prison university shaped how its graduates would return to politics when large numbers of prisoners were released following the Good Friday Agreement of 1998. Some of the Loyalist prisoners slunk away from the prison gate, covering their faces. IRA prisoners paraded out to a confetti and champagne welcome.[113]

Time behind bars produces political communities and leadership, and some lessons last beyond the moment the gates to freedom finally open. From every political prison emerge men and women who have not only survived but have gained renewed commitment to the struggle. Both ruling and opposition parties and organizations in dozens of countries are shaped by the prison experience of their members and supporters.

Conclusion

The Politics of Prisoners' Stories

The political prison differs in one fundamental way from most other total institutions that are the bulwarks of modern states, all of which produce something of value or promise to remake the people interned within. An ordinary prison may not actually rehabilitate its inmates, but the ostensible goal of reform nonetheless frames prison policy. In contrast, in the political prison the state demonstrates its power to detain, confine, name, and torture or at the very least discomfort and inhibit a group of people who claim to oppose it. There is no further possible development to the story, no rehabilitation or redemption. Some prisoners may yield useful information; some appear at trial, are released, or executed. But the collective narrative of opposition to a regime, as far as the state is concerned, is intended to come to an end.

Similarly, concentration camps might tell new inmates that their term is indefinite or that the only way out is "feet first." Especially since World War I, prison administration and guards have humiliated and debased their captives, letting them know that they are not political, perhaps even not worthy of being called human. The order and discipline they impose appears arbitrary to political prisoners precisely because it does not aim to rehabilitate or transform these inmates. To imprison is to punish, but that is not the same thing as saying that punishment, and still less rehabilitation, is the purpose of imprisonment. From the perspective of a purely rational regime, incarceration of one's opponents would seem to be less effective, and thus less preferable, than execution. Instead of getting rid of troublesome figures, regimes instead choose to incarcerate them, sometimes for decades. This book has shown why that is the case. Having them under lock and key allows states to categorize these prisoners clearly and to demonstrate the regimes' power over opposition. Above all, they can destabilize the prisoners' very sense of self and make them illegible or unrecognizable to themselves and to their comrades. In choosing this path, though, states have no way of declaring that the task has been completed.

The result is a kind of narrative confusion: what is to be done with political prisoners?

Political incarceration thus challenges the state as well as the opposition. The long-term outcome, especially in the late twentieth-century cases, is often that state leaders learn they have to negotiate with prisoners and treat them as potential partners—first in the prison itself, later in the broader political arena. In some of these cases, the prisoners emerge victorious. How does this happen? This book argues that a crucial transformation takes place within the prison that is actually impossible outside prison. Rendered illegible by the state's prison, prisoners create their own illegibility and confuse the prison, refusing its terms. Denied the possibility of human agency, of having any influence on their future, prisoners make their own. As they devise communal structures, engage in protest, and invent prison universities, political prisoners create a new narrative and wrest back their own agency, forcing the regime to respond.

Consider Nelson Mandela, instructing the prison governor on how he intended to speak during visits; Barbara Sadowska, inventing a novel form of hunger strike; Bobby Sands, devising a fiendishly frustrating hunger strike calendar. Recall the early Polish socialists engineering complex escapes, or the manacled Patrick Fleming throwing his clothes out through the cell door. The students mastering the Mrabulo Syllabus on Robben Island or enacting the pedagogical theory of Paulo Freire in the H-Blocks are declaring their ability to craft their own story of their imprisonment, just as much as those who burned down Long Kesh or who mastered the *przeplatanka*. O'Donovan Rossa tossing his hammer over the prison wall, Mohandas Gandhi or Hanna Sheehy-Skeffington refusing food, Ludwik Waryński composing a *mazurka* for his chained comrades—each reclaims agency in a place where there should be none. The narrative does not have to be about release and revolution for the political prisoner to reverse politics.

The political prison thus has a crucial if unexpected role to play in opposition to a regime. The prisoner community develops in parallel to the movement outside prison. Sometimes that movement is very far away—or has even ceased to exist, such as in Stalinist Poland. Other times, as in revolutionary Ireland or in Gandhi's Transvaal, the movements inside and out overlap significantly. More often, the two learn from each other, engaged in different but complementary actions. Even where the movement for political change has been successful, those who have spent many years in prison for the cause do not always partake in that success. But in the one place where the state seeks to render its opponents illegible and stripped of any agency, those opponents deploy their own strategies of illegibility, reclaim the power to act, and, by making one state institution their own, make political change real. Collective action, as is possible where regimes allow some minimal space for it, accomplishes this most clearly. Yet even where a powerful state is determined to disaggregate and disable prisoners, limiting their actions to the barest forms of personal dignity—the hidden diary, the collective prayer, the whispered lesson, the lonely hunger strike—such prisoners find ways to recapture initiative and thus to deny their incapacitation.

This book argues for recognizing the political prisoner and political incarceration as participants in politics in the modern state. Political prisoners are not merely evidence that a regime exerts repression against its opponents and displays a disregard for human and civil rights. The political prisoner—often incarcerated in a few square meters, behind thick walls and guarded gates—embodies the confining and silencing of a whole cause. As they regain agency and assert their ability to control the narrative of their prison lives, these prisoners reconstitute the movement and its goals within prison. Beginning with smuggled letters, furtive hand waves, and coded conversations, they escalate to widespread individual and collective actions. Prisoners also inspire movements of their own, from local prisoner aid groups to international organizations.

Not all political prisoners or political movements have the same opportunities. The cell of the political prisoner concentrates oppositional and repressive politics in one place; those two forces produce various kinds of actions, though the general framework of illegibility, confusion, and control is consistent. The lonely prisoners in Stalinist Poland could hardly have employed the same repertoire of actions as the inmates of the H-Blocks, and yet their efforts often resemble each other. When numbers overwhelmed the prison—as in the POW camps in Frongoch or Szczypiorno, or in Pawiak Prison under the Nazis—prisoners have had a greater chance of denying access to their identity, making it difficult for the regime to know even whom they have incarcerated. When regimes feel constrained by international or domestic observers—as in the Irish War of Independence or in regimes closely watched by Amnesty International and other critics—prisoners can discomfort their captors to a much greater extent than would be possible in a regime confident that it can ignore such pressures.

In each prison, a community of prisoners takes shape, and a contest with the regime emerges. Regardless of whether that contest ends in victory for the opposition—perhaps even the elevation of a former inmate to the president's office—that community reshapes the political conflict precisely at a place where the state's power appears most complete. The apparently demobilized and depoliticized demonstrate agency and control over their bodies, the spaces they inhabit, and their lives. They build community structures, educate each other, and conceptualize the world beyond prison. Prison communities, born in the politicized collectives and in protest, contribute to a transformation of political opposition more generally. The "prison university," offering education that ranges from the basic and practical to the explicitly political and theoretical, makes the cell an incubator of politics. The political prison cell is a dynamic place. A communist ditty composed in Poland in the early 1920s sums it up, in words that would make sense to many of the protagonists of this book:

> Prison, o Prison/what a palace it is/even the toughest guys/long for you
> The toughest guys,/the bravest men,/the coolest kids,/the most spirited girls.
> Prison, o Prison/you have such force/that anyone who meets you/will surely return
> Will surely return/leaving mother and dad/for the prison walls/and the iron bars.
> Prison, o Prison/a wearied guest/will in your cells/find some rest
> Will find some rest/and with spirit revived/go out to serve/under the banner held high.[1]

Peace Dividends: Prisoners beyond Prison

Great Britain, Ireland, Poland, and South Africa today hold very few if any of their opponents.[2] From the late 1980s to the late 1990s, political opponents streamed out of the prisons of these countries. South Africa and Poland boasted iconic prisoner figures, especially Nelson Mandela and Lech Wałęsa, whose moral authority evoked both the regime's cruelty and the movement's principles, who could then play an important role after prison. But the paths from prison to politics were complicated. The ambitious reforms of President F. W. de Klerk, which would lead to a Nobel Peace Prize shared with Nelson Mandela in 1993, looked from within prison like preservation tactics for apartheid. Promises of amnesty turned out merely to be a way for the regime to redefine "political prisoner," releasing some but not others. A wave of hunger strikes among detainees and convicted prisoners swept the country in the first months of 1989; Robben Island inmates announced their own in February 1990. In lengthy press releases—the one from Robben Island stretched to four typewritten pages, followed by twelve pages of numbered demands—they presented themselves as conscious and politically engaged, ready "to serve the oppressed and exploited community in furtherance of our people's aspirations," yet driven to extreme measures by broken promises of freedom. Using the network of prisoner support organizations very effectively, they became visible players in the political transformation.[3]

The fall of communism in Poland did not hinge on events in prison themselves, as no talks took place until most Solidarity leaders, like Wałęsa, were long out of prison. But when senior communist officials, including Minister of Internal Affairs General Czesław Kiszczak, sat down with Solidarity to discuss political and economic change at the Round Table negotiations of February–April 1989, they confronted men and women who had been their captives a few years before. Some, like Adam Michnik and Jacek Kuroń, were judged by the regime to be so dangerous that it attempted to exclude them from the Round Table. The depth of transformation during those talks, which precipitated the communists' surrender of power that summer, can be measured by the prison background of many participants.[4] But no less a measure is the lesson learned by the regime, which had less to gain than its former captives by negotiating with them. The communists had assumed their adversaries came prepared to string them up; instead, the ex-prisoners of the new democratic government would often invoke their experiences of repression to oppose any settling of scores.

Northern Ireland did not have such leaders; Bobby Sands might have been such a figure, but his death at twenty-seven makes it impossible to guess how his prison leadership would have translated into ordinary politics. Many former prisoners who did go on to play central roles in the peace process of the 1990s, like Martin McGuinness, Gerry Adams, or David Ervine of the Ulster Volunteer Force (UVF), had left prison a decade or more earlier. Jail politics over the last fifteen years of the Troubles had diverged from trends outside; prisoners' interest in communism came to seem antiquated after the fall of Soviet-backed regimes in 1989. In contrast to the success of East European dissenters or of the African National Congress (ANC), Northern Ireland's prisoners were unable to adapt to dramatic political change.[5] Traditional political structures were favored; the Nobel Prize for ending the Northern Ireland conflict went to two men, John Hume and David Trimble, who had never been in prison. Prison university graduates have made an impact primarily at the community level.

As a democratic regime, the British government had in some ways less leeway to listen to and learn from the prison; the government would not fall if they didn't, and indeed any hint of negotiation could and did anger political allies. By making prison administration negotiate with them, Republican prisoners nevertheless made prison into a school for the regime. The political prisoner and the prison governor do not need to become comrades (in fact, the IRA assassinated senior officers of the H-Blocks as late as 1984–85). But having demonstrated control, the Republican prisoners forced the administration to deal with them differently. Negotiations over the mundane details of prison life then provided a template for negotiation with the regime outside. Republican and Loyalist prisoners alike urged this next step: " 'Sure if you can talk to us in here you can talk to them out there,' " as Chris Ryder captured the sentiment.[6]

The rehabilitation of released prisoners and the interpretation of their experience has challenged many post-transition societies. Debates about the reparations owed for imprisonment and about the adequacy of social services for those reentering society stand in for the question of the place political imprisonment held in the fight for regime change. The thousands of uncelebrated prisoners who simply returned home, trying either to resume interrupted lives or to find a role in the revolution for which they gave their freedom, force reevaluation of why political imprisonment matters. Long after the political cells are empty, the legacy of incarceration lives on in each country. Decades of incarceration by quite varied regimes have provided an understanding of how states, prisons, prisoners, and opposition movements shape and are shaped by the experience. Those regimes' opponents are now free, and information about their travails is freely available. But to end with the opening of iconic prison gates in the 1990s might leave the false impression that the story is concluded.

Epilogue

"Nobody Survives Guantanamo": A Political Prison Today

One day in the winter of 2005, after nearly three years in American custody, Moazzam Begg decided to play a trick on his captors. He and other detainees considered the most valuable in Guantanamo had recently been moved to Papa Block in Camp Delta and issued new tan uniforms to replace the hated orange ones. Though they were still kept isolated from one another, many had met in the American prisons in Afghanistan or Iraq. Somehow, claims Begg, this group "built up quite a deep and unusual comradeship, . . . sharing this special, unbelievable experience." They had finally been allowed to consult with lawyers, in anticipation of planned military tribunals. Some had refused to cooperate with this new system; all wondered what purpose the tribunals would serve. The sense of being denied information—a constant from the moment of detention—had grown palpable. "We all wanted to antagonize the guards a little," admits Begg. So he composed a note filled with "complete nonsense": random sentences in nearly a dozen languages, decorated with flags of different countries. He then hid it in the recreation yard, where he knew the guards would find it. Within an hour, a general came to inspect the block, and soon all detainees there were subject to special searches. Begg apologized to his comrades for the inconvenience these caused, but "enjoyed my little joke on the Americans."[1]

The meaningless message that apes politics while exposing the prison regime's impotence and lack of knowledge has appeared in numerous versions in camps and prisons over the last 150 years. Moazzam Begg used the very conditions of his solitary confinement to take advantage of the US government's belief that he was a talented and well-connected activist of "significant intelligence value" in order to expand the zone of uncertainty in Papa Block.[2] While he played his game alone, he was confident that his fellow detainees would appreciate it, even at the cost of a few more searches of their cells and bodies.

The world today does not lack for political prisoners of all ideologies, in a wide range of regimes. Any attempt to quantify political imprisonment worldwide is impossible, given that many regimes hold hundreds, even thousands of people about whom little or nothing is known—some detained for a few days after a demonstration and others disappearing for years.[3] It is also foolhardy to try to assess whether the number of political prisoners has changed over time. Perhaps, with the Gulag and the Chinese *laogai* both smaller than they were a few decades ago, this kind of repression affects fewer people than before. Countries that once incarcerated thousands of opponents—for example, Spain, Greece, Chile, and Yugoslavia—no longer use this tactic of mass control. On the other hand, more countries are capable of holding larger numbers of people—sometimes with funding from the United States[4]—and have found that the language of anti-terrorism is as effective as the old language of anti-communism in justifying repressive measures.

This epilogue applies the analysis of political prisoners historically to one contemporary case: the nearly 800 men imprisoned by the United States Armed Forces at Guantanamo Bay since January 2002. To say that the detention facility at Guantanamo Bay holds political prisoners is not a value statement about either the detainees or the regime. Many do use the term that way, either honoring the detainees or indicting the regime, or as a marker of rights violations. Guantanamo deserves analysis as a political prison on the grounds of whether its inmates act and are treated like political prisoners.

Guantanamo differs from many other cases in that the prisoners did not, at the outset, represent a cohesive group. Despite the assertions of US officials at the time, many had no connection either to the Taliban or al Qaeda but were random people caught up in the post-9/11 dragnet. Some were sold out to settle political or other scores, or simply to earn the bounty Americans offered.[5] Nor could they all communicate with one another, as some spoke little or no Arabic and no English upon entering the camp. Despite American political rhetoric about the danger of terrorist attacks should the men be transferred to federal prisons, there is no evidence of an outside movement coordinating or communicating with them. The community, as it came together, lacked any recognized or preexisting leaders, men whose authority among others in a movement predated their incarceration.

It is not easy to know the world of Guantanamo the way we can know Robben Island, the H-Blocks, or Pawiak. This prison is still in operation, and most of the evidence on its operation remains secret. Even parts of court proceedings are kept hidden, while the monitoring of client-lawyer communications ensures that some information is withheld. The early photographs of rows of kneeling, hooded men revealed little about life in Guantanamo's cages. Journalistic accounts have focused on the shocking facts of detention, rendition, and mistreatment, and on the legal proceedings; everyday life in the prison is frustratingly hidden. Detainee Assessment Briefs (leaked by Wikileaks) prepared for nearly all detainees provide only the barest of glimpses into camp society; the same is true for the few reports by governmental bodies or human rights organizations. There are, however, five rich, detailed memoirs, four written by men after their release and one composed in prison by a man who was released much later.[6] These sources, which focus mainly on the first five years of the camp, present their own problems, of course. For example, reviewers have noticed that several elide or minimize the author's path to detention in Afghanistan or Pakistan. More important, there is little or no corroboration for their stories. Only Moazzam Begg himself provides the story of his little prank, for example. All prisons are underdocumented, but for now memoirs and a few other accounts have to suffice for a comparison between Guantanamo and other political prisons.

The Regime

A political prison regime seeks to isolate and infantilize the prisoner, depriving him of information and predictability and breaking a sense of connection to a community or even to oneself. The experience of Mohamedou Ould Slahi at Guantanamo is emblematic. A Mauritanian who lived much of his adult life in Germany, Slahi arrived at Guantanamo in August 2002 after more than eight months in a Jordanian prison. In June 2003, he was moved from the main prison area, Camp Delta, to a punishment section known as India Block. "Brothers, pray for me, I am being transferred," he called to his cell neighbors. Slahi found his new home "completely empty of any signs of life. I was put at one end of the block and the Yemeni fellow was at the beginning, so there was no interaction whatsoever between us . . . . Later . . . the whole block was reserved for me, only me, ALLAH, [the American officers], and the guards who worked for them." Everything was taken away except some bedding. Isolation was so complete, he writes, that "I was forbidden from seeing the light of the day; every once in a while they gave me a rec-time at night to keep me from seeing or interacting with any detainees."[7] Soon after, a representative from the International Committee of the Red Cross (ICRC) was permitted to visit Slahi and to take a letter from him to his mother; the ICRC was subsequently unable to visit him for more than a year, despite requests. Guards even endeavored, for over a year, to prevent Slahi from performing ritual prayers, leaving him spiritually isolated.[8]

Some other prisoners have been kept even more isolated than Slahi at a site known as Camp Platinum whose exact location has not been disclosed. Other forms of isolation include wire mesh so thick one cannot see through it; solitary exercise periods; and rules against communicating with one's neighbor. The legal system itself imposes isolation on all prisoners, as lawyers advocate for individual clients, not prisoners as a group, so their collective plight cannot be represented. The most intimately isolating component of the entire War on Terror incarceration was the hood. Sometimes an ordinary bag, sometimes a specially made part of the prisoner uniform, it was at first worn by all prisoners during rendition or while being transferred between cells and sometimes even by visitors. It completely cuts the wearer off from the environment and puts him at the mercy of those who lead him.

Prison and transport personnel devise such treatment in part because they fear their charges, whom they believe are capable of abnormal and inhuman acts. Murat Kurnaz, a Turkish German detained in Pakistan and sold to the Americans by local officials as a dangerous fighter, was stripped and manacled when he arrived at Kandahar Base in Afghanistan. The war was at its most intense then, and yet, he writes, "It seemed to me that [the soldiers] were less afraid of the bombs than of me, although I was naked, bound, and unarmed."[9] Legend imbued another detainee, David Hicks, with almost superhuman powers: he had, his guards believed, escaped from his chains in the plane from Afghanistan and then tried to crash it by chewing through its electrical wiring.[10] Even less fearsome prisoners are very closely guarded. Especially in the early years (from which most recollections come), five or more soldiers would be sent to collect a detainee for interrogation or to punish him for an infraction. This reinforced the idea that the prisoners were not only "the worst of the worst," in the formulation of the US administration, but capable of incredible physical feats, too. The young guards displayed little understanding of their captives, fearing both them and the unfamiliar cultures they are believed to have come from. Ahmed Errachidi—who says soldiers even removed the paper wrappers from water bottles because they had been told the terrorists could fashion weapons from them, and covered their name tags to protect themselves from terrorist retribution—astutely observes that the prison administration used such suggestions "to sow fear in the soldiers' minds so they wouldn't be tempted to get to know us."[11]

The brutality of the treatment of Guantanamo prisoners has been well documented in memoirs and legal documents. Subjection to extreme cold, waterboarding, weeks of sleep deprivation, confinement in airless containers, shackling, pepper spraying, systematic physical abuse, and mental torture such as sexual humiliation and continuous loud music all contribute to reducing detainees to an infantile or animal level.[12] Memoirists report crying excessively and being unable to understand simple commands. They become unused to the sun. Unable to walk, they have to be led by the hand, whether or not they are wearing a hood. They do things that their adult selves find shameful, like having to defecate in sight of the guards or in their pants. In the short term, these brutal tactics may be intended to "soften up" the prisoners. But they are also a response to the irrational fears the guards have of the prisoners, a way to reduce the prisoners to manageable states. This reinforces, of course, the sense of cultural or racial superiority that guards repeatedly express to their captives.

Some practices, like the use of numbers instead of names or the requirement that prisoners crouch down and/or face away when guards enter the cell or when encountering a prisoner under escort, are the same practices that have enabled many other political prisons to deny information about inmates. Interrogators used false names; guards too hid such information. The United States military has taken secrecy to novel extremes, particularly during transport The prison regime has rendered detainees, when in transport around the prison or to/from Guantanamo, completely and literally insensate to even their immediate environment. In addition to hoods, prisoners have been fitted with painted-over goggles, headphones, and thick gloves. Like the windowless shipping containers used for solitary confinement, these accessories denied even the existence of the outside world. Many detainees were also prevented from knowing the day or time. While not unusual in a prison, at Guantanamo this has prevented detainees (nearly all practicing Muslims) from knowing when to pray. Even when this restriction was relaxed, the prison administration at times imposed its own rituals over the prayers by broadcasting the American national anthem at the same time as a call to prayer. Prisoners' practice of their faith remained dependent upon prison administration; distrusting the camp schedule, they demanded clocks in their cells.

During the first three years, the only outside contact was through the ICRC, which does not seem to have shared much information with the prisoners. A few lawyers were finally allowed to see prisoners in late 2004, but they too were restricted in what they could tell prisoners.[13] One of the first of these came to meet Murat Kurnaz and brought clippings from German and American newspapers. That night, Kurnaz relayed news to others in his block—by yelling when the generators were quiet—and in return received six weeks' solitary confinement in one of the airless cells.[14] This denying of information also helped to deprive prisoners of social ties. Having knowledge about a comrade's court proceedings might enable a prisoner to prepare his own strategy; knowing the name of the prisoner in an adjacent cell could allow one to report torture.

The regime has gone to elaborate lengths to make its hooded, isolated, sleep-deprived, tortured prisoners, disoriented in time and space, illegible to each other and to observers. Among its most significant innovations is rendition, in which prisoners are flown to secret sites around the world for interrogation and torture.[15] Disappearance itself is crucial to this strategy. "I bet you don't know where you are," an American soldier taunted Moazzam Begg and was surprised when Begg correctly guessed Kandahar Airport.[16] Many detainees could not figure out where they had ended up; David Hicks reports that some at Guantanamo were convinced they were in China. As he put it, the interrogators twisted and withheld information to "create a new reality for us."[17] The prison regime has also endeavored to maintain the uncertainty, even pretending that prisoners might again be renditioned, this time out of Guantanamo. On the afternoon of August 26, 2003, Mohamedou Ould Slahi was meeting with a "friendly" interrogator, when "suddenly a commando team consisting of three soldiers and a German Shepherd broke into our interrogation room." One shouted "Motherfucker, I told you, you're gone!" while his partner punched Slahi all over. They put him in goggles and headphones, fitted a bag over his head, tightened his chains, and threw him into the back of a truck, and then onto a boat. For three hours, he estimates, they drove him around the bay, making him drink salt water. Then they turned him over to an Egyptian-Jordanian torture team, for another three-hour tour on a different boat. This team talked about taking Slahi to one of their countries. Late that night, Slahi found himself in Camp Echo, a five-minute ride from where he had started. Slahi—whose account is backed up by a US Senate Armed Services Committee report—says this performance was supposed to make him think he "was being transferred to some far, faraway secret prison. We detainees knew all of that; we had detainees reporting they had been flown around for four hours and found themselves in the same jail where they started."[18]

The practices at Guantanamo offer a combination of brutal certainty and uncertainty, in which it becomes extremely difficult to tell who is who, where is where, and when is when. The US military has thus created a classic political prison. The logic is clear, if all detainees are assumed to be fighters for Al Qaeda or other related groups. Disorientation and isolation break up an otherwise impenetrable cabal; infantilization renders harmless their presumedly inaccessible, alien, hostile culture; illegibility neutralizes their supposedly devilish abilities and conspiratorial nature. We cannot determine whether US interrogators really believed that detainees might somehow know, after years in captivity, where Osama bin Laden or other leaders were hiding, but only a formidable prison like Guantanamo could allow the regime to master its fear.

The Prisoners

Hundreds of the inmates of Guantanamo cannot tell their stories. Some are still there; others have been imprisoned in their home countries (as David Hicks was for eight months in Australia); many more are very unlikely to share their memories in print. The existing stories offer explanations for their fate, accounts of the mistreatment they personally suffered, and (for the most part) stories of redemption and release. Lawyers, translators, and other witnesses see one inmate at a time, and government documents treat them individually, which

Blackened glass, gates. One ties the sheet into a shawl One listens to MP3s. One speaks to a guard

Fig. E. 1 Molly Crabapple, sketch of prisoners at Guantanamo, 2013. Crabapple was forbidden to draw the prisoners' faces. Her sketches appeared originally at vice.com. Courtesy of the artist.

does not allow for a reconstruction of the everyday life of a community of prisoners. Memoirists have often spent much of their time in total solitude and simply cannot describe the prison community. Moazzam Begg did not so much as glimpse another detainee until he was hospitalized, some eighteen months after he came to Guantanamo.[19] Finally, each memoirist exercises a good deal of caution. Murat Kurnaz does not use anyone else's name—nor does Slahi. They have experienced enough of the long arm of US vengeance not to risk anyone's exposure.

Nevertheless, a community formed among the Guantanamo prisoners. Again, the men lacked a common cause, as many had no connection with extremist groups and still fewer seem to have engaged directly with al Qaeda. But all had been captured by the Americans or turned over to them; most had been tortured; all had been transported against their will to an unfamiliar place. So all had a common foe. Furthermore, their shared Muslim faith, albeit with some sectarian variations, provided a common cultural framework for protest. For example, protests concerning prayer times and treatment of the Koran erupted with some frequency. Murat Kurnaz knew exactly what had happened when he heard "a long, tortured cry . . . different from the cries of people being beaten," and saw a guard in a prisoner's cage. "This guard must have thrown the Koran on the ground—otherwise the prisoner wouldn't have howled like that. I saw the guard trampling on something." Kurnaz watched as men throughout the block stood up and started "wailing . . . . It was as though lightning had struck a zoo. Some of the prisoners tried to kick down the cage doors, others shook the fencing, trying to tear or bite their way through the chain links. Suddenly, the guard was afraid. He left the Koran on the ground and ran away."[20]

In this telling, the protest emerges spontaneously, and the men, as if possessed, whirl around "like dervishes." But Kurnaz (whose Turkish-German background may have given him an unconscious Western cultural bias) dimly realized that something more was going on. As helicopters gathered overhead and snipers took their positions on the perimeter, he noticed one prisoner, a Chechen whom he calls "Isa," neither tearing at his cage nor rolling on the floor. Instead he was standing "with a clenched fist, smiling."[21] Other prisoners, meanwhile, called out what seem to be instructions, in Arabic. One of these quieted the hubbub; then, when the pacification teams arrived and began beating the men in their cages, prisoners began dumping their water buckets or toilet buckets on soldiers as they passed by or entered neighboring cells.

Other glimpses of collective action and identity appear. Begg reported hearing his first call to prayer in nearly two years, having finally been moved to Camp Delta from the isolation section in October 2004. First, a call came over the loudspeakers, but then prisoners began their own call. Begg learned, "from shouted conversations over the cell blocks," that a "unanimous decision" had been taken to "reject the prayer call the Americans put over the loudspeakers."[22] Begg adds that the prisoners also doubted that their food is halal and that they have been given the correct orientation toward Mecca. But on second reading the "unanimous decision" is quite striking. How was this consensus reached, in a chaotic, almost random group of men kept forcibly apart from one another?

The emergence of leadership is one of the enduring mysteries of Guantanamo, but its presence is undeniable. One of these leaders is Isa the Chechen. Moazzam Begg also introduces Uthman al-Harbi, a Yemeni, who was "not only the most influential person in our block, but probably one of the most influential in the whole of Guantánamo Bay. He also happened to be on the side of the block that was closest to [the next block of cages], which bolstered his theory that the Americans had placed us, or him, strategically so that whatever was said would be recorded."[23] Begg's understanding of how Uthman acquired authority is revealing, as much for its obvious reliance on hearsay as for the pride of place it gives politics. He "had always refused to speak to the interrogators. He'd also said openly in the military commission that he was a member of al-Qa'idah, and he'd sacked his military-appointed lawyer .... So he'd thrown a big spanner in their works."[24] Uthman thus represents a politics that Begg and others are cautious about or even disclaim; he tells Begg he has met Osama bin Laden and argues for the righteousness of the 9/11 attacks. This stance appears to give him a different relationship with the American jailers. While Begg claims that he and others argue with Uthman, the latter's erudition, his commitment to practices of his faith, and his ability to deal with the regime all gave him authority which, Begg suggests, the Americans acknowledged.

The best-known leadership figure at Guantanamo was Shaker Aamer, a British citizen arrested in Afghanistan and released in late 2015. It is probably Aamer whom Murat Kurnaz describes during a hunger strike that followed the Koran riot:

> On the fourth day of the hunger strike, the general who was in charge of Guantanamo in the early days arrived and talked with one of the English-speaking prisoners. The prisoner refused to stand up in the general's presence. The general took his cap off and sat on the ground in the corridor in front of the cage. At that moment, I realized that we were not utterly powerless .... The general and the prisoner talked .... The prisoner explained how important the Koran was to us and what it meant. The general said he would punish the soldier who had defiled the Koran.[25]

Kurnaz places this scene in early 2002, but it closely resembles an encounter between Colonel Michael Bumgarner and Shaker Aamer in 2005, also during a hunger strike, when Aamer was "giving his guards fits, pressing one of the sporadic civil disobedience campaigns for which he was famous." Bumgarner went to confront him in his cell: "'You're either gonna start complying with the rules ... or life's gonna get really rough.' ... Aamer, who wore a thick black beard and had his hair pulled back in a ponytail, was unimpressed. The prisoner, who was not wearing his glasses, squinted for a moment, trying to read the officer's insignia. 'Colonel,' he finally said, 'don't come in here giving me that.'" Bumgarner sat down, and he and Aamer talked for five hours.[26]

Whenever this meeting took place, it offers further clues to the origins of leadership on Guantanamo. First, the prison regime, like all others, found that it could not simply reduce all its captives to an undifferentiated mass. There were so many of them, so widely different in cultures and in background, that authorities needed to create some structure. Naturally, they chose articulate English speakers, and Aamer was one.[27] But the detainees' efforts to organize came first, not the authorities' search for possible leaders. A 2002 CIA report raised the alarm that movement leaders were among those detained, making Guantanamo seem like a favor done for al Qaeda. "Terrorists approach incarceration as an opportunity to advance the interests of their groups through forming new connections or reinforcing existing ones. Prison culture is conducive to these goals because institutional life is similar to the outside operating environment where they conduct clandestine activity, face a hostile security service, and are forced to create or join tight-knit groups to survive." The report notes such features emerging at Guantanamo, cautions against allowing freedom of movement, and warns of attempts to "corrupt . . . intimidate . . . or manipulate" guards.[28] According to the report, al Qaeda—like many of the movements discussed in this book—produced a manual on organizing in prison; however, elaborate structures would not have been possible in the Guantanamo cages. Given that the vast majority of the detainees were very unlikely to have read such a manual, the prison community most likely crystallized independently.

It seems probable that organization cohered at different times in different parts of the prison camp. Tim Golden interviewed a released Bahraini prisoner who described how Shaker Aamer organized prisoners "through sheer force of personality." Very early on, perhaps in the first week, Aamer boycotted the routine weighing of prisoners by the medical staff and convinced others to join him.[29] This was a brilliant choice, as the refusal to be weighed could be cast as an entirely personal decision, not political, yet the bureaucratic routine required this minor task. Moreover, each individual prisoner would have the opportunity to refuse, and short of beating each inmate unconscious, guards could not compel them to stand on a scale.

In Golden's account, Aamer's actions led to further organizing, block by block. When Colonel Bumgarner came to meet Aamer during the 2005 hunger strike, Aamer convinced him that he could help control the camp: "If you can get me to go around the camp, I can turn this off." In Bumgarner's company, Aamer visited several blocks and brought the hunger strike to an end. Several interesting things emerge from the story. First, Aamer portrayed the prisoners as otherwise impenetrable: he told Bumgarner of a vision prisoners have had in which three would have to die so the others would be freed. This would have played on the Americans' assumptions about mystical, less rational Muslims, and made them dependent upon leaders like Aamer to interpret such stories. Second, he casually let Bumgarner know of the extent of prisoner networks, by declining to meet with more than "a handful of the most influential detainees." That Aamer was greeted like a "rock star" in several of the blocks they visit further indicated how far news could travel. Finally, Aamer proposed an elected representation system and got Bumgarner to agree to a meeting of six leaders who discuss how to improve prison conditions.[30] A well-developed prisoner community had clearly emerged, despite efforts of the prison regime to isolate the men in accordance with the CIA's warnings.

Bumgarner also met with another leader, Ahmed Errachidi, "the General." Like Aamer, Errachidi used his knowledge of English to advance protest. He devised actions in which prisoners put the administration on the defensive, thus giving prisoners a sense of "control over our destinies." The common thread in these protests was that prisoners appeared to act against their interests. Errachidi proposed that they protest the defilement of Korans by simply returning their Korans to the prison library. This way, he argued, "the administration wouldn't be able to keep up their pretence of giving us full religious freedom and, at the same time, they'd also not be able to use our holy book as leverage against us."[31] The action appeared to succeed: soon the prison guards were trying to force prisoners to take the Koran, for example, by slipping copies into their cells when they were summoned away for interrogation. Another tactic, during the very heated conflicts of 2003, similarly exposed the ridiculous prison rules. Errachidi proposed that prisoners neglect to return the plastic spoons after a meal—and then push them out of their cages into an inaccessible spot behind the mesh. The soldiers had been told the terrorists could use the spoons as weapons, so they descended on Errachidi's block to get the spoons. Errachidi was dragged off to interrogation, where he gave a "nonsensical answer" to explain the action: "I told [my interrogator] that we'd noticed that they were obsessed with the spoons, so we decided that spoons must hold some special importance for them, which is why we hid them in a place where neither we nor they could get at them." But now he had a chance to articulate several of the prisoners' demands.[32]

Errachidi's leadership—generally confirmed by Bumgarner's account—is, like Aamer's, rooted in personality and cultural advantage. Murat Kurnaz, however, claims that prisoner organization was more complex than that, with a second, hidden layer of prisoner authority under the visible layer. In response to the early incidents with the Koran, he writes, "we went ahead and elected a leader. All of the prisoners were allowed to nominate a candidate. It was a secret vote—the Americans knew nothing about it." The vote took several weeks; the 500 prisoners chose ten, who then chose three, who somehow communicated

among themselves to choose an "emir." Kurnaz describes an elaborate system
designed to thwart further repressions.

> No one but the three men who elected him knew who he was. Officially
> this man was not our leader. He chose a spokesperson to deal with the
> Americans and appear as our leader. In that way, the real emir could
> remain in the background, undetected.
>
> We strung the Americans along. We acted as though we had elected
> an emir, the spokesperson, and let his name be known. Before long
> the spokesperson disappeared for months. The Americans thought
> they had broken our resistance, and there wouldn't be any more hun-
> ger strikes. But the real emir was still making the decisions behind the
> scenes. He collected opinions from all the prisoners' representatives
> and decided what the figurehead emir would tell the Americans.[33]

Later, each block elected an emir; Kurnaz served several times "when I wasn't
being transferred or spending time in solitary confinement."[34]

If Kurnaz's story is accurate, we can imagine that Aamer or Errachidi may
have been designated as the spokesman/emir, working with a clandestine emir
of whom Kurnaz writes: "The man that we had first elected in Camp X-Ray
remained the real emir without the Americans ever catching on. Indeed, very
few of the prisoners knew who the real emir was. I know his name, but I'm not
saying anything. As of 2007 he's still in Guantanamo, and he's still the prisoners'
true leader."[35] On the other hand, the story could be a fabrication, designed to
imbue "visible" leaders with greater powers, since they purportedly have access
to a secret whose existence the Americans had not suspected. Thus the prisoner
community becomes still more inscrutable to the prison regime.

This is certainly a performance of prisoner illegibility. The prison authorities
are shown that where leadership exists, they may not even recognize it. Where
protest occurs, they may not understand it. During the 2003 Koran protests, as
soldiers ignored prisoners' pleas to allow them to take the Koran to punishment
cells, a new shout emerged from the din: "Osama bin Laden." "All the prisoners took up the chant," Errachidi recalled. "I joined in as well. It was very scary
at first to shout like this . . . . Our shouts enraged the soldiers. They wanted to
take something from us but we had so little: in the end they could only demand
that we give up our towels."[36] This is an astonishing conflict: the prisoners have
been grilled about bin Laden through months of interrogations and have mostly
denied any connection to al Qaeda, but they collectively risked punishment
with a chant that taunted the guards for their ignorance and helplessness.

Thus the prisoners of Guantanamo make use of the illegibility they are given
by the prison regime. Some are told they belong to an organization despite their

denials, and then adopt the forbidding name as a weapon. They are assumed to belong to a secretive, alien culture (Muslim, or Arab, or terrorist, or Taliban). Many prisoners try to explain their traditions and beliefs to their captors, but they also revel in their ability to confound guards' expectations. Thus Moazzam Begg overheard a soldier joking about letting his dog chase "orange meat"—a prisoner—around a cage like a mouse. "Yes," he interrupted, "but this mouse has two legs and speaks English better than you do."[37] All the memoirists give examples of prisoners using language barriers or assumptions to their benefit, hinting at capabilities beyond those of their guards.

The punishments inflicted by the prison regime could also be used to the detainees' benefit. The constant movement of prisoners, as several of the memoirists point out, expanded the prison network and spread information around the camp. In terms of uncertainty of outcome, the detainees of Guantanamo are quintessential political prisoners. Very few have been sentenced, while rumors of transfer and release, of a hearing, or even just a meeting with a lawyer, linger for years.[38] Prisoners are left with very little. As a result, the Guantanamo authorities have relatively little leverage over inmates who have, writes journalist Tim Gordon, "much less incentive to obey the rules" than do those in an ordinary prison. For some prisoners, "exile to the discipline or segregation blocks was a source of status and pride," while "there was no such thing as getting a few more years tacked on to your sentence." Compliance, in turn, "brought only prayer beads, packets of hot sauce, a slightly thicker mattress."[39] At least as long as some of the Geneva Convention rules are observed their indeterminate future gives the prisoners of Guantanamo leverage over their captors, albeit within the narrow confines of their cages.

Less than a year after the leadership discussions with Colonel Bumgarner, Shaker Aamer was taken by force to a secret location—called "Camp No" because its existence was denied—outside the camp perimeter. There he was tortured for hours, even dryboarded: the torturers stuffed a rag in his mouth and taped up his nose to induce asphyxiation. The next morning, three other prisoners who had also been taken away that day were found dead in their cells, hanged—with bound hands and feet, and with rags down their throats.[40] Since early 2013, dozens of Guantanamo prisoners have been on a series of hunger strikes, begun in response to renewed mishandling of Korans during searches; they are kept alive by force-feeding. The rhetoric around these strikes in some ways recalls that of the early days of the prison.[41] After nine months of the protest, the prison administration imposed an information blackout; there is no evidence that the fifteen men still striking when the blackout began have since ceased.[42] The camp still holds forty-one prisoners, and it now seems unlikely that any of them will be released. While the relentless physical and mental torture of the early years seems to have abated, abuses continue. There is a new term for the remaining prisoners: they are the "forever prisoners."[43]

So what can be taken away from the depraved story of Guantanamo? First, a community of political prisoners emerged from the institutional experience, despite disparate backgrounds and lack of a supporting movement. Guantanamo gave them the shared consciousness of a common experience. This community then used the prison to advance a common politics. That politics had relatively little to do with the *jihad* for which they were incarcerated, despite the "Osama bin Laden" chant. Instead, it centered on the prison as an emblem of the deterioration of human rights in the twenty-first century. Some of those released have joined or built prisoner-assistance movements to help their comrades left in Guantanamo.[44] The experience of rendition, torture, and isolation has transformed the Guantanamo detainees, but in a way that has little in common with rehabilitation. Guantanamo is quintessentially a site of politics.

It has been nearly a century since the United States arrested so many ostensible opponents of the regime. Unlike many of the prisoners portrayed in this book, none of the Guantanamo prisoners will become president of the country that has held them or win the Nobel Peace Prize; it is doubtful that any will speak before a Truth and Reconciliation Commission. Some have returned to the fight against the American presence in the Middle East; at least one has died as a suicide bomber. Many have sought to retreat as far as possible from politics. Yet it is doubtful that the prison has achieved its intended objectives. An examination of 150 years of modern political incarceration indicates that, if in the short term a regime can use incarceration to weaken its opponents and disintegrate their psyches and their bodies, over the long term the effort fails. The creation of a political prison has transformed the United States; this is what Shaker Aamer meant when he told Michael Bumgarner, "Nobody survives Guantanamo. You won't survive, either."[45] Although the United States, like all the regimes before it, could impose its will, it could not impose a narrative upon its prisoners. Not only is there no conceivable journey toward rehabilitation, there has rarely been even a path toward a redemptive day in court. Instead, the prisoners themselves have created narratives of control and of illegibility. Those stories, still very much in development, will in the end be more powerful and enduring than the story the regime tried to write.

NOTES

Introduction

1. It is inscribed, for example, on the back cover of Sighle Humphreys's 1928 jail journal and echoed in Ruta Czaplińska's observation that she could sing patriotic songs in a Stalinist prison, being "more free than those at liberty." Humphreys Papers, UCD P106/1067-68; Czaplińska quoted in Tadeusz Wolsza, *W cieniu Wronek Jaworzna i Piechcina 1945–1956* (Warsaw: Instytut Historii PAN, 2003), 91.

2. The history and reception of the "Mazurka in Chains" is fully explored by Bogdan Zakrzewski, *Arka przymierza. O najgłośniejszych pieśniach narodowych* (Wrocław: Wydawnictwo Dolnośląskie, 2001), 157-201.

3. This book does take a European model, produced by a common set of institutions—states, police, prisons, media, parties, and so on—as a norm that of course varies in form around the world. On the use of European models as norms in global history, see Sebastian Conrad, *What Is Global History?* (Princeton, NJ: Princeton University Press, 2016), 32.

4. Peter Zinoman, *The Colonial Bastille: A History of Imprisonment in Vietnam, 1862–1940* (Berkeley: University of California Press, 2001), ch. 4. See also Frank Dikötter, *Crime, Punishment and the Prison in Modern China* (New York: Columbia University Press, 2002).

5. Ervand Abrahamian, *Tortured Confessions: Prisons and Public Recantations in Modern Iran* (Berkeley: University of California Press, 1999), ch. 1.

6. Lila Caimari, *Apenas un Delincuente: Crimen, Castigo y Cultura en la Argentina, 1880–1955* (Buenos Aires: Siglo Veintiuno Editores, 2004). I am grateful to Jonathan Warner for summarizing this work for me. Marguerite Feitlowitz, *A Lexicon of Terror: Argentina and the Legacies of Torture* (New York: Oxford University Press, 1998). The word "appears" is used advisedly; only extensive work in the archives can confirm the patterns presented here.

7. Jean-Claude Vimont, *La prison politique en France: genèse d'un mode d'incarcération spécifique XVIIIe–XXe siècles* (Paris: Anthropos, 1993); Laurent Boscher, *Histoire des prisonniers politiques, 1792–1848: le châtiment des vaincus* (Paris: Harmattan, 2008).

8. Other works on European cases include Warren Rosenblum, *Beyond the Prison Gates: Punishment and Welfare in Germany, 1850–1933* (Chapel Hill: University of North Carolina Press, 2008); Polymeris Voglis, *Becoming a Subject: Political Prisoners during the Greek Civil War* (New York: Berghahn, 2002); and works on Russia cited in Chapter 1. See also Mary Gibson, "Global Perspectives on the Birth of the Prison," *American Historical Review* 116: 4 (October 2011), 1040-63.

9. Darius Rejali, *Torture and Democracy* (Princeton, NJ: Princeton University Press, 2007).

10. See Yang Xiguang and Susan McFadden, *Captive Spirits: Prisoners of the Cultural Revolution* (Hong Kong: Oxford University Press, 1997); Philip F. Williams and Yenna Wu, *The Great Wall of Confinement: The Chinese Prison Camp through Contemporary Fiction and Reportage* (Berkeley: University of California Press, 2004).

11. Erving Goffman, *Asylums: Essays on the Social Situation of Mental Patients and Other Inmates* (Garden City, NY: Anchor, 1961), 17.

12. One recent exception is Colin Dayan, *The Law Is a White Dog: How Legal Rituals Make and Unmake Persons* (Princeton, NJ: Princeton University Press, 2011).

13. Michel Foucault, *Discipline and Punish: The Birth of the Modern Prison* (New York: Pantheon, 1977); Giorgio Agamben, *Homo Sacer: Sovereign Power and Bare Life* (Stanford, CA: Stanford University Press, 1998).

14. James C. Scott, *Domination and the Arts of Resistance: Hidden Transcripts* (New Haven, CT: Yale University Press, 1990). Scott, *Seeing Like a State: How Certain Schemes to Improve the Human Condition Have Failed* (New Haven, CT: Yale University Press, 1998). Though we diverge on "resistance," I am indebted to Fran Lisa Buntman's essential study of prisoner politics on Robben Island: *Robben Island and Prisoner Resistance to Apartheid* (Cambridge: Cambridge University Press, 2003).

Chapter 1

1. Zofia Kirkor-Kiedroniowa, *Wspomnienia,* ed. Alina Szklarska-Lohmannowa (Kraków: Wydawnictwo Literackie, 1986), 98.

2. Aryeh Neier, "Confining Dissent: The Political Prison," in *The Oxford History of the Prison,* ed. Norval Morris and David J. Rothman (New York: Oxford University Press, 1995), 350–80; John Laffin, *The Anatomy of Captivity* (London: Abelard-Schuman, 1968).

3. Leon Radzinowicz and Roger Hood, "The Status of the Political Prisoner in England: The Struggle for Recognition," *Virginia Law Review* 65:8 (December 1979), 1421–81.

4. On the concept of the "imprisoned political," see Padraic Kenney, "'I felt a kind of pleasure in seeing them treat us brutally.' The Emergence of the Political Prisoner, 1865–1910," *Comparative Studies in Society and History* 54:4 (2012), 863–89.

5. Henry Hunt, *A Peep into a Prison, or, the Inside of Ilchester Bastile* (London: T. Dolby, 1821).

6. Michael Ignatieff, *A Just Measure of Pain: The Penitentiary in the Industrial Revolution, 1750–1850* (New York: Penguin, 1978), 159. As Cobbett's polemic reminds us, the category of "criminal" is itself an uncertain one, encompassing offenders who are merely indigent, those who have committed violent crimes, and, possibly, those whose crimes might elsewhere be labeled "political."

7. John Mitchel, *Jail Journal: With an Introductory Narrative of Transactions in Ireland* (London: Sphere Books, 1983), 1–3.

8. George Kennan, *Siberia and the Exile System* (New York: Praeger, 1891); George Rudé, *Protest and Punishment: The Story of the Social and Political Protesters Transported to Australia, 1788–1868* (Oxford: Clarendon Press, 1978).

9. While most places of exile were under the control of the exiling ruler, this was not always the case; some Irish were allowed to go to the United States.

10. Elżbieta Kaczyńska, *Siberia, największe więzienie świata* (Warsaw: Gryf, 1991), 51–52.

11. This is not to suggest that Siberian exile constituted a light sentence. See Alan Wood, "Crime and Punishment in the House of the Dead," in *Civil Rights in Imperial Russia,* ed. Olga Crisp and Linda Edmondson (Oxford: Clarendon Press, 1989), 215–33.

12. Rudé, *Protest and Punishment;* Stephen A. Toth, *Beyond Papillon: The French Overseas Penal Colonies, 1854–1952* (Lincoln: University of Nebraska Press, 2006); Christian G. DeVito and Alex Lichtenstein, eds., *Global Convict Labour* (Leiden: Brill, 2015).

13. The proportion among Irish only was rather higher, almost 6 percent (of about 40,000 transported). Rudé, *Protest and Punishment,* 9.

14. The rest may have received short sentences and been released immediately after conviction; a few were executed. Rudé, *Protest and Punishment,* 77.

15. Zygmunt Bauman, *Modernity and the Holocaust* (Cambridge: Polity, 1989), ch. 4.

16. Randall McGowen, "The Well-Ordered Prison: England, 1780–1865," in *Oxford History of the Prison,* ed. Morris and Rothman, 71–99.

17. Bruce F. Adams, *The Politics of Punishment: Prison Reform in Russia, 1863–1917* (DeKalb: Northern Illinois University Press, 1996), 9.

18. See Peter Zinoman, *The Colonial Bastille: A History of Imprisonment in Vietnam, 1862–1940* (Berkeley: University of California Press, 2001); Florence Bernault, ed., *A History of Prison and Confinement in Africa* (Portsmouth, NH: Heinemann, 2003).

19. See works cited earlier and Patricia O'Brien, *The Promise of Punishment: Prisons in Nineteenth-Century France* (Princeton, NJ: Princeton University Press, 1982).

20. See Charles Tilly and Lesley J. Wood, *Social Movements, 1768–2008* (Boulder, CO: Paradigm, 2009), ch. 3; Philip Nord, "Introduction," in *Civil Society before Democracy: Lessons from Nineteenth-Century Europe*, ed. Nancy Bermeo and Philip Nord (Lanham, MD: Rowman & Littlefield, 2000), xiii–xxxiii; Miroslav Hroch, *Social Preconditions of National Revival in Europe: A Comparative Analysis of the Social Composition of Patriotic Groups among the Smaller European Nations* (New York: Columbia University Press, 2000).

21. Michael Barnett, *Empire of Humanity: A History of Humanitarianism* (Ithaca, NY: Cornell University Press, 2011).

22. Margaret DeLacy, *Prison Reform in Lancashire, 1700–1850: A Study in Local Administration* (Stanford, CA: Stanford University Press, 1986).

23. Ignatieff, *A Just Measure of Pain*; Michel Foucault, *Discipline and Punish: The Birth of the Prison* (New York: Pantheon, 1977).

24. Herman Franke, *The Emancipation of Prisoners: A Socio-historical Analysis of the Dutch Prison Experience* (Edinburgh: Edinburgh University Press, 1995), 32–33.

25. See Howard C. Payne, *The Police State of Louis Napoleon Bonaparte, 1851–1860* (Seattle: University of Washington Press, 1966); Roger Price, *The French Second Empire: An Anatomy of Political Power* (Cambridge: Cambridge University Press, 2001), 166; "Amnesty," in *Historical Dictionary of the French Second Empire, 1852–1870*, ed. William E. Echard (Westport, CT: Greenwood, 1985), 18.

26. NAI CSORP 1869, Box 9, File 4789R.

27. Dublin Metropolitan Police Report, November 10, 1869, NAI CSORP 1869, Box 9, File 4902R.

28. On the Italian prisoners: Steven C. Soper, *Building a Civil Society: Associations, Public Life, and the Origins of Modern Italy* (Toronto: University of Toronto, 2013); *My Prisons: The Memoirs of Silvio Pellico* (Cambridge, MA: C. Folsom, 1836).

29. Seán McConville, *Irish Political Prisoners, 1848–1922: Theatres of War* (London: Routledge, 2003), 4.

30. Otto Kirchheimer, *Political Justice: The Use of Legal Procedure for Political Ends* (Princeton, NJ: Princeton University Press, 1961), 241.

31. The emergence of modern terrorism parallels the emergence of political prisoners, as changing meanings of political violence and the character of its perpetrators posed similar problems for the state. Claudia Verhoeven names Dmitrii Karakozov, who attempted to assassinate Czar Alexander II in 1866, as the first terrorist. Premodern political assassinations, she argues, were singular, individual acts aimed at the removal of a particular hated figure, in contrast to the modern act of terrorism aimed at a class of people or representatives of an idea. Claudia Verhoeven, *The Odd Man Karakozov: Imperial Russia, Modernity, and the Birth of Terrorism* (Ithaca, NY: Cornell University Press, 2009), 175. See also Michael Burleigh, *Blood and Rage: A Cultural History of Terrorism* (London: Harper, 2008).

32. Kirchheimer, *Political Justice*, 34, n24; Zeev Sternhell, "Paul Déroulède and the Origins of Modern French Nationalism," *Journal of Contemporary History* 6:4 (1971), 67.

33. Walerian Łukasiński, *Pamiętnik*, ed. Rafał Gerber (Warsaw: Państwowe Wydawnictwo Naukowe, 1986).

34. Contrast to Foucault's analysis of public executions in the Early Modern period, in *Discipline and Punish*, ch. 1.

35. Foucault, *Discipline and Punish*, 135.

36. Andrzej Budzyński, " 'Pawiak' jako więzienie polityczne w latach 1880–1915," PhD diss., Warsaw University, 1987, 112–18.

37. Brian Jenkins, *The Fenian Problem: Insurgency and Terrorism in a Liberal State, 1858–1874* (Montreal: McGill-Queen's University Press, 2008), 40–42.

38. McConville, *Irish Political Prisoners, 1848-1922*, 123–24, 146–47.

39. McConville, *Irish Political Prisoners, 1848-1922,* 140.
40. McConville, *Irish Political Prisoners, 1848-1922,* 140.
41. McConville, *Irish Political Prisoners, 1848-1922,* 153.
42. Jenkins, *Insurgency and Terrorism,* ch. 6.
43. Quoted in McConville, *Irish Political Prisoners, 1848-1922,* 173, n146.
44. Jeremiah O'Donovan Rossa, *My Years in English Jails,* ed. Sean Ua Cearnaigh (Tralee: Anvil, 1967), 101.
45. Rossa, *My Years,* 105.
46. Rossa, *My Years,* 106.
47. Rossa, *My Years,* 111; McConville, *Irish Political Prisoners, 1848-1922,* 173.
48. McConville, *Irish Political Prisoners, 1848-1922,* 193–94.
49. McConville, *Irish Political Prisoners, 1848-1922,* 363–65, 372.
50. McConville, *Irish Political Prisoners, 1848-1922,* 364, 367–68. See also a later newspaper from Mountjoy, *The Trumpeter* (1922, in NLI Ms. 21121).
51. Martin Phillip Johnson, *The Paradise of Association: Political Culture and Popular Organizations in the Paris Commune of 1871* (Ann Arbor: University of Michigan Press, 1996), 286–87.
52. Norman M. Naimark, *The History of the "Proletariat": The Emergence of Marxism in the Kingdom of Poland, 1870-1887* (Boulder, CO: East European Quarterly, 1979), 107.
53. Quoted in Naimark, *History of the "Proletariat,"* 72.
54. Zygmunt Heryng, "X Pawilon przed pięćdziesięciu laty," in *Pamiętnik X Pawilonu,* ed. Aleksander Kozłowski and Henryk J. Mościcki (Warsaw: Wydawnictwo Ministerstwa Obrony Narodowej, 1958), 118.
55. Naimark, *History of the "Proletariat,"* 176. On the Russian penal system generally, see Boris N. Mironov, *The Social History of Imperial Russia, 1700–1917,* vol. 2 (Boulder, CO: Westview, 2000), 247–64, esp. 261–64.
56. Feliks Kon, "Ze wspomnień," in *Pamiętnik X Pawilonu,* ed. Aleksander Kozłowski and Henryk J. Mościcki (Warsaw: Wydawnictwo Ministerstwa Obrony Narodowej, 1958), 167–69.
57. Kon, "Ze wspomnień," 152.
58. Kirkor-Kiedroniowa, *Wspomnienia,* 108.
59. Budzyński, "'Pawiak' jako więzienie polityczne w latach 1880–1915," 106–7. See Jan Tomicki, *Polska Partia Socjalistyczna, 1892–1948* (Warsaw: Książka i Wiedza, 1983), 77–79, 101–105; Robert Blobaum, *Rewolucja: Poland, 1904–1907* (Ithaca, NY: Cornell University Press, 1995).
60. Marian Płochocki, "Za działalność w szeregach SDKPiL," in *Pamiętnik X Pawilonu,* ed. Aleksander Kozłowski and Henryk J. Mościcki (Warsaw: Wydawnictwo Ministerstwa Obrony Narodowej, 1958), 264–65.
61. Wacław Koral, *Przez partje, związki, więzienia i Sybir. Wspomnienia drukarza z działalności w ruchu socjalistycznym i zawodowym 1898–1928* (Warsaw: Robotnik, 1933), 51–52. Kazimierz Pielat offers a comparable story from Płock Prison, where his assassination of a Russian colonel had landed him in 1907. On one of his first nights there, he writes, "I heard in my sleep the porthole open, and the watchman's hand appeared and threw something on the floor. It was money, two silver rubles wrapped in paper. The next day I heard . . . that those two rubles I received from the organization. So there were even comrades or supporters, deeply hidden, among the watchmen." Kazimierz Pielat, "Z pamiętnika bojowca," *Niepodległość* 17:1 (1938), 89–90.
62. Bronisław Fijałek, *Lata walki. Wspomnienia SDKPiL-owca* (Warsaw: Książka i Wiedza, 1955), 100–102. Prisoners in Mountjoy in 1923 got up to similar shenanigans: Anonymous letter, October 4, 1923, Ernest O'Malley Papers, UCD P17a/163, 135. See also Con Casey, in *Survivors,* ed. Uinseann MacEoin (Dublin: Argenta, 1980), 377.
63. Robert E. Blobaum, "Under Lock and Key? Prisons and Prison Conditions in Russian Poland, 1906–1914," *Społeczeństwo w dobie przemian. Wiek XIX i XX. Księga jubileuszowa profesor Anny Żarnowskiej,* ed. Maria Nietyksza et al. (Warsaw: DiG, 2003), 298.
64. S. B. Spies, *Methods of Barbarism? Roberts and Kitchener and Civilians in the Boer Republics, January 1900–May 1902* (Cape Town: Human and Rousseau, 1977), 182, 215; Elizabeth van Heyningen, "The Concentration Camps of the South African (Anglo-Boer) War, 1900–1902," *History Compass* 7:1 (2009), 22–43.

65. H. W. J., "The Concentration Camps," January 16, 1902, *British Documents in Foreign Affairs*, Part 1, Series G: Africa, 1885–1914, ed. David Throup, vol. 9: *Anglo-Boer War II: Attitude of European Powers and Post-War Reconstruction, 1901–1905* (Bethesda, MD: University Publications of America, 1995), document 54, pp. 53–56.

66. On concentration camps and camps for prisoners of war, see Chapter 6.

67. See, for example, Department of Prisons correspondence, December 13, 1901, NASA CS Correspondence files, 7049.

68. John S. Galbraith, "British War Measures in Cape Colony, 1900–1902: A Study of Miscalculations and Mismanagement," *South African Historical Journal/Suid-Afrikaanse historiese joernaal* 15:1 (1983), 71. See also documents in *British Documents in Foreign Affairs*, Part 1, Series G: Africa, 1885–1914.

69. For use of the term, see, for example, David Tennant (Agent General of the Cape of Good Hope), letter to the Home Office, London, October 30, 1900, quoting a cable from the Cape Town Attorney General. WCPA CO 2356, Ref 1615.

70. High Commissioner Alfred Milner, Telegram 260 to Governor of Natal, November 7, 1900. WCPA CO 2356, Ref 1615.

71. HB Shawe, letter to H. Orpen, July 1901. WCPA CO 2360 (Administrative and Convict Service), Ref. Folio 1615, vol. 7.

72. A similar case involved the right of certain prisoners to smoke, or to have their lights kept on later in the evening. See letters between prison administrators and the Colonial Secretary's office in WCPA CO 2357, Ref. 1615, vol. 4.

73. Letters between Shawe and Orpen, August–September 1901, in WCPA CO 2357, Ref. Folio 1615, vol. 4, and CO 2362, Ref Folio 1615, vol. 9 (October 1902).

74. Sophia A. van Wingerden, *The Women's Suffrage Movement in Britain, 1866–1928* (New York: St. Martin's Press, 1999), 87.

75. See Peter Brock, *Pacifism in the Twentieth Century* (Toronto: University of Toronto Press, 1999); W. J. Forsythe, *Penal Discipline, Reformatory Projects and the English Prison Commission, 1895–1939* (Exeter, UK: University of Exeter Press, 1991), 108–10.

76. "Speech at Hamidiya Islamic Society," doc. 308 in *The Collected Works of Mahatma Gandhi* [hereafter *CWMG*] vol. 5 (Delhi: Ministry of Information and Broadcasting, 1958–84), 332.

77. "Johannesburg Letter," *Indian Opinion*, September 22, 1906, doc. 324 in *CWMG*, vol. 5, 359–60.

78. "Deeds Better than Words," *Indian Opinion*, November 24, 1906, doc. 383 in *CWMG*, vol. 5, 431–32; "The Duty of Transvaal Indians," *Indian Opinion*, October 6, 1906, doc. 344 in *CWMG*, vol 5, 384.

79. He addressed some practical concerns in essays in *Indian Opinion*. See, for example, "Johannesburg Letter," *Indian Opinion*, July 20, 1907, doc. 48 in *CWMG*, vol. 7, 68; "Some Questions," *Indian Opinion*, October 20, 1906, doc. 353 in *CWMG*, vol. 5, 396–98; and "Johannesburg Letter," *Indian Opinion*, April 27, 1907, doc. 355 in *CWMG*, vol. 6, 406–11. On the campaign in general, see Maureen Swan, *Gandhi: The South African Experience* (Johannesburg: Ravan Press, 1985), 126–52.

80. "Johannesburg Letter," *Indian Opinion*, October 5, 1907, doc. 197 in *CWMG*, vol. 7, 240.

81. Swan, *Gandhi*, 142.

82. "My Experience in Gaol, III," *Indian Opinion*, March 21, 1908, doc. 108 in *CWMG*, vol. 8, 217–19 (quote on p. 219). Gandhi saw the fear of hardship as a national shortcoming, concluding that "nations which have progressed are those which have given in on inessential matters," 220. On the development of *satyagraha*, see Paul F. Power, "Gandhi in South Africa," *Journal of Modern African Studies* 7:3 (1969), 452, and Mohandas K. Gandhi, *Satyagraha in South Africa* (Ahmedabad: Navjivan Publishing House, 1972).

83. "My Second Experience in Gaol, III," *Indian Opinion*, January 16, 1909, doc. 155 in *CWMG*, vol. 9, 253.

84. H. S. L. Polak, letter to D. Pollock, March 27, 1909, NASA GOV 1193, 15/1/42/09; Transvaal Prime Minister Louis Botha, Minute 223, May 21, 1909, NASA GOV 1193, 15/1/61/09; Mohandas Gandhi, "My Third Experience in Gaol, II," *Indian Opinion*, June 5, 1909, doc. 215 in *CWMG*, vol. 9, 356.

85. See, for example, "Memorandum on Indians in Prison," n.d., NASA GEV 4/141; and Sir MM Bhownaggree, letter to Undersecretary of State Lord Crewe, December 31, 1909, NASA GOV 1234, 15/1/7/10.
86. A. M. Cachalia, chair of Transvaal British Indian Association, letter to Governor's Office, n.d. (late December 1908), NASA GOV 1192, 15/1/6/09. Gandhi himself suggested as much, according to H. S. L. Polak; see his letter to D. Pollock, March 27, 1909, NASA GOV 1193, 15/1/42/09.
87. D. O. Malcolm (for Lord Selborne) to D. Pollock (responding to the letter by H. S. L. Polak, noted above), March 27, 1909, NASA GOV 1193 15/1/42/09.
88. Office of the Prime Minister, Minute 123 to Office of the Governor-General, June 29, 1910, NASA GG 886 15/13.
89. Gladstone, letter to General Botha, October 3, 1910, NASA GG 887, 15/51, 2, 7.
90. In October 1913, the *Rand Daily Mail* reported that "eleven ladies—six with babies in arms" who had courted arrest by selling wares without a license had been sentenced to three months hard labor and "received their sentences smilingly." Clipping in files of the Governor-General, NASA GG 897 15/496. On Gandhi's changing tactics as the struggle continued and the Indian community became generally less eager to go to prison, see various documents in NASA GG 897 15/480, and Swan, *Gandhi*, 226–54. Gladstone continued to urge caution upon the South African government. See, for example, his "Urgent" telegram to General Botha of November 25, 1913, NASA GG 898 15/551.

Chapter 2

1. Mike Nicol, *A Good-Looking Corpse* (London: Secker & Warburg, 1991), 1. The unnamed woman quotes the 1642 Richard Lovelace poem "To Althea, from Prison."
2. Sheehy-Skeffington, undated notes (1912), NLI 33618 (6). She also describes relations in the women's prison as "spinstery" and like a convent.
3. Letter from Government Prisons Office to Undersecretary of State, Dublin, February 25, 1867, NAI CSORP 1867, carton 1732, document 3402. Andrzej Budzyński, "Pawiak jako więzienie polityczne w latach 1880–1915," PhD diss., Warsaw University, 1987, 112–31.
4. Mateusz Wyrwich, *W celi śmierci* (Warsaw: Rytm, 2012), 101. His response would not be out of place even in a prison in a liberal state. In the words of a member of the Northern Ireland Prison Management Committee: the administration seeks "ways to impose our will on . . . prisoners and force them to behave." Prison Management Committee meeting minutes, May 31, 1977, PRONI NIO/10/2/5, n.p.
5. Most political prisoners are not in a separate prison that could be called a "political prison"; this term is used here to denote the set of rules and practices that apply particularly to political prisoners, whether or not they are separated.
6. Letter, October 20, 1964, quoted in Benjamin Pogrund, *How Can Man Die Better: Sobukwe and Apartheid* (London: Halban, 1990), 215.
7. Moses Dlamini, *Hell-Hole, Robben Island: Reminiscences of a Political Prisoner in South Africa* (Trenton, NJ: Africa World Press, 1984), 15–16.
8. Barbara Skarga, *Po wyzwoleniu . . . 1944–1956* (Kraków: Znak, 2008), 11–12.
9. Peadar O'Donnell, *The Gates Flew Open* (London: Jonathan Cape, 1932), 135–36; see also p. 157. Henryk Nakielski makes a similar point in *Jako i my odpuszczamy* (Warsaw: Iskry, 1989), 162.
10. Pogrund, *How Can Man Die Better*, 164.
11. Letter signed by forty-six Robben Island prisoners, October 1972, in Brian Bunting papers, Mayibuye Archives, MCH 7, 2.40 (Box 122). Emphasis in original. The petition and subsequent case are discussed in Lin Menge, "The Right to 'Privileges' in Jail," *Rand Daily Mail*, April 14, 1973.
12. Neville Alexander, *Robben Island Prison Dossier, 1964–1974* (Rondebosch, South Africa: University of Cape Town Press, 1994), 74–75. Similar confrontations in later years can be traced in meetings of Robben Island prisoner groups: General meeting minutes, November 19, 1982 and May 17, 1988, and Executive Committee meeting minutes September 24, 1976, April 3, 1977, and June 5, 1978, in MCH 64, Box 1, Folder 1.4; Seddick Isaacs report, January

27, 1977, MCH 64, Box 1A, Folder 1.2. See also Makana Football Association, Chairman's Annual Report, reprinted in Roberts, *Sport in Chains*, 22.

13. Jan Krzesławski, "Więzienie w Ratuszu za rządów Nazarowa," *Kronika Ruchu Rewolucyjnego* 1:2 (1935), 84–85.

14. Budzyński, "Pawiak jako więzienie polityczne," 129–31.

15. WCPA CO 2356, Ref Folio 1615.

16. See Alexander, *Robben Island Prison Dossier*, 78.

17. "Wytyczne Krajowej Narady Czerwonej Pomocy w Polsce," AAN 175/I-1, k. 12; also *Biuletyn Komitetu Centralnego Czerwonej Pomocy w Polsce (MOPR)*, n.d. (c. August/September 1932), AAN 175/I-8, kk. 12-12a.

18. See Red Help Communiqué #35, December 24, 1928, AAN 175/I-6, 21–22; Communiqué #27, March 15, 1927; *gryps* from Grudziądz Prison, January 1937, Ministry of Internal Affairs AAN Mf 25749 (sygn. 1176), kk. 186–87; Letter from Białystok Prison, in Biuletyn Informacyjny Komitetu Centralnego Czerwonej Pomocy w Polsce, #8, March 1934, AAN 175/I-16, k. 4.

19. Quoted in Edward Crankshaw, *Gestapo: Instrument of Tyranny* (New York: Viking, 1956), 215; on the Nacht und Nebel prisoners: Nikolaus Wachsmann, *Hitler's Prisons: Legal Terror in Nazi Germany* (New Haven, CT: Yale University Press, 2004), 271–74.

20. Marguerite Feitlowitz notes that the Argentine dictatorship in the 1970s used the same language. Feitlowitz, *A Lexicon of Terror: Argentina and the Legacies of Torture* (New York: Oxford University Press, 1998), 49; see also ch. 2, which is entitled „Night and Fog."

21. On the Argentine disappeared, see *The Disappeared of Argentina: List of Cases Reported to Amnesty International, March 1976–February 1979* (London: Amnesty International, 1979); Comisión Nacional sobre la Desaparición de Personas, *Nunca más: The Report of the Argentine National Commission on the Disappeared* (New York: Farrar, Straus and Giroux, 1986).

22. Text of decree in *Johannesburg Star*, March 31, 1960.

23. John Laffin, *The Anatomy of Captivity* (London: Abelard-Schuman, 1968), 31.

24. Aleksander Solzhenitsyn, *The Gulag Archipelago 1918–1956: An Experiment in Literary Investigation* (New York: Harper & Row, 1974), vol. 1, ch. 1; Adam Michnik, quoted in John Keane, *Violence and Democracy* (Cambridge: Cambridge University Press, 2004), 1.

25. Gaweł, "Wspomnienia," Ośrodek Karta, AO II/442w, 7.

26. Hirson, *Revolutions in My Life* (Johannesburg: Witwatersrand Univerity Press, 1995), 34.

27. Sowińska, "Gorzkie lata," Biblioteka Narodowa mps. 14257, k. 102.

28. Kulczyk, "Wspomnienia," Ośrodek Karta, AO II/380, 7–8.

29. "Where Criminals Are Made: The English Prison System," *Irish Nation*, October 6, 1917. To be "Bertillioned" meant to be measured according to the biometric system developed by Alphonse Bertillon in the late nineteenth century.

30. Rostworowski, *Zaraz po wojnie. Wspomnienia duszpasterza (1945–1956)* (Paris: Spotkania, 1986), 104. The question uses the second-person plural favored by communists and otherwise uncommon in Polish.

31. See, for example, Marian Płochocki, "Za działalność w szeregach SDKPiL," in *Pamiętnik X Pawilonu*, ed. Aleksander Kozłowski and Henryk J. Mościcki (Warsaw: Wydawnictwo Ministerstwa Obrony Narodowej, 1958), 258; Feliks Kon, "Ze wspomnień," in *Pamiętnik X Pawilonu*, ed. Aleksander Kozłowski and Henryk J. Mościcki (Warsaw: Wydawnictwo Ministerstwa Obrony Narodowej, 1958), 220; Ed Moloney, *A Secret History of the IRA* (New York: W. W. Norton, 2002), 109; "Closed Circuit TV: A New Form of Torture," DPSC press release, 1984, WHP AG 2523 M1.9; Eunan O'Halpin, *Defending Ireland: The Irish State and its Enemies* (New York: Oxford University Press, 1999), 58.

32. Sowińska, "Gorzkie lata," 153.

33. Particularly thoughtful on this is Kulczyk, "Wspomnienia," 40–41. An explosive scandal surrounded the 1990 publication of a book showing that the British had succeeded in destabilizing IRA prison networks in the mid-1970s despite elaborate precaution among prisoners. Martin Dillon, *The Dirty War* (New York: Routledge, 1990).

34. Tadeusz Wolsza, *W cieniu Wronek, Jaworzyna i Piechcina, 1945–1956. Życie codzienne w polskich więzieniach, obozach i ośrodkach pracy więźniów* (Warsaw: Instytut Historii PAN, 2003), 50.

35. The pattern would have been roughly similar in Nazi-occupied Poland. See Report, July 12, 1944. Komórka więzienna, Departament Spraw Wewnętrznych, Delegatura Rządu, AAN 202/II-17 (Mf 2225/3A), k. 133; the report's authors admitted that they inflated the danger so that prisoners would be careful about what they said. See also Leon Wanat, *Za murami Pawiaka* (Warsaw: Książka i Wiedza, 1958), 268–75. On informers in the czarist period, see Gustaw Daniłowski, *Wrażenia więzienne* (Lwów: Bernard Połoniecki, 1908), 113–16; Ludwik Śledziński, "Przejścia więzienne w Łowiczu i w Warszawie," *Niepodległość* 2:1 (1930), 129–30; Bronisław Fijałek, *Lata walki. Wspomnienia SDKPiLowca* (Warsaw: Książka i Wiedza, 1958), 110–12.

36. Cell report, November 19, 1946, "Augustyński i inni. Akta kontrolno-śledcze," IPN BU 02136/567 (mf 1030-3), f. 3, k. 250.

37. Cell reports November 20–21, 1946, in "Augustyński i inni. Akta kontrolno-śledcze," IPN BU 02136/567 (mf 1030-3), f. 3, kk. 251–53.

38. Natoo Babenia, *Memoirs of a Saboteur* (Cape Town: Mayibuye, 1995), 96.

39. Zofia Owczarek-Jagodzińska, who conspired to kill Warsaw Governor-General Georgii Skalon in 1906, confessed to a visitor who posed as her lawyer's assistant. Adam Próchnik, "Zamach na Skalona," *Kronika Ruchu Rewolucyjnego* 1:1 (1935), 22. Other examples in *Więzienia polityczne w Rosji* (Kraków: Latarnia, 1903), 13.

40. Cell report January 2, 1947, "Augustyński i inni," IPN BU 02136/567 (mf 1030-3), f. 3, k. 221.

41. Anonymous cell report, March 14, 1951, in Jarosław Pałka, "Cele Mossora," *Karta* 44 (2005), 132.

42. Cell report, July 3, 1950, in Pałka, "Cele Mossora," 120.

43. Cell report, August 28, 1951, in Pałka, "Cele Mossora," 132.

44. Mac Maharaj, "Where Thought Remained Unprisoned," in *Reflections in Prison*, ed. Mac Maharaj (Cape Town: Robben Island Museum, 2001), x.

45. Babenia, *Memoirs of a Saboteur*, 98.

46. Andrzej Friszke, *Czas KOR-u. Jacek Kuroń a geneza Solidarności* (Kraków: Znak, 2011), 557–58.

47. See Helen Suzman's polemic with Minister of Justice John Vorster in 1964, in Suzman, *In No Uncertain Terms: A South African Memoir* (New York: Knopf, 1993), 74–76. A lengthier exploration of the confusion of detention is in Paweł Bryszkowski's story of women interned in the Polish city of Wałbrzych in December 1981: *Getto w Gołdapi* (Bydgoszcz: Świadectwo, 1999), 22–27.

48. Inspection report, May 6, 1953, AAN Prokurator Generalny 509/102, kk. 3–9.

49. Bartoszewski, *Warto być przyzwoitym. Szkic do pamiętnika* (Paris: Spotkania, 1986), 65. On sudden trials in the Irish Free State, see Maud Gonne MacBride, letter in the *Irish Independent*, October 23, 1928, NAI Taoiseach S5752, n.p.

50. Report on Gomułka, September 10, 1951, AAN 509/147, k. 44; also reports from August 7 and November 29. Nakielski, *Jako i my odpuszczamy*, 162.

51. Chris Ryder, *Inside the Maze: The Untold Story of the Northern Ireland Prison Service* (London: Methuen, 2001), 294–96.

52. Hugh Lewin, *Bandiet: Out of Jail* (Johannesburg: Random House, 2002), 48.

53. Padraic Kenney, "A Parade of Trick Horses: Work and Physical Experience in the Political Prison," in *Global Convict Labour*, ed. Christian G. DeVito and Alex Lichtenstein (Leiden: Brill, 2015), 380–99.

54. Alexander, *Robben Island Prison Dossier*, 31.

55. Dlamini, *Hell-Hole*, 15.

56. Alexander, *Robben Island Prison Dossier*, 21.

57. Affidavit by Thandi Ruth Modise, July 14, 1981, Helen Suzman Papers, WHP A 2084 Ab1.3, file 1.

58. Sowińska, "Gorzkie lata," 74–75.

59. On Soviet use of psychiatric hospitals, see Sidney Bloch and Peter Reddaway, *Psychiatric Terror: How Soviet Psychiatry Is Used to Suppress Dissent* (New York: Basic Books, 1977).

60. Bogdan Ciszak, "Dziennik," Ośrodek Karta, CzP 19w, k. 39.

61. Ciszak, "Dziennik." See also report from Commissioner of Prisons J. C. Steyn to the Minister of Justice, January 26, 1973, in response to a request from Helen Suzman. CSA 1/3/6: Dissipline en Beheer. Klagte en Vertoë. Deel 5.

62. Lehane, statement to Commission of Inquiry for the Treatment of Political Prisoners, June 1936. Elgin O'Rahilly Papers, UCD P200/8, n.p. See also Seán McConville, *Irish Political Prisoners, 1920–1962: Pilgrimage of Desolation* (Abingdon: Routledge, 2014), 529.

63. Wolsza, *W cieniu*, 108.

64. Darius Rejali, *Torture and Democracy* (Princeton, NJ: Princeton University Press, 2007), 153.

65. Rejali, *Torture and Democracy*, 427–31. A key work on the topic is Sanford Levinson, ed., *Torture: A Collection*, rev. ed. (New York: Oxford University Press, 2006).

66. Nicol, *A Good-Looking Corpse*, 184–94.

67. Wolsza, *W cieniu*, 32–33; Brian Campbell, Laurence McKeown, and Felim O'Hagan, eds., *Nor Meekly Serve My Time: The H-Block Struggle 1976–1981* (Belfast: Beyond the Pale, 1998), ch. 7.

68. Polymeris Voglis, *Becoming a Subject: Political Prisoners during the Greek Civil War, 1945–1950* (New York: Berghahn, 2002), 131.

69. Jacobo Timerman, *Prisoner without a Name, Cell without a Number*, trans. Toby Talbot (Madison: University of Wisconsin Press, 1981), 32–33, 38–39. Also Henri Alleg, *The Question*, trans. John Calder (Lincoln: University of Nebraska Press, 2006).

70. Quoted in Regina Domańska, *Pawiak—kaźń i heroizm* (Warsaw: Książka i Wiedza, 1988), 291–92.

71. "Biko on Death," *New Republic*, January 7, 1978, 12.

72. Oleh Razyhraev, "Policja Państwowa II Rzeczypospolitej Polskiej wobec ruchu komunistycznego na Wołyniu w latach 1926-1939," Annales Universitatis Mariae Curie-Skłodowska, Sectio F, Historia, 65:1 (2010) 451–54. Proces Łucki. Relacje Zakład Historii Partii (1966), AAN R-196, kk. 32–33.

73. AAN R-196, kk. 139–40.

74. AAN R-196, k. 164.

75. AAN R-196, kk. 32–33.

76. Zarząd komuny więźniów politycznych, Grudziądz, April 23, 1936, in Czerwona Pomoc, AAN 175/III-5, k. 4. On the significance of Łuck, see Krzysztof Urbański, *System penitencjarny II Rzeczypospolitej a więźniowie polityczni (na przykładzie województwa kieleckiego* (Kielce: Kieleckie Towarzystwo Naukowe, 1997), 38.

77. Martin J. McCleery, *Operation Demetrius and Its Aftermath: A New History of the Use of Internment without Trial in Northern Ireland, 1971–75* (Manchester: Manchester University Press, 2015), 61–66.

78. Father Denis Faul and Father Raymond Murray, *The Hooded Men: British Torture in Ireland, August, October 1971* (Dungannon, Co. Tyrone: The Authors, 1974), 24, 27. Hannaway: John McGuffin, *The Guineapigs* (London: Penguin, 1974), 55–56.

79. McNally: in Faul and Murray, *The Hooded Men*, 59–60; see also 27, 8, 11.

80. Faul and Murray, *The Hooded Men*, 38, 23. Also John Conroy, *Unspeakable Acts, Ordinary People: The Dynamics of Torture* (Berkeley: University of California Press, 2006), ch. 1; and McGuffin, *Guineapigs*.

81. This is not to suggest that South African police and prison guards had not practiced torture before this. Torture had not featured in the internment of ANC and PAC activists in 1960–1964; with the Terrorism Act, prison practices appear to have evolved from ordinary racist cruelty into systematic torture of political detainees.

82. *South Africa: Trial by Torture. The Case of the 22* (London: International Defence and Aid Fund, 1970), 23, 24. See also Hilda Bernstein, *South Africa: The Terrorism of Torture* (London: Christian Action Publications, 1972).

83. *South Africa: Trial by Torture*, 38–39.

84. Bernstein, *South Africa: The Terrorism of Torture*, 35.

85. Bernstein, *South Africa: The Terrorism of Torture*, 40–41.

86. Rejali, *Torture and Democracy*, ch. 15, 316–33, esp. 316; on standing in South Africa, see pp. 16–17, for which Rejali cites the report of South Africa's Truth and Reconciliation Commission.

87. *South Africa: Trial by Torture*, 31. While Bernstein's name does not appear in the book, similarities to the 1972 International Defence and Aid Fund pamphlet cited elsewhere point to her authorship.

88. See, for example, cell reports on Adam Stanowski, 1951, IPN BU 0259/579, t. 2 k. 57; and on Józef Kirchmayer, 1952, IPN BU 0298/347, k. 89. Also Sighle Humphreys, journal entry January 13, 1932, UCD P106/1096, n.p.

89. Quoted in Wyrwich, *W celi śmierci*, 96; see also "Maria Szelągowska ps. 'Rysia,'" *Nike* 15 (1994), 15–18.

90. Sowińska, "Gorzkie lata," 70.

Chapter 3

1. Entry of December 24, 1987, "Surviving Section 29: The Detention Diary of Chris Giffard," Mayibuye Archives, MCH 23.

2. Tomasz Rostworowski, *Zaraz po wojnie. Wspomnienia duszpasterza (1945–1956)* (Paris: Spotkania, 1986), 89, 85.

3. Antoni Lange, "Wspomnienia więzienne," *Niepodległość* 4:1 (1932), 103–4.

4. Hugh Lewin, *Bandiet: Out of Jail* (Johannesburg: Random House, 2002), 29; Marek Kulczyk, "Wspomnienia," Ośrodek Karta, AO II/380, 30.

5. Scholars of the Holocaust have also grappled with the problem of accessing common experiences and identities through the possibly exceptional accounts of individuals who have not been consumed by shame or guilt and who have survived.

6. Nelson Mandela, letter to Commissioner of Prisons, July 12, 1976. Reprinted in Verne Harris, ed., *A Prisoner in the Garden: Opening Nelson Mandela's Prison Archive* (Johannesburg: Penguin, 2005), 130.

7. Irena Cieślińska-Skrzypiec, "Inowrocław. Długie miesiące—ciężkie lata . . ." *Nike* 6 (June 1993), 12.

8. Letter to Benjamin Pogrund, April 20, 1966, Sobukwe Papers, WHP A2618 Ba3.

9. Ireneusz Polit, *Miejsce odosobnienia w Berezie Kartuskiej w latach 1934–1939* (Toruń: Adam Marszałek, 2003), 121; Jewhen Wreciona quoted in Agnieszka Knyt, ed., "Bereza Kartuska," *Karta* 59 (2009), 43.

10. Patrick Lekota, interview with Julie Frederikse, SAHA AL 2460, 332.

11. Tokyo Sexwale, interview with John Carlin, at http://www.pbs.org/wgbh/pages/frontline/shows/mandela/interviews/sexwale.html.

12. See photograph in Richard English, *History of Ireland* (Dublin: Gill and MacMillan, 1991), 158.

13. Jacek Kuroń, *Wiara i wina: Do i od komunizmu* (London: Aneks, 1989), 14.

14. Interview by author with Jacek Kuroń, Warsaw, June 2004. Ironically, Henryk Kuroń apparently was never imprisoned—and Jacek began smoking anyway.

15. General Georgi Skalon, Governor-General of Warsaw. Antoni Lange, "Wspomnienia więzienne," *Niepodległość* 3:2 (1931), 280–81.

16. Lewin, *Bandiet: Out of Jail*, 36.

17. Hanczak, "Za kratami Cytadeli i Mokotowskiego więzienia," in *Za kratami więzień i drutami obozów. Wspomnienia i notatki więźniów*, vol. 1 (Warsaw: Komitet Organizacyjny Zjazdu b. Więźniów Ideowych z lat 1914–1921, 1927), 82.

18. Robert Sobukwe, letter to Benjamin Pogrund, April 12, 1967. Sobukwe papers, WHP, A 2618 Ba5.

19. Ewa Ludkiewicz, *Siedem lat w więzieniu, 1948–1955* (Gdańsk: BiT, 2005), 110–11.

20. Barbara Harlow, *Barred: Women, Writing, and Political Detention* (Hanover, NH: University Press of New England, 1992); see also Ioan Davies, *Writers in Prison* (Oxford: Basil Blackwell, 1990); and Paul Gready, *Writing as Resistance: Life Stories of Imprisonment, Exile, and Homecoming from Apartheid South Africa* (Lanham, MD: Rowman & Littlefield, 2003).

21. Vladimir Petrovich Makhnovets, *Kak derzhat' sebia na doprosakh* (Geneva: Rabochee Delo, 1902).

22. Wacław Koral, *Przez partje, związki, więzienia i Sybir . . . Wspomnienia drukarza z działalności w ruchu socjalistycznym i zawodowym 1898–1928* (Warsaw: Związek Zawodowy Drukarzy i Pokrewnionych Zawodów w Polsce, 1933), 53.
23. "Instrukcja więzienna," AAN 202/II-13, 133.
24. "Instrukcja więzienna," AAN 202/II-13, 134.
25. Zdzisław Jędrzejewicz, "Dziennik z lat 1945–50," Ośrodek Karta, AO CzP 234w, 1–2.
26. Baruch Hirson, *Revolutions in My Life* (Johannesburg: Witwatersrand University Press, 1995), 336.
27. Gerry Adams, *Cage Eleven* (Dingle: Brandon, 1990), 151.
28. Thomas Mathiesen, *The Defences of the Weak: A Sociological Study of a Norwegian Correctional Institution* (London: Tavistock, 1965); Gresham M. Sykes, *The Society of Captives: A Study of a Maximum Security Prison,* 2nd ed. (Princeton, NJ: Princeton University Press, 2007).
29. Marek M. Kaminski, *Games Prisoners Play: The Tragicomic Worlds of Polish Prison* (Princeton, NJ: Princeton University Press, 2004).
30. Władysław Bartoszewski, *Warto być przyzwoitym. Szkic do pamiętnika* (Paris: Spotkania, 1986), 33.
31. Bartoszewski, *Warto być przyzwoitym,* 11–12.
32. Bogdan Ciszak, "Dziennik," Ośrodek Karta, AO CzP 19w, 2.
33. Jerzy Stokowski, "Dziennik pisany w pamięci. 758 dni," Ośrodek Karta, AO CzP 193w, 60.
34. Stokowski, "Dziennik pisany w pamięci," 8, 37–43.
35. Stokowski, "Dziennik pisany w pamięci," 11–12. Thirty years later Marek Kaminski would encounter the same game among his cellmates. Kaminski, *Games Prisoners Play,* 18.
36. *Gryps* to the Regional Committee of MOPR, no date, but probably 1932. AAN 175/III-16, 3–4.
37. Mathibedi added that her "sense of humour" told her she was being "tested." Letter, n.d. [c. June 1982] CSA, Pretoria, 1/3/2/1: Dissipline en Beheer. Afsondering. v. 4.
38. Władysława Osińska, "W celi matek na Mokotowie," *Nike* 12 (May 1994), 19.
39. Letter from Jan Sosnkowski to Jan Klempiński, April 2, 1911, in *Listy nieprawomyślne. Wybór z akt Warszawskiego Gubernialnego Zarządu Żandarmerii 1886–1914* (Warsaw: Akademia Nauk Społecznych PZPR, 1989), 251–52.
40. Quoted in the *San Francisco Examiner,* December 7, 1919.
41. Zofia Kirkor-Kiedroniowa, *Wspomnienia* (Kraków: Wydawnictwo Literackie, 1986), 198. See also p. 187, where Grabska attempts to refuse an order to stand when the prison chief enters the cell, because "we politicals are not bound by the rules for criminals."
42. Kulczyk, "Wspomnienia," 27.
43. Galelekile W. Sitho, in Jan K. Coetzee, *Plain Tales from Robben Island* (Pretoria: Van Schalk, 2000), 96.
44. On this term, see Kieran McEvoy, *Paramilitary Imprisonment in Northern Ireland* (Oxford: Oxford University Press, 2001).
45. Maggie Resha, *My Life in the Struggle* (Johannesburg: Congress of South African Writers, 1991), 166.
46. Bartoszewski, *Warto być przyzwoitym,* 59.
47. Gustaw Daniłowski, *Wrażenia więzienne,* (Lwów: Bernard Połoniecki, 1908), 90–91.
48. Daniłowski, *Wrażenia więzienne,* 136–37. Lange, "Wspomnienia więzienne," *Niepodległość* 4:1 (1932), 91. See also Letter from Łomża District Court prosecutor, 1908, APWOP 6623, k. 110.
49. Jan Kwapiński, *Moje wspomnienia 1904–1939* (Paris: Księgarnia Polska, 1965), 71–72.
50. Stefania Sempołowska, *Z dna nędzy* (Warsaw: K. Kowalewski, 1909), 35–36. Other examples from the czarist period: Daniłowski, *Wrażenia więzienne,* 99–103; Andrzej Jerzy Budzyński, "'Pawiak' jako więzienie polityczne w latach 1880–1915" (PhD diss., Warsaw University, 1987), 142.
51. Władysław Szczypa, "Z więziennych chwil za okupacji austriackiej," *Niepodległość* 7 (1933), 410–12.
52. Rostworowski, *Zaraz po wojnie,* 208.

53. Janusz Horodniczy, *Młodsi od swoich wyroków* (Warsaw: Volumen, 1997), 47–48. See also Barbara Otwinowska, "Z naszych rozmów," 24; Barbara Szwarczyk-Janicka, *Za kratami. Wspomnienia więźniarki okresu stalinowskiego* (Lublin: Author, 1992), 16.
54. See Moses Dlamini, *Hell-Hole, Robben Island: Reminiscences of a Political Prisoner* (Trenton, NJ: Africa World Press, 1984), esp. 131–33; Indres Naidoo, *Island in Chains: Ten Years on Robben Island* (London: Penguin, 1982); Coetzee, *Plain Tales*.
55. Dlamini, *Hell-Hole*, 164.
56. Lewin, *Bandiet*, 98.
57. Lewin, *Bandiet*, 99.
58. Kulczyk, "Wspomnienia," 16, 13–14.
59. McEvoy, *Paramilitary Imprisonment*, 40.
60. Kwapiński, *Moje wspomnienia*, 73–74. Ignacy Hańczak contrasted the utter lack of order among criminals in Mokotów Prison in 1918 with the sharing of goods among politicals. "Za kratami Cytadeli i mokotowskiego więzienia," 72–74.
61. Marek Kulczyk, "Wspomnienia," Ośrodek Karta AO II/380, 21–22.
62. H. Duljasz, "Praca wychowawcza wśród więźniów" (n.d., c. 1953), Departament Więziennictwa, AAN MBP 1744/1/92, 4.
63. Horodniczy, *Młodsi od swoich wyroków*, 102–3.
64. Tadeusz Wolsza, *W cieniu Wronek, Jaworzna i Piechcina... 1944–1956. Życie codzienne w polskich więzieniach, obozach i ośrodkach pracy więźniów* (Warsaw: Instytut Historii PAN, 2003), 106–7.
65. Horodniczy, *Młodsi od swoich wyroków*, 103.
66. Departament Więziennictwa, n.d. (c. 1949–50), AAN MBP 1744/1/37, 121–22.
67. Janina Jelińska, "Na ogólniaku," *Nike* 31 (October 1996), 16.
68. Frank Gallagher, *Days of Fear: Diary of a 1920s Hunger Striker* (Cork: Mercier, 2008), 73–74.
69. Quoted in Tim Carey, *Mountjoy: The Story of a Prison* (Cork: Collins, 2000), 187. See also threats made to doctors treating hunger-striking Terence MacSwiney in 1920: Francis J. Costello, *Enduring the Most: The Life and Death of Terence MacSwiney* (Dingle: Brandon, 1995), 182–83.
70. Examples: Marja Chmieleńska, "Wrażenia z rewolucji w 1905 r. w 'Serbji,'" *Niepodległość* 8:2 (1933), 287–88; *Z doświadczeń aresztowanego* (Warszawa: Polska Partya Socyalistyczna, n.d.), 25–28; Aleksander Ringman, "Z Zagłębia, więzienia i emigracji," *Niepodległość* 4:2 (1931), 277; Budzyński, "'Pawiak' jako więzienie polityczne," 97, 101.
71. Jan, "Z więzienia sieradzkiego," *Z dawnych dni* 1:1, 18–20.
72. Letter from MacDermot, General Prisons Board, to Ministry of Home Affairs, December 30, 1922. NAI H 170/113, n.p.
73. Peadar O'Donnell, *The Gates Flew Open* (London: Jonathan Cape, 1932), 160.
74. Besides O'Donnell's memoir, O'Keeffe figures prominently in Margaret Buckley, *The Jangle of the Keys* (Dublin: J. Duffy, 1938).
75. See Republican Political Prisoners Committee, handbill, n.d. (1929), UCD P200/12(2); Department of Justice notes, June 1, 1932, in NAI Taoiseach S 6296, n.p.
76. While white South African political prisoners also experienced cruel and sadistic treatment, they could also form closer bonds with their jailers, for the gulf between them was not racial. On the other hand, white politicals tended to be English speakers, while guards most likely spoke Afrikaans. For examples, see Lewin, *Bandiet*, 78–79; Giffard, "Surviving Section 29," entry for December 27, 1987. Baruch Hirson taught mathematics to a black warder. Hirson, *Revolutions*, 184–85. On language and cultural barriers in Polish prisons in the Stalinist period, where some guards were poorly educated Polish communists who had grown up in France and spoke little Polish: Wolsza, *W cieniu*, 42.
77. In 1977, 40 percent of white wardens in South Africa were under twenty, and annual turnover exceeded 15 percent. *Rand Daily Mail*, July 20, 1977.
78. James Gregory, with Bob Graham, *Goodbye Bafana, Nelson Mandela: My Prisoner, My Friend* (London: Headline, 1995).
79. Dlamini, *Hell-Hole*, 105–6, 125–26.
80. Mmutlanyane Stanley Mogoba, *Stone, Steel, Sjambok: Faith Born on Robben Island* (Johannesburg: Ziningweni Communications, n.d.), 43.
81. Joseph Faniso Mati, in Coetzee, *Plain Tales*, 21.

82. Mosibudi Mangena, *On Your Own: Evolution of Black Consciousness in South Africa/Azania* (Braamfontein: Skotaville, 1989), 84–85.

83. Neville Alexander, *Robben Island Prison Dossier, 1964–1974* (Rondebosch, South Africa: University of Cape Town Press, 1994), 16.

84. Alexander, *Robben Island Prison Dossier*, 15.

85. Ngxiki, in Coetzee, *Plain Tales*, 86–87. Black prisoners elsewhere were not as fortunate. As late as 1990, black staff at Johannesburg Prison were protesting the continued use of "baas" (and "nona" for wardresses) for white staff, asking that all warders be addressed by rank. "Petition for the Grievances of the Johannesburg Command," February 9, 1990, SAHA Original Collection AL 2457 F4.2

86. Naidoo, *Island in Chains*, 177.

87. Gregory, *Goodbye Bafana*, 97, 112–13. Also Nelson Mandela, *Long Walk to Freedom* (London: Abacus, 1994). See also, on warder respect for Mandela, Walter Sisulu, *I Will Go Singing* (Cape Town: Robben Island Museum, 2002), 163.

88. Emphasis in the original. Letter to Robben Island O/C, c. October 1972. Brian Bunting Papers, Mayibuye Archives MCH 7, 2.40, Box 122.

89. Mira Zimińska-Sygietyńska, *Nie żyłam samotnie* (Warsaw: WAiF, 1985), 191. See also Leon Wanat, *Za murami Pawiaka*, 4th ed. (Warsaw: Książka i Wiedza, 1967), 22–24, 298–99; Regina Domańska, *Pawiak—kaźń i heroizm* (Warsaw: Książka i Wiedza, 1988), 226.

90. *Gryps*, March 1943, AAN 212/I/13, kk. 19–23.

91. Wanat, *Za murami Pawiaka*, 44.

92. On the contempt Protestant guards showed Loyalist prisoners: McEvoy, *Paramilitary Imprisonment*, 197–99.

93. Colin Crawford, *Defenders or Criminals? Loyalist Prisoners and Criminalisation* (Belfast: Blackstaff, 1999), 167; also 32–33.

94. Crawford, *Defenders or Criminals*, 171. See also McEvoy, *Paramilitary Imprisonment*, 133–36. For South Africa, see Gregory, *Goodbye Bafana*, 99–101.

95. Chris Ryder, *Inside the Maze: The Untold Story of the Northern Ireland Prison Service* (London: Methuen, 2001), 267, also 301–309. Kieran McEvoy mentions similar intimidation by Loyalist prisoners, who were more likely to know the neighborhoods where the guards, mostly Protestant themselves, lived. McEvoy, *Paramilitary Imprisonment*, 198.

96. Ryder, *Inside the Maze*, 118.

97. See Ryder, *Inside the Maze*, 161–64, 171, 176–78, 184–91; Wanat, *Za murami Pawiaka*, 38–43. Also Lwów: *Gryps* from Żrun, March 28, 1943, AAN 203/XV/33, 82. In the internment camps of martial-law Poland, some guards were told that Solidarity had drawn up a list of guards to be executed along with their families. Ciszak, "Dziennik," 2.

98. Ryder, *Inside the Maze*, 160, 172.

99. Ryder, *Inside the Maze*, 174–75.

100. Jacobo Timerman, *Prisoner without a Name, Cell without a Number* (Madison: University of Wisconsin Press, 2002); Kulczyk, "Wspomnienia," 7–8; Stanisława Sowińska, "Gorzkie lata," Biblioteka Narodowa, Dział rękopisów, Sygn. 14257, 102; and many more.

101. Ernie O'Malley, *The Singing Flame* (Dublin: Anvil, 1992), 249.

102. Wojciech Duklanowicz, "Wspomnienia," Ośrodek Karta AO II/439, 16.

Chapter 4

1. Hugh Lewin, *Bandiet: Out of Jail* (Johannesburg: Random House, 2002), 197–203.

2. Kulczyk, "Wspomnienia," Ośrodek Karta, AO II/380, 45–46; reprinted in *Polityczni* (Warsaw: Ośrodek Karta, 2010).

3. Quoted in Padraic Kenney, *Carnival of Revolution: Central Europe, 1989* (Princeton, NJ: Princeton University Press, 2002), 27–28. Władysław Frasyniuk had a similar experience in Wrocław: Kenney, *Carnival of Revolution*, 23–24.

4. As their prison record sentenced them to life above ground, Nowak and others like him began to wonder about the value of an underground. They decided to oppose the regime openly, using new methods of defiance. In this way, prison experience in the 1980s had an unexpected effect on the anti-communist movement.

5. Marek Niedziewicz, interview with author, 1997, Biblioteka Ossolineum, Wrocław, Ośrodek Dokumentacji Życia Społecznego.

6. Sighle Humphreys, journal entry December 23, 1931, UCD P106/1096, n.p. A similar note from late 1922 bears the same sentiment (and may have been written by Humphreys): "The women prisoners in Mountjoy Jail hope that sympathetic friends will not go to any expense to send them in parcels for Christmas." Male prisoners had not been allowed to receive packages, and they hoped that they might be treated equally, the letter continued. Letter from Republican Women Prisoners' Council, n.d., IRA Publicity Reports, NLI, ms. 43, 125/1, n.p.

7. One form of writing, the interrogation protocol, severely tests the political prisoner's autonomy. Whether a lengthy autobiographical statement or simply a signature on a conversation summary prepared by the interrogator, the document is important to regimes precisely because it can be attributed to the prisoner. They are usually quite formulaic, often dictated by the interrogator. On the interrogation protocol, see Paul Gready, *Writing as Resistance: Life Stories of Imprisonment, Exile, and Homecoming from Apartheid South Africa* (Lanham, MD: Rowman & Littlefield, 2003), 25–28; Anna Muller, "If the Walls Could Talk: Women Political Prisoners in Stalinist Poland, 1945–1956," PhD diss. Indiana University, 2010. The prisoner-interrogator relationship is explored in Breytenbach, *True Confessions of an Albino terrorist* (New York: Mariner Books, 1994), 341–44; and it is the subject of Arthur Koestler's classic novel *Darkness at Noon* (New York: MacMillan, 1941).

8. See works in Chapter 3, note 20.

9. Joachim C. Fest, *Hitler* (New York: Harcourt Brace Jovanovich, 1974), 199–203.

10. Komórka Więzienna report April 24, 1944, AAN 202/II-17, k. 92. Regina Domańska, *Pawiak—kaźń i heroizm* (Warsaw: Książka i Wiedza, 1988), 373–74.

11. See Domańska, *Pawiak—kaźń i heroizm*, 134.

12. Letter from Sean Harling, C Wing Mountjoy, April 9, 1923. Ernest O'Malley Collection, UCD P17a/163, CD, 93–94.

13. On smuggled letters, see Director of Intelligence (Free State), letter, n.d. [1923], UCD P17a/190, CD, 29. Circular, Commissioner of Prisons Cilliers, August 13, 1980: Central Prison Archives, 1/3/3: Dissipline en Beheer. Visentering, vol. 1.

14. Nikolaus Wachsmann, *Hitler's Prisons: Legal Terror in Nazi Germany* (New Haven, CT: Yale University Press, 2004), 273.

15. Breyten Breytenbach, *True Confessions of an Albino Terrorist* (New York: Harcourt Brace, 1983), 149–50, 172. Breytenbach's wife and mother agreed to alternate letters each month; when an unknown admirer sent him a letter, he had to choose whether to receive that in place of one from his wife.

16. James Gregory, with Bob Graham, *Goodbye, Bafana: Nelson Mandela, My Prisoner, My Friend* (London: Headline, 1995), 116, 126; also 169.

17. Or into a box of toys: Andrew Jacobs, "Behind Cry for Help from China Labor Camp," *New York Times*, June 11, 2013.

18. Sighle Humphreys, May 1928, UCD P106/1079, n.p.; see also Nell Humphreys, letter to Sighle, n.d. (1923), UCD P106/1054, n.p.

19. See, for example, Małgorzata Szejnert, *Śród żywych duchów* (London: Aneks, 1990), 195–96.

20. Mandela, letter to Mrs. Bhilla, WHP AG 2510 E3.4.1. See also *A Prisoner in the Garden: The Nelson Mandela Foundation* (Johannesburg: Studio, 2006), 136.

21. Quoted in Domańska, *Pawiak—kaźń i heroizm*, 295.

22. HB Shawe, Under Colonial Secretary, letter to Assistant Resident Magistrate Orpen, Tokai, August 29, 1901; reply from Orpen, September 5, 1901. WCPA CO 2357 Ref Folio 1615, v. 4, n.p.

23. Michael Warner, *The Rise and Fall of Intelligence: An International Security History* (Washington, DC: Georgetown University Press, 2014), ch. 2.

24. Francis J. Costello, *Enduring the Most: The Life and Death of Terence MacSwiney* (Dingle: Brandon, 1995), 80–81.

25. See Jeffrey A. Keshen, *Propaganda and Censorship during Canada's Great War* (Edmonton: University of Alberta Press, 1996), ch. 6; William G. Rosenberg, "Reading Soldiers' Moods: Russian Military Censorship and the Configuration of Feeling in World War I," *American Historical Review* 119:3 (2014), 714–40.

26. Criminal prisoners might of course also try to continue to keep control of activities outside, though it would be difficult to speak of commitment to a cause in this case.

27. Michael Burrough, *Blood and Rage: A Cultural History of Terrorism* (New York: Harper, 2009), 7–8.

28. Ludwik Śledziński, "Przejścia więzienne w Łowiczu i w Warszawie (rok 1906–1907)," *Niepodległość* 2:2 (1930), 260–64.

29. Stanisław Czarnecki, "O wyprowadzeniu dziesięciu z Pawiaka," *Niepodległość*, 6:1 (1932), 124–28. On escapes in this period in general, see Robert Blobaum, "Under Lock and Key? Prisons and Prison Conditions in Russian Poland, 1906–14," in *Społeczeństwo w dobie przemian. Wiek XIX i XX. Księga jubileuszowa profesor Anny Żarnowskiej*, ed. Maria Nietyksza et al. (Warsaw: DiG, 2003), 300–304; Elżbieta Kaczyńska, *Ludzie ukarani. Więzienia i system kar w Królestwie Polskim 1815–1914* (Warsaw: Państwowe Wydawnictwo Naukowe, 1989), 434–36.

30. Quoted in Tim Carey, *Mountjoy: The Story of a Prison* (Cork: Collins, 2000), 189. See also the *Irish Independent*, March 17, 1919.

31. Seán McConville, *Irish Political Prisoners, 1848–1922: Theatres of War* (London: Routledge, 2005), 710–12.

32. Frank O'Connor, *The Big Fellow: Michael Collins and the Irish Revolution* (London: Picador, 1998), 59–60. Collins "carried a plan of each prison in his mind," O'Connor adds (121).

33. Seán MacBride, *That Day's Struggle: A Memoir, 1904–1951* (Blackrock, Co. Dublin: Currach Press, 2005), 74, 75–76. On disorder in the camps, see the files of the Adjutant General of General Headquarters, 1923, in IMA, CW/P/08/07 and CW/P/02/01/6A.

34. General Prison Board reports, NAI H78/64. Thirty-one men failed to escape but began a hunger strike the very next day.

35. Domańska, *Pawiak—kaźń i heroizm*, 194–217; Leon Wanat, *Za murami Pawiaka*, 4th ed. (Warsaw: Książka i Wiedza, 1967), 369–78.

36. Tadeusz Wolsza, *W cieniu Wronek, Jaworzna i Piechcina . . . 1944–1956. Życie codzienne w polskich więzieniach, obozach i ośrodkach pracy więźniów* (Warsaw: Instytut Historii PAN, 2003), 70–74.

37. Kazimierz Moczarski, *Zapiski*, ed. Andrzej Krzysztof Kunert (Warsaw: Państwowy Instytut Wydawniczy, 1990), 66–67.

38. Denis Herbstein, *White Lies: Canon Collins and the Secret War against Apartheid* (Cape Town: James Currey, 2004); Steven Friedman, *Race, Class and Power: Harold Wolpe and the Radical Critique of Apartheid* (Durban: University of KwaZulu-Natal Press, 2015).

39. Tim Jenkins, *Inside Out: Escape from Pretoria Prison* (Johannesburg: Jacana Press, 2005). Also see WHP AD 1912, 202.8.

40. Chris Ryder, *Inside the Maze: The Untold Story of the Northern Ireland Prison Service* (London: Methuen, 2001), 268–72.

41. Quoted in Ryder, *Inside the Maze*, 278–79.

42. Kieran McEvoy, *Paramilitary Imprisonment in Northern Ireland* (Oxford: Oxford University Press, 2001), 69–70.

43. McEvoy, *Paramilitary Imprisonment*, 50–55, 64–66; he notes that a Loyalist escapee could not flee to a welcoming country as easily as could a Republican.

44. One exception is the escape of four women from Mountjoy in October 1921. Carey, *Mountjoy*, 190–91.

45. See Ryder, *Inside the Maze*, 95–96, 128–45. One escapee in 1943 appeared on the stage of a Belfast cinema for a dramatic reading of the Easter Proclamation of 1916. Ryder, *Inside the Maze*, 64.

46. Annemieke van Drenth and Francisca de Haan, *The Rise of Caring Power: Elizabeth Fry and Josephine Butler in Britain and the Netherlands* (Amsterdam: Amsterdam University Press, 1999).

47. Owen McGee, *The IRB: The Irish Revolutionary Brotherhood, from the Land League to Sinn Féin* (Dublin: Four Courts Press, 2005).

48. Zofia Zbyszewska, *Ministerstwo polskiej biedy. Z dziejów Towarzystwa Opieki nad Więźniami 'Patronat' w Warszawie, 1909–1944* (Warsaw: Państwowy Instytut Wydawniczy, 1983); Zofia Kirkor-Kiedroniowa, *Wspomnienia* (Kraków: Wydawnictwo Literackie, 1986), 158, n49.

49. One of Sempołowska's young protegees, lawyer Aniela Steinsbergowa, continued Sempołowska's work helping prisoners and others repressed by communist Poland until the 1980s. Szejnert, *Śród żywych duchów*, 6.

50. Jan Krzesławski, "Więzienie w Ratuszu za rządów Nazarowa," *Kronika Ruchu Rewolucyjnego* 1:2 (1935), 87.

51. Andrzej Ajnenkiel, "Memoriały Stefanii Sempołowskiej dotyczące położenia więźniów politycznych w Polsce w 1920 i 1922r.," *Teki archiwalne* 6 (1959), 10–12; "Pierwsze pięciolecie więziennictwa polskiego," *Księga jubileuszowa więziennictwa polskiego 1918–1928* (Warsaw: Związek Pracowników Więziennych Rzeczypospolitej Polskiej, 1929), 53–54.

52. Zarządzanie Ministerstwa Sprawiedliwości, May 26, 1937. AAN Ministerstwo Spraw Wojskowych, 296/III-53, k. 163.

53. On the Soviet case, see Stuart Finkel, "The 'Political Red Cross' and the Genealogy of Rights Discourse in Revolutionary Russia" *Journal of Modern History*, 89:1 (2017), 79-118.

54. Zofia Wankowiczowa, "Kombatantki," *Kultura* (Paris) 10 (1954), 80–81; Wanat, *Za murami*, 119, 284, 307–12.

55. Delegat Rządu, Departament Spraw Wewnętrznych, AAN 202/II/63 (Mf 2225/11), kk. 148–50.

56. "Sprawozdanie z opieki nad więźniami drogą Opium," AAN 203/XV/32, k. 103; Domańska, *Pawiak—kaźń i heroizm*, 351–72; A.S., report October 6, 1941, AAN 202-II/19, k. 1.

57. On Cumann na mBan: Cal McCarthy, *Cumann na mBan and the Irish Revolution* (Cork: Collins Press, 2007).

58. In December 1971, Humphreys helped to establish an Association of Committees for Aiding Internees' Dependents and found that her name made an impact in Belfast. Committee records in UCD P106/1585-1595.

59. See Margaret Ward, *Unmanageable Revolutionaries: Women and Irish Nationalism* (London: Pluto Press, 1989).

60. Comerford to Humphreys, May 1927, UCD P106/1086.

61. Margaret Ward, *Hanna Sheehy-Skeffington: A Life* (Dublin: Attic Press, 1997), ch. 11; Costello, *Enduring the Most*, 77–79; Director of Intelligence, report to Minister of Defence, October 27, 1923, IMA CW/P/02/02/34, n.p. William Murphy, *Political Imprisonment and the Irish, 1912–1921* (Oxford: Oxford University Press, 2014), esp. 70–79, 117–18.

62. UCD P106/1286-1310, 1333, 1342, 1353, 1358–65.

63. See materials of Republican Prisoners Reception Committee, 1932, UCD P200/13.

64. Humphreys's notes from meetings of the Political Prisoners' Committee, Dublin (n.d.), UCD P106/1310.

65. Government Information Bureau, July 10, 1936, NAI S9044. See also Elgin O'Rahilly Papers, UCD P200/9, 1–3, 8.

66. Surveillance reports in NAI JUS 8/387.

67. David Welsh, "A Tribute to Helen Suzman," in *Opposing Voices: Liberalism and Opposition in South Africa Today*, ed. Milton Shain (Johannesburg: Jonathan Ball, 2006), 10.

68. See Helen Suzman, letter to Hildegard Falk, October 19, 1981, WHP A2084, Aa1.2.5; Suzman, *In No Uncertain Terms: A South African Memoir* (New York: Knopf, 1993), 234; Suzman, letter to Minister of Law and Order Louis le Grange, October 7, 1985, WHP A2084 Aa1.2.9.

69. Suzman, letter to Minister of Justice John Vorster, September 4, 1965, WHP A2084, Aa1.2.1.

70. Letters in Suzman Papers, WHP A2084, Aa1.1.1 and Ad 1.1.

71. Letter, December 29, 1978, WHP A2084 Ad 1.1.

72. Suzman, *In No Uncertain Terms*, 153–54. Her letter of February 16, 1967 to Minister of Justice Petrus Cornelius Pelser—who, unlike his immediate predecessor John Vorster, had not been interned for Nazi sympathies during World War II—is in WHP A2084 Aa 1.2.1.

73. WHP A2084 Ad10.

74. WHP A2084 Aa1.1.1, n.d.

75. "Więźniowie polityczni do proletarjatu Polski," AAN 175/III-24, kk. 1–2.

76. Quoted in James Ryle, "International Red Aid 1922–1928: The Founding of a Comintern Front Organization," PhD diss., Emory University, 1967, 37.

77. "Statut 'Pomocy Czerwonej' w Polsce—organizacji pomocy więźniom," ed. Henryk Wajn, *Z pola walki. Kwartalnik póswięcony dziejom ruchu robotniczego* 10:2 (1967), 169.

78. "Wczoraj i dziś. Ci co walczą do tych, co walczyli," *Więzień polityczny* 7–8 (1925), 8–9.
79. "W walce o amnestję dla więźniów politycznych," ed. Helena Zatorska, *Z pola walki. Zeszyty wydziału historii partii KC PZPR*, 1 (1956), 5–15.
80. Ministry of Justice report, February 1928, AAN 361/2, k. 189; *Jednolity Front Pomocy* 2 (February 15, 1934), AAN 175/I-16, k. 3a; "W walce," 18–19; MOPR Central Committee, "List do więzień, No. 1," October 18, 1931, AAN Mf 25749, kk. 72–73.
81. "O masowej pracy Czerwonej Pomocy," circular issued by the MOPR Central Committee in Poland, November 1935, AAN 175/I-5, kk. 22–23, 25.
82. "O masowej pracy Czerwonej Pomocy," k. 21.
83. "Do wszystkich organizacji Komunistycznej Partii Rzeczpospolitej Polski!" *Więzień polityczny* 1, 1924, 1.
84. "Uchwały Pierwszej Krajowej Narady Wydziałów Gospodarczych Czerwonej Pomocy w Polsce," June 1936, AAN 175/I-1, k. 17a.
85. *Amnestji!* ... Nr 3, 1926. AAN 179/3. See also "Plan akcji amnestyjnej," n.d., AAN 179/2, kk. 1–2. The government announced a partial amnesty in July; in some cases, it seems, pardons were offered. The pressure for full amnesty continued. Międzypartyjny Sekretariat dla Walki o Amnestię, Circular 2, August 1, 1926, AAN 179/2, kk. 5–7.
86. Red Help Press Communiqué 35, 24 December 1928, AAN 175/I-6, k. 22.
87. AAN 175/1 and 175/III, *passim*.
88. AAN 175/I-5, k. 9. See also "Wytyczne krajowej narady Czerwonej Pomocy w Polsce," December 1931. AAN 175/I-1, kk. 1–13.
89. Quoted in Red Help circular, 1928, AAN 175/I-13, k. 26.
90. Memo, General Staff, Ministry of Military Affairs, September 15, 1926, AAN 296/II-22, k. 56.
91. "Do robotników i robotnic PPS," n.d. (early 1926), AAN 175/I-9, k. 10.
92. Seminar discussion transcript, March 7, 1966 at Zakład Historii Partii, AAN R-196, kk. 116–19.
93. Open letter from women political prisoners, Fordon Prison, to the workers and peasants of Poland, n.d. (1932-33), AAN 175/III-4, kk. 1-1a.
94. Open letter to the people of Kraków, 1934. AAN 175/III-9, k. 1.
95. Wolsza, *W cieniu*, 25–26; Wyrwich, *W celi śmierci* (Warsaw: Rytm, 2012), 31–32.
96. Maria Sobocińska, "Dr. Czesław Zagorski," *Nike* 31 (October 1996), 14.
97. Regina Mikulska, "Autobiogram," *Nike* 52 (February–March 2000), 16; Wolsza, *W cieniu*, 108–109.

Chapter 5

1. The suffragettes are an exception; their cause resonated with activists in Europe and North America.
2. Daniel Ryan, Chief Superintendent to Commissioner of Police, Dublin, October 22, 1869. NAI CSORP 1869, Box 9, File 4803R. On American support, see Owen McGee, *The IRB: The Irish Republican Brotherhood from the Land League to Sinn Féin* (Dublin: Four Courts Press, 2005); David Brundage, *Irish Nationalists in America: The Politics of Exile, 1798–1998* (Oxford: Oxford University Press, 2016), ch. 4.
3. "Organizowanie pomocy więziennej," *Więzień polityczny* 1:1 (February 1911), 17. See Halina Kiepurska, *Warszawa w rewolucji 1905–1907* (Warsaw: Wiedza Powszechna, 1974), 329–34.
4. See, for example, William Murphy, *Political Imprisonment and the Irish, 1912–1921* (Oxford: Oxford University Press, 2014), ch. 8; and documents in NAI Taoiseach S1369/9.
5. James Joll, *The Second International, 1889–1914* (London: Routledge and Kegan Paul, 1974).
6. Margaret Ward, *Hanna Sheehy-Skeffington: A Life* (Dublin: Attic, 1997), ch. 11. Sheehy-Skeffington, letter October 24, 1912, NLI 33618 (6).
7. See, for example, MT Kaderbhoy, London All-India Muslim League, letter to Undersecretary of State, January 17, 1911, NASA GG 888 15/109. Sean Scalmer, *Gandhi in the West: The Mahatma and the Rise of Radical Protest* (Cambridge: Cambridge University Press, 2011).
8. See Isabel V. Hull, *A Scrap of Paper: Breaking and Making International Law during the Great War* (Ithaca, NY: Cornell University Press, 2014), chs. 3 and 9.

9. Among the movements that have made use of the prisoner of war frame are the prisoners of the Irish War of Independence and Civil War and Afrikaaner nationalists during World War II.

10. J. D. Armstrong, "The International Committee of the Red Cross and Political Prisoners," *International Organization* 39:4 (Autumn, 1985), 622–23.

11. Armstrong, "International Committee," 624, 622.

12. Quoted in Armstrong, "International Committee," 624.

13. Seán McConville, *Irish Political Prisoners, 1920–1962: Pilgrimage of Desolation* (London: Routledge, 2014), 260–63.

14. Memo, Counsel to President, December 29, 1922, NLI Ms. 43, 124.

15. See Choi Chatterjee, "Imperial Incarcerations: Ekaterina Breshko-Breshkovskaia, Vinayak Savarkar, and the Original Sins of Modernity," *Slavic Review* 74:4 (Winter 2015), 850–72.

16. Leaflet, March 1930, in Elgin O'Rahilly Papers, UCD P200/12 (8).

17. RPPC, Letter to Gandhi, 1931. Sighle Humphreys papers, UCD P106/1314.

18. James Martin Ryle, "International Red Aid 1922–1928: The Founding of a Comintern Front Organization," PhD diss., Emory University, 1967, 73–74.

19. *Więzień polityczny* 9 (1926), 14.

20. Michael Barnett, *Empire of Humanity: A History of Humanitarianism* (Ithaca, NY: Cornell University Press, 2011), 39–41.

21. Baldwin, Memo in reply to Kenneth Durant, ICPP Papers, New York Public Library ZL 281, reel 1.

22. The ICPP published four books from its New York offices: *Letters from Russian Prisons* (1925); *The Fascist Dictatorship in Italy* (1926); *Political Prisoners in Poland* (1927); *Political Persecution Today* (1925).

23. International Committee for Political Prisoners, letter to President de Valera, July 15, 1936, NAI Taoiseach, S1964.

24. Minutes of ICPP meeting, March 30, 1925, ICPP papers, NYPL ZL 281, Reel 1.

25. *Letters from Russian Prisons*, xiii.

26. Baldwin, in *Letters from Russian Prisons*, xiii.

27. Von Eltz, letter to Baldwin, April 18, 1925. ICPP papers, NYPL, ZL 281, Reel 1.

28. "To our friends," November 27, 1927. ICPP papers, NYPL ZL 281, Reel 1.

29. See, for example, 1933 report, ICPP papers, NYPL ZL 281, Reel 1.

30. A webpage on the origins of the quote and its many versions is maintained by Harold Marcuse: www.history.ucsb.edu/faculty/marcuse/niem.htm.

31. Jan Eckel, "The International League for the Rights of Man, Amnesty International, and the Changing Fate of Human Rights Activism from the 1940s through the 1970s," *Humanity: An International Journal of Human Rights, Humanitarianism, and Development* 4:2 (Summer 2013), 186.

32. Aaron Levenstein, *Escape to Freedom: The Story of the International Rescue Committee* (Westport, CT: Greenwood Press, 1983).

33. Jonathan D. Bloom, "The Workers' Defense League," in *The Oxford Encyclopedia of American Business, Labor, and Economic History*, ed. Melvin Dubofsky (Oxford: Oxford University Press, 2013).

34. Tom Buchanan, "'The Truth Will Set You Free': The Making of Amnesty International," *Journal of Contemporary History* 37:4 (October 2002), 579–80.

35. Eckel, "International League for the Rights of Man," 190–91.

36. See Daniel C. Thomas, *The Helsinki Effect: International Norms, Human Rights, and the Demise of Communism* (Princeton, NJ: Princeton University Press, 2001).

37. International Committee of the Red Cross, *Commission of Experts for the Examination of the Question of Assistance to Political Detainees* (Geneva: ICRC, 1953), 2.

38. Benenson, "The Forgotten Prisoners," *Observer*, May 28, 1961. Text available at http://www.amnestyusa.org/about-us/amnesty-50-years/peter-benenson-remembered/the-forgotten-prisoners-by-peter-benenson.

39. On the "prisoner of conscience" idea in theory and practice, see Edy Kaufman, "Prisoners of Conscience: The Shaping of a New Human Rights Concept," *Human Rights Quarterly* 13:3 (August 1991), 339–67.

40. *Threes Newsletter* 14 (September 1966), at https://www.amnesty.org/en/documents/nws21/013/1966/en/. See similar commentary, among many that could be cited, on the "confused war situation in Nigeria," *Newsletter for Groups* 18 (September 1967), at https://www.amnesty.org/en/documents/nws21/015/1967/en/.

41. Egon Larsen, *A Flame in Barbed Wire: The Story of Amnesty International* (New York: Norton, 1979), 24.

42. Larsen, *Flame in Barbed Wire*, 24–25; Amnesty International, *Annual Report, June 1, 1964—May 31, 1965* (London: Amnesty International, 1965), 3–4. Jonathan Power, *Like Water on Stone: The Story of Amnesty International* (Boston: Northeastern University Press, 2001), 125, reports that Amnesty employed a similar compromise in later cases. This distinction has also become the basis for Amnesty's subsequent campaigns against the death penalty.

43. Benenson, "The Forgotten Prisoners."

44. Discussed in Buchanan, "'The Truth Will Set You Free,'" 589–94.

45. Wei Jingsheng, *The Courage to Stand Alone: Letters from Prison and Other Writings* (New York: Penguin, 1997); Kim Dae-jung, *Prison Writings* (Berkeley: University of California Press, 1987); Nawal el Saadawi, *Memoirs from the Women's Prison* (Berkeley: University of California Press, 1987); Natan Sharansky (Anatoly Shcharansky), *Fear No Evil* (London: Weidenfeld and Nicholson, 1988); Jacobo Timerman, *Prisoner without a Name, Cell without a Number* (New York: Knopf, 1981).

46. Amnesty International, *Journalists and Writers in Prison* (London, 1977).

47. The terminology of Amnesty International has been misappropriated, famously so in the title of the prison memoir of Mumia Abu-Jamal, who may or may not have shot a policeman but who was certainly a member of a group advocating violence. Mumia Abu-Jamal, *Death Blossoms: Reflections from a Prisoner of Conscience* (Farmington, PA: Litmus, 1997).

48. *Amnesty International Newsletter* 8:2 (February 1978), 4, at https://www.amnesty.org/en/documents/nws21/002/1978/en/.

49. *Card Scheme Newsletter*, December 1966, at https://www.amnesty.org/en/documents/nws21/010/1966/en/. See also *Postcards for Prisoners Campign* newsletter, July 1967, at https://www.amnesty.org/en/documents/nws21/008/1967/en/.

50. *Amnesty International* [Card Scheme Newsletter], 1 (June 1965), 1, at https://www.amnesty.org/en/documents/nws21/009/1965/en/.

51. *Postcards for Prisoners Campaign Newsletter*, March 1967. www.amnesty.org/en/library/info/NWS21/004/1967/en; *Newsletter for Groups* 17 (June 1967), 4, at https://www.amnesty.org/en/documents/nws21/014/1967/en/.

52. *Amnesty International* [Card Scheme Newsletter] 1 (June 1965), 4. On Amnesty's use of sometimes controversial sources of information, see Tom Buchanan, "Amnesty International in Crisis, 1966–7," *Twentieth-Century British History* 15:3 (2004), 267–89.

53. *Newsletter for Groups* 17 (June 1967), 3.

54. A 1966 scandal over support for political detainees in Rhodesia, involving funds channeled from the British government, nearly destroyed Amnesty International and led to Peter Benenson's departure from the organization. Tom Buchanan, "Amnesty International in Crisis."

55. Victoria Brittain, "Michael Tobin: Visionary or Inciter to Disaffection?" *The Times* (London), April 16, 1973.

56. Victoria Brittain, "Last Hope for the Prisoners of Conscience: Amnesty International after a Decade of Painstaking Vigilance," *The Times* (London), May 1, 1971.

57. Amnesty International, *Report of an Enquiry into Allegations of Ill-Treatment in Northern Ireland* (London: Amnesty International, 1972). On AI and Northern Ireland: Power, *Like Water on Stone*, ch. 5.

58. Brice Dickson, *The European Convention on Human Rights and the Conflict in Northern Ireland* (Oxford: Oxford University Press, 2010).

59. See, for example, Prisons Management Committee, Minutes September 6, 1979 and July 19, 1979. PRONI NIO 10/2/8, n.p. #584.

60. See Jeri Laber, *The Courage of Strangers: Coming of Age with the Human Rights Movement* (New York: Public Affairs, 2002); Samuel Moyn, *The Last Utopia: Human Rights in History* (Cambridge, MA: Belknap Press, 2010), ch. 4.

61. Włodzimierz Domagalski and Radosław Peterman, *Studenci '81. NZS w oczach Partii i SB* (Łódź: Archiwum Opozycji Niepodległościowej, 2006), 176–80; Andrzej Friszke, *Czas KOR-u. Jacek Kuroń a geneza Solidarności* (Kraków: Znak, 2011), 571–74; Andrzej Friszke, *Rewolucja Solidarności* (Kraków: Znak, 2014).

62. Tadeusz Mazowiecki, *Internowanie* (London: Aneks, 1983); Adam Michnik, *Letters from Prison and Other Essays* (Berkeley: University of California Press, 1987).

63. Kristi S. Long, *We All Fought for Freedom: Women in Poland's Solidarity Movement* (Boulder, CO: Westview, 1996), ch 7.

64. Władysław Bartoszewski was one of those so released: Władysław Bartoszewski, *Warto być przyzwoitym. Szkic do pamiętnika* (Paris: Spotkania, 1986), 81–82.

65. Władysław Rodowicz, *Komitet na Piwnej. Fakty, dokumenty, wspomnienia* (Warsaw: Biblioteka 'Więzi,' 1994), 20–28. Marek Żukowski, *Ośrodki odosobnienia w Polsce w latach 1981–1982* (Warsaw: Trio, 2013), 216–17.

66. *Arcybiskupi Komitet Charytatywny we Wrocławiu "pod czwórką"* (Wrocław: Arcybiskupi Komitet Charytatywny, 1997); Padraic Kenney, *A Carnival of Revolution: Central Europe, 1989* (Princeton, NJ: Princeton University Press, 2001), ch. 1.

67. Kenney, *Carnival of Revolution*, ch. 1.

68. Bogdan Ciszak, "Dziennik," Ośrodek Karta, AO CzP 19w.

69. *Amnesty International Annual Report, 1971–1972*, 27, at https://www.amnesty.org/en/documents/pol10/001/1972/en/.

70. South African History Online, "The International Defence and Aid Fund (IDAF)," http://www.sahistory.org.za/topic/international-defence-and-aid-fund-idaf-3; Denis Herbstein, *White Lies: Canon Collins and the Secret War against Apartheid* (Cape Town: James Currey, 2004). The necessary secrecy has meant that the scale of IDAF's support, and any coordination with Amnesty International or the Red Cross, remain hidden even today.

71. Margaret Lenta, "History Effaced: The International Defence and Aid Letters," *Social Dynamics: A Journal of African Studies* 34:2 (September 2008), 205.

72. International Defence and Aid Fund, *Prisoners of Apartheid: A Biographical List of Political Prisoners and Banned Persons in South Africa* (London: IDAF, 1978). Amnesty International has also published surveys of imprisonment and torture in many countries, including South Africa: Amnesty International, *Political Imprisonment in South Africa* (London: Amnesty International, 1978).

73. Amnesty International did not found chapters in South Africa until the early 1990s.

74. Anthony W. Marx, *Lessons of Struggle: South African Internal Opposition, 1960–1990* (New York: Oxford University Press, 1992), 110–15.

75. A key source on and by the Detainees' Parents Support Committee (DPSC) is *Crime against Humanity: Analysing the Repression of the Apartheid State*, ed. Max Coleman (Johannesburg: Human Rights Committee, 1998).

76. *DesCom Newsletter* 2 (January 13, 1982).

77. Ad Hoc Detention Action Committee (ADAC) report, n.d., WHP AG 2523 P1.1.1 Two predecessors were both partly or wholly under regime influence: the Prisoners Support Trust and the South African Prison Education Trust. See Mayibuye Archives MCH 121-1: Mac Maharaj Security Files, ch. 3, subchapter M, n.p.

78. Jeremy Seekings, *The UDF: A History of the United Democratic Front in South Africa, 1983–1991* (Athens: Ohio University Press, 2000).

79. Draft commentary for *Johannsburg Star*, November 4, 1987. DPSC Papers, WHP AG 2523 M1.10.

80. Accounts in F. Stuart Ross, *Smashing H-Block: The Rise and Fall of the Popular Campaign against Criminalization, 1976–1982* (Liverpool: Liverpool University Press, 2011), ch. 6; and in Denis O'Hearn, *Bobby Sands: Nothing but an Unfinished Song* (London: Pluto Press, 2006), 352.

81. David Bereford, *Ten Men Dead: The Story of the 1981 Irish Hunger Strike* (London: Pluto, 1987), 82.

82. Aran Molloy, "Remembering 1981: Francie Molloy on the Bobby Sands Election Campaign," *An Poblacht*, April 13, 2006.

83. Quoted in Thomas Hennessey, *Hunger Strike: Margaret Thatcher's Battle with the IRA, 1980–81* (Kildare: Irish Academic Press, 2014), 167.
84. Quoted in Hennessey, *Hunger Strike*, 169.
85. Richard English, *Armed Struggle: The History of the IRA* (Oxford: Oxford University Press, 2003), 200.
86. O'Hearn, *Bobby Sands: Nothing but an Unfinished Song*, 356.
87. IRA prisoners could still stand for election in Ireland, as some did.
88. English, *Armed Struggle*, 204.
89. Chris Ryder, *Inside the Maze: The Untold Story of the Northern Ireland Prison Service* (London: Methuen, 2001), 301.
90. Micheál Mac Giolla Ghunna, "Cultural Struggle and a Drama Project," in *Writing as Resistance: The Journal of Prisoners on Prison Anthology (1988–2002)*, ed. Robert Gaucher (Toronto: Canadian Scholars' Press, 2002), 72; Laurence McKeown, *Out of Time: Irish Republican Prisoners, Long Kesh 1972–2000* (Belfast: Beyond the Pale, 2001), 209–10.

Chapter 6

1. Adam Grzymała-Siedlecki, quoted in Regina Domańska, *Pawiak—kaźń i heroizm* (Warsaw: Książka i Wiedza, 1988), 110.
2. Appeal decision, Supreme Court of South Africa, September 9, 1966. Violet Weinberg papers, SAHA, 9.
3. Zdzisław Jędrzejewicz, "Dziennik z lat 1945–50," Ośrodek Karta, AO CzP 234w, 19.
4. Kieran McEvoy, *Paramilitary Imprisonment in Northern Ireland* (Oxford: Oxford University Press, 2001), 39, n22.
5. See Marek Kaminski, *Games Prisoners Play* (Princeton, NJ: Princeton University Press, 2004).
6. Stokowski, "Dziennik pisany w pamięci. 758 dni," Ośrodek Karta, AO CzP 193w, 17–18.
7. Thus Adam Michnik, pressed in an interview several years after the end of communist rule to explain how he not only wrote and published essays from within the prison of the secret police but even gave an interview, declined: "You never know what yet might happen in my life." Adam Michnik, Józef Tischner, and Jacek Żakowski, *Między panem a plebanem* (Kraków: Znak, 1998), 429.
8. Bronisław Pluciński to F. Himmenfarb, c. October 13, 1902. *Listy nieprawomyślne. Wybór z akt Warszawskiego Gubernialnego Zarządu Żandarmerii, 1886–1914*, ed. Małgorzata Pleskaczyńska (Warsaw: Akademia Nauk Społecznych PZPR, 1989), 139–40.
9. Kłosowicz, survey response in AAN 34/III-1, 67–68; see also Stanisław Bobrowski's account in AAN 34/III-1, 8–10. Zygmunt Heryng, "X Pawilon przed pięćdziesięciu laty," in Aleksander Kozłowski and Henryk J. Mościcki, eds. *Pamiętnik X Pawilonu* (Warsaw: Wydawnictwo Ministerstwa Obrony Narodowej, 1958), 118–20. For a later example, see a 1943 *gryps* in AAN 212/I/13, 28–30. The 5x5 code is specific to prisons, while prisoners with backgrounds in the military or scouting might bring in knowledge of Morse code. Zdzisław Jędrzejewicz makes this point in "Dziennik z lat 1945–50," Ośrodek Karta, AO CzP 234w; see also Tadeusz Wolsza, *W cieniu Wronek, Jaworzna i Piechcina . . . 1944–1956. Życie codzienne w polskich więzieniach, obozach i ośrodkach pracy więźniów* (Warsaw: Instytut Historii PAN, 2003), 98–100.
10. Sławek, "W Cytadeli Warszawskiej," *Za kratami więzień i drutami obozów. Wspomnienia i notatki więźniów*, vol. 1 (Warsaw: Komitet Organizacyjny Zjazdu b. Więźniów Ideowych z lat 1914–1921, 1927), 48.
11. On the use of and struggles over the toilet, see Stokowski, "Dziennik pisany w pamięci," 16–17; Domańska, *Pawiak—Kaźń i heroizm*, 315–16; Natoo Babenia, *Memoirs of a Saboteur* (Cape Town: Mayibuye, 1995), 121; Feliks Koń, "Ze wspomnień," in *Pamiętnik X Pawilonu*, ed. Aleksander Kozłowski and Henryk J. Mościcki (Warsaw: Wydawnictwo Ministerstwa Obrony Narodowej, 1958), 159–60.
12. On the body and its messages, see Maud Ellmann, *The Hunger Artists: Starving, Writing, and Imprisonment* (Cambridge, MA: Harvard University Press, 1993), 84–85; she cites in particular David Beresford, *Ten Men Dead: The Story of the 1981 Irish Hunger Strike* (New York: Atlantic Monthly Press, 1989).

13. Maria Czernikowa, "Halina Sadowska," *Nike* 19 (January 1995), 27–28; Wolsza, *W cieniu,* 100; see also Urke Nachalnik, *Życiorys własny przestępcy* (Łódź: Wydawnictwo Łódzkie, 1989).

14. Irena Cieślińska-Skrzypiec, "Inowrocław. Długie miesiące—ciężkie lata . . ." *Nike* 6 (June 1993), 8.

15. Małgorzata Szejnert, *Śród żywych duchów* (London: Aneks, 1990), 5; Anna Muller, "If the Walls Could Talk: Women Political Prisoners in Stalinist Poland, 1945–1956," PhD diss., Indiana University, 2010, ch. 4

16. Marek Kulczyk, "Wspomnienia," Ośrodek Karta, AO II/380, 17–18.

17. Chris Ryder, *Inside the Maze: The Untold Story of the Northern Ireland Prison Service* (London: Methuen, 2001), 252.

18. James Gregory, *Goodbye Bafana, Nelson Mandela: My Prisoner, My Friend* (London: Headline, 1995). Language could reflect class. To learn Xhosa or Irish could seem demeaning to a guard; conversely, poorly educated guards might not know foreign languages. When Andrzej Sołdrowski and his cellmates practiced English, writing with matchsticks on their soup bowls (which they first smeared with soap and sprinkled with tooth powder), a watchful guard interrupted them: "It is not allowed in the cell to speak to one another in unintelligible words." Sołdrowski, *Spisani na straty* (Wrocław: Nortom, 1996), 74.

19. AAN MSW 1176, k. 190.

20. *Gryps* in Regina Domańska, *Pawiak—kaźń i heroizm,* 249–50. Metelski added some urgent advice: "Don't be afraid of interrogation, just don't allow them to link you to anything, and you know nothing about others because you were working the whole time."

21. Szejnert, *Śród żywych duchów,* 67.

22. Sołdrowski, *Spisani na straty,* 54. See also Wolsza, *W cieniu,* 86–89 and 93, on Masses and Catholic ritual in the Stalinist prison.

23. AAN 34/III-1, k. 162.

24. Sowińska, "Gorzkie lata," Biblioteka Narodowa ms. 14257, 154–55.

25. Aleksander Ringman, "Z Zag, więzienia i emigracji," *Niepodległość* 4:2 (1931), 278.

26. Ngxiki, in Jan K. Coetzee, *Plain Tales from Robben Island* (Pretoria: Van Schalk, 2000), 84–86. Even guards in Polish Stalinist prisons would take messages outside, collecting fees for their service at both ends. Wolsza, *W cieniu,* 43.

27. Tomasz Rostworowski, *Zaraz po wojnie. Wspomnienia duszpasterza (1945–1956)* (Paris: Spotkania, 1986), 110–13.

28. Domańska, *Pawiak—kaźń i heroizm,* 133.

29. Leon Wanat, *Za murami Pawiaka,* 4th ed. (Warsaw: Książka i Wiedza, 1967), 265–68 (quote on 267); 286–90.

30. Wanat, *Za murami Pawiaka,* 288.

31. Wanat, *Za murami Pawiaka,* 285–86.

32. Wanat, *Za murami Pawiaka,* 206.

33. Stanisław Miedza-Tomaszewski, *Benefis konspiratora. Umarłem, aby żyć* (Warsaw: Krajowa Agencja Wydawnicza, 1985), 80–92; Wanat, *Za murami Pawiaka,* 226.

34. Franciszek Wojciechowski, *Polska Niepodległa. Organizacja konspiracyjna* (Warsaw: Adiutor, 1996), 194–97.

35. Wanat, *Za murami Pawiaka,* 292–94.

36. Wanat, *Za murami Pawiaka,* 223.

37. Domańska, *Pawiak—kaźń i* heroizm, 225–26. She calls the *gryps* a "bridge over the walls."

38. Letter, Orpen to Under Colonial Secretary, October 10, 1901 and January 10, 1902. WCPA CO 2358, Ref Folio 1615, v. 5, n.p.

39. Letters, Prisoner JC Strydom, PJ Perold, Assistant Resident Magistrate Orpen, Under Colonial Secretary HB Showe, December 1901–February 1902, WCPA CO 2358 and 2359, ref folio 1615, vv. 5–6, n.p. The theme of "prayer" as a metaphor for community appears on Robben Island seventy years later, to describe communal reading of newspapers. Mosibudi Mangena, *On Your Own: The Evolution of Black Consciousness in South Africa/Azania* (Florida Hills, SA: Vivlia, 1989), 86.

40. See Antoni Lange's recollections from Warsaw, 1907, in "Wspomnienia więzienne," *Niepodległość* 4:1 (1932), 289–91; and Robert E. Blobaum, "Under Lock and Key? Prisons

and Prison Conditions in Russian Poland, 1906–1914," *Społeczeństwo w dobie przemian. Wiek XIX i XX. Księga jubileuszowa profesor Anny Żarnowskiej*, ed. Maria Nietyksza et al. (Warsaw: DiG, 2003).

41. Jonathan Hyslop, "The Invention of the Concentration Camp: Cuba, Southern Africa and the Philippines, 1896–1907," *South African Historical Journal* 63:2 (June 2011), 251–76; Klaus Mühlhahn, "The Concentration Camp in Global History," *History Compass* 8:6 (2010), 543–61.

42. Linda Colley notes that Mysore authorities during the Anglo-Mysore wars of the late eighteenth century broke up British captured soldiers and officers into smaller groups, in a "deliberate assault on the cohesion of those British individuals experiencing it." Colley, *Captives: Britain, Empire, and the World, 1600–1850* (New York: Pimlico, 2002), 282. See also similar tactics in the American War of Independence; Colley, *Captives*, 210.

43. Nikolaus Wachsmann, *KL: A History of the Nazi Concentration Camps* (New York: Farrar, Straus and Giroux, 2015).

44. See, for example, Isabel Hull, *Absolute Destruction: Military Culture and the Practices of War in Imperial Germany* (Ithaca, NY: Cornell University Press, 2004).

45. Letter to Governor, Reading Prison, February 1, 1919, NAB HO 144/1496/362269.

46. Heather Jones, "The Prisoner of War Camp, the Modern State and the Radicalization of Captivity, 1914–1918," unpublished manuscript in author's possession; see Jones, *Violence against Prisoners of War in the First World War: Britain, France and Germany, 1914–1920* (Cambridge: Cambridge University Press, 2011); Alan Kramer, "Prisoners in the First World War," in *Prisoners in War*, ed. Sibylle Scheipers (Oxford: Oxford University Press, 2010).

47. On Frongoch, see Lyn Ebenezer, *Frongoch and the Birth of the IRA* (Llanwrst, Wales: Gwasg Carreg Gwalch, 2006); Sean O Mahony, *Frongoch: University of Revolution* (Dublin: Teoranta, 1987); Seán McConville, *Irish Political Prisoners, 1848–1922: Theatres of War* (London: Routledge, 2003), 466–80.

48. S. B. Spies, *Methods of Barbarism? Roberts and Kitchener and Civilians in the Boer Republics, January 1900–May 1902* (Johannesburg: Human & Rousseau, 1977); Wim Hopford, *Twice Interned: Transvaal 1901–12, Germany 1914–18* (London: John Murray, 1919).

49. For example, "Notice No. 2," prepared by Heygate-Lambert in early June, in NAB HO 144/1455/313106/8; and Lambert memo to Secretary of State, July 20, 1916, in HO 144/1455/313106/222. W. J. Brennan Whitmore, *With the Irish in Frongoch* (Dublin: Talbot Press, 1917), 1, 23, 49.

50. Brennan Whitmore, *With the Irish*, 23.

51. Brennan Whitmore, *With the Irish*, 54.

52. Brennan Whitmore, *With the Irish*, 32.

53. Brennan Whitmore, *With the Irish*, 33; see also 37.

54. Irish revolutionary Roger Casement made a futile attempt to convince Irish soldiers in the British Army interned by the Germans at Limburg to form a fighting unit to liberate Ireland. Andreas Roth, "'The German Soldier Is not Tactful': Sir Roger Casement and the Irish Brigade in Germany during the First World War," in *The Irish Sword. The Journal of the Military History Society of Ireland* 19:78 (Winter 1995). NAB WO 141/9, WO 141/15 and WO 141/49. I am grateful to Heather Jones for bringing this episode to my attention.

55. See Irena Homola-Skąpska, "Polska prasa w obozach jenieckich we Włoszech w czasach I wojny światowej," *Rocznik history prasy polskiej* XIII (2010), nr. 1–2.

56. See Włodzimierz Suleja, *Józef Piłsudski* (Wrocław: Zakład Narodowy im. Ossolińskich, 1995).

57. Ludwik Dudziński, *Ofiarny stos. Dziennik legionisty* (Kalisz: Kaliskie Towarzystwo Przyjaciół Nauk, 2006), 51.

58. Jan Snopko, *Finał epopei Legionów Polskich 1916–1918* (Białystok: Wydawnictwo Uniwersytetu w Białymstoku, 2008), 224–25.

59. Dudziński, *Ofiarny stos,* 82.

60. Dudziński, *Ofiarny stos,* 83.

61. Dudziński, *Ofiarny stos,* 111.

62. See, for example, Michał Tadeusz Brzęk-Osiński, *Ze wspomnień legionisty i piłsudczyka, 1905–1939* (Warsaw: Rytm, 2003), 146.

63. Brzęk-Osiński, *Ze wspomnień legionisty,* 154.

64. Snopko, *Finał epopei,* 231; Brzęk-Osiński, *Ze wspomnień legionisty,* 155.

65. House of Commons debate July 26, 1916, *Hansard's Parliamentary Debates,* vol. 84 (1916), column 1765.

66. Szczypiorno's fame lived on long after the camp was forgotten: sports journalists still refer to players of handball as "szczypiorniści." Whether the Poles learned this game from German guards or from POWs from other countries, the accepted legend is that Poles first played the game in the camp.

67. See, for example, "Przemówienie na Zjeździe Legionistów w Kaliszu," August 7, 1927, in Piłsudski, *Pisma zbiorowe,* vol. 9 (Warsaw: Krajowa Agencja Wydawnicza, 1937), 78–92.

68. Helena Zatorska, *Marian Buczek* (Warsaw: Iskry, 1980).

69. Widlicki also imagined that the bedbugs keeping him awake were blades of grass tickling him in a meadow. Quoted in Domańska, *Pawiak—kaźń i heroizm,* 282.

70. "Back to Normal after the Emergency," *Johannesburg Star,* August 31, 1960, 1, 9.

71. Baruch Hirson, *Revolutions in My Life* (Johannesburg: Witwatersrand University Press, 1995), 141. Hirson was imprisoned 1964–73.

72. Their experiences are almost absent in South African memory today. One rare volume, *Agter Tralies en Doringdraad* (Pretoria: Die Bond van Oud-Geinterneerdes en Politieke Gevangenes, 1953), collected memories of the camps. I am indebted to my colleague Betsi Grabe for reading and summarizing this book for me.

73. Report from Commanding Officer, RI to Commissioner of Prisons JC Steyn, February 9, 1973. CSA, Pretoria. 1/3/6: Dissipline en Beheer, Klagte en Vertoë, Deel 4, n.p. A more important model for black South African prisoners would have been the training camps (in exile) of *Umkhonto we Sizwe,* the armed wing of the African National Congress.

74. Jan Snopko, "Szczypiorno 1917—drugie Santo Domingo?," *Dzieje najnowsze* 40:4 (2008), 41; Ebenezer, *Frongoch,* ch. 11; John McGuffin, *Internment* (Tralee: Anvil, 1973), 26–28.

75. On British prisoner terminology: Michael Tatham (British Ambassador to Ireland), telegram 310 to FCO, August 27, 1981. NAB FCO 87/1263.

76. McConville, *Irish Political Prisoners, 1848–1922,* 715.

77. Emmet Humphreys, memoir, UCD P106/648, 124–27; McConville, *Irish Political Prisoners, 1848–1922,* 763–64.

78. On the camp and the POW in the twentieth century: Sibylle Scheipers, "Introduction: Prisoners in War," in *Prisoners in War,* 1–20; Joël Kotek and Pierre Rigoulot, *Le siècle des camps: Detention, Concentration, extermination: cent ans de mal radical* (Paris: Lattes, 2000).

79. Frank Gallagher, diary entries for January 6–7, 1923, NLI 18356(2). See also *The Trumpeter,* prisoner's handwritten newspaper, n.d. [1922], NLI ms. 21121.

80. O'Brennan diary, UCD P13/1. Most of these women would have served in Cumann na mBan, Sinn Féin's auxiliary women's paramilitary organization.

81. J. J. Layng, letters to Military Governor Sean Hayes, November 21 and 30, 1922. IMA, CW/P/10/01. See also Emmet Humphreys memoir of Gormanstown Camp's "military police," UCD P106/648, 225–26. At Newbridge, prisoners were parading so much that one military governor was forced to arrange to count prisoners in their rooms. Notice posted at Newbridge, Curragh, July 4, 1923. IMA, CW/P/10/01, n.p.

82. Letter, O/C Tomas MacM to Governor, Newbridge Military Barracks, February 17, 1923. IMA, CW/P/10/01, n.p. Similarly, Frank Aiken instructed all internees at Tintown, via an order read out in each hut, not to sign the "Form of Understanding" that the regime was pressing on its captives. Letter from Director of Intelligence, GHQ, to Minister of Defence, August 21, 1923, IMA, CW/P/02/01/02, n.p.

83. Krzysztof Pol, "Sylwetki wybitnych adwokatów. Adwokaci warszawcy w Cytadeli 1905–10," *Adwokatura. Strony adwokatury polskiej,* http://web.archive.org/web/20071128011015/ http://www.adwokatura.pl/aktualnosci_sylwetkicytadela_91003.htm (last accessed June 10, 2013).

84. Sempołowska, memo to Minister of Justice Bronisław Sobolewski, in Andrzej Ajnenkiel, "Memoriały Stefanii Sempołowskiej dotyczące położenia więźniów politycznych w Polsce w 1920 i 1922r.," *Teki archiwalne* 6 (1959), 16–17.

85. Gustaw Daniłowski, *Wrażenia więzienne* (Lwów: Bernard Połoniecki, 1908), 74–75.

86. Jan Kwapiński, *Moje wspomnienia 1904–1939* (Paris: Księgarnia Polska, 1965), 76–77. See also Daniłowski, *Wrażenia*, 76, on reluctance to admit criminal prisoners to the *komuna*.

87. Ludwik Śledziński, "Przejścia więzienne w Łowiczu i w Warszawie (rok 1906–1907)," *Niepodległość* 2:2 (1930), 255–56. More examples of the pre-war *komuna*: Zdzisław Dębicki, *Grzechy młodości* (Warsaw: Trzaska, Evert, i Michalski, 1930), 33; Jan Krzesławski, "Więzienie w Ratuszu za rządów Nazarowa," *Kronika Ruchu Rewolucyjnego* 1:2 (1935), 93–94.

88. *Gryps* December 15, 1927, MN 2801. See also *gryps* MN 2096.

89. "Regulamin więźniów politycznych więzienia," 1933. In *Korespondencja i notatki więźniów politycznych. Katalog zbiorów Muzeum Historii Polskiego Ruchu Politycznego*, ed. Alina Gabara and Anna Dymek (Warsaw: Muzeum Historii Polskiego Ruchu Rewolucyjnego, 1964), 171.

90. Undated *gryps* [1927–28], MN 4446. Bohun calls the proposed structure a "Department of Distribution and Management" (*Wydział Aprowizacyjno-Gospodarczy*).

91. Białystok Prison *komuna*, *gryps* October 18, 1927. MN 2474. For a letter by an excluded prisoner asking to be returned to the *komuna*, see *gryps* from Ludwik Kołasiński to "prison comrades," Piotrków Prison, April 7, 1938. MN 3929.

92. See, for example, *gryps*, Białystok Prison, December 26, 1926, MN 2096; and *gryps* from collective of cell elders, n.d. (December 1926), MN 2838. Also Krzysztof Urbański, *System penitencjarny II Rzeczypospolitej a więźniowie polityczni (na przykładzie województwa kieleckiego)* (Kielce: Kieleckie Towarzystwo Naukowe, 1997), 125.

93. *Gryps* May 4, 1927, Białystok Prison. MN 2199 Xa.

94. Secretariat, Red Help Central Committee, to all *komunas* and all political prisoners, June 1928. AAN MSW Mf 25749, kk. 29–30. Also Franciszka Świetlikowa, "Więźniowie polityczni 'Mokotowa' w latach 1918–1939," *Z pola walki* 15:2 (1972), 273; and Białystok Prison *grypsy*, August 1927, MN 2442 and MN 2881.

95. Circular on prison tactics, n.d. [c. 1936], AAN MSW Mf 25749, kk. 123–24. Resolutions of the First National Conference of Economic Sections of Red Help in Poland, June 1936, AAN 175/I-1, kk. 14–19.

96. Barbara Ochinowska, "Nauczycielka," *Nike* 43 (May–June 1998), 12–13.

97. Aleksander Solzhenitsyn, *The Gulag Archipelago: An Experiment in Literary Investigation* (New York: Harper & Row, 1974), part IV; Elżbieta Kaczyńska, *Syberia. Największe więzienie świata* (Warsaw: Gryf, 1991), chs. 8–9.

98. On Soviet and Nazi camps: Steven Barnes, *Death and Redemption: The Gulag and the Shaping of Soviet Society* (Princeton, NJ: Princeton University Press, 2011); Wolfgang Solsky, *The Order of Terror: The Concentration Camp*, trans. William Templer (Princeton, NJ: Princeton University Press, 1997).

Chapter 7

1. Jan Kwapiński, *Moje wspomnienia 1904–1939* (Paris: Księgarnia Polska, 1965), 75–76.

2. Regina Mikulska z d. Ostojska, "Autobiogram," *Nike* 52 (2000), 14.

3. Leon Wanat, *Za murami Pawiaka*, 4th ed. (Warsaw: Książka i Wiedza, 1967), 369.

4. See W. J. Brennan Whitmore, *With the Irish in Frongoch* (Dublin: Talbot Press, 1917), 82–89, for one such effort to evade identification, by a prisoner suspected of having deserted.

5. Journal entry for January 8, 1932, Humphreys Papers UCD P106/1096.

6. Cieślińska-Skrzypiec, "Inowrocław. Długie miesiące, ciężkie lata . . ." *Nike* 6 (1993), 13.

7. Hugh Lewin, *Bandiet: Out of Jail* (Johannesburg: Random House, 2002), 164.

8. Regina Domańska, *Pawiak—kaźń i heroizm* (Warsaw: Książka i Wiedza, 1988), 139–40.

9. Bill Kissane, *The Politics of the Irish Civil War* (Oxford: Oxford University Press, 2005), 87–92.

10. Wanat, *Za murami*, 236–38.

11. Mateusz Wyrwich, *W celi śmierci* (Warsaw: Rytm, 2012), 133–41; Stanisław Harasymiuk, "Zofia Wilczyńska-Wlizło," *Nike* 29 (1996), 16.

12. Feliks Kon, "Ze wspomnień," in *Pamiętnik X Pawilonu*, ed. Aleksander Kozłowski and Henryk J. Mościcki (Warsaw: Wydawnictwo Ministerstwa Obrony Narodowej, 1958), 218.

13. Lewin, *Bandiet*, 185–92; quotes on 189 and 187.

14. There are numerous examples in the memoirs of czarist Russia and Stalinist Poland, as well as in Nazi prisons.

15. Krzesławski, "Więzienie w ratuszu za rządów Nazarowa," *Kronika Ruchu Rewolucyjnego* 1:2 (1935), 85.

16. Ludwik Śledziński, "Przejścia więzienne w Łowiczu i w Warszawie," *Niepodległość* 2:1 (1930), 122–23. See also Franciszek Mrozowski, "Z przeżyć więziennych w Warszawie," *Niepodległość* 6:3 (1932), 380–81.

17. Kazimierz Pietkiewicz, "Zarząd X Pawilonu Cytadeli Warszawskiej," *Niepodległość* 5:3 (1932), 458–59.

18. Wiesław Chrzanowski, *Pół wieku polityki, czyli rzecz o obronie czynnej*, ed. Piotr Mierecki and Bogusław Kiernicki (Warsaw: ad astra, 1997), 221.

19. Prison Management Committee, meeting minutes January–February 1977, PRONI NIO 10/2/5, n.p.

20. John Nkadimeng, interview by Julie Friederikse. Friederikse papers, SAHA AL 2460, 26.

21. Marek Kulczyk, "Wspomnienia," Ośrodek Karta, AO II/380, 36–37; quote on 45.

22. Jacek Kuroń, *Wiara i wina. Do i od komunizmu* (London: Aneks, 1989), 237–38.

23. Kuroń, *Wiara i wina*, 294–95. Andrzej Friszke, *Anatomia buntu. Kuroń, Modzelewski i komandosi* (Kraków: Znak, 2010), 666–68.

24. Sadowska, "Raport Barbary Sadowskiej," *Niepodległość i pamięć* 4:1 (1997), 171.

25. Halina Waszczuk-Bazylewska, "Od WW-72 do 'Liceum,'" *Niepodległość i pamięć* 4:1 (1997), 159.

26. Sadowska, "Raport Barbary Sadowskiej," 172.

27. Seán McConville, *Irish Political Prisoners, 1848–1922: Theatres of War* (London: Routledge, 2003), 518–21, quote 520–21.

28. Interviews by Kieran McEvoy, *Paramilitary Imprisonment in Northern Ireland* (Oxford: Oxford University Press, 2001), 163.

29. Mandela, letter January 1970. ANC Papers, WHP AG 2510 e 3.4.1, pp. 1–2, 7.

30. Report from Commanding Officer, Robben Island to Commissioner of Prisons J. C. Steyn, February 9, 1973. CSA, Pretoria, 1/3/6: Dissipline en Beheer. Klagte en Vertoë. Deel 4.

31. Mac Maharaj, in Maharaj, ed., *Reflections in Prison* (Cape Town: Penguin, 2001), 5.

32. *Więzienia polityczne w Rosyi* (Kraków: Latarnia, 1903), 7. Emphasis in original.

33. Frequent examples can be found during the Irish Civil War: for example, Tintown Camp, April 1923, IMA CW/P/08/05, n.p.; Newbridge Prison, September–November 1922, IMA CW/P/10/01-02, n.p.; Mountjoy Prison, April 11, 1922, NAI H8/79. Examples from Polish socialists in the Russian Empire have been cited elsewhere.

34. Neville Alexander, *Robben Island Prison Dossier, 1964–1974* (Rondebosch, South Africa: University of Cape Town Press, 1994), 38–39; on the conflict over short pants, see also Disciplinary Hearing, Robben Island, February 5, 1970. CSA, 1/3/8: Dissipline en Beheer. Departementele Verhore deur Offisiere en Hersiening van Sake. Deel 2, n.p.

35. Wanat, *Za murami*, 34.

36. Undated report [c. January 1936], Sighle Humphreys papers, UCD P106/1316, n.p. Seán McConville, *Irish Political Prisoners, 1920–1962*, 300–302.

37. McEvoy, *Paramilitary*, 86; Chris Ryder, *Inside the Maze: The Untold Story of the Northern Ireland Prison Service* (London: Methuen, 2001), 252; Sighle Humphreys, Mountjoy journal entry December 22, 1931, Humphreys Papers UCD P106/1096.

38. Adam Stanowski, Akta kontrolno-śledcze, IPN BU 0259/579, t. 2, k. 56.

39. Jacobo Timerman, *Prisoner without a Name, Cell without a Number* (Madison: University of Wisconsin Press, 2002), 40–41.

40. "Okólnik w sprawie kampanji kongresowej," August 1932, AAN 175/I-5, kk. 9-9a.

41. See, for example, Walery Sławek's account of an escape from Sieradz Prison in 1903: Sławek, *Ku wolności. Karta z życia* (Warsaw: Drukarnia Mazowiecka, 1933), 13–14.

42. The Earl of Longford and Thomas P. O'Neill, *Eamon de Valera* (London: Hutchinson, 1970), 59. See also McConville, *Irish Political Prisoners 1848–1922*, 517–18, 531–35.

43. Cumann na mBan statement, November 6, 1922, Sighle Humphreys papers, UCD P106/1056, n.p.; McConville, *Irish Political Prisoners, 1920–1962: Pilgrimage of Desolation* (Abingdon: Routledge, 2014), 188. A similar example from 1928: Leaflet, "Hunger Strikes of Republican Women in Mountjoy jail," Sighle Humphreys papers, UCD P106/1094, n.p.

44. For example, Ministerstwo Sprawiedliwości, memo to state prosecutors, April 7, 1927, AAN Prokuratora przy Sądzie Apelacyjnym w Katowicach, 361/2, k. 142; Mysłowice prison head, letter November 12, 1927, AAN 261/2, k. 181; *gryps*, Białystok Prison, 1927, MN 2671 Xa.
45. "Sekretariat, KC CzP do Zarządu Komun Więźniów Politycznych," June 1928. AAN MSW Mf 25749 (sygn 1176), kk. 31–33. See similar arguments in a *gryps* in Białystok Prison, August 1928. MN 4438.
46. MOPR Central Committee, "List do więzień," October 18, 1931. AAN MSW Mf 25749 (sygn 1176), kk. 69–71. Also memos from September 1931, in AAN 362/II, kk. 145–46; and, from c. 1936, AAN MSW Mf 25749 (sygn 1176), k. 123.
47. MOPR Central Committee, Letter to Zarząd Komuny Grudziądz, November 21, 1933. AAN MSW Mf 25749 (sygn 1176), k. 92.
48. *Gryps* from Sandomierz Prison, May 1936, MN 4249.
49. *Gryps* from Kielce Prison, MN 3314. On Sandomierz, see also a *gryps* from 1934, MN 2921. A *przeplatanka* in nearby Radom is discussed in *Biuletyn Informacyjny KCCzP w Polsce*, 8 (March 1934), AAN 175/I-16, k. 6.
50. AAN 363/I, kk. 80–81. Thanks to Mirosława Pałaszewska for finding this document.
51. Caesarina Makhoere, *No Child's Play: In Prison under Apartheid* (London: Women's Press, 1988), 30–47.
52. Kulczyk, "Wspomnienia," 3–4, 26, 45; also Zbigniew Kamiński, "Raptularz internowanego," Ośrodek Karta, AO CzP113dz, 34–5.
53. Minutes of the Prison Management Committee meetings, in PRONI, NIO 10/2/5, n.p.
54. Leo Kuper, *Passive Resistance in South Africa* (New Haven, CT: Yale University Press, 1957), 103; a history of the campaign is on pp. 122–45.
55. Julia C. Wells, *We Now Demand! The History of Women's Resistance to Pass Laws in South Africa* (Johannesburg: Witwatersrand University Press, 1993), 120–21.
56. Wells, *We Now Demand!*, 122.
57. Zoe A. Colley, *Ain't Scared of Your Jail: Arrest, Imprisonment, and the Civil Rights Movement* (Gainesville: University Press of Florida, 2012), 29–30.
58. Padraic Kenney, *A Carnival of Revolution: Central Europe, 1989* (Princeton, NJ: Princeton University Press, 2002), ch. 5.
59. Documents in Prokuratura Sądu Apelacyjnego, AAN 359.
60. Lt. Gen. Martinus Brink, affidavit (n.d.), Prison Archive, Pretoria, 1/3/2/1: Dissipline en Beheer. Afsondering. Deel 2, n.p.
61. Makhoere affidavit, n.d., Prison Archive, Pretoria, 1/3/2/1: Dissipline en Beheer. Afsondering. Deel 2, n.p. See also Suzman Papers, WHP A2084 Ab 1.3, file 1.
62. Makhoere, *No Child's Play*, 59, referring to a punishment of sixty days on "spare diet."
63. Gerry Adams, *Cage Eleven* (Dingle: Brandon, 1990), 138–44.
64. Jerzy Stokowski, "Dziennik pisany w pamięci. 758 dni," 15–16. Ośrodek Karta, AO CzP193w.
65. Nelson Mandela, *Long Walk to Freedom* (London: Abacus, 1994), 39–40.
66. See, for example, Medical Officer's notes on Mary Leigh and Gladys Evans, NAI, GPB Suffragettes, Box 1, Folder C, n.p. Prison-issue mugs, Sighle Humphreys and Maire Comerford found in 1923, were also good for breaking windows. Chief Wardress, Mountjoy Prison, report March 26, 1923, NAI, H170/113.
67. Examples from Mountjoy Prison: GPB Minutes, September 20 and 21, 1917, NAI GPB DORA Box 1, n.p.; Tim Carey, *Mountjoy: The Story of a Prison* (Cork: Collins, 2000), 184–85, 198. Kilmainham Gaol and Curragh Camp: Letter from Director of Organization to Commander in Chief, September 12, 1922, IMA, CW/P/02/01/05, n.p.; Longford and O'Neill, *Eamon de Valera*, 59.
68. *Gryps* from Białystok Prison, 1926, MN 2841. Reprinted in *Korespondencja i notatki więźniów politycznych. Katalog zbiorów Muzeum Historii Polskiego Ruchu Politycznego*, ed. Alina Gabara and Anna Dymek (Warsaw: Muzeum Historii Polskiego Ruchu Rewolucyjnego, 1964), plates 12–13. Serbia was the women's section of Pawiak Prison.
69. On destruction generally, see letter from Director of Organization to Commander in Chief, September 12, 1922, IMA, CW/P/02/01/05, n.p.; Carey, *Mountjoy*, 198. For a contemporary example from Będzin Prison, Poland: *Więzień polityczny* 10 (1926), 6–7.

70. Solidarity internees in Poland sometimes attacked guards or barricaded themselves in their cells but did not engage in mass cell destruction. One incident of burning mattresses in Uherce in April 1982 is considered to have been a security police provocation. Marek Żukowski, *Ośrodki odosobnienia w Polsce latach 1981–1982* (Warsaw: Trio, 2013), 444–45.

71. Kieran McEvoy observes an analogy between these "self-governed communities" and the "no-go" areas in Northern Ireland's cities. McEvoy, *Paramilitary*, 218–19.

72. Adams, *Cage Eleven*, 28; McEvoy, *Paramilitary*, 122.

73. Ed Moloney, *Voices from the Grave: Two Men's War in Ireland* (New York: Public Affairs, 2010); McEvoy, *Paramilitary*, 121–23.

74. McEvoy, *Paramilitary*, 123.

75. McEvoy, *Paramilitary*, 56; J. Bowyer Bell, *The Irish Troubles: A Generation of Violence, 1967–1992* (New York: St. Martin's Press, 1993), 427. Secretary of State for Northern Ireland Merlyn Rees did report "an early attempt . . . to storm the main gate" during the mayhem. House of Commons debate, October 30, 1974, *Hansard's Parliamentary Debates*, volume 880, col. 212.

76. See Gerry Adams's lightly fictionalized account in *Cage Eleven*, 28–32.

77. Jeremiah O'Donovan Rossa, *Irish Rebels in English Prisons*, ed. Sean Ua Cearnaigh (Tralee: Anvil, 1967), 83–84, 298; quote at 84. It is not clear that O'Donovan Rossa is actually naked. He describes being forced to remove his "shirt and stockings," but does not mention undershorts when he says he stands "quite naked." Regardless, he manipulates ideas of shame and impropriety just as he does with physical brutality.

78. Antoni Lange, "Wspomnienia więzienne," *Niepodległość* 3:2 (1932), 293–94.

79. "An Irish Priest" [Piaras Béaslaí], *In Maryboro' and Mountjoy: The Prison Experiences and Prison-Breaking of an Irish Volunteer (Padraic Fleming)*, n.d., n.p., 14. Fleming did dress to receive a visit from his mother, but they abruptly terminated their conversation when forbidden to discuss his treatment.

80. Quoted in Patrick Bishop and Eamonn Mallie, *The Provisional IRA* (London: Heinemann), 279.

81. Tim Pat Coogan, *On the Blanket: The Inside Story of the IRA Prisoners' 'Dirty' Protest* (New York: St. Martiin's Press, 2002), 95.

82. Campbell et al., *Nor Meekly Serve My Time*, ch. 1.

83. Campbell et al., *Nor Meekly*, 12, 16.

84. Campbell et al., *Nor Meekly*, 17. Ned Flynn (in Campbell et al., *Nor Meekly*, 11) reports that one prisoner attended Mass naked.

85. Quoted in Bishop and Mallie, *The Provisional IRA*.

86. Jaz McCann, in Campbell et al., *Nor Meekly,* 26, 28–29.

87. One possible factor in the decision to escalate, though omitted in the memoirs, was that some Loyalists had also refused the prison uniform and "gone on the blanket." Colin Crawford, *Defenders or Criminals? Loyalist Prisoners and Criminalisation* (Belfast: Blackstaff, 1999), 55; Ryder, *Inside the Maze*, 160; Tim Coogan, *On the Blanket*, 194–98. Loyalism—allegiance to a British Ulster, opposed not to the state but to the republican movement—was difficult to square with prison protest, for while protest attested to Loyalists' claim to be political, any protest tactic they adopted made them like the Republicans.

88. Sean Lennon, Peter Cunningham, and Jaz McCann, in Campbell et al., *Nor Meekly*, 33, 32.

89. Campbell et al., *Nor Meekly*, 41–42.

90. Campbell et al., *Nor Meekly*, ch. 3, esp. 41–43. Bishop and Mallie, *The Provisional IRA*, 280.

91. Coogan, *On the Blanket*, ch. 10.

92. McEvoy, *Paramilitary Imprisonment*, 88.

93. McEvoy, *Paramilitary Imprisonment*, 153–55 (quote at 154); also Ryder, *Inside the Maze*, 195–96.

94. Bobby Sands, *Writings from Prison* (Boulder, CO: R. Rinehart, 1997), 152.

95. Prisons Management Committee, meeting September 27, 1977. PRONI, NIO 10/2/5, n.p.

96. Prison Management Committee, meeting April 12, 1979. PRONI, NIO 10/2/8, n.p.; Campbell et al., *Nor Meekly*, ch. 4.

97. Fran Lisa Buntman, *Robben Island and Prisoner Resistance to Apartheid* (Cambridge: Cambridge University Press), 47.

98. Letter from Bongani Manzini, Barberton Maximum Prison, January 1985. CSA 1/3/6: Dissipline en Beheer. Klagte en Vertoë. vol. 96; see also letter from Bethel Prison (anonymous) n.d. (June 1985), Suzman Papers, WHP A 2084 Aa 1.1.11
99. Klara Schillinger, letter May 26, 1937, MN 4104.
100. R., letter September 2, 1937, Czerwona Pomoc, AAN 175/III-4, kk. 71–72; Rywa Kac, letter May 29, 1937, MN 4091; Anastazja Kulesza, letter June 2, 1937, MN 4099.
101. Franka, letter October 1937. Czerwona Pomoc, AAN 175/III-4, k. 54.
102. Ciller, letter to family in Brooklyn, New York, n.d. (late 1937), AAN 175/III-4, kk. 26–27.
103. GPB minutes, June 27, 1912. NAI, GPB Suffragettes, Box 1, Folder A, n.p.
104. Hanna Sheehy-Skeffington letters/journal, June 1912, NLI 33618 (6).
105. Śledziński, "Przejścia więzienne," 256–57. See also Andrzej Jerzy Budzyński, "'Pawiak' jako więzienie polityczne w latach 1880–1915," PhD diss. Warsaw University, 1987, 207–8.
106. Quoted in Henryk Nakielski, *Jako i my odpuszczamy* (Warsaw: Iskry, 1989), 167.
107. For two poignant examples, see Jarosław Pałka, "Cele Mossora," *Karta* 44 (2005), 137–38; and note on Adam Boryczka, July 30, 1954, Akta kontrolno-śledcze: Adam Boryczka, IPN BU 0330/258, v. 1 (5169/III), kk. 38–39.
108. Benjamin Pogrund, *How Can Man Die Better: Sobukwe and Apartheid* (London: Halban, 1990), 302–4; Sobukwe Papers, WHP A2618, Ba7.
109. Coogan, *On the Blanket,* 222.
110. Coogan, *On the Blanket,* 170, 223, 226.

Chapter 8

1. Krzysztof Bińkowski, Tylko jeden rok. Pamiętnik z więzienia 14.XII.1981-14.XII.1982 (Radom, 1983).
2. Kulczyk, "Wspomnienia," Ośrodek Karta, AO II/380, 44.
3. On the necessary conditions for a hunger strike, see Seán McConville, *Irish Political Prisoners, 1920–1962: Pilgrimage of Desolation* (Abingdon: Routledge, 2014), 405.
4. General Prisons Board to Prison Governors, September 25, 1917. NAI GPB DORA Box 1, n.p. See William Murphy, *Political Imprisonment and the Irish, 1912–1921* (Oxford: Oxford University Press, 2014), ch. 4, esp. p. 88.
5. Kulczyk, "Wspomnienia," 20.
6. Maud Ellmann, *The Hunger Artists: Starving, Writing, and Imprisonment* (Cambridge, MA: Harvard University Press, 1993), 21–22.
7. Nelson Mandela, *Long Walk to Freedom,* vol. 2 (London: Abacus, 1994), 135–36.
8. Jerzy Stokowski, "Dziennik pisany w pamięci. 758 dni." Ośrodek Karta, AO CzP193w. k. 43.
9. Murphy, *Political Imprisonment and the Irish,* 11–12; Ellmann, *Hunger Artists,* 12; Anthony Bradley, "Nation, Pedagogy, and Performance: WB Yeats's *The King's Threshhold* and the Hunger Strikes," *Literature and History,* 18:2 (2009), 21–27; Joseph Lennon, "Fasting for the Public: Irish and Indian Sources of Marion Wallace Dunlop's 1909 Hunger Strike," in *Enemies of Empire: New Perspectives on Imperialism, Literature and Historiography,* ed. Eóin Flannery and Angus Mitchell (Dublin: Four Courts, 2007), 19–39.
10. See, for example, Laurence McKeown, *Out of Time: Irish Republican Prisoners, Long Kesh, 1970–2000* (Belfast: Beyond the Pale, 2001), 18.
11. June Purvis, "The Prison Experiences of the Suffragettes in Edwardian Britain," *Women's History Review* 4:1 (1995), 103–33; William Murphy, "Suffragettes and the Transformation of Political Imprisonment in Ireland, 1912–1914," in *Irish Women and the Vote: Becoming Citizens,* ed. Louise Ryan and Margaret Ward (Dublin: Irish Academic Press, 2007), 114–35; Kevin Grant, "British Suffragettes and the Russian Method of Hunger Strike," *Comparative Studies in Society and History* 53:1 (2011), 113–43.
12. On Chernyshevskii: Mikhail Nikorevich Gernet, *Istoriia tsarskoi tiur'my,* vol. 2: *1825–1870* (Moscow: Gosizdat iuridicheskoi literatury, 1961), 264–314, esp. 273; on the 1878 strike: Grant, "British Suffragettes," 113. Chernyshevskii aside, the history of political prisoners in Russia begins at the same time as in Poland: hundreds of Russian populists and anarchists in St. Petersburg's House of Preliminary Detention in 1878 simply overwhelmed prison staff and impeded prosecution efforts with a variety of raucous protests

that displayed contempt for the prison. Ana Siljak, *Angel of Vengeance: The Girl Who Shot the Governor of St. Petersburg and Sparked the Age of Assassination* (New York: St. Martin's Press, 2008), 175–81.

13. See Franciszek Ludwik Sadz (1885), AAN 34/III-1, k. 130; Zofia Grabska (1894): Zofia Kirkor-Kiedroniowa, *Wspomnienia* (Kraków: Wydawnictwo Literackie, 1986), 199–200; Franciszek Lewandowski (1907), AAN 34/III-1, k. 89.

14. Murphy, *Political Imprisonment and the Irish*, 18.

15. Dr. Edgar Flinn to Sir James Dougherty, Undersecretary for Ireland, September 9, 1912. NAI GPB Suffragettes, Box 1, Folder C, n.p.

16. Maud Gonne, April 1923, quoted in Margaret Ward, *Maud Gonne: Ireland's Joan of Arc* (London: Pandora, 1990), 140.

17. General Prisons Board Chair to Undersecretary, October 19, 1912, NAI GPB Suffragettes, Box 1, Folder C, n.p.

18. Margaret E. Cousins, "In Tullamore Jail. A Prisoner's Story," *Irish Independent*, February 28, 1913. [NAI GPB Suffragettes, Box 1, Folder F, n.p.]

19. Cousins, "In Tullamore Jail"; Cousins, in *Freeman's Journal*, February 28, 1913 [NAI GPB Suffragettes, Box 1, Folder F, n.p.]; documents on hunger strikers in Belfast Prison, March–April 1914, NAI GPB Suffragettes, Box 1, Folder J, n.p.; Governor of Mountjoy, letter October 10, 1912, NAI GPB Suffragettes, Box 1, Folder C, n.p.

20. Frank Gallagher, *Days of Fear: Diary of a 1920s Hunger Striker* (Cork: Mercier, 2008), 81.

21. Murphy, *Political Imprisonment and the Irish*, ch. 4.

22. Quoted in Murphy, *Political Imprisonment and the Irish*, 83. See Ian Miller, *A History of Force-Feeding: Hunger Strikes, Prisons, and Medical Ethics 1909–1974* (London: Palgrave Macmillan, 2016).

23. Seán McConville, *Irish Political Prisoners 1848–1922: Theatres of War* (London: Routledge, 2003), 614–16.

24. Murphy, *Political Imprisonment*, 89; McConville, *Irish Political Prisoners 1848–1922*, 610.

25. General Prisons Board to all prisons, March 7, 1918, NAI GPB DORA Box 2, Folder F, n.p. A more practical letter was sent to prison governors and medical officers on October 29, 1917, outlining the steps they should take in evaluating the possible release of a hunger-striking prisoner. NAI GPB DORA Box 1, n.p.

26. David Hogan [Frank Gallagher], *The Four Glorious Years* (Dublin: Irish Press, 1971), 162.

27. Murphy, *Political Imprisonment and the Irish*, 164.

28. Munro, Governor of Mountjoy Prison, to General Prisons Board, April 11 and 12, 1920. NAI GPB DORA, Box 4, n.p.

29. McConville, *Irish Political Prisoners 1848–1922*, 720; Murphy, *Political Imprisonment and the Irish*, 166; Gallagher, *Days of Fear*, 125–27.

30. Gallagher, *Days of Fear*, 148. Gallagher throughout refers to Clancy as "Philip."

31. John Irwin, letter to Mr. Duke, Chief Secretary's Office, March 7, 1918. NAI Taoiseach S14059.

32. Quoted in Costello, *Enduring the Most*, 149.

33. Costello, *Enduring the Most*, 171; McConville, *Irish Political Prisoners 1848–1922*, 739–40; Murphy, *Political Imprisonment and the Irish*, 184–85; Dave Hannigan, *Terence MacSwiney: The Hunger Strike That Rocked an Empire* (Dublin: O'Brien Press, 2010), 149–50.

34. Quoted in McConville, *Irish Political Prisoners 1848–1922*, 738.

35. McConville, *Irish Political Prisoners 1848–1922*, 755; Costello, *Enduring the Most*, 179–80, 231; quote at 153.

36. McConville, *Irish Political Prisoners 1920–1962*, 626–27.

37. Gallagher, *Days of Fear*, 44.

38. For example, Gallagher, *Days of Fear*, 76, 98; see also Costello, *Enduring the Most*, 157–58.

39. Mandela, *Long Walk to Freedom*, 136.

40. Journal entry for August 16, 1912, Sheehy Skeffington Papers, NLI 33618 (6).

41. Moses Dlamini, *Hell-Hole, Robben Island: Reminiscences of a Political Prisoner in South Africa* (Trenton, NJ: Africa World Press, 1984), 181.

42. Documents in NASA GOV 1194, 15/1/82-92/09; see also letter from N. Govindasamy Pillay and N. Kanabathy Pillay to Transvaal British Indian Association, January 1911, NASA

GG 888 15/101. Paul F. Power, "Gandhi in South Africa," *Journal of Modern African Studies* 7:3 (1969), 452.

43. Gandhi, *Satyagraha in South Africa* (Ahmedabad: Navajivan, 1950 [1928]); Gandhi, letters to Director of Prisons, November 19 and 22, 1910, in *The Collected Works of Mahatma Gandhi,* vol. 11 (Delhi: Ministry of Information and Broadcasting, 1958–84), 174–75.
44. On spontaneity, see, for example, Indres Naidoo, *Island in Chains: Ten Years on Robben Island* (London: Penguin, 1982), 153.
45. Dlamini, *Hell-Hole,* 181–82.
46. Dlamini, *Hell-Hole,* 182.
47. Dlamini, *Hell-Hole,* 183.
48. Naidoo, *Island in Chains,* 153–54.
49. At some point the guards themselves began their own hunger strike. Natoo Babenia says this strike took place three months later, while Moses Dlamini places it during the prisoners' strike. Natoo Babenia, *Memoirs of a Saboteur: Reflections on My Political Activity in India and South Africa* (Cape Town: Mayibuye, 1995), 159–60; Dlamini, *Hell-Hole,* 186.
50. Babenia, *Memoirs of a Saboteur,* 161.
51. Dlamini, *Hell-Hole,* 189–92.
52. See, for example, Hogan, *Four Glorious Years,* 166–67.
53. *Mokotowianin,* n.d. [early 1928], copy in AAN 175/I-13, k. 41.
54. *Mokotowianin,* kk. 41–42.
55. *Mokotowianin,* 41–43; list of forty-two deaths on pp. 37–39.
56. Komunikat, n.d., Międzypartyjny Sekretariat dla Walki o Amnestję, AAN 179/5, kk. 2–3; see also letters from Mokotów Prison, *Więzień polityczny* 1 (1924), 6–7; letter from Łuck Prison, *Więzień polityczny* 5–6 (1925), 11; letter, M. P. Ballin, Łuck Prison, September 1926, Ministerstwo Spraw Wewnętrznych, AAN 296/II-22, k. 60.
57. Prosecutor of District Court, letter to Prosecutor of Appeals Court, Katowice, November 12, 1923 (and subsequent updates), AAN 361/1. k. 38; also kk. 43, 48.
58. See, for example, Bela Frankel, letter to Prison Head, Poznań, September 20, 1932, MN 4074.
59. "Przebieg akcji wewnętrzno-więziennej 20–22 września [1931], in AAN, MSW Mf 25749 (sygn. 1176), kk. 74–76. See also Uchwały Pierwszej Krajowej Narady Wydziałów Gospodarczych Czerwonej Pomocy w Polsce, June 1936, AAN 175/I-1, k. 17.
60. Jan Krzesławski, "Więzienie w Ratuszu za rządów Nazarowa," *Kronika Ruchu Rewolucyjnego* 1:2 (1935), 86.
61. See, for example, Red Help Secretariat to all prison *komunas,* June 1928, AAN MSW Mf 25749 (sygn. 1176), k. 32.
62. Marek Żukowski, *Ośrodki odosobnienia w Polsce latach 1981–1982* (Warsaw: Trio, 2013), 451–58.
63. Andrzej Friszke, *Czas KOR-u. Jacek Kuroń a geneza Solidarności* (Kraków: Znak, 2011), 231–33.
64. Żukowski, *Ośrodki odosobnienia,* 452–53.
65. Henryk Wujec, in *Polityczni. Więźniowie polityczni w Polsce lat 1981–1983* (Warsaw: Przedświt, 1986), 16.
66. Bogdan Ciszak, "Dziennik," Ośrodek Karta, AO CzP 19w, 21–23.
67. Kulczyk, "Wspomnienia," 34–35.
68. Kulczyk, "Wspomnienia," 43–44.
69. Bill Kissane, *The Politics of the Irish Civil War* (Oxford: Oxford University Press, 2005).
70. Gallagher diary, entries October 24–26 and November 3, 1922. NLI 18356(2).
71. IRA GHQ to Commanding Officers of all prisons and camps. Mulcahy Papers, UCD P7a/87, 34.
72. Michael Kilroy, Communiqué October 12, 1923. NAI Taoiseach S1369/10, n.p.
73. Gallagher diary, entries October 12–13 and December 11, 1923, NLI 18356(4).
74. Tim Carey, *Mountjoy: The Story of a Prison* (Cork: Collins, 2000), 202–3. Sean MacBride also joined, though he knew that would lead to the discovery of an escape tunnel he was working on. Seán MacBride, *That Day's Struggle: A Memoir, 1904–1951* (Dublin: Currach, 2005), 81.
75. Anna O'Rahilly, letter to Nell Humphreys, October 28, 1923, Sighle Humphreys papers, UCD P106/197.

76. "Suggestions for immediate action," n.d., O'Malley Papers, UCD P17a/43, n.p. (CD, p. 14) See Bandon Board of Guardians (Ref. IE CCCA/BG/42), http://www.corkarchives.ie/media/BG42web.pdf, 26; *Republican Bulletin*, October 18, 1923, Humphreys Papers, UCD P106/1724.

77. Chief of Staff Frank Aiken, letter October 28, 1923, reprinted in *No Surrender Here! The Civil War Papers of Ernie O'Malley, 1922–1924*, ed. Cormac K. H. O'Malley and Anne Dolan (Dublin: Lilliput, 2007), 388.

78. Intercepted letter, October 28, 1923, and attached report to IRA Director of Intelligence. NAI Taoiseach S1859, n.p.

79. Military Governor, Newbridge, to Director of Intelligence (Free State), in Ernest O'Malley Papers, UCD P17a/192, n.p. (CD, 27–28).

80. Aiken, to "all volunteers on hungerstrike," November 5, 1923. O'Malley Papers, UCD P17a/43, n.p. (CD, 18).

81. Ernie O'Malley, November 7, 1923, in *Republican Bulletin*, November 9, 1923. NAI Taoiseach S1369/10, n.p.

82. See NAI Taoiseach S1369/10, n.p.; and reports of the Adjutant General in IMA, CW/P/02/02/20, n.p.

83. *Daily Sheet* [Sinn Féin], in Elgin O'Rahilly Papers, UCD P200/258; hunger strikers' letter to Archbishop of Dublin, October 17, 1923, in Richard Mulcahy Papers, UCD P7a/87, doc. 2.

84. Letter, October 28, 1923, in Mulcahy Papers, UCD P7a/94.

85. Micheal Mac Giollaruaidh, letter to Military Governor Kilmainham, November 22, 1923, NAI Taoiseach S1369/10, n.p.

86. She added that any strike in which even one person "continues to the end cannot be called a failure, any more than one would call Calvary a failure." Mary MacSwiney, press confeence, n.d., NAI Taoiseach S1369/10, n.d.

87. Quoted in McConville, *Irish Political Prisoners, 1922–1962*, 255.

88. Kit Byrne, intercepted letter, November 8, 1923, IMA, CW/P/08/08, n.p.; Seamus O'Rourke, intercepted letter, November 15, 1923, Mulcahy Papers, UCD P7a/87, 139.

89. *Sinn Fein*, December 1, 1923. NAI Taoiseach S1369/10, n.p.

90. Frank Aiken, letter in *Sinn Fein*, December 1, 1923. NAI Taoiseach S1369/10, n.p.

91. John McGuffin, *Internment* (Tralee: Anvil, 1973), 147–49; Richard English, *Armed Struggle: The History of the IRA* (New York: Oxford University Press, 2003), 193.

92. Kieran McEvoy, *Paramilitary Imprisonment in Northern Ireland: Resistance, Management, and Release* (Oxford: Oxford University Press, 2001), 78–79.

93. Ruán O'Donnell, *Special Category: The IRA in English Prisons*, vol. 1, *1968–1978* (Dublin: Irish Academic Press, 2012), ch. 4; McEvoy, *Paramilitary Imprisonment*, 79–82. See also files in NAI Taoiseach 2003/16/132. On Frank Stagg's strike as understood in prison: Gerry Adams, *Cage Eleven* (Dingle: Brandon, 1990), 116–24.

94. Thomas Hennessey, *Hunger Strike: Margaret Thatcher's Battle with the IRA, 1980–1981* (Sallins, Kildare: Irish Academic Press, 2014), ch. 3; McEvoy, *Paramilitary Imprisonment*, 91–92.

95. Ed Moloney, *Voices from the Grave: Two Men's War in Ireland* (New York: Public Affairs, 2010), 236–37; O'Hearn, *Bobby Sands: Nothing but an Unfinished Song*, 275–76.

96. David Beresford, *Ten Men Dead: The Story of the 1981 Irish Hunger Strike* (New York: Atlantic Monthly, 1997), 28; Moloney, *Voices from the Grave*, 238–40.

97. Text in Chris Ryder, *Inside the Maze: The Untold Story of the Northern Ireland Prison Service* (London: Methuen, 2001), 218–21.

98. It also inspired pity, and even sympathy, among loyalist prisoners. Ryder, *Inside the Maze*, 210; Colin Crawford, *Defenders or Criminals? Loyalist Prisoners and Criminalisation* (Belfast: Blackstaff, 1999), 150–51.

99. Quoted in Richard O'Rawe, *Blanketmen: An Untold Story of the H-Block Hunger Strike* (Dublin: New Island Books, 2005), 124.

100. Quoted in Laurence McKeown, *Out of Time: Irish Republican Prisoners, Long Kesh 1972–2000* (Belfast: Beyond the Pale, 2001), 79.

101. Padraig O'Malley, *Biting at the Grave: The Irish Hunger Strikers and the Politics of Despair* (Boston: Beacon Press, 1990), 208.

102. McEvoy, *Paramilitary Imprisonment*, 97.

103. McKeown, *Out of Time*, 86.
104. McKeown, *Out of Time*, 88.
105. McKeown, *Out of Time*, 94–95; also McEvoy, *Paramilitary Imprisonment*, 265, n18.

Chapter 9

1. Tomasz Ochinowski, "Nauczycielka (Wstępna analiza materiału autobiograficznego)," *Nike* 43 (1998), 16.
2. Baruch Hirson, *Revolutions in My Life* (Johannesburg: Witwatersrand University Press, 1995), 160. See also Stefania Sempołowska, letter to Minister of Justice Bronisław Sobolewski, in Andrzej Ajnenkiel, "Memoriały Stefanii Sempołowskiej dotyczące położenia więźniów politycznych w Polsce w 1920 i 1922r." *Teki archiwalne* 6 (1959), 26.
3. Marian Płochocki, "Za działalności w szeregach SDKPiL," in *Pamiętnik X Pawilonu*, ed Aleksander Kozłowski and Henryk J. Mościcki (Warsaw: Wydawnictwo Ministerstwa Obrony Narodowej, 1958), 258–62. See also Zofia Kirkor-Kiedroniowa, *Wspomnienia* (Kraków: Wydawnictwo Literackie, 1986), 193–94.
4. Anna Muller, "If the Walls Could Talk: Women Political Prisoners in Stalinist Poland, 1945–1956," PhD diss., Indiana University, 2010; Denis O'Hearn, *Nothing but an Unfinished Song: Bobby Sands, the Irish Hunger Striker Who Ignited a Generation* (London: Pluto Press, 2006), 218–21.
5. Quoted in Henryk Nakielski, *Jako i my odpuszczamy* (Warsaw: Iskry, 1989), 106. See also Leon Macherowski, "Wspomnienia," Ośrodek Karta, AO II/374, k. 190; and Muller, "If These Walls Could Talk."
6. Aleksander Szetlich, survey response, AAN 34/III-1, k. 149.
7. Eugenia Zochniak (Ustrońska), in *Zawołać po imieniu. Księga kobiet-więźniów politycznych 1944–1958*, vol. 1, ed. Barbara Otwinowska (Nadarzyn: Vipart, 1999), 338–39.
8. Gallagher diary entry, October 12–13, 1923, NLI 18356(4). Nell Humphreys boasted in a letter to her sister that "one could leave Kilmainham the most accomplished woman in Ireland," with classes in Irish, German, French, shorthand, dancing, and more. Letter, February 2, 1923, in Sighle Humphreys papers, UCD P106/396.
9. Sowińska, "Gorzkie lata," Biblioteka Narodowa ms. 14257, k. 191.
10. Andrzej Sołdrowski, *Spisani na straty* (Wrocław: Nortom, 1996), 68.
11. Gallagher diary, entry December 17, 1922, NLI 18356 (2).
12. Marek Kulczyk, "Wspomnienia," Ośrodek Karta, AO II/380, 47–48.
13. Irena Cieślińska-Skrzypiec, "Inowrocław. Długie miesiące—ciężkie lata . . . ," *Nike* 6 (1993), 15–16.
14. Galelekile W. Sitho, in Jan K. Coetzee, *Plain Tales from Robben Island* (Pretoria: Van Schalk, 2000), 103.
15. Quoted in Eva Hoffman, *Exit into History: A Journey through the New Eastern Europe* (New York: Penguin, 1994), 51.
16. Letter, June 1912, in *Listy nieprawomyślne. Wybór z akt Warszawskiego Gubernatora Zarządu Żandarmerii 1886–1914*, ed. Małgorzata Pleskaczyńska (Warsaw: Akademia Nauk Społecznych PZPR, 1989), 256–57.
17. See, for example, Franciszek Mrozowski, "Z przeżyć więziennych w Warszawie," *Niepodległość* 6:3 (1932), 375–79; Ludwik Śledziński, "Przejścia więzienne w Łowiczu i w Warszawie (rok 1906–1907)," *Niepodległość* 2:2 (1930), 259–60; Leon Berenson, *Z sali śmierci. Wrażenia obrońcy politycznego* (Warsaw: Księgarnia F. Hoesicka, 1929), 23–24; Józef Kłosowski, Questionnaire response, AAN 34/III-1, k. 69; as well as many of the essays in *Za kratami więzień i drutami obozów. Wspomnienia i notatki więźniów ideowych z lat 1914–1921*, 2 vols., ed. Julian Stachewicz (Warsaw: Komitet Organizacyjny Zjazdu b. Więźniów Ideowych z lat 1914–1921, 1927–1931).
18. Quoted in Francis J. Costello, *Enduring the Most: The Life and Death of Terence MacSwiney* (Dingle: Brandon, 1995), 150.
19. Armia Krajowa, Komenda Obszaru Lwów. AAN 203/XV/33 (Mf 2400/6), k. 99. See also Regina Domańska, *Pawiak—kaźń i heroizm* (Warsaw: Książka i Wiedza, 1988), 123.

20. Examples in Małgorzata Szejnert, *Śród żywych duchów* (London: Aneks, 1990); Mateusz Wyrwich, *W celi śmierci* (Warsaw: Rytm, 2002); and Sołdrowski, *Spisani*.
21. See "Biko on Death," *New Republic*, January 7, 1978, 12; O'Hearn, *Bobby Sands: Nothing but an Unfinished Song*, 345.
22. Władysław Bartoszewski, *Warto być przyzwoitym. Szkic do pamiętnika* (Paris: Spotkania, 1986), 14.
23. See Eoghan Davis, "The Guerrilla Mind," in *Revolution? Ireland 1917–1923*, ed. David Fitzpatrick (Dublin: Trinity College History Workshop, 1990), 43–59.
24. de Valera, May 22, 1923, NAI Taoiseach S1859, n.p.
25. de Valera, July 18, 1923, IMA, CW/P/02/02/34, n.p. See generally The Earl of Longford and Thomas P. O'Neill, *Eamon de Valera* (London: Hutchinson, 1970), 216–26.
26. *The Book of Cells*, November 1922. NLI 20849(1). The name was a pun on the famous medieval manuscript on display nearby in Trinity College.
27. Gallagher diary, entries for August 29, 1923 and later. NLI 18356(3).
28. Davis, "The Guerrilla Mind," 57.
29. Postcard from Piotr Górczyński to Franciszka Górczyńska, Ostrowiec Kielecki, November 15, 1931. MN 3915.
30. KC KPP, Circular November–December 1930. Prokuratura Sądu Okręgowego w Suwałkach, AAN 362/II, kk. 32–33. See Franciszka Świetlikowa, "Więźniowie polityczni 'Mokotowa' w latach 1918–1939," *Z pola walki* 58: 2 (1972), 272–73.
31. "Więzienie—szkoła proletariatu," *Więzień polityczny* 7–8 (1925), 6. The curriculum also included arithmetic, Polish, and geography. Wednesdays were devoted to lectures on various political or scientific topics.
32. *Gryps* from Mars to Młot, December 15, 1927. MN 2781. See also *gryps* to the "Lecturers' Group" in Białystok Prison, December 27, 1926, MN 2028Xa.
33. *Gryps*, Sieradz Prison, n.d. (1932) MN 3589. On self-criticism in the cell: Szymon Szwarc, in Zakład Historii Partii, seminar on the *komuna* in Grudziądz Prison, January 14, 1964. AAN R-145, k. 12.
34. Saul Hersz Weindling, *gryps* to Janek, February 14, 1932. MN 4039. Also Maria Eiger, letter to Appeals Court Prosecutor, Kalisz, 1924. MN 4303; Alfred Lampe, letter to Minister of Justice, March 31, 1924, AAN 250/1 (Mf 2732/1), kk. 7–9; *gryps*, Grudziądz Prison, May 10, 1933, Czerwona Pomoc, AAN 175/I-8, k. 15.
35. On communist discipline, see Igor Halfin, *Stalinist Confessions: Messianism and Terror at the Leningrad Communist University* (Pittsburgh: University of Pittsburgh Press, 2009).
36. *Gryps*, n.d. [1931], from Piotrków Prison to MOPR, Piotrków, AAN 175/III-16, kk. 6–7.
37. *Gryps*, n.d. [1931], Sieradz Prison, MN 3416.
38. See Andrzej Friszke, *Czas KOR-u. Jacek Kuroń a geneza Solidarności* (Kraków: Znak, 2011); and Friszke, *Rewolucja Solidarności* (Kraków: Znak, 2013).
39. Jan Mur [Andrzej Drzycimski and Adam Kinaszewski], *Dziennik internowanego. Grudzień 1981-grudzień 1982* (Gdańsk: Modem, 1989), 128–33; Marek Żukowski, *Ośrodki odosobnienia w Polsce w latach 1981–1982* (Warsaw: Trio, 2013), 598.
40. Żukowski, *Ośrodki odosobnienia w Polsce*.
41. Interview in Grzegorz Wołk, *Ośrodki odosobnienia w Polsce południowo-wschodniej (1981–1982)* (Rzeszów: Instytut Pamięci Narodowej, 2009), 183. Maksim Gorkii's autobiographical *My Universities* (1923) is not about such formal education but the school of life among ordinary prisoners.
42. Bogdan Ciszak, diary entry May 18, 1982. Ośrodek Karta, AO CzP19w.
43. Bartoszewski, *Warto być przyzwoitym*, 13.
44. Mur, *Dziennik internowanego*, 114.
45. Kulczyk, "Wspomnienia," 32.
46. Andrzej Paczkowski, *Wojna polsko-jaruzelska. Stan wojenny w Polsce* (Warsaw: Prószyński, 2006).
47. See Mur, *Dziennik internowanego*, 133–34; also Zbigniew Kamiński, "Raptularz internowanego," Ośrodek Karta, AO CzP113dz, k. 21.
48. Quoted in Ciszak diary, cover page. Ośrodek Karta, AO CzP19w.

49. Marek Niedziewicz joined the Freedom and Peace movement in 1987 after coming to watch a demonstration and being locked in a cell with many participants. Padraic Kenney, *Wrocławskie zadymy* (Wrocław: Atut, 2007), 179–80.

50. Paweł Bryszkowski, *Getto w Gołdapi* (Bydgoszcz: Świadectwo, 1999), 75; *Kobiety internowane. Gołdap 1982*, ed. Ewa Rogalewska (Białystok: Instytut Pamięci Narodowej, 2009).

51. Krystyna Ziółkowska, interview by author, July 2006. Ziółkowska is my mother-in-law.

52. See Neville Alexander, *Robben Island Prison Dossier* (Rondebosch: University of Cape Town Press, 47–65. Fran Lisa Buntman, *Robben Island and Prisoner Resistance to Apartheid* (Cambridge: Cambridge University Press, 2003), 62–65.

53. Joseph Faniso Mati, in Coetzee, *Plain Tales from Robben Island*, 24.

54. Quoted in Colin Bundy, "Introduction," in Govan Mbeki, *Learning from Robben Island: The Prison Writings of Govan Mbeki* (Cape Town: D. Philip, 1991), xx.

55. Quoted in Buntman, *Robben Island*, 131; on recruitment generally, 130–47. Bundy, "Introduction," xxi; Mati, in Coetzee, *Plain Tales*, 26–27.

56. Mati, in Coetzee, *Plain Tales*, 27. See also Natoo Babenia, *Memoirs of a Saboteur: Reflections on My Political Activity in India and South Africa* (Cape Town: Mayibuye, 1995), 179–80, 192; Bundy, "Introduction," xxiii.

57. "Secretary's Hand-Over Paper," Makana Football Association, June 19, 1973, Mayibuye Archives, MCH 64, Box 17, Folder 17.1, n.p.; Cheryl Roberts, *Sport in Chains* (Cape Town: Township Publishing Co-operative, 1994), 46. See also Buntman, *Robben Island*, 66–70.

58. Logbook entries in Mayibuye Archives, MCH 64, Box 1, Folder 1.4.

59. Indres Naidoo, *Island in Chains: Ten Years on Robben Island* (London: Penguin, 1982), 165.

60. Liaison meeting with Major Harding, September 25, 1979, Mayibuye Archives, MCH 64, Box 1A, Folder 1.2.

61. Quoted in Roberts, *Sport in Chains*, 33.

62. Chairman's report, MFA General Meeting, May 28, 1974, Mayibuye Archives, MCH 64, Box 17, Folder 17.1. See also comments by Anthony Suze at a meeting of tennis players, May 14, 1978, MCH 64, Box 1, Folder 1.4.

63. Minutes of Executive Meeting, March 17, 1971, Mayibuye Archives, MCH 64, Box 1, Folder 1.4.

64. Minutes, Federal Council, August 2, 1974, Mayibuye Archives, MCH 64 Box 1, Folder 1.4.

65. Minutes of Executive Committee meeting, November 27, 1974, Mayibuye Archives, MCH 64, Box 1, Folder 1.4.

66. Documents in Mayibuye Archives, MCH 64, Box 2, Folders 2.2–2.4.

67. Not entirely unsung; one referee was Jacob Zuma, later president of South Africa (2009–).

68. Letter, Referees Union to Secretary, General Recreation Committee, September 5, 1990, Mayibuye Archives, MCH 64, Box 2, Folder 2.4. Judges at the prisoners' Summer Olympics threatened to quit in 1986: Meeting of directorate and clubs, December 7, 1986, MCH 64, Box 1, Folder 1.4.

69. Minutes of 9th Federal Council Meeting, November 22, 1974. Mayibuye Archives, MCH 64, Box 1, Folder 1.4.

70. Minutes, Special Meeting August 9, 1981, Mayibuye Archives, MCH 64, Box 1, Folder 1.4.

71. Chibane, letter to Directorate, March 6, 1978, Mayibuye Archives, MCH 64, Box 1, Folder 1.4.

72. Naidoo, letter to Commanding Officer, February 19, 1968, Mayibuye Archives, MCH 64, Box 2, Folder 2.1.

73. Ad Hoc Committee, letter to Commanding Officer, July 23, 1972, Mayibuye Archives, MCH 64, Box 17, Folder 17.3.

74. Report by Sedick Isaacs, March 20, 1977, Mayibuye Archives, MCH 64, Box 1A, Folder 1.2.

75. See, for example, Meeting of Directorate with Commanding Officer Harding, January 18, 1981; Directorate meeting with Commanding Officer, July 31, 1984; and other minutes 1981–86, in Mayibuye Archives, MCH 64, Box 1, Folder 1.4.

76. Minutes of meeting with Deputy Officer Commanding Major Lombard, December 9, 1982, Mayibuye Archives, MCH 64, Box 1, Folder 1.4.

77. Minutes of MDC, August 14, 1983, Mayibuye Archives, MCH 64, Box 1, Folder 1.4.

78. Minutes of general meeting, January 7, 1985, Mayibuye Archives, MCH Box 1, Folder 1.4.

79. E-Section, "To All the Membership," n.d. [1989–90], Mayibuye Archives, MCH 64, Box 79. See also "A statement of intent and declaration made by political prisoners in the Robben Island Maximum Prison," n.d. [February 1990], SAHA AL 2457 F 4.2.

80. See, for example, "Evaluative meeting of Mrabulo, 1989," Mayibuye Archives, MCH 64, Box 76.

81. Untitled intelligence report, "compiled by K. Z. Edwards, NIS Head Office," May 1980, subchapter G, unpaginated. Mac Maharaj Security Files, Mayibuye Archives, MCH 121-1.

82. Gerry Kelly, quoted in Laurence McKeown, *Out of Time: Irish Republican Prisoners, Long Kesh 1972–2000* (Belfast: Beyond the Pale, 2001), 41.

83. Ed Moloney, *Secret History of the IRA* (New York: Norton, 2002), 77.

84. David Sharrock and Mark Devenport, *Man of War, Man of Peace: The Unauthorised Biography of Gerry Adams* (London: Pan, 1998), 125. See also Ed Moloney, *Secret History*, 147–49.

85. McKeown, *Out of Time*, 41. See also Jacqueline Dana and Seán McMonagle, "Deconstructing 'Criminalisation': The Politics of Collective Education in the H-blocks," *Journal of Prisoners on Prisons* 8:1–2 (1997), 418–21; Eunan O'Halpin, *Defending Ireland: The Irish State and Its Enemies since 1922* (Oxford: Oxford University Press, 1999), 300–302.

86. Ed Moloney, *Voices from the Grave: Two Men's War in Ireland* (New York: Public Affairs, 2010), 201.

87. McKeown, *Out of Time*, 131.

88. Richard English, *Armed Struggle: The History of the IRA* (New York: Oxford University Press, 2003), 209; Brian Campbell, Laurence McKeown, and Felim O'Hagan eds., *Nor Meekly Serve My Time: The H-Block Struggle 1976–1981*, eds. (Belfast: Beyond the Pale, 1998).

89. Mickey Culbert, quoted in McKeown, *Out of Time*, 122.

90. McKeown, *Out of Time*, 123–25.

91. McMullan, in McKeown, *Out of Time*, 131.

92. McMullan, in McKeown, *Out of Time*, 131.

93. McKeown also mentions the psychoanalytic theories of Carl Rogers; *Out of Time*, 245, n6. On Freire's influence: Richard English, *Armed Struggle*, 229–31.

94. McKeown, *Out of Time*, 130.

95. McMullan in McKeown, *Out of Time*, 133.

96. English, *Armed Struggle*, 231–37; McKeown, *Out of Time*, 137–38, 141–45.

97. Raymond McCartney, in McKeown, *Out of Time*, 140.

98. English, *Armed Struggle*, 230; McKeown, *Out of Time*, 140.

99. McKeown, *Out of Time*, ch. 12; Chris Ryder, *Inside the Maze: The Untold Story of the Northern Ireland Prison Service* (London: Methuen, 2001), 292–94.

100. Murray, in McKeown, *Out of Time*, 148.

101. Patrick Magee, quoted in English, *Armed Struggle*, 228.

102. Declan Moes, quoted in English, *Armed Struggle*, 235; McKeown, *Out of Time*, 208–10.

103. McKeown, *Out of Time*, 145–46; Simona Sharoni, "Gendering Resistance within an Irish Republican Prisoner Community: A Conversation with Laurence McKeown," *International Feminist Journal of Politics* 1:2 (1999).

104. John Stevenson, *"We Wrecked the Place": Contemplating an End to the Northern Irish Troubles* (New York: Free Press, 1996), 140–43; Kieran McEvoy, *Paramilitary Imprisonment in Northern Ireland: Resistance, Management, and Release* (Oxford: Oxford University Press, 2001), 39, 102–104.

105. McEvoy, *Paramilitary Imprisonment*, 103 and 135.

106. McEvoy, *Paramilitary Imprisonment*, 286–88. See McKeown, *Out of Time*, 215.

107. Roy Garland, *Gusty Spence* (Belfast: Blackstaff, 2001); Colin Crawford, *Defenders or Criminals? Loyalist Prisoners and Criminalisation* (Belfast: Blackstaff, 1999), 158–59; Moloney, *Voices from the Grave*, 367.

108. Quoted in Moloney, *Voices from the Grave*, 367; also 334–35.

109. Ryder, *Inside the Maze*, ch. 14.

110. Quoted in Ryder, *Inside the Maze*, 321.

111. McKeown, "'Unrepentant Fenian bastards': The Social Construction of an Irish Republican Prisoner Community," PhD diss., Queen's University Belfast, 1998, 96.
112. See Martin Snodden, quoted in Ryder, 291; also Crawford, *Defenders or Criminals?*, 11.
113. Ryder, *Inside the Maze*, 342–43.

Conclusion

1. *Więzień polityczny* 1 (1924), 5.
2. In some cases, especially South Africa, there are still prisoners whom some consider to be political prisoners. See, for example, Gugu Myeni, "Call to Free Political Prisoners Still Languishing in SA Jails," *New Age (South Africa)*, March 16, 2012.
3. Documents in SAHA AL2457 F4.2, F 4.3; Suzman Papers, WHP A2084 Ad 1.7; Detainees' Parents Support Committee Papers, WHP AG 2523 Q2.1.1; Similo Wonci Papers, Mayibuye Archives, MCH 260; Thomas Winslow Papers, UCTMA, BC1210, E7.
4. In early 1990, these former prisoners, now in Parliament, reponded to a wave of prison protests by approving an amnesty for ordinary criminal convicts whose conditions they had experienced in 1981–83. Małgorzata Kozera, "Lambada dla recydywy," *Newsweek Polska—Historia*, November 26, 2014.
5. Richard English, *Armed Struggle: The History of the IRA* (New York: Oxford University Press, 2003), 304–306, 331–32.
6. Chris Ryder, *Inside the Maze: The Untold Story of the Northern Ireland Prison Service* (London: Methuen, 2001), 321.

Epilogue

1. Moazzam Begg, *Enemy Combatant: My Imprisonment at Guantánamo, Bagram, and Kandahar* (New York: New Press, 2006), 333–34.
2. Department of Defence, Joint Task Force Guantanamo Bay, Detainee Assessment Brief: Moazzam Begg, November 11, 2003. Obtained from wikileaks.ch/gitmo.
3. See Human Rights Watch, *World Report 2015*, www.hrw.org/sites/default/files/wr2015_web.pdf.
4. James P. Jordan, "Empire of Prisons," *Counterpunch*, June 5, 2014, at www.counterpunch.org/2014/06/05/empire-of-prisons/.
5. Kathy Gilsinan, "The Economics of Terrorist Bounties," The Atlantic, May 19, 2015, https://www.theatlantic.com/international/archive/2015/05/the-economics-of-terrorist-bounties/393461/.
6. Other memoirs include Mamdouh Habib, *My Story: The Tale of a Terrorist Who Wasn't* (Melbourne: Scribe, 2008); and Abdul Salam Zaeef, *My Life with the Taliban*, ed. and trans. Alex Strick van Linschoten and Felix Kuehn (New York: Columbia University Press, 2010).
7. Mohamedou Ould Slahi, *Guantánamo Diary*, ed. Larry Siems (New York: Back Bay Books, 2015), 217–18.
8. Slahi, *Guantánamo Diary*, 231. He was released in October 2016.
9. Murat Kurnaz, *Five Years of My Life: An Innocent Man in Guantanamo*, trans. Jefferson Chase (New York: Palgrave, 2007), 52. See also Begg, *Enemy Combatant*, 120: "they were terrified of us."
10. David Hicks, *Guantanamo: My Journey* (Sydney: Random House, 2010), 217–18.
11. Ahmed Errachidi, *The General: The Ordinary Man Who Challenged Guantánamo* (London: Random House, 2013), 136.
12. Mark Danner, "Our State of Exception," *New York Review of Books*, October 13, 2011, 44–48.
13. Jonathan Hafetz, *Guantanamo Lawyers: Inside a Prison Outside the Law* (New York: New York University Press, 2011).
14. Kurnaz, *Five Years*, 203–207.
15. See documents available at www.therenditionproject.org.uk/documents/index.html.
16. Begg, *Enemy Combatant*, 114.

17. Hicks, *Guantanamo,* 244.
18. Slahi, 250–63; quote on p. 253. Slahi prides himself on his ability to keep track of time and the date, glimpsing interrogators' watches or the date stamps on printouts.
19. Begg, *Enemy Combatant,* 245–46.
20. Kurnaz, *Five Years,* 148–49.
21. Kurnaz, *Five Years,* 149.
22. Begg, *Enemy Combatant,* 290.
23. Begg, *Enemy Combatant,* 292. Uthman is probably Uthman Abdul Rahim Mohammed Uthman.
24. Begg, *Enemy Combatant,* 301–2.
25. Kurnaz, *Five Years,* 250–51. Karen Greenberg backs up this story in *The Least Worst Place: How Guantanamo Became the World's Most Notorious Prison* (New York: Oxford University Press, 2009).
26. Tim Golden, "The Battle for Guantánamo," *New York Times,* September 17, 2006.
27. There seem to have been others. See Errachidi, *The General.*
28. Central Intelligence Agency, Directorate of Intelligence, *Terrorists: Recruiting and Operating Behind Bars,* August 20, 2002. www.thesmokinggun.com/file/coming-prison-near-you.
29. Golden, "The Battle for Guantánamo."
30. Golden, "The Battle for Guantánamo."
31. Errachidi, *The General,* 90–91.
32. Errachidi, *The General,* 100.
33. Kurnaz, *Five Years,* 152.
34. Kurnaz, *Five Years,* 153.
35. Kurnaz, *Five Years,* 154.
36. Errachidi, *The General,* 93.
37. Begg, *Enemy Combatant,* 206.
38. See Tyler Cabot, "The Prisoners of Guantanamo," *Esquire,* September 2011, www.esquire.com/news-politics/a10760/guantanamo-prisoner-0911/.
39. Golden, "The Battle for Guantánamo."
40. See Golden, "The Battle for Guantánamo;" Scott Horton, "'Dryboarding' and Three Unexplained Deaths at Guantánamo," *Harper's Magazine,* November 2011, harpers.org/blog/2011/11/dryboarding-and-three-unexplained-deaths-at-guantanamo/.
41. Jason Leopold, "Déjà vu: Defense Officials Downplay Growing Guantanamo Hunger Strike with Bush-Era Talking Points," *Truthout,* April 1, 2013, www.truth-out.org/news/item/15442-defense-officials-downplay-growing-guantanamo-hunger-strike-with-bush-era-talking-points.
42. Carol Rosenberg, "Tracking the Hunger Strike," *Miami Herald,* media.miamiherald.com/static/media/projects/gitmo_chart/.
43. See Carol Rosenberg, "Final Obama Transfer Leaves 41 Prisoners at Guantánamo Bay," *Miami Herald,* January 19, 2017, http://www.miamiherald.com/news/nation-world/world/americas/guantanamo/article127537514.html Declaration of Clive A. Stafford Smith, March 31, 2013, archived at humanrights.ucdavis.edu/projects/the-guantanamo-testimonials-project/testimonies/prisoner-testimonies/prisoner-testimonies/declaration-of-clive-a-stafford-smith-march-31-2013.
44. See, for example, the work of CAGE Advocacy in Great Britain: www.cageuk.org.
45. Shaker Aamer, quoted in Golden, "The Battle for Guantánamo."

ARCHIVES CONSULTED

Poland
    Ośrodek Karta, Warsaw
        AO: Archiwum Opozycji
    Biblioteka Narodowa, Warsaw
    Muzeum Niepodległości, Warsaw (MN)
    Archiwum Akt Dawnych, Warsaw
    Archiwum Akt Nowych, Warsaw (AAN)
        MSW: Ministerstwo Spraw Wewnętrznych
        MBP: Ministerstwo Bezpieczeństwa Publicznego
    Instytut Pamięci Narodowej, Warsaw (IPN)
    Archiwum Państwowe w Warszawie, Oddział w
        Pułtusku (APWOP)
    Muzeum Władysława Broniewskiego, Warsaw
Ireland
    National Archive of Ireland, Dublin (NAI)
        CSORP: Chief Secretary's Office, Registered Papers
        DORA: Defence of the Realm Act
        GPB: General Prisons Board
    National Library of Ireland, Dublin (NLI)
    University College Archives, Dublin (UCD)
    Military Archives, Dublin (IMA)
Northern Ireland
    Public Record Office, Belfast (PRONI)
        NIO: Northern Ireland Office
    Linen Hall Library, Belfast

Great Britain
  National Archive of Britain (NAB)
    FCO: Foreign and Commonwealth Office
    HO: Home Office
    WO: War Office
  British Library
South Africa
  Witwatersrand University, Historical Papers, Johannesburg (WHP)
    DPSC: Detainees' Parents Support Committee
  South African History Archive, Johannesburg (SAHA)
  National Archive of South Africa, Pretoria (NASA)
    CS: Colonial Secretary
    GEV: Director of Prisons
    GG: Governor-General
    GOV: Governor of the Transvaal Colony
  Correctional Services Archive, Pretoria (CSA)
  Mayibuye Archives, Cape Town
    MCH: Mayibuye Centre Historical Papers
  Robben Island Museum, Cape Town
  University of Cape Town, Manuscripts and Archives (UCTMA)
  Western Cape Provincial Archives, Cape Town (WCPA)
    CO: Colonial Office
United States
  New York Public Library, Manuscript Division (NYPL)
    ICPP: International Committee for Political Prisoners

INDEX

Aamer, Shaker, 276–81
Adams, Gerry, 64, 72, 86, 110, 191, 255, 266
Agamben, Giorgio, 5
Aiken, Frank, 100, 224–26
Alexander, Neville, 48–49, 83–84
Alexander I, Emperor, 16
American Civil Liberties Union (ACLU), 122
Amnesty International. *See* prisoner aid and advocacy.
Andaman Islands penal colony, 13
Andrzejewski, Mirosław, 148
Anglo-Irish Treaty, 82, 106, 223, 238
Argentina, prisoners in, 4, 41, 53, 56, 136, 289n20
Ashe, Thomas, 81, 118, 207, 211
Asiatic Registration Act, 31–32, 118
Augustyński, Zygmunt, 45
Australia, transport to, 12, 15, 17–19

Babenia, Natoo, 45, 217
Badenhorst, Colonel Piet, 84, 253
Baldwin, Roger, 122–24, 126–27, 130
Barton, Robert, 98
Bartoszewski, Władysław, 47, 72–73, 75–76, 238, 243, 245
Barylewska-Hajdo, Halina, 53–54
Béaslaí, Piaras, 196, 214
Begg, Moazzam, 268, 270, 272, 274–76, 280
Benenson, Peter, 3, 126–27, 129–30, 134, 301n54
Bermuda, transport to, 12, 163
Bernstein, Hilda, 59–60, 234
Bertillon, Alphonse, 289n29
Biko, Steve, 54, 238
bin Laden, Osama, 273, 276, 279, 281
Bojko, Stefan, 55
Bosch, Lieutenant, 215, 217
Brennan-Whitmore, W.J., 157
Breytenbach, Breyten, 93

Brezhnev, Leonid, 50
Britain. *See* political movements *and* prisons.
British Army, 56, 175, 255
Brodsky, Josef, 130
Brok, General Nikolai, 9
Brugha, Caitlin, 106
Brugha, Cathal, 106, 237
Brussels Conference (1874), 118
Brzęk-Osiński, Michał, 160–161
Buczek, Marian, 162, 191
Bumgarner, Colonel Michael, 276–78, 280–81
Burke, Richard, 19, 97
Byrne, Kit, 225

camp, concentration, 14, 27, 154, 163, 172–73, 262
camp, prisoner-of-war, 7, 87, 154–55, 158–59, 172
Carron, Owen, 141–42
Casement, Roger, 305n54
Cat and Mouse Act, 29–30
Central Prison Board (Russia), 40
Chernyshevskii, Nikolai, 24, 64, 209
Chile, prisoners in, 169
China, prisoners in, 5, 269
Chrzanowski, Wiesław, 178
Cieślińska-Skrzypiec, Irena, 64, 176, 236
Ciller, Zisla, 201
Ciszak, Bogdan, 50, 138, 221–22, 245
Clancy, Peadar, 212
Clarke, Philip, 141
Clarke, Thomas, 22
class relations in the prison, 10, 16, 22, 24–26, 28, 73–78, 80, 168, 241
clothing strikes and protests, 69, 164, 183, 187, 191, 194–201, 204, 208, 229–30, 310n77
Cobbett, William, 11
Collins, John, 138

Collins, Michael, 98–99, 164, 239
Comerford, Marie, 106
Coogan, Tim Pat, 203–204
Cosgrave, President W.T., 119, 226
Cousins, Margaret, 210
Cyrankiewicz, Józef, 3
Czaplińska, Ruta, 283n1

Daniłowski, Gustaw, 76, 167
de Klerk, President F. W., 265
Déroulède, Paul, 16
Despard, Charlotte, 106
de Valera, Éamon, 3, 98, 101, 118, 181,
    185, 238–39
Devine, Sleepy, 196
Dlamini, Moses, 38, 48, 77, 83, 216
Długoszowski, Tadeusz, 192
Dobrzyński, Szymon, 55
Domańska, Regina, 153
Donnelly, Michael, 56, 57
Downarowicz, Medard, 146
Dudziński, Ludwik, 159–60
Duklanowicz, Wojciech, 88
Duljasz, Hipolit, 79
Dutkiewicz, Sławomir, vii
Dwaba, Lungile, 250
Dymarski, Lech, 67

Errachidi, Ahmed, 271, 278–79
Ervine, David, 260, 266
escape from prison, 18–19, 26, 97–104, 152, 174,
    194, 257, 259
European Court of Human Rights (ECHR),
    135–36, 200
execution, 6, 26–27, 36, 41, 47, 64, 82, 88, 118,
    149, 151–52, 154, 176–77, 238, 262

Feldpolizei (Prussian secret police), 110
Fijałek, Bronisław, 26
Fitzgerald, Séamus, 164
Fleming, Patrick, 195–96, 263, 310n79
Flynn, Ned, 196
Foucault, Michel, 5, 17
France, prisoners in, 4, 15, 16
Freire, Paolo, 257–58, 263
Fursa, Lt., 23, 178
Fry, Elizabeth Gurney, 104

Gallagher, Frank, 81, 165, 211–12, 215, 223, 233,
    236, 240
Gandhi, Mohandas, 31–35, 40, 70, 118, 173, 195,
    215, 263, 287n82, 288n90
    influence of, 63, 94, 101, 121, 157, 163, 189–90
gender and the prison, 37, 63, 75, 103–109, 186,
    189–90, 199–201, 297n44
General Prisons Board (Ireland), 82, 195, 202,
    207, 210

Geneva Conventions, 155
Gestapo, 44, 54, 71, 97, 101, 104, 144,
    151–52, 175
Giffard, Chris, 61–62
Gladstone, Governor-General Herbert,
    34–35, 288n90
Gladstone, Prime Minister William, 22
Goffman, Erving, 5
Gomułka, Władysław, 48, 133
Gonne, Maud, 210–11
Górczyński, Piotr, 240
Gorkii, Maksim, 245, 316n41
Gosani, Bob, 52
Grabska, Zofia, 9–10, 11, 24, 64, 75
Greece, prisoners in, 269
Green, Max, 81
Gregory, James, 82, 84, 93
Grzymała-Siedlecki, Adam, 144
Guantanamo Bay detention camp, 4, 8, 173, 268–81

Habib, Hajee, 31
Hague Conventions, 118–19, 155
Hales, Tom, 164
Hańczak, Ignacy, 294n60
Hannaway, Kevin, 56
Harling, Sean, 92
Hart, Jean, 37
Havel, Václav, 130
Healy, Tim, 162
Heryng, Zygmunt, 23, 146
Heygate-Lambert, Colonel, 156
Hicks, David, 271–73
Hilditch, Stanley, 203–204
Himmler, Heinrich, 41
Hirson, Baruch, 42, 72, 163, 232
Hitler, Adolf, 3, 91, 124
Ho Chi Minh, 64, 72
honor, 2, 46, 76, 79, 144, 150, 154, 176, 183, 186,
    237–38, 242
Horodniczy, Janusz, 77, 79–80
Howard, John, 14
Hughes, Brendan "The Dark," 197, 227–28
Hughes, Francis, 229
Humphreys, Sighle, 91, 93, 106–107, 120,
    175–76, 185, 199, 226, 283n1
hunger strikes, 203, 205–207, 209
    at Guantanamo Bay, 276–277, 280
    in Ireland and Northern Ireland, 63, 81, 118,
        140–42, 207–208, 210–14, 222–31,
        237, 240, 256, 297n34
    in Poland, vii, 25, 75 161, 167, 180, 185, 188,
        205, 207–209, 218–22
    in South Africa, 108, 150, 191, 208, 214–17,
        265, 313n49
    by suffragettes, 29–30, 202, 209–10
Hunt, Henry, 11, 20
Hussein, Saddam, 3

illegibility, 5–6, 8, 36–37, 41, 60, 180–81, 184–
    85, 200–201, 204, 262–63, 272, 279
India, prisoners in, 13, 118, 163
Indonesia, prisoners in, 134
informers, 44–47, 70–71, 104, 151, 177, 179,
    184, 203
international prisoner support. *See* prisoner aid
    and advocacy.
interrogation, 45–47, 51, 56–60, 70–71, 73,
    151, 176–77, 179–80, 184, 235,
    272–73, 296n7
Iran, prisoners in, 4
Ireland. *See* political movements *and* prisons.
Israel, prisoners in, 109
Italy, prisoners in, 15

Jakubowicz, Andrzej, 73
Jaruzelski, Gen. Wojciech, 244
Jędrzejewicz, Zdzisław, 71, 144
Jelińska, Janina, 80
Jenkins, Tim, 102
Jesus Christ, 10
Junczys, Andrzej, 190

Kac, Rywa, 201
Kamiński, Marek, 72, 293n35
Kandahar detention facility, 271–72
Kathrada, Ahmed, 191
Kelus, Jan Krzysztof, 67
Kenney, Annie, 28
Kilroy, Michael, 223, 226
Kim Dae-jung, 130
King, Jr., Martin Luther, 136
Kizny-Gaczyński, Roman, 152
Kłosowicz, Józef, 146
Koc, Leon, 160
Koestler, Arthur, 64
Kołłątaj-Srednicki, Jan, 159–60
komuna, 40, 94, 145, 167–73, 185–87,
    219–20, 241–42
Kon, Feliks, 23–24, 110, 177
Koral, Wacław, 25–26, 70
Kossak-Szczucka, Zofia, 175
Krzesławski, Jan, 39, 177–78, 220
Kulczyk, Marek, 43, 62, 75, 78–79, 89–90, 147–
    48, 179, 189, 205, 207, 222, 236, 245
Kuresza, Anastazja, 201
Kurnaz, Murat, 271–272, 274–276, 278–279
Kuroń, Henryk, 65–66
Kuroń, Jacek, 65–67, 110, 132–33, 179–81,
    244, 266
Kwapiński, Jan, 79, 174

Lamert-Mianowska, Eliza, 176
Lang, Herzel, 190
Lange, Antoni, 62, 67, 195
Layng, J.J., 165

Lee, Stephen, 102
Lehane, Con, 50
Leigh, Mary, 29, 30, 210
Lekota, Patrick, 65
Lewin, Hugh, 48, 62, 68, 77–78, 89–90, 176–77
Lewis, John, 190
Liebbrandt, Robey, 163
Luby, Thomas, 20
Ludkiewicz, Ewa, 69
Łukasiński, Walerian, 16

MacBride, Sean, 99, 136, 313n74
MacSwiney, Mary, 106, 226
MacSwiney, Terence, 81, 96, 106, 118, 164, 211,
    213–14, 226, 229, 237–38
    as legend, 63, 197, 218, 223–24
madness, 200–202, 207, 210
Maharaj, Mac, 46, 182, 238
Majewska, Kama, 237
Majewski, Edward, 237
Makana Football Association (MFA),
    248–249, 252
Makhoere, Caesarina, 50, 188–89, 191
Malone, Thomas, 164
Mancewicz, Michał, 178
Mandela, Nelson, 3, 48, 110, 150, 191, 208, 215,
    217, 254, 263
    and Amnesty International, 129–30, 138
    and the apartheid regime, 63, 82, 84, 94–95,
    163, 181–83
    influence of, 65, 85, 91, 183, 238, 253, 265
Mangena, Mosibudi, 83
Manzi, Gladys, 109
Marchlewski, Julian, 110
Markievicz, Countess Constance, 74–75
Marsh, Charlotte, 29
martial law (Poland), 137–38, 205, 220–21,
    244–46, 295n97
Matanzima, Chief George Mzivubu, 163, 182
Mathibedi, Elsie, 74
Matta, Don, 250
Mazowiecki, Tadeusz, 3, 137, 244
Mbeki, Govan, 191, 247–48
McCreesh, Raymond, 229
McDonnell, Joe, 229
McFarlane, Bik, 229
McGrath, Joseph, 164
McGuigan, Francis, 56–57
McGuinness, Martin, 3, 266
McKee, Billy, 226
McKenna, Sean, 228
McKeown, Laurence, 230, 256–57, 259, 261
McMullen, Jackie, 196, 256–59
McNally, Patrick, 56
Meehan, Martin, 204
Metelski, Marian, 149
Michnik, Adam, 42, 137, 244, 266, 303n7

Michnik-Szechterowa, Helena, 115
Miedza-Tomaszewski, Stanisław, 100, 152
Mikulska, Regina, 175
Milošević, Slobodan, 3
Mitchel, John, 12, 17, 19, 20
Mitchell, Thomas, 141
Ministry of Public Security (Poland), 44, 60, 79–80, 265
Moczarski, Kazimierz, 101
Modise, Thandi Ruth, 49, 191
Modzelewski, Karol, 132–33
Mogoba, Stanley, 83
Moran, Patrick, 100, 164
Morgiewicz, Emil, 131
Morley, David, 193
Moseneke, Ernest Dikgang, 249
Mossor, General Stefan, 46
Mrabulo Syllabus, 254, 263
Mulcahy, Denis, 20
Mulcahy, Richard, 164, 166, 226
Mur, Jan (Andrzej Drzycimski and Andrzej Kinaszewski), 245
Murphy, Jane, 202
Murphy, Margaret, 202
Murray, Seán, 259
Mthimunye, Isaac, 253

Naidoo, Indres, 84, 217, 249, 252
Nakielski, Henryk, 48
Napoleon III, Emperor, 15
Ndzonga, Rita, 58
Netherlands, prisoners in, 14
Ngxiki, Canzibe Rosebury, 84, 150
Nicholas I, Emperor, 16
Nicholas II, Emperor, 26
Niedziewicz, Marek, 316n49
Niemoeller, Martin, 124
Night and Fog prisoners, 41
Nhlapo, Elizabeth, 191
Nkadimeng, John, 178–179
Nobel Peace Prize, 136, 141, 265, 266, 281
North Korea, prisoners in, 5
Northern Ireland. *See* political movements *and* prisons.
Northern Ireland Prison Service, 194, 288n4
Nowak, Edward, 90
Nugent, Kieran, 196–97, 200
Nyanda, Raymond, 46

O'Brennan, Lily, 165
O'Donnell, Peadar, 39, 82, 236
O'Donovan Rossa, Jeremiah, 18, 19–21, 24, 63, 161, 195, 263, 310n77
O Fiaich, Cardinal Tomás, 204
O'Hara, Patsy, 229
O'Keeffe, Paudeen, 82, 164–65
Okhrana (Russian secret police), 105, 110, 178

Okrzeja, Stanisław, 150
O'Leary, Michael, 183–84
O'Malley, Ernie, 88, 225, 227
Onyszkiewicz, Janusz, 67
O'Rahilly, Anna, 224
Osińska, Władysława, 74
Owczarek-Jagodzińska, Zofia, 290n39

Pajdak, Wiesława, 147
Pankhurst, Christabel, 28
Paszkowska, Maria, 105
Patek, Stanisław, 105
Pawlina, Fr. Leon, 45–46
Peter, Apostle/Saint, 10, 43
Petrusewicz, Marta, 237
Pielat, Kazimierz, 286n61
Pilecki, Witold, 64, 100
Piłsudski, Józef, 3, 24, 54, 64, 113, 158, 161–62, 240
Pellico, Silvio, 15
Perold, P.J., 153
Płochocki, Marian, 24, 232–33
Pluciński, Bronisław, 146
Pogrund, Benjamin, 68
Polak, H.S.L., 31, 33
Poland. *See* political movements *and* prisons.
political movements (imprisoned)
    African National Congress (ANC), 8, 57, 61, 72, 75, 101–102, 109, 129, 139, 190, 254, 266
        on Robben Island, 77, 182, 216–17, 236, 247–48
    Black Consciousness Movement (BCM), 54, 139, 247–48
    Boer War treason prisoners, 27–28, 40, 153, 155, 163
    British Indian Association, 31, 34
    Chartists (Britain), 10, 18
    Communist Party of Great Britain, 125
    Communist Party of Poland, 168, 171
    Communist Youth League (Poland), 55
    Cumann na mBan, 106–107, 213
    Dynamitards, 22, 28
    Fenian Brotherhood (IRB), 15, 17, 18–22, 23, 24, 28, 29, 97, 104, 117–18, 153, 185
    Freedom and Peace (Poland), vii, 316n49
    Home Army (Poland), 38, 44, 104, 180, 233
    Irish Republican Army (IRA), 69, 88, 92, 97, 99, 119, 141–42, 164, 199, 213, 223, 227, 249, 255, 266
        IRA prisoners, 56, 75, 78, 86–87, 102–103, 135, 143, 147–49, 181, 189, 193, 198, 205, 226
        See also Republicans (Ireland).
    Irish Republican Brotherhood (IRB). *See* Fenian Brotherhood.
    London Corresponding Society, 10

Loyalists (Northern Ireland), 72, 86–88, 102, 227, 260–61, 295n95, 310n87
Orange Alternative (Poland), 190
Ossewabrandwag (South Africa), 163, 300n9
Pan-African Congress (PAC), 39, 68, 72, 83, 109, 215–17, 247–48
Polish Communist Party, 40, 44, 74, 100, 110–15, 162, 168–71, 186–88, 190–91, 193, 200, 218–20, 232, 240–43, 249, 265
Polish Legions (World War I), 158–61, 162, 164
Polish Military Organization, 77
Polish Socialist Party, 10, 24, 97, 105, 112
Proletaryat, 22–23, 178
Provisional IRA. *See* Irish Republican Army.
Republicans (Ireland), 72, 104, 156, 214, 218, 224–31, 239–40, 255–61, 266
  See also Sinn Féin; Irish Republican Army.
satyagraha/satyagrahis, 31–35, 70, 118, 157, 163, 189, 215
Sinn Féin, 81, 98, 106, 155, 162, 211, 227
  See also Republicans (Ireland)
Solidarity (Poland), 2, 72, 79, 89–90, 104, 137–38, 147, 205, 220–21, 238, 244–46, 265, 295n97, 309n70
South African Communist Party, 4, 101, 109, 247, 254
Stormjaers, 163
suffragettes (Britain and Ireland), 28–31, 32, 40, 70, 118, 121, 192, 207, 209–10, 299n1
Ulster Volunteer Force, 260, 266
Umkhonto we Sizwe, 45, 129, 306n73
Western Ukrainian Communist Party (KPZU), 55, 115
Women's Social and Political Union (WSPU), 28–29
Workers' Defense Committee (KOR), 137
Young Irelanders, 17
political prisoner
  as legal category, 15–17, 27, 47–48, 119, 284n6
  and terrorism, 7, 57, 269, 271, 277, 285n31
Popiełuszko, Fr. Jerzy, 138
Portugal, prisoners in, 126
Prange, Walburga Urszula, 149
Prins, Lt. Piet, 252
prison
  censorship in, 28, 92–96, 247
  as institution, 5, 13–14, 36–38, 262, 283n3
  labor, 20, 33, 43, 48, 76, 79, 125, 133, 158, 216–17, 230, 257
  reform and rehabilitation in, 13–14, 17, 33, 40, 48, 78, 262, 281
prisoner aid and advocacy, 14–15, 104, 116, 117
  Ad Hoc Detention Action Committee (ADAC), 139
  Amnesty International (AI), 3, 7, 121, 122, 125–39, 142–43, 264, 301n54
  Appeal for Amnesty in Spain, 125–26

Commission for Intervention and Legality (Poland), 138
Detainees' Parents Support Committee (DPSC), 139–140
Foreign Union of Assistance for Political Victims, 118
Human Rights Watch/Helsinki Watch, 136, 137
International Committee for Political Prisoners (ICPP), 122–24, 128, 132
International Committee of the Red Cross (ICRC), 83, 119–20, 122–23, 126, 129, 250, 270, 272
International Defence and Aid Fund (IDAF), 138–39, 302n70
International League for the Rights of Man/ International League for Human Rights, 124–26
International Organization for Aid to Revolutionaries (MOPR), 110–12, 114, 122
International Rescue Committee, 125
IRB Ladies' Club, 104
League for Defense of Human and Civil Rights (LOPCziO), 111–112
Patronat (Poland), 105–106, 110, 112
Primate's Committee in Support of Those Deprived of Freedom and Their Families, 137–38
Political Defenders' Circle, 166
Red Help (Poland), 7, 40, 110–15, 121–22, 168, 171, 185–87, 201, 220
Republican Political Prisoners Committee, 107, 120–121
Society for the Moral Improvement of Prisoners (Netherlands), 14
Women's Prisoners' Defence League (WDPL), 106–107, 122
Workers' Defense League, 125
prisons and camps
  in Britain
    Brixton, 211, 213, 229, 237
    Chatham Prison, 20, 21, 195
    Clerkenwell Prison, 19, 97
    Dartmoor Prison, 181
    Frongoch internment camp, 155–59, 161–64, 166, 172, 175, 244, 258, 264
    Ilchester Prison, 11
    Lincoln Prison, 98
    Manchester Prison, 98
    Newgate Women's Prison, 104
    Northampton Prison, 43
    Pentonville Prison, 164, 195
    Portland Prison, 20, 153
    Reading Gaol/Reading Prison, 28, 155, 164
    Richmond Bridewell, 18
    Wakefield Prison, 227
    Wormwood Scrubs, 164

prisons and camps (*cont.*)
  German/Nazi. *See also* Pawiak Prison, under
      Nazi occupation.
    Auschwitz concentration camp, 72, 93, 100,
        151, 172, 175, 220
    Landsberg Prison, 91
    Limburg (POW camp), 305n54
    Magdeburg Fortress, 158
    Ravensbrück concentration camp, 151
    Szczypiorno internment camp, 159–62,
        164, 172, 264, 306n66
    Szucha Avenue, 86
  in Ireland
    Arbour Hill Prison, 50
    Cork Prison, 211, 213
    Curragh prison/camp, 193, 225
    Dundalk Prison, 100
    Finner Camp, 82
    Gormanstown Camp, 223
    Kilmainham Prison, 74, 100, 106,
        164, 225–26
    Mountjoy Prison,
      during the Irish Revolution, 75, 211–13,
          215, 218
      in the Irish Free State, 82, 91–92, 99, 106,
          164–66, 223–24, 239–40, 286n62
      in the Republic of Ireland, 97
      suffragettes in, 202, 210
    Newbridge Camp, 99, 165, 225–26
    North Dublin Union, 224
    Tullamore Gaol, 210
  in Northern Ireland
    Armagh Prison, 142, 199–200, 227
    Crumlin Road Prison (Belfast), 224,
        226–227
    H-Blocks (Maze Prison), 102–103, 140,
        173, 194, 196–97, 199–200, 203–204,
        227–31, 255–59, 264
      See also Long Kesh.
    Long Kesh Detention Centre, 51, 62, 64,
        65, 86–88, 142, 144, 147–48, 173,
        191, 193, 202, 208, 227, 255, 259, 260
      See also H-Blocks (Maze Prison)
    Magilligan Prison, 88
  in Poland
    Arsenal Prison (Warsaw), 79
    Będzin Prison, 241
    Bereza Kartuska camp, 51, 54, 64, 115, 172
    Białołęka Prison, 67, 221
    Białystok Prison, 94, 168–69, 170–71, 241
    Brześć Fortress, 115
    Bydgoszcz. *See* Fordon Prison.
    Citadel, Warsaw, 2, 9, 17, 23–24, 26,
        146–47, 178, 192, 232–33
    Fordon Prison, 51, 69, 88, 180,
        200–201, 232–33
    Głogów Prison, 90

Gołdap (internment center), 246
Grodno Jail, 219
Grudziądz Prison, 55, 186
Hrubieszów Prison, 101, 179, 205, 222, 245
Inowrocław Prison, 116, 176
Jaworze internment camp, 238
Jaworzno internment camp, 79
Kamienna Góra Prison, 90
Katowice Prison, 113, 149, 219
Kielce Prison, 71, 101, 170, 186
Kraków, prison in, 101, 115
Kwidzyń Prison, 245
Łęczyca Prison, 79, 207
Łódź, prison in, 62, 110
Łomża Prison, 168, 174
Lublin Castle prison, 76
Łuck prison, 55, 115
Lwów Prison, 121
Mokotów Prison, 294n60
    in interwar Poland, 218, 242
    during martial law, 62, 78
    in Stalinist Poland, 44, 47, 48,
        49–50, 147, 175, 184,
        232–233
Montelupich Prison (Kraków), 105
Mostowski Palace, 73, 208–209
Mysłowice Prison, 113
Nysa Prison, 90
Opole Prison, 90
Ostrów Wielkopolski, 221
Pawiak Prison,
    in the Russian Empire, 25–26, 97, 146
    in interwar Poland, 167, 218
    under Nazi occupation, 53, 85–86, 92,
        95, 97, 100–101, 149, 151–53, 162,
        175–76, 183, 264
Piotrków Prison, 74, 242–43
Płock Prison, 286n61
Potulice Prison, 245
Radom Prison, 101
Rawicz Prison, 44, 101, 186, 202
Sandomierz Prison, 186, 240
"Serbia" (Pawiak Prison), 193
Siedlce Prison, 114
Sieradz Prison, 81, 241, 243–44
Strzebielinek, 244
Strzelce (Opolskie) Prison, 90
Uherce Prison, 309n70
Warsaw City Jail, 76
Wronki Prison, 121, 150, 178, 186, 191,
    219, 235
in Russia/Soviet Union
    Gulag. *See* Siberia, exile to.
    House of Preliminary Detention,
        St. Petersburg, 311n12
    Kresty Prison, 24
    Lubyanka Prison, 145

Petropavlovsk Fortress, 209
Shlisselburg Fortress, 16–17
in South Africa
Diepkloof Penal Settlement, 215
Hillbrow police station, 37
Johannesburg Fort/Central Prison, 32, 39, 52, 75, 109, 215, 234
Klerksdorp Prison, 191
Paarl Prison, 109
Point Prison (Durban), 45
Pretoria prisons (Central and Local), 62, 74, 77–78, 89, 102, 109, 163, 177, 191, 215, 232
Robben Island Prison, 39, 44, 62, 65, 68, 75, 85, 96, 101, 136, 138, 181–83, 191, 203, 208
discipline on, 40, 48–49, 51, 84, 93
guard-prisoner relations on, 82–84, 87, 109, 149, 304n18
hunger strikes on, 150, 215–17, 265, 313n49
prisoner organization on, 150, 163, 173, 236, 247–55, 304n39
Tokai Prison, 28, 95, 153
Progressive Party (South Africa), 109
Pundit, Ram Sundar, 32
Pużak, Kazimierz, 145
psychiatric hospitals, use of, 50

al Qaeda, 269, 275–77, 279

race in the prison, 37, 40, 49, 77–78, 83–85, 190, 200, 247, 272, 294n76, 295n85
Ramoshaba, John, 249
resistance, 3, 6, 134, 174–75, 196, 202–205
Rhodesia, prisoners in, 301n54
Ringman, Aleksander, 150
Romaszewski, Zbigniew, 138
Rostworowski, Tomasz, 44, 61–62, 77, 149–150
Royal Ulster Constabulary (RUC), 55, 255
Rulewski, Jan, 67
Ryan, James, 164

el Saadawi, Nawal, 130–131
Sadowska, Barbara, 180–181, 263
Sands, Bobby, 63–65, 141–42, 200, 227–29, 238, 263, 266
Sawczyński, Wasylij, 170
Schillinger, Klara, 201
Schlapobersky, John, 58–59
Scott, James, 6
Security Bureau/Security Police (Poland). *See* Ministry of Public Security.
Segal, Captain Szymon, 46
Selborne, Lord, Governor of Transvaal Colony, 34

Sempołowska, Stefania, 76, 104–107, 110–11, 167–68
Serokolo, Kate, 191
Sexwale, Tokyo, 65
Shcharansky, Anatoly, 131
Sheehan, Pat, 230
Sheehy-Skeffington, Francis, 30
Sheehy-Skeffington, Hanna, 30, 37, 104, 106, 118, 199, 202, 209, 263
Siberia, exile to, 2, 10, 12, 13, 15, 17, 23–24, 26, 37, 62, 172, 174, 209
Sieradzka, Helena, 232
Sieradzki, Makary, 232
Sisulu, Walter, 85
Sitho, Galelikile, 236
Skalon, General Georgii, 68, 290n39
Skalski, Stanisław, 202–203
Skarga, Barbara, 38
Skokowski, Jerzy, 167
Slahi, Mohamedou Ould, 270, 273–74
Sławek, Walery, 146–147
Śledziński, Ludwik, 97, 168, 202
Śliwińska, Myra, 149
Śliwiński, Władysław, 69, 149
Śmiechowski, Jerzy, 147
Sobolewski, Bronisław, 166–67
Sobukwe, Robert, 38, 64, 68, 132, 203, 217
Socrates, 10
Sołdrowski, Andrzej, 149, 235–36, 304n18
Solzhenitsyn, Aleksander, 42, 172
Sosnkowski, Jan, 74
Soszyński, Jerzy (George d'Ostoya), 25
South Africa. *See* political movements *and* prisons.
South African National Intelligence Service, 254
South African Prison Service, 250, 254
Soviet Union, prisoners in, 37, 50, 136, 269
Sowińska, Stanisława, 42–43, 44, 49–50, 60, 150, 173, 235
Spain, prisoners in, 269
Special Category (Northern Ireland), 193–94, 196–97, 227, 229, 255
Spence, Gusty, 260
Spratt, Reverend John, 15
Stack, Austin, 98
Stagg, Frank, 227
Stanford Prison Experiment, 82
Stanowski, Adam, 184, 194
Steinsbergowa, Aniela, 298n49
Stephens, James, 18
Steyn, Colonel J.C., 84
Stokowski, Jerzy, 73, 191, 208–209
strip strike. *See* clothing strike.
Suliński, Józef, 152
Suzman, Helen, 107–109, 253, 290n47
Swanepoel, Theunis, 57–59, 191
Świrski, Kazimierz, 60

Szczypa, Władysław, 76–77
Szczyrbowa, Rozalia, 55
Szechter, Ozjasz, 55
Szetlich, Aleksander, 233
Szostkiewicz, Adam, 245

Taliban, 269, 280
tauza, 51–52, 216
Terrorism Act (South Africa), 57, 291n81
Thatcher, Prime Minister Margaret, 141,
        227–28, 230
Thoreau, Henry David, 2, 32
Timerman, Jacobo, 53, 131, 184–85
Tobin, Michael, 134
Tolstoy, Lev, 33
torture, 45, 49–60, 65, 71, 86, 115, 134–35,
        184–85, 227, 271–273, 280
        291n81
Traugutt, Romuald, 9
Tshabangu, Elliott, 57
Tshwete, Steve, 249
Turkey, prisoners in, 136
Turkowski, Krzysztof, 90–91
Twomey, Seamus, 98

United Democratic Front (South Africa), 139
Ustrońska, Genia, 233–34

Vietnam, prisoners in, 4
von Beseler, General Hans Hartwig, 158

von Eltz, Eleonore, 123–24
Vorster, John, 3, 290n47, 298n72

Walsh, Séanna, 230–31
Wanat, Leon, 100–101, 151–53, 173, 175
Waryński, Ludwik, 2, 22–23, 24, 64, 65, 183, 263
Wałęsa, Lech, 265
Walter-Janke, Zygmunt, 233
Wei Jingsheng, 130
Weinberg, Violet, 144
Weindling, Saul Hersz, 242
Wentzel, Ernie, 108
Weremowicz, Jan, 150
Whelan, Peadar, 199
Widlicki, Eugeniusz, 162
Wilczewska, Wanda, 92
Wilde, Oscar, 28
Wohlfarth, Halina, 183
Wrzos, Ignacy, 219
Wujec, Henryk, 67, 221

Yeats, W. B., 209
Yugoslavia, prisoners in, 269

Zalewski, Grzegorz, 95
Zimbardo, Philip, 82
Zimińska-Sygietyńska, Mira, 85
Ziółkowska, Krystyna, 246
Zuma, Jacob, 317n67
Zylbersztajn, Teofila, 243–44